Political Illustration

BLOOMSBURY VISUAL ARTS
Bloomsbury Publishing Plc
50 Bedford Square, London, WC1B 3DP, UK
1385 Broadway, New York, NY 10018, USA
29 Earlsfort Terrace, Dublin 2, Ireland

BLOOMSBURY, BLOOMSBURY VISUAL ARTS and the Diana logo are trademarks of Bloomsbury Publishing Plc

First published 2025

For legal purposes the Acknowledgements on p. 245 constitute an extension of this copyright page.

Cover illustration: Krishna Chavda, NANU Studio;
Secondary illustration and design by Catherine A. Moore

A catalogue record for this book is available from the British Library.

A catalog record for this book is available from the Library of Congress.

ISBN:	HB:	978-1-3503-3715-2
	PB:	978-1-3503-3714-5
	ePDF:	978-1-3503-3717-6
	eBook:	978-1-3503-3716-9

Typeset by Typo•glyphix, Burton-on-Trent, DE14 3HE, UK
Printed and bound in India

Political Illustration

The Visual Language of Propaganda, Censorship, and Dissent

Catherine A. Moore
and Megan Hauser

BLOOMSBURY VISUAL ARTS
LONDON • NEW YORK • OXFORD • NEW DELHI • SYDNEY

Contents

3

Media, Censorship, & Taboo 93

4

Contentious Politics and the Art of Dissent 159

Introduction

Political illustration can take many forms, from editorial illustration on political subjects, to political cartoons printed in a newspaper, to posters displayed in a subway, to campaign materials. However, we can also find political illustration in more unexpected places, such as the illustrations used to help us vote for our governments on ballots, the illustrations on our currency and stamps, and the illustrated graffiti on the streets where we walk. Images have a special power to help us remember and recall information and play an important role in influencing our beliefs and decisions.

Political illustration has been created for millennia and has a wide variety of applications. This book will show how encoders of political illustrations have attempted, both successfully and unsuccessfully, to sway and influence the political thoughts, ideas, and actions of the public. In this book, four categories have been identified in which to present the readers with a survey of political illustration and its applications. The first section, *An Introduction to Visual Language*, discusses how signs, symbols, and semiotics can be used to interpret visual messages. The second section, *Propaganda: The Art of the State*, discusses how visual methods of propaganda and different media can be used by governments to take hold of the public. This section discusses how propaganda was used from the time of Julius Caesar to Napoleon, to more modern applications during the world wars and in post-war communist countries such as the Soviet Union and China. This section discusses how propaganda was used by European Imperialism throughout the 18th–20th centuries will be discussed, and also how it was used by new dictatorships filling leadership roles in newly independent states. This book will also cover how propaganda continues to be used in the contemporary and post-contemporary era, including its applications in American politics. The third section, *Media, Censorship, & Taboo*, discusses the role of the media and popular press in political illustration, including how social media has changed this dynamic in recent years. Issues of taboo, censorship, the commercialization of media, and its effects on political imagery will also be discussed. This section will also cover how reportage illustration has been used in the political realm, the role of political satire and its real-life consequences, and misinformation and disinformation in the media. The final section, *Contentious Politics and the Art of Dissent*, discusses the terms and definitions of contentious politics and dissent, and the multiple media political dissent illustration has been used in throughout history. This section focuses on anti-regime activities perpetrated by non-governmental forces, which can range from well-established, legal organizations to groups operating beyond the legal confines of the government, to individual people. This section will explain the menu of contentious politics, including nonviolent behaviors and violent tactics. This section will differentiate between the dynamics of protest and speech in democratic and non-democratic societies. Topics covered include early Latin American protest art, the Vietnam War, Black Civil Rights and Black Lives Matter, LGBTQ+, Indigenous Americans, the Arab Spring, and Women's Rights. Finally, the conclusion of the book will discuss technology and its potential impact on political illustrations and the future of political illustration's role in society.

Throughout the book, we will tie these examples of political illustration back to how they are created and how they are interpreted, discussing the visual grammar they use and how an audience understands and deciphers the code inherent in political illustrations. Oftentimes, a misinterpreted visual code is the basis for political conflict, clarifying the importance of education in visual interpretation. We hope this book will not only educate about political events, history, and issues through imagery, but also about the nuances of reading images, expanding upon your foundation of visual grammar.

Defining Illustration

In this book, we will be using a variety of examples of illustration, from editorial illustration, to political cartoons, to graphic novels, to murals, to paintings and sculptures, to unpublished works, but all will be defined as illustrations in the context of this book. We feel it is important to clarify the sometimes ambiguous definition of illustration and discuss what other authors have posited in terms of its definition.

Author and professor of design Aggie Toppins makes a strong case for legitimizing design that exists beyond the professional sphere. Toppins posits that while graphic design needed to rely on professional practice for its legitimization as a discipline, once it was accepted as a field of study, its role as a cultural practice could be expanded.[1] Although the term "graphic design" was not used commonly until after World War II, the term illustration has existed since the 1400s, and by the early 1800s adopted its contemporary definition of an illustrative picture. Instead of the field of illustration originating out of a professional practice, a professional practice has grown from a cultural one. Illustration did not require the legitimization process that graphic design had to endure to establish itself as a commercial discipline, although it's taken awhile to establish itself as an academic one. However, its return to defining itself as a cultural practice is increasingly necessary as the term becomes further associated with published works and professional practice. Illustration is often limited by the misnomer "commercial art," although illustration does not have to be commercial. As David Craven notes about some of the best Latin American posters from the 1960s and 1970s, *"they have nothing to sell,"* but instead create "icons of popular struggle, … public policy, and … shared popular experience."[2] The importance of acknowledging non-professional work as illustration is increasingly necessary so that our field can fully embrace the diversity of contributions to the field by marginalized groups that may not have succeeded in the professional realm of illustration but thrived in the cultural realm. As political history favors the victors, the history of illustration favors the published.

Guerilla and ephemeral art movements are particularly important in contentious politics and the art of dissent, and we strive in this book to balance the art of the oppressor with the art of the oppressed. We need not look far for examples of the cultural practice of illustration, including the protest posters of Latin America, the social justice street art of Atlanta growing from the Black graffiti and AfriCOBRA movements, and the self-authored graphic novels of refugees, incarcerated persons, and political dissenters across the world. Not only is a broadening definition of illustration necessary for the future of the field, but it is also accurate to the history of the field, which encompasses a variety of mediums, techniques, and applications of visual communication. Unlike fine art's "precious objects for exhibition," to quote visual culture historian Alan Gowans, illustration is often ephemeral, printed on cheap newsprint or spray-painted on a wall, emphasizing even more the importance of documenting its existence.[3]

Are there any limits to what illustration could encompass? Alan Male argues that "context" is the driver of what warrants the moniker of illustration vs. the term "fine art." Unlike subjective fine art, Male asserts that illustration exists in an objective context, a context that drives the creation of illustration. He writes that in illustration, "context defines the reason for the image in the first place and underpins the essence of the whole brief."[4] Susan Doyle, Jaleen Grove, and Whitney Sherman expand on this definition, that illustration communicates specific messages with an intended audience in mind, and that this *intent* to communicate this particular message is key. They posit that illustration "is inherently in service of an idea." Many paintings, prints, and other artworks that exist in fine art museums today were originally created with a specific communication or context in mind. Albrecht Dürer, Katsushika Hokusai, and Käthe Kollwitz, to name a few, were all illustrators, although we would now associate their names with fine art. Therefore, in this book, we choose to be liberal with our definition of the term "illustration." While some of our examples may be co-categorized as fine art, graphic design, or photography, we will examine images in which a particular message has been sought to be communicated, to a specific audience, and in a specific context.

Endnotes

1 Aggie Toppins, "We Need Graphic Design Histories That Look Beyond the Profession," *AIGA Eye on Design*, June 10, 2021, https://eyeondesign.aiga.org/we-need-graphic-design-histories-that-look-beyond-the-profession/.

2 Russ Davidson and David Craven, *Latin American Posters: Public Aesthetics and Mass Politics* (Santa Fe: Museum of New Mexico Press, 2006), 16.

3 Susan Doyle, Jaleen Grove, and Whitney Sherman, *The History of Illustration* (New York: Fairchild Books, 2018), xvii.

4 Alan Male, *The Power and Influence of Illustration: Achieving Impact and Lasting Significance through Visual Communication* (London: Bloomsbury Visual Arts, 2019), 9.

1

An Introduction to Visual Language

Symbols and Global Ballots

One of the most fundamental activities in a democracy is voting. Depending on the political system, voters may directly elect a president or executive figure, in addition to members of a legislative body like Congress or a Parliament. They may elect local leaders like a mayor, or regional positions like a governor. In some countries, voters select a particular candidate, while in others, voters may just vote for a particular party. In all these cases, the ballot is a crucial tool with serious implications. Thus, it is important that the ballot is clear and effectively able to offer voters the ability to participate. One way that a ballot can do this is through illustrated symbols.

Imagine walking into a voting booth and placing your vote not just next to the name of your favored politician, but next to a picture of a bunch of bananas. Or a wedge of cheese. Or an 8-ball. Or a chess piece. In dozens of countries with low-literacy rates, voting by symbols is an integral part of their democracy. (Figure 1.1) In Afghanistan's 2005 parliamentary elections, illiteracy rates for women were approximately 85 percent and for men were approximately 55 percent.[1] Many provinces had dozens of candidates listed on the ballot, each paired with a seemingly randomly associated symbol. (In Farrah province, for instance, 46 different candidates and symbols were listed on the ballot.) For months prior to the elections, these candidates had been handing out pamphlets and flyers associating these symbols with their name, picture, and campaign promises. Afghan television had also been using these symbols to associate the candidates with the ballot symbols. These symbols were also particularly important because candidates in Afghanistan competed without political parties, so voters could not rely on the cue of a party endorsement or campaign when choosing for whom to vote.[2] While symbols on ballots were not new in Afghanistan, this election differed because the JEMB (Joint Electoral Management Body) assigned the symbols to the candidates instead of letting the candidates choose these. In fact, the JEMB disallowed any historical or religious symbols to avoid candidates from receiving an advantage by utilizing the associations made with these symbols. Ultimately, the symbols were in fact randomly chosen, at least in part, by each candidate, who would draw three of the approved symbols from a hat and then select which symbol meant the most to them.[3] Does a system of illustrated symbols reduce errors and increase voting accuracy?

While some Afghans joked that some voters may have thought they'd receive a car or plane from the candidate with that particular symbol, the system created by the JEMB had attempted to resolve visual biases in electoral ballots. Multiple studies on ballot photographs have been conducted in Ireland and Britain, many concluding that photographs had the most impact on uninformed voters and may favor younger candidates and those of a preferred ethnic phenotype. Dr. Devra Moehler, a professor in communications, conducted a survey in Uganda prior to the country's February 2011 elections on party symbols on ballots, and similarly found that symbols identifying a political party could unduly influence elections.[4] The U.S. Election Assistance Commission recommends many best practices when it comes to polling place materials around the world. They suggest that illustrations are better than photographs when providing instructions to illiterate voters, because photographs often do not reproduce well. They too caution against using political party icons. Their recommendations focus on illustrations that supplement the instructions rather than ones that identify candidates and parties.[5] Illustrated symbols can help move democracy in the right direction, nevertheless, voters may still be unconsciously influenced by these seemingly random visual signs.

Inevitably, whenever we see a visual sign of any type, we associate that sign with the plethora of memories of every image we have ever seen. These signs may unearth memories that may be positive or may be negative, and they may bring about certain expectations based on our experiences. We may project our own mental state onto these objects. Certain signs may have a certain association with our job, profession, or interests. Some signs may have cultural or personal meaning to us. Often unconsciously, whenever we see a visual sign, it has the opportunity to influence our thoughts and behaviors, even our voting behaviors, and, in turn, our governments.

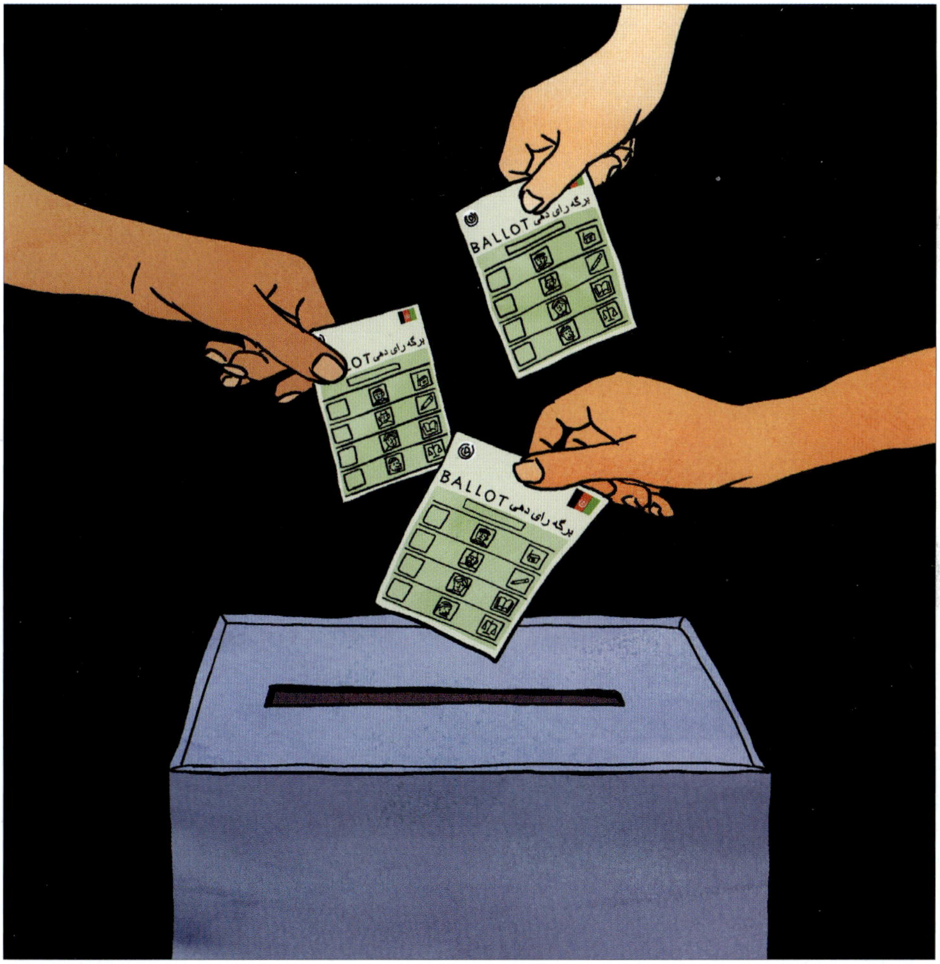

Figure 1.1
In dozens of countries with low-literacy rates, voting by symbols is an integral part of their democracy. © Krishna Chavda, NANU Studio

Reception Theory: An Introduction to Visual Signs

Illustration has commonly been condescendingly referred to as mere decorations supplementing a text, but the illustrations printed onto a ballot clearly do much more than decorate. Instead, they are employed as tools for visual communication. Even when used for a seemingly neutral purpose, persuasion and influence are inherent to illustrative visual forms. All types of political illustration, regardless of their practical applications, use semiotics, Gestalt principles, and the universal principles of design to motivate, persuade, dissent, offend, or enlighten.

This process is not solely the role of the author but extends through the communication path of author to viewer as described in Stuart Hall's reception theory. Called the "**encoder**," the author is not working within a void, but within a specific historical and cultural context. When the author and the viewer (referred to as the "**decoder**") share the same cultural context, the message is easily communicated, but when gaps in history and culture widen, this communication can be misinterpreted and even repurposed. (Figure 1.2)

For example, in 2014, an African American U.S. Postal Service employee filed a complaint with the Equal Employment Opportunity Commission (EEOC) regarding a coworker wearing a yellow hat with the "Gadsden flag" on it: a coiled rattlesnake on a yellow background, with the words "DON'T TREAD ON ME" boldly placed underneath it. (Figure 1.3) The EEOC initially dismissed the complaint, but later reversed this ruling to request the Postal Service investigate the claim.[6] Although there was no definitive ruling on this claim, it sparked a series of media articles and discussion about the racial and racist nature of the flag. Of course, historically, there was no such association. While the flag was created as an overtly anti-British symbol, racial connotations were absent. (The rattlesnake, interestingly, came from a satirical comment by Ben Franklin that Americans should ship rattlesnakes to Britain in response to them shipping convicts to America… a good example of how obscure the connotations of signs and symbols can be.) However, the flag became increasingly associated with right-wing anti-government movements over time, being adopted as a Libertarian symbol in the 70s, and eventually as a Tea Party symbol after the group's formation in 2009. With this, it became associated with opposition to the election of America's first African American president, sealing its racist connotations. It has even been compared to the Confederate flag as a racist symbol, and, along with the Confederate flag, was displayed during the January 6th attacks on the U.S. Capitol. As a symbol gains historical distance from its initial purpose, its meaning can evolve and change. Author and journalist Rob Walker muses, "no symbolic meaning is locked in time."[7]

When we scroll past images without giving our brains time to process those images, we build up a subconscious repertoire of selections from these images, devoid of context. Without taking time to learn this context and the faults of our immediate subconscious perception of images, we cannot fully comprehend them. An example

comes from a 2016 satirical illustrative logo design entitled *Trump 24K Gold-Plated* by Angie Wang and Mark Fox of Design is Play. (Figure 1.4) The logo won *Communication Art's* 7th Annual Typography Contest. A statement by the artists explained the visual metaphor at play: "Trump 24K Gold-Plated is an unauthorized presidential campaign poster for Donald Trump. Composed of four T monograms, the poster uses the visual tension between foreground and background to reveal the metaphoric negative spaces created by Trump's rhetoric."[8] The visual trick at play here is that in the negative space of the four T's, a swastika appears, referring to the racist rhetoric of Donald Trump. Nevertheless, it was widely believed on the internet that this was a logo actually created by the Trump campaign, so much so, that it warranted an article on Snopes.com to fact-check this belief as false.[9] However, the logo continued to cause confusion. When Letterform Archive, a respected design nonprofit center, reshared Design is Play's logo design on their Instagram account in 2021, their largely anti-Trump fanbase rebelled. Some asked if Trump had commissioned this logo. Many people expressed shock and dislike at the post, and many even unfollowed the account. What was clear is that many people, if not most, had not taken the time to read the context of the image. They didn't even *see* the swastika in the negative space. However, even those who *did* see the swastika took issue with the visual rhetoric in play. Jewish commentors decried the comparison of Nazi mass murder to Trump's rhetoric. Others commented how Hindus, Buddhists, and Jains may take issue with the use of the continued appropriation of the swastika, originally a spiritual symbol, by the Nazis, another classic example of a symbol evolving throughout time.[10]

This case reminds us that, by definition, a visual sign is only a sign if it is a *communicated* sign. Although the swastika in the Design is Play logo was arguably obvious for a seasoned viewer, other signs may not be as clearly communicated, and the importance of the decoder of an image comes into play. Stuart Hall describes three ways of decoding, the "dominant," the "negotiated," and the "oppositional." In the dominant reader, the decoder of the image reads the image directly and literally, without any confusion of the intended message, and accepts the message that is presented before them. In the negotiated reader, the decoder of the image may accept the message from the author without necessarily agreeing with it. The oppositional reader, however, disagrees and rejects the image being presented to them. When looking at one image, a viewer may experience all of these types of readerships in one sitting, and the encoder has little control over this messaging. Time and context can also change a reader's view of this image. The creator of any image does not necessarily get to dictate how it will be processed and perceived by an audience. German illustrator Christoph Niemann addressed this topic in his 2018 TED Talk, in which he states that "The real magic doesn't happen on paper, it happens in the mind of the viewer when your expectations and your knowledge clash with my artistic intentions. Your interaction with an image, your ability to read, question, be bothered, or bored, or inspired is as important as my artistic contribution. Because that's what turns an artistic statement... into a creative dialogue."[11] The encoder, decoders, and context work together to create any visual communication.

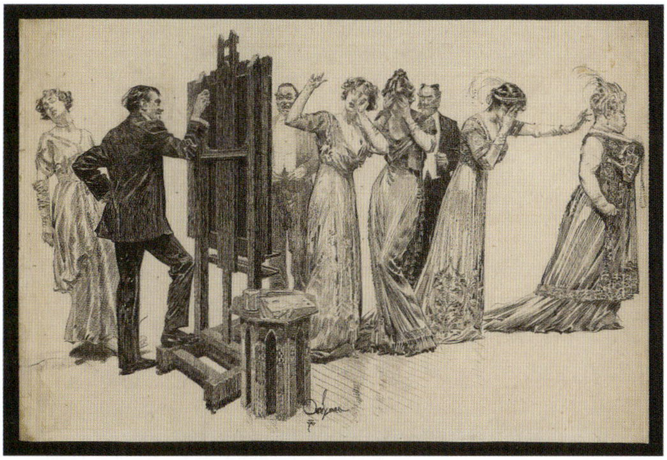

Figure 1.2
In Stuart Hall's reception theory, an "encoder" is the author of a message who uses their visual medium to communicate their message, which is then transmitted to the "decoder," or audience, who interprets the message. In this 1913 illustration by Orson Lowell, the encoder, or artist, seems to have had a different intent with his message than what was interpreted by the decoders, his audience.

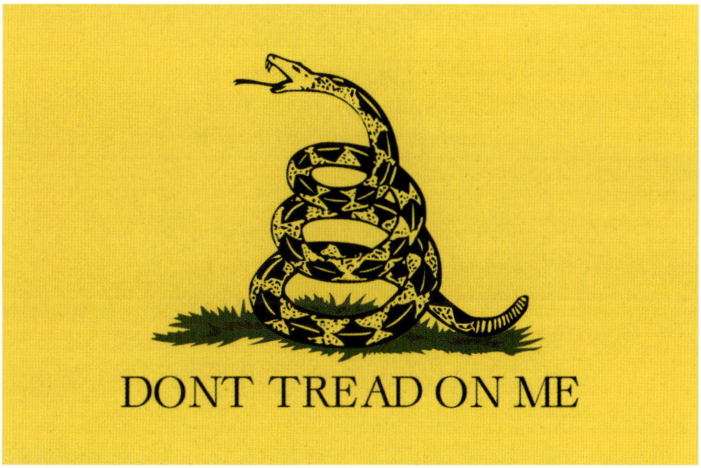

Figure 1.3
The Gadsden Flag, originally created by Christopher Gadsden, was originally created as an anti-British symbol during the Revolutionary War, but has evolved in the 21st century into a racist and right-wing symbol.

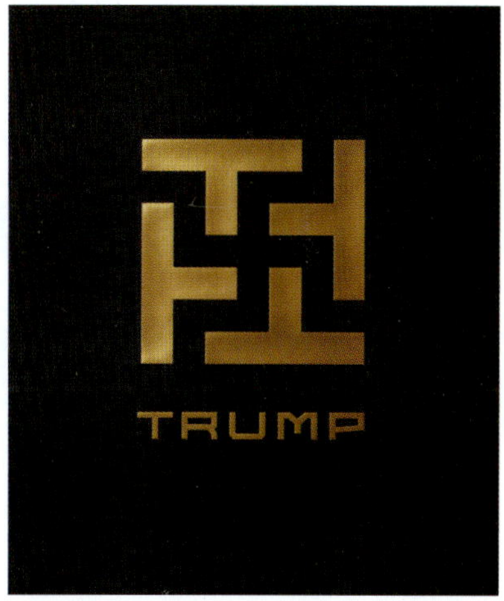

Figure 1.4
In *Trump 24K Gold-Plated* by Angie Wang and Mark Fox of Design is Play, the artists utilized visual metaphor to encode a hidden message into the negative space of the design.
Design © 2016 Mark Fox and Angie Wang, Design is Play

Visual Grammar & Technique

If the author of an image doesn't have full control over the message of their image, what do they have control of? They have control over what Christian Leborg calls **visual grammar**: how they construct and present the initial visual code in the first place. Leborg writes that, like in written or spoken language, visuals have processes and patterns that create relationships between the elements of the language.[12] These elements and their relationships to each other are how we encode visual ideas for the most universal understanding. Many of these relational elements of visual grammar are included in **Gestalt theory**. Gestalt theory states that as human beings, we need to eliminate chaos and create order out of our environments in order to achieve equilibrium. As natural pattern seekers, humans will seek this order, this *visual grammar* in their environments, by seeing the whole over the sum of the parts. For example, think of the word puzzles in which you receive a paragraph with the first letter and last letter of the words the same, but the middle of the word is gibberish. (Figure 1.5) Even though the middle of the word is chaos, we still can find the order and read these paragraphs. Likewise, when we see an illustration, if the encoder has done their job properly, we can get enough visual clues that we can fill in the gaps and read the image as we would read the message in the word puzzle. In the Design is Play Trump logo, the creators perhaps only marginally provided enough clues for the image, since some of their audience couldn't decode it.

There are several different elements of Gestalt theory, depending on the author, but this book highlights four of the most critical elements: **closure**, **continuation**, **similarity**, and **proximity**. (Figure 1.6) In the Gestalt principle of closure, the viewer seeks to take unrelated elements and see them as a complete whole or shape. The logo of the conservative party of Canada consists of three individual shapes which our brains visually link to perceive the letter "C." (Figure 1.7) Another example is in an image by Edel Rodriguez of Kim Jong Un and Trump riding a nuclear bomb like a toy horse outside a grocery store. In this image, although the bodies of each figure are physically disconnected from their legs, our brains read the negative white space as diapers, and, therefore, we don't see the legs as (rather gruesomely) being detached from the torsos, but we read the legs, diaper, and torso as being one whole body. (Figure 1.8) In Doug Chayka's *Let's See Some I.D.*, we perceive the individual figures as forming the whole of an anonymous head and shoulders. (Figure 1.9)

In the Gestalt principle of continuation (also called good continuation), a series of related elements on a line or path are seen as one connected whole. When this is applied to motion, it is called **common fate**. We perceive continuation whenever we look at a dotted line: although the elements are not physically connected, our brain fills in the gaps to see them as one continuous line or path. In a North Korean propaganda poster, a diagonal line of people extends from the bottom right to the top left, and our brain perceptually connects them as one path. (Figure 1.10) In a Thomas Nast cartoon lampooning the Tammany Hall corruption case, we see individual men standing in a circle as one continuous ring. (Figure 1.11)

In the Gestalt principle of similarity, we connect visual elements that are similar to one another. In similarity, there is a hierarchy of visual cues that will make parts of an

image seem to be more connected: shape, then size, and then color. The first cue is shape. Objects with a similar shape within an image will be seen as one group or chunk. An even stronger cue is size. Objects that have a similar size, even if they have different shapes, will be seen as one group or chunk. The strongest visual cue is color, objects that have a similar color will be seen as one group or chunk, even if they have the same size or shape. Illustrators can strategically use these visual cues to create visual connections and groups within an image. When objects are similar, we will see them as more connected. In the British *Together* posters from the 1940s, the soldiers are similar in their direction (or common fate), shape of their faces, shape of their guns, and by their hats. (Figure 1.12) These similarities help them read as a group even when their nationalities differ. (As the British propaganda machine intended!) In Jaime Anderson's illustration *Two Party System*, the fighting teams of Republican elephants and Democratic donkeys are seen as distinct groups because of the similarity of the characters. (Figure 1.13)

Finally, in the Gestalt principle of proximity, we connect visual elements that are closer in space to one another, while we may see other elements that are less close together as disconnected. Overlap can also be used to show items in proximity to one another. In the Chinese propaganda poster from 1969, *Long Live to the Red Sun of the World's People, Chairman Mao,* the group of people seem connected to one another because of proximity and overlap. (Figure 1.14) Despite the world's people being different colors, shapes, and sizes, because of their proximity, they still appear connected as a group. Proximity is in fact the strongest grouping principle, more so than size, shape, or color, and can be used to connect items within imagery when similarity cannot be used. Proximity is also what makes the remainder of the Gestalt principles work. Closure only works when the elements forming the group are close enough to read as a whole. Continuation only works if the dots in the line are close enough for the brain to visually connect. Proximity is also often paired with similarity to create strong groupings within images as well.

In Takashi Kono's 1953 poster *Sheltered Weaklings*, which critiques the allyship between the US and Japan after World War II, America is seen as a shark, leading a group of small fish decorated with the rising sun of the Japanese flag. (Figure 1.15) The fish share a common fate as they're led in one direction by the shark, and the communist Russian fish are seen to break from the capitalist direction of America and Japan because they face in a different direction. The Japanese fish are seen as a group through similarity in shape, size, and color, but are also grouped through proximity. The American shark stands out as a focal point because it contrasts in size, shape, and pattern from the other fish. Kono was one of the founders of the Japanese Advertising Artists Club, which created post-war images using artistic and modern Japanese design techniques in their work. This example of his poster is an excellent illustration of how Gestalt principles can be used in political illustration to communicate a message.

In her book "Picture This," Molly Bang describes many Gestalt principles, but also other psychological principles that affect how we view images. Diagonals in images indicate tension and motion. Points in images activate our amygdala, the fear center of our brain, evoking an evolved aversion to the teeth of a predator or the point of a knife. Dark colors can evoke our fears of the unknown, and bright and light colors can evoke feelings of happiness.[13] Our brains work in a myriad of predictable ways to help us interpret visual images and form our innate sense of visual grammar. When creating an illustration, the artist can pull from these principles in order to construct a clear and understandable message.

Figure 1.5
Can you raed the mgsseae?

Fuor srcoe and seevn yraes ago
our frhtaes bhguort ftroh on
tihs cnontient, a new notian,
cecvnioed in Lterbiy, and
decditaed to the piposoitorn
taht all men are certaed eauql.

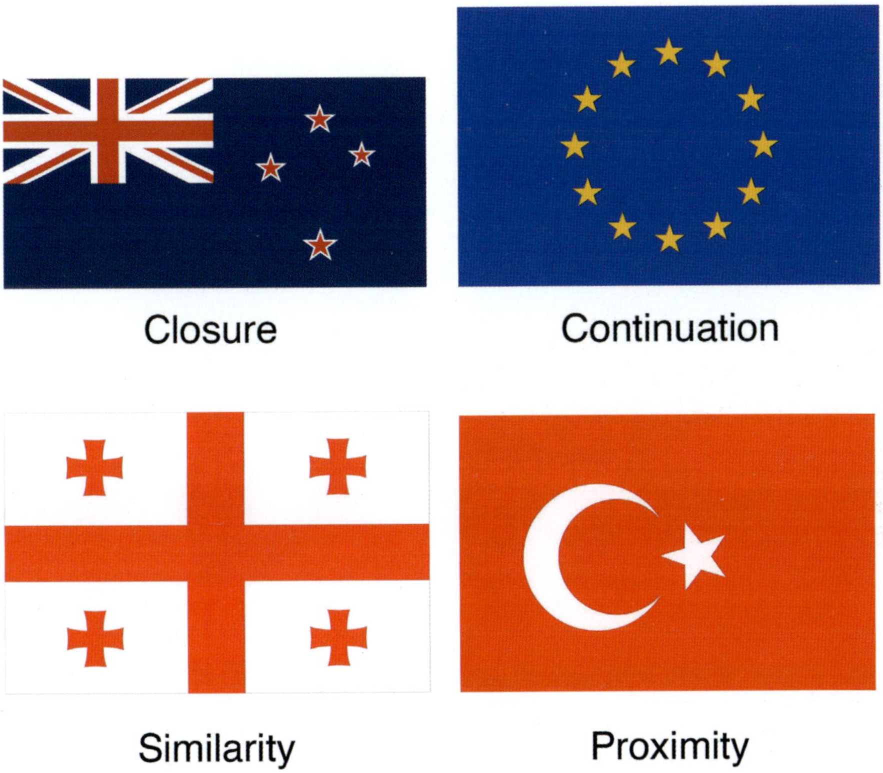

Figure 1.6
Closure, continuation, similarity, and proximity are all examples of how Gestalt principles form patterns that cause the viewer of an image to perceive a whole instead of separate parts. The Southern Cross constellation on the New Zealand flag utilizes closure by reading as a cross instead of four separate stars. The stars in the EU flag read as a continuous circular path, demonstrating continuation. The four crosses in the flag of Georgia unite the four quadrants through similarity. The crescent and star on the flag of Turkey are close together, demonstrating proximity, and therefore the two shapes are united as one symbol.

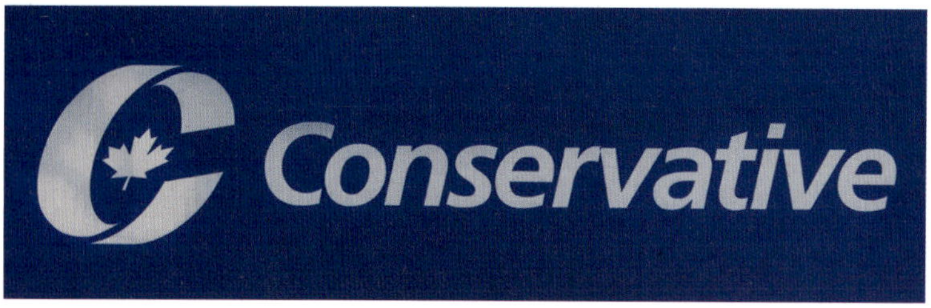

Figure 1.7
The three ribbon-like pieces of the Conservative Party of Canada logo are not physically connected, but the brain mentally connects the separate pieces, so the viewer perceives an uppercase letter C.

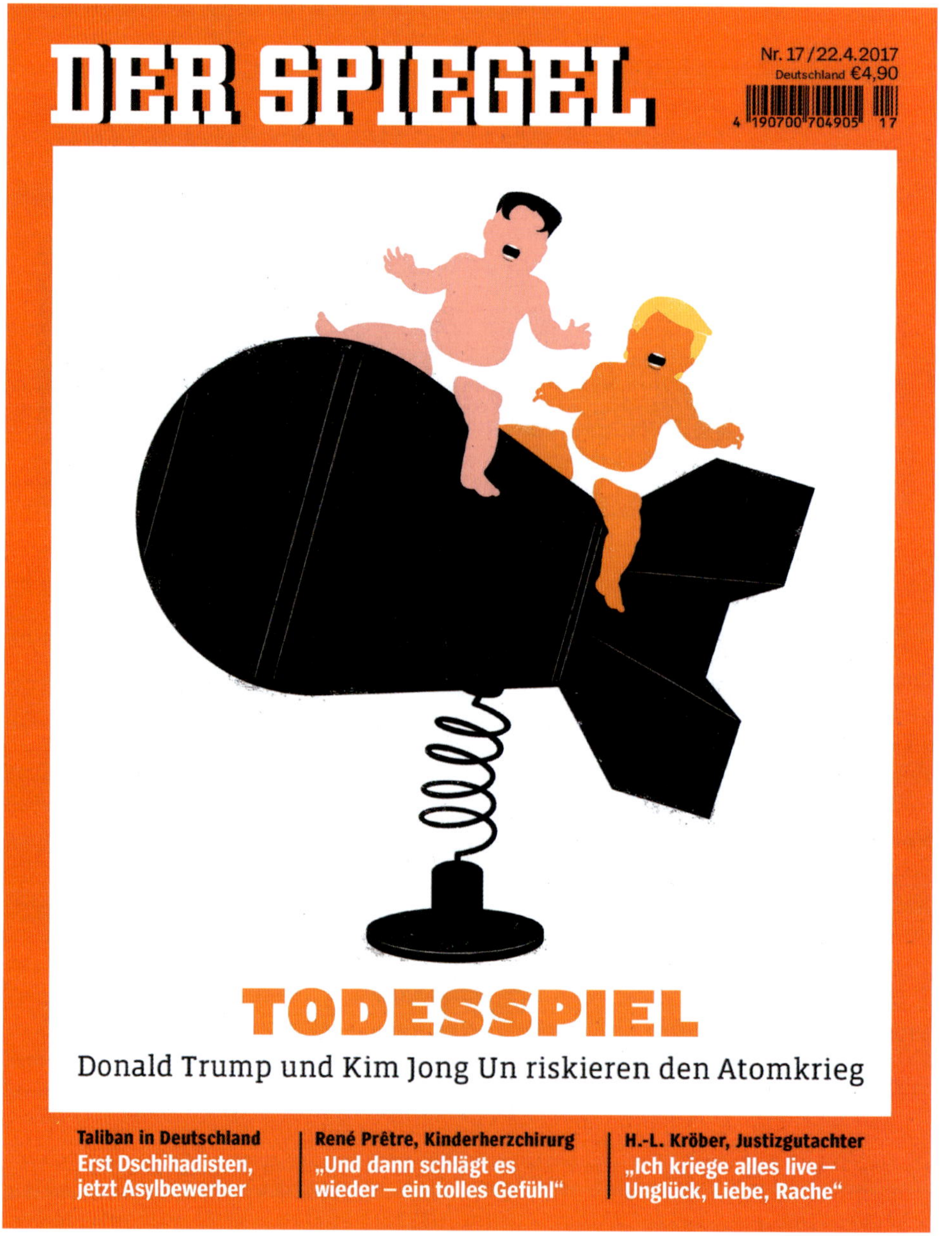

Figure 1.8
Edel Rodriguez' image *Todespiel* (2017) uses the Gestalt principle of closure to interpret the legs, negative white space, and torso as being one whole body. © Edel Rodriguez

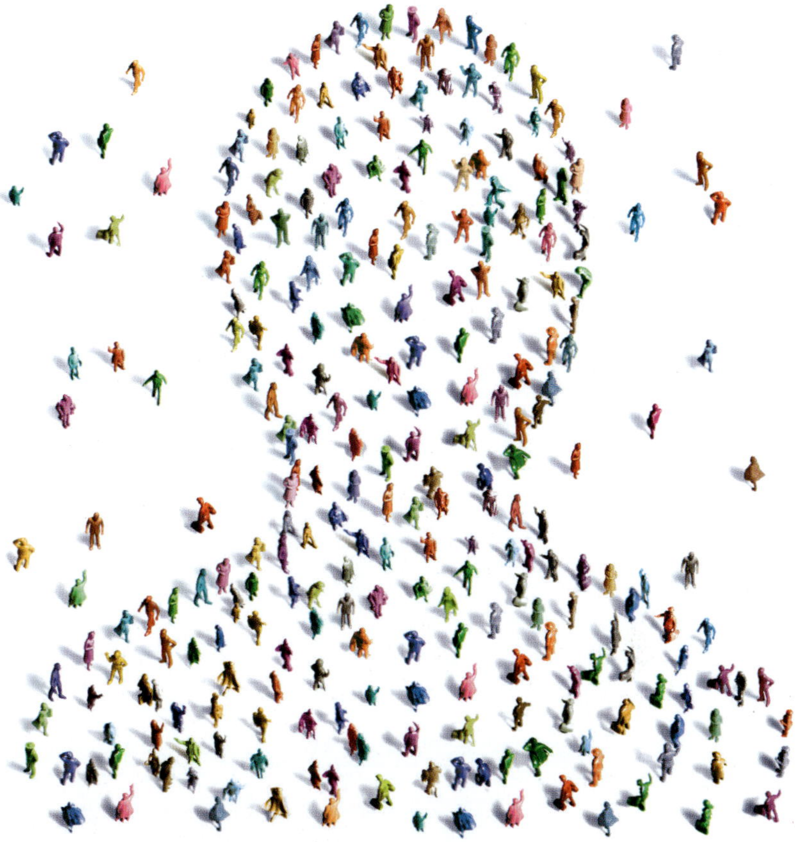

Figure 1.9
Doug Chayka's *Let's See Some I.D.* (2018) uses the Gestalt principle of closure so that the viewer perceives the individual figures as forming the whole of an anonymous head and shoulders.
© Doug Chayka

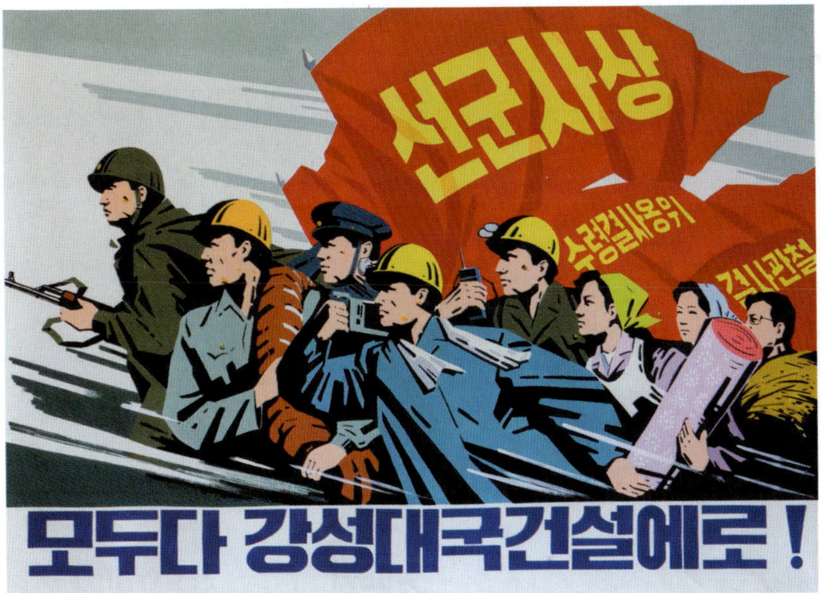

Figure 1.10
In this North Korea propaganda poster, a diagonal line of people extends from the bottom right to the top left, and our brain uses the Gestalt principle of continuation to perceive them as one path.

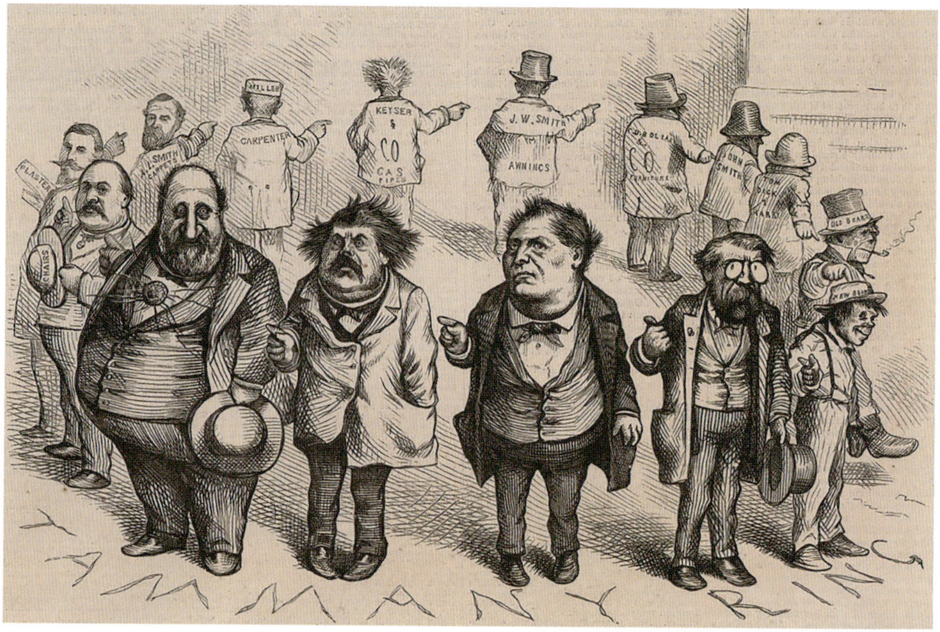

Figure 1.11
In this 1871 Thomas Nast cartoon lampooning the Tammany Hall corruption case, our brain uses the Gestalt principle of continuation to perceive the individual men standing in a circle as one continuous ring.

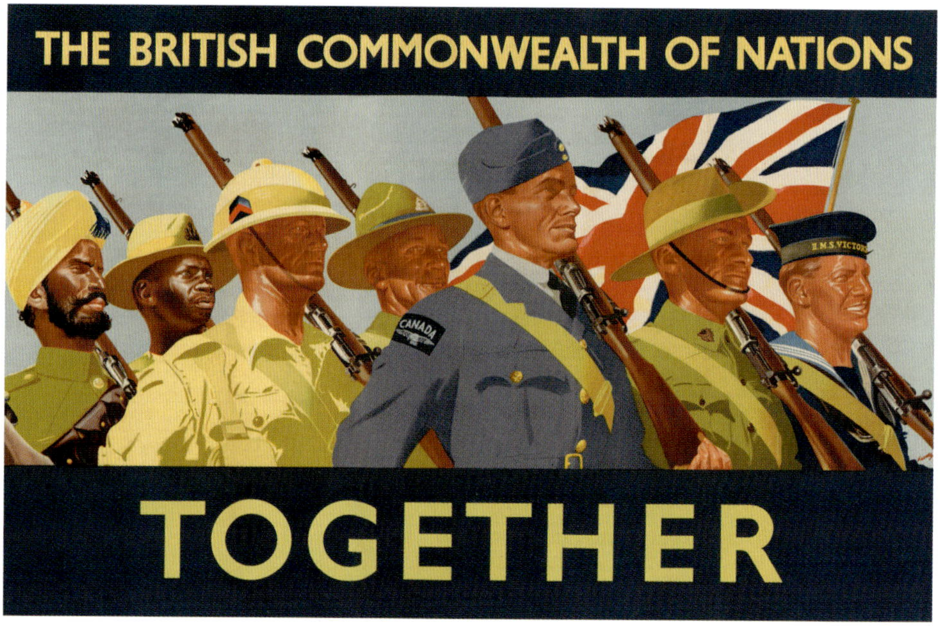

Figure 1.12
In the British *Together* posters from the 1940s, the soldiers show the Gestalt principle of similarity through their direction (or common fate), shape of their faces, shape of their guns, and by their hats.

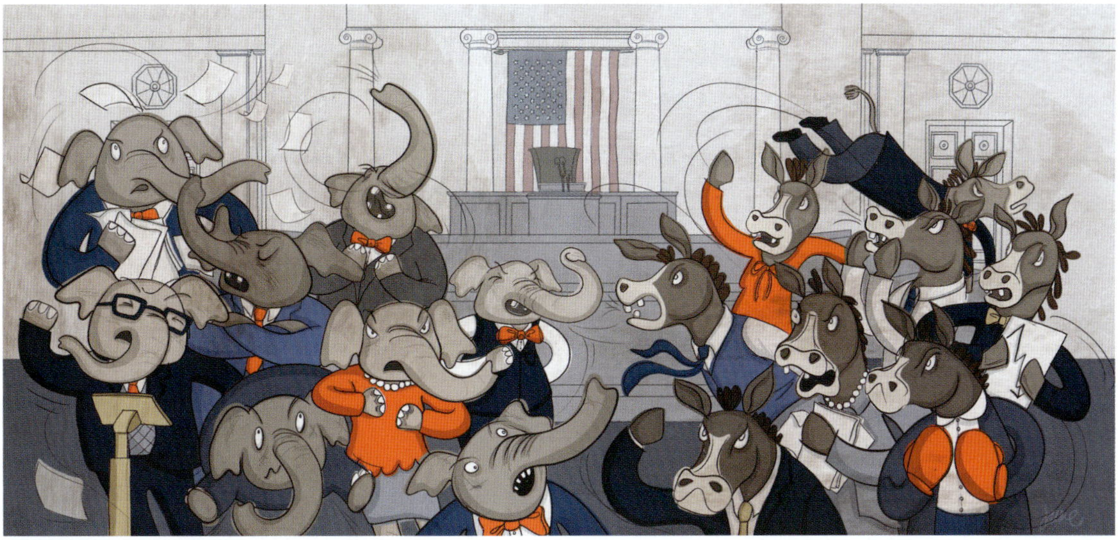

Figure 1.13
In Jaime Anderson's illustration *Two Party System*, the fighting teams of Republican elephants and Democratic donkeys are seen as distinct groups because of the Gestalt principle of similarity.

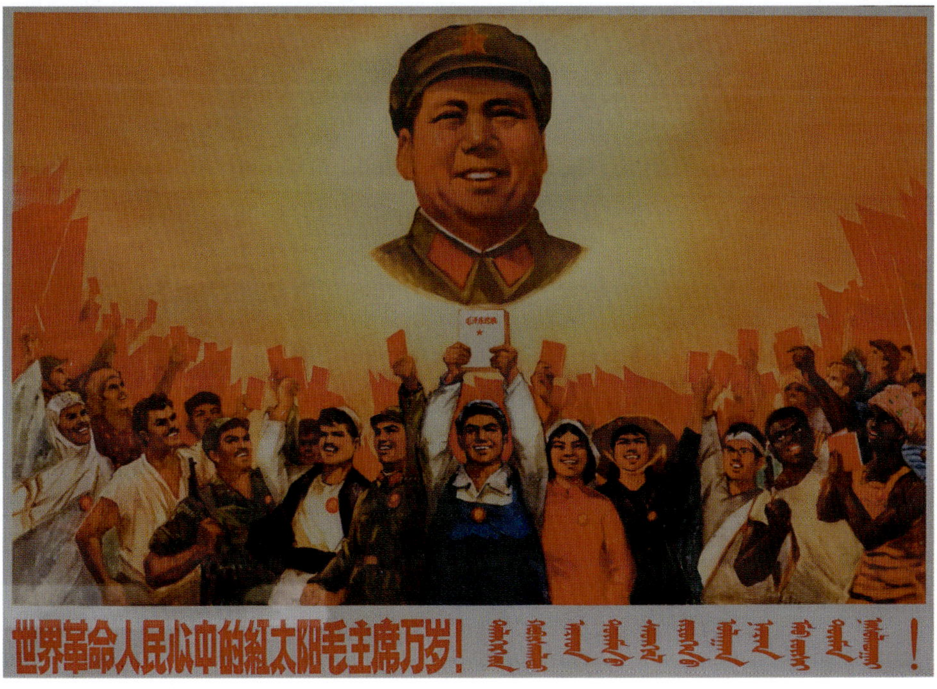

Figure 1.14
In the Chinese propaganda poster from 1969, *Long Live to the Red Sun of the World's People, Chairman Mao*, the group of people seem connected to one another because of the Gestalt principle of proximity.

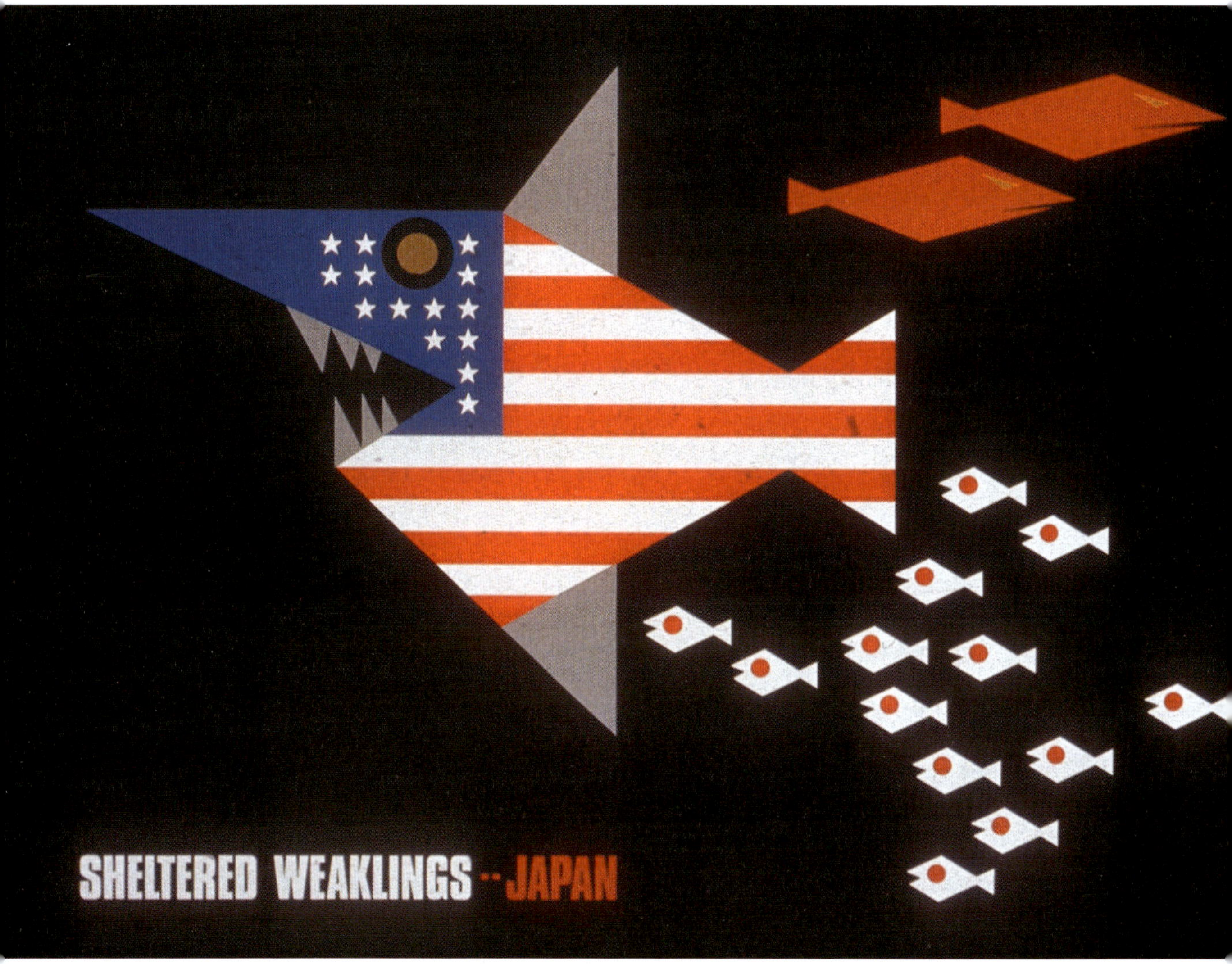

Figure 1.15
Takashi Kono's 1953 poster *Sheltered Weaklings* exemplifies the Gestalt principles of similarity, proximity, and common fate.

Semiotics: Connotation and Denotation

The process of encoding and decoding a visual message must pass through what is called **semiotics**. Semiotics is another approach to visual grammar. Initially developed by linguists Ferdinand de Saussure and Charles Sanders Peirce, semiotics is defined as the study of signs: the idea that an image can be more than just an image, but a signifier of something else. The relationship between a sign and what it signifies is often, but not always, arbitrary, and needs to be culturally learned. Whenever we see an image, we understand that an image isn't the actual object or thing it signifies, but it is simply a signifier of the object or thing. Peirce divided signs into three categories: icons, indexes, and symbols. (Figure 1.16) **Icons** are a direct representation of the signified. A photograph of a woman is not the woman herself but signifies that person. A child's drawing of the same woman would also be an icon, even though it is abstracted, the signifier is a direct representation of the signified. A drawing, photograph, sculpture, or other type of medium that directly represents the signified acts as an icon.

An **index** has more nuance than an icon. In an index, the signifier gives evidence of the signified, without directly representing it. The classic representation of this would be smoke indicating, or giving evidence of, a fire. Indexes tend to refer to concrete, non-abstract objects or concepts. This is important in distinguishing an index from a symbol. **Symbols** often refer to more abstract or arbitrary associations, such as a diamond necklace symbolizing wealth or love. Symbols must be learned in order to be a symbol, while indexes are more directly communicated. All letters and numbers for instance, are learned and arbitrary representations of a subject. Regardless of the type of sign, remember the meaning of the sign must be communicated in order to be a sign. If a toddler draws a portrait of you, but you don't understand what it is supposed to signify, it is not a sign until it is communicated.

In the 1960s, Roland Barthes' explored and expanded on the types of messages that images can communicate. Barthes, a longtime follower of semiotics, proposed that any image has two meanings to it: the **denotation** and the **connotation**. (Figure 1.17) The denotation is the literal, fixed meaning of the signifier. The connotation is the underlying, second meaning of an image. Barthes' asserts that connotations, unlike denotations, are arbitrary and depend on the experience and background of the viewer.

The use of semiotics is inherent to the efficacy of political illustration. Often, full understanding of political illustration is dependent on the decoder of an image having a working knowledge of the political situations behind the images. For this reason, this book gives its readers enough background knowledge that they can fully appreciate the impact of some of the illustrations we share. The interpretation of political images is also dependent on the decoder's background and viewpoint. As will be discussed in section two of the book, *Media, Censorship, & Taboo*, the difference of these interpretations can lead to censorship and even dangerous conflict. The denotation of a smiling dictator may be interpreted at face value by a happy subject but may take on an ominous connotation by an opposition political party or a political dissident.

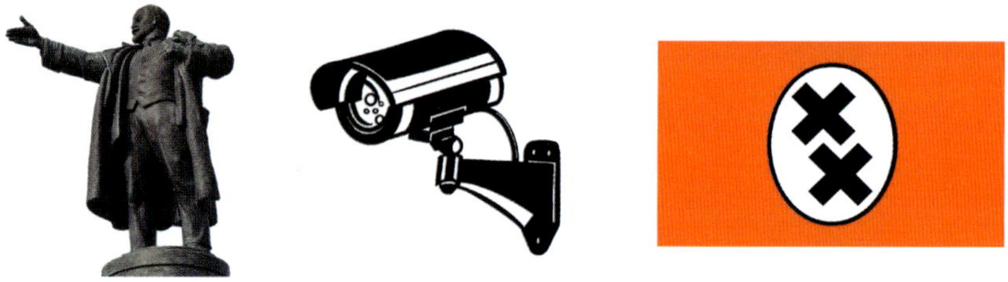

Figure 1.16
In semiotics, signs are divided into three categories: icons, indexes, and symbols. Any concept, such as "dictator," can be represented iconically, indexically, or symbolically. An icon is a direct representation of the signified. A statue of a dictator is an icon of a dictator. An index indicates or gives evidence of the thing being represented. A surveillance camera indicates evidence of a dictatorship surveilling the public. A symbol represents the signified, but has to be culturally learned. The "double x" flag from Charlie Chaplin's 1940 film *The Great Dictator*, meant to mock the Nazi swastika, is a symbol of a dictatorship.

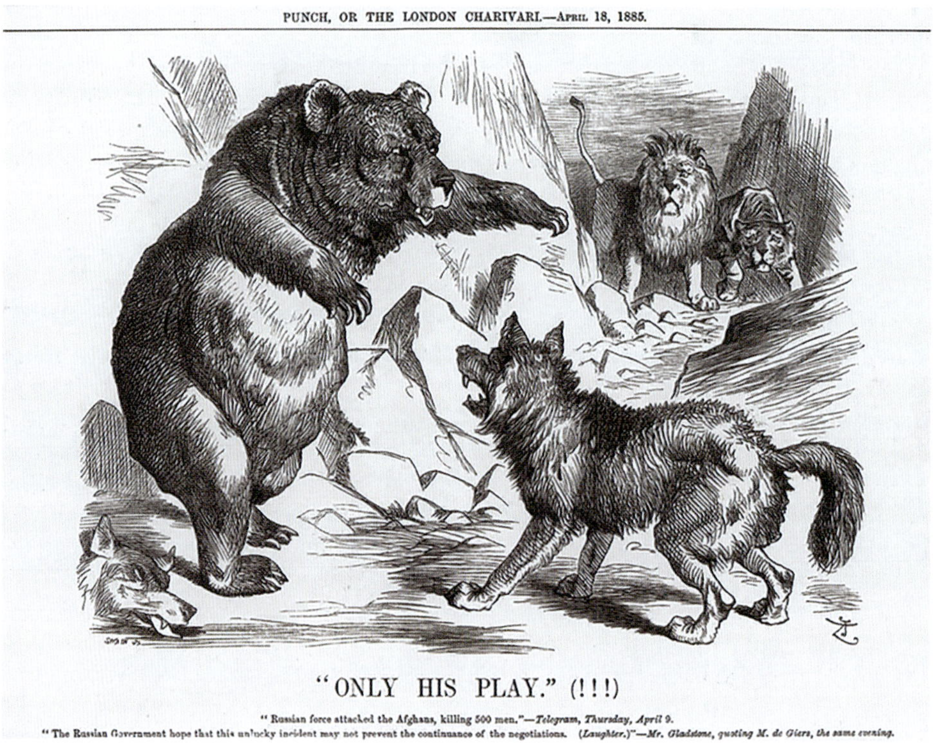

Figure 1.17
An image's denotation is the literal, fixed meaning of the signifier. The connotation is the underlying, second meaning of an image. In this 1885 cartoon from *Punch* magazine, the denotation is a bear fighting a wolf. The connotation is that Russia attacked Afghanistan, while Britain (the lion) and India (the tiger) look on nervously.

Metaphor & Metonym

The connotations of political illustrations can be hinted at in numerous ways, but a common technique of illustrators is to use what is called visual **metaphor**. In visual metaphors, like linguistic metaphors, images take on multiple meanings, using a variety of techniques including visual similarities or visual symbolism. In her book, "Picture This," Molly Bang discusses how as humans we assign meaning to any visual, based on our biology and life experiences. A simple circle could become a pie, a basketball, a period at the end of a sentence, the pupil of an eye, or a black hole, depending on the meaning you assign to it. Scott McCloud also addresses this in his book "Understanding Comics," stating the more we simplify an object, the more meanings it can take on.[14] (Figure 1.18) The art of an illustrator is to find the perfect balance between complexity and simplicity in order to communicate an idea, as described by Christoph Niemann. A heart that is too simple can't be recognized and fails to communicate a sign, an overly realistic heart is too specific (and grotesque!), but a heart that strikes that balance brings along with it a symbol that can be interpreted by a wide variety of audiences.[15] (Figure 1.19)

The importance of metaphor in human understanding and communication is also discussed by George Lakoff and Mark Johnson in "Metaphors We Live By." In this book, Lakoff and Johnson discuss how our language and linguistic experience is formed by metaphors that relate back to our physical experience. For instance, when we say we are "feeling down," it is a metaphor for the physical experience of laying prostrate, for instance when we are sick or we are tired.[16] We also create these metaphors based on our visual experience. We may say we are "feeling blue," because of our association of blue and cool colors with melancholy, or we are "seeing the world through rose colored glasses" when we are feeling happy or optimistic, because of our association with warm colors and life and happiness. This again is based on our physical experience. A rainstorm or a cold, bleak day are all physical experiences that include cool colors, while a warm fire or a sunny day include warm colors. We can feel "shiny," "bright," or "sparkly," or, in contrast, we can feel "dull," "dim," or "cloudy." When we see these visual concepts in illustration, they evoke metaphors that relate us to our physical experience. This is, in essence, how art makes us feel emotions.

In political illustration, metaphor is used extensively. In her illustration *End Sex Trafficking*, illustrator Erin Burns, provocatively uses the shape of pubic hair to become a bar code, indicating the commercial transactions involved with sex trafficking. (Figure 1.20) In another image by Burns about bullying in the LGBTQ+ community, *End Bullying*, she uses the color of the target presented as a metaphor for the rainbow flag, a symbol of the queer community. (Figure 1.21) The trickle of red represents more than a physical injury, but as a symbol of the suffering victims of bullying endure. Illustrator Jonathan Cumberland also uses a visual metaphor in his illustration, *Target Guns, Not our Future*, which calls for political action against gun violence. (Figure 1.22) By comparing the circular shape of a tricycle's wheel, a symbol of childhood, to the circular shape of a target, he illustrates how children have become victims of the gun epidemic. In his illustration *Gas Tank,* illustrator JP Kelly uses a visual similarity of the top of a military tank becoming the handle of a gas pump, with a drip of oil from it being colored

red to show a further metaphor of it being a drop of blood. The metaphor is intended to illustrate to the audience how wars can be fought for economic interests such as oil. (Figure 1.23)

Metonym is another concept frequently used in editorial and political illustration. In metonym, unlike metaphor, a singular object represents a totality: not just one other thing, object or idea, but a group of other things, objects, or ideas. As Christoph Niemann describes, a graduation cap may not just signify a graduation cap, but any college graduate. Use of the symbol of a woman wearing a dress (or a cape, it's to be disputed) on a bathroom door, is a metonym for all women, not just one specific woman. In America, a red elephant is a metonym for all Republicans, not just a specific Republican. In Anita Kunz' illustration for *The Nation*, *Whistleblower's Mother*, the woman in the illustration is not just a metaphor for one woman, but is a metonym for women in Texas seeking an abortion after the 2021 state law allowing whistleblowers or vigilantes to sue those aiding and abetting in an abortion. (Figure 1.24) When an encoder has considered visual grammar, Gestalt, semiotics, the principles of design, and the context with which the readers of the image are familiar with, they can create political illustrations that can be successfully decoded by their audience.

With this introduction to the vocabulary necessary to discuss and interpret visual messages, we can now analyze how encoders employed by governments have used these techniques in the past and the present for political gain.

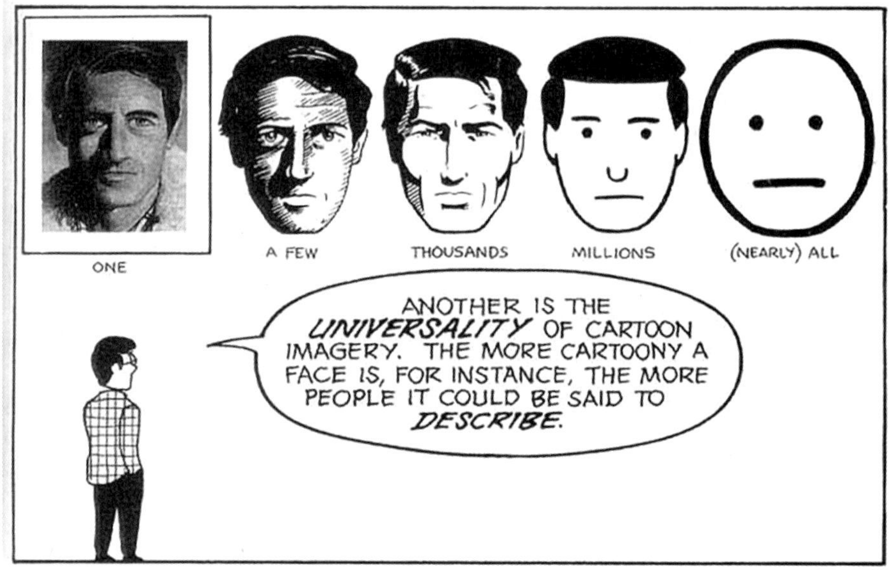

Figure 1.18
According to Scott McCloud, the more we simplify an object, the more meanings it can take on.

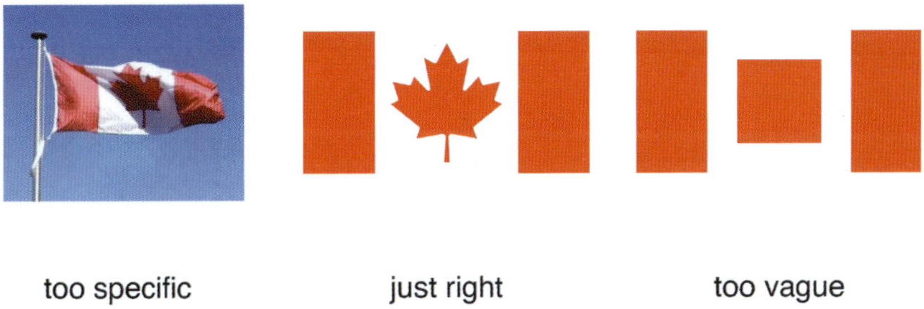

Figure 1.19
The art of an illustrator is to find the perfect balance between complexity and simplicity in order to communicate an idea. A realistic drawing of a flag blowing in the wind may obscure the design of the flag. A simplified color block version of a flag may be difficult to interpret. The best representation is a flat version of the flag with enough details to be understood.

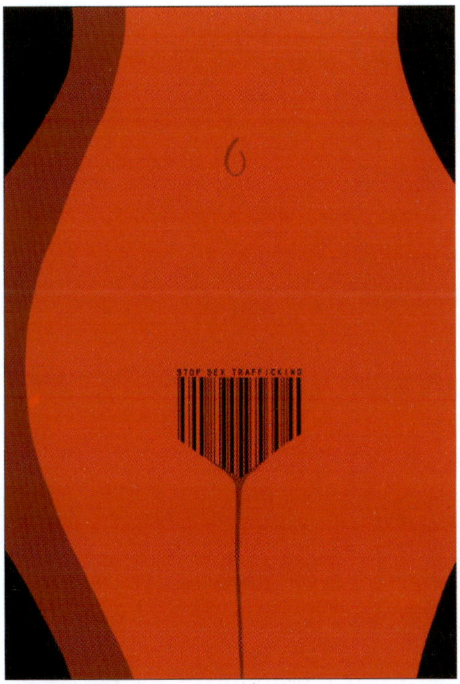

Figure 1.20
Visual metaphor is key to illustrator Erin Grace Burns' work. In her illustration *Stop Sex Trafficking*, the shape of pubic hair becomes a bar code.
© Erin Grace Burns, 2011

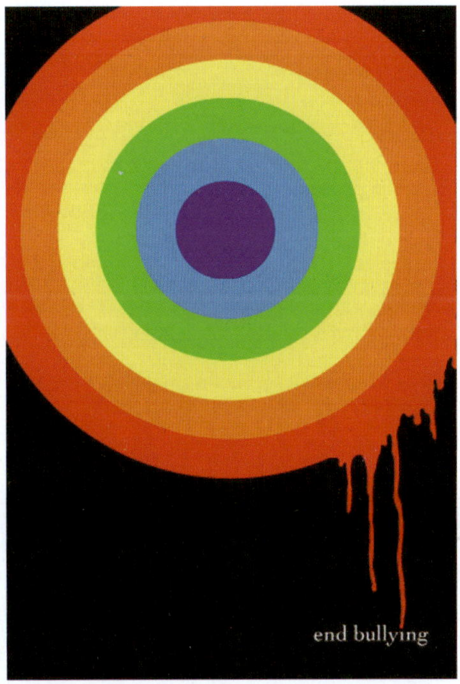

Figure 1.21
In this illustration by Erin Grace Burns about queer bullying, the colors of the target are a metaphor for the pride flag.
© Erin Grace Burns, 2011

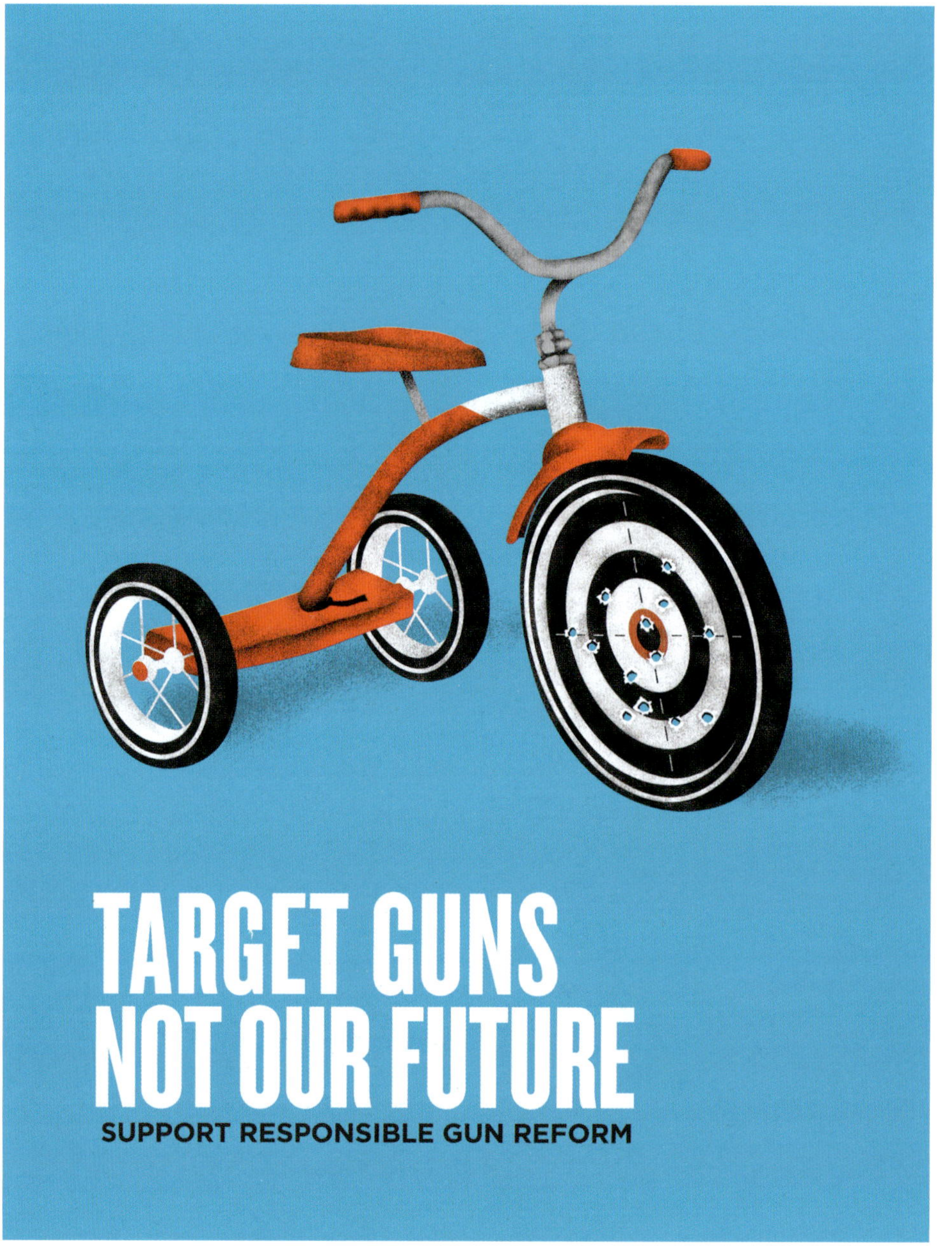

Figure 1.22
In his work *Target Guns, Not Our Future*, illustrator Jonathan Cumberland uses visual metaphor to compare the wheel of a tricycle with a target.

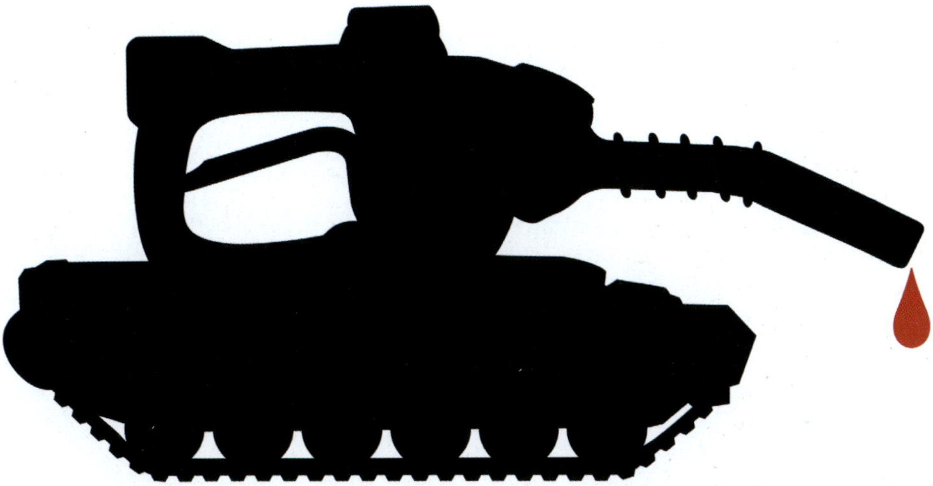

Figure 1.23
In his illustration *Gas Tank*, illustrator JP Kelly uses a visual similarity of the top of a military tank becoming the handle of a gas pump, with a drip of oil from it being colored red to show a further metaphor of it being a drop of blood.
© JP Kelly

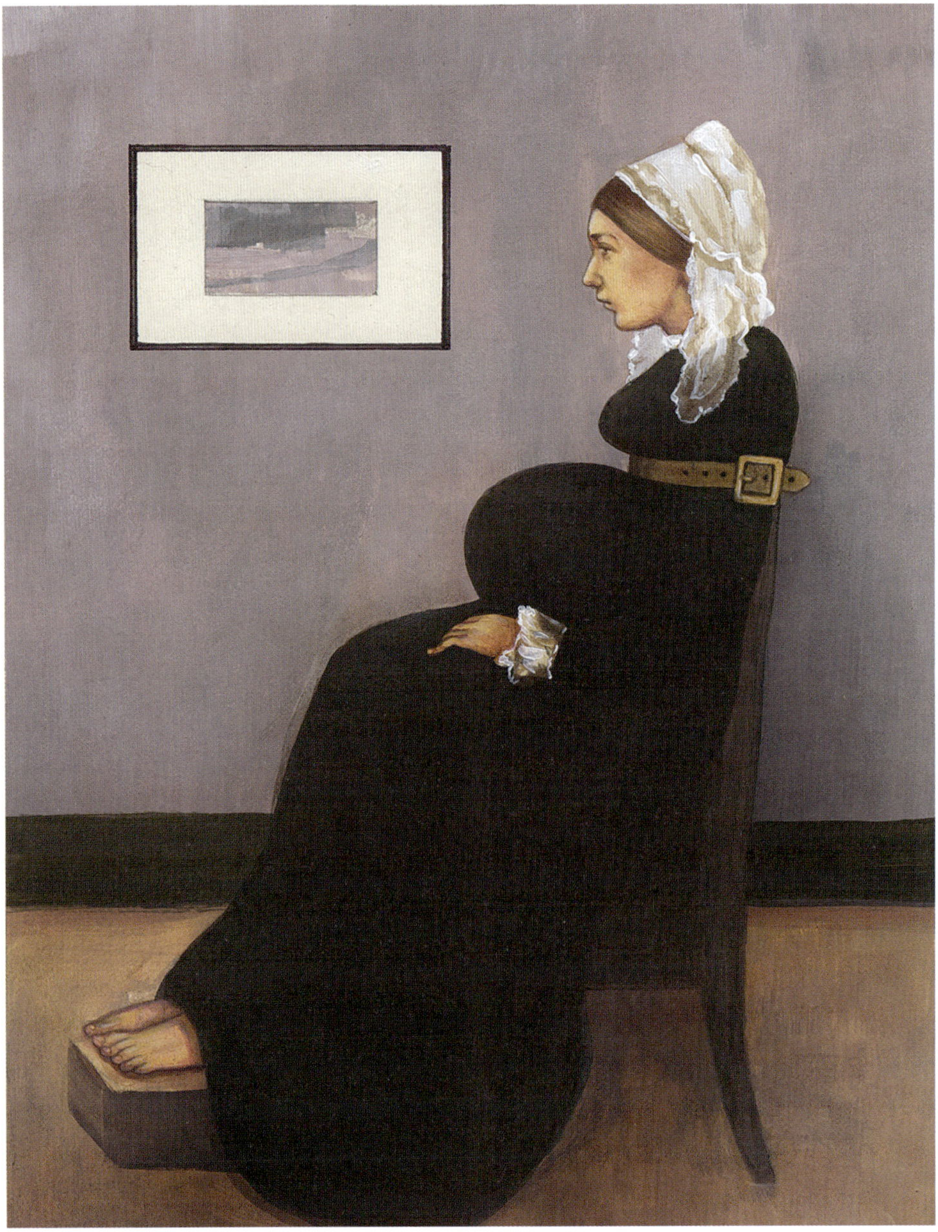

Figure 1.24
In Anita Kunz' illustration for *The Nation*, *Whistleblower's Mother*, the woman in the illustration is not just a metaphor for one woman, but is a metonym for women in Texas seeking an abortion after a 2021 state law was passed.
© Anita Kunz

Endnotes

1 Ron Synovitz, "Afghanistan: Ballot Papers Feature Unique System Of Candidate Symbols," *RadioFreeEurope/RadioLiberty*, September 14, 2005, https://www.rferl.org/a/1061384.html.

2 As of publication, Afghanistan does not currently hold elections, given the return of the Taliban to power.

3 Synovitz, "Afghanistan: Ballot Papers Feature Unique System Of Candidate Symbols"

4 "Designing Polling Place Materials: Top 10 election design guidelines," *United States Election Assistance Commission,* March 11, 2022, https://www.eac.gov/election-officials/designing-polling-place-materials.

5 Synovitz, "Afghanistan: Ballot Papers Feature Unique System Of Candidate Symbols"

6 "What You Should Know about EEOC and Shelton D. v. U.S. Postal Service (Gadsden Flag case)," *U.S. Equal Employment Opportunity Commission,* accessed January 1, 2024, https://www.eeoc.gov/wysk/what-you-should-know-about-eeoc-and-shelton-d-v-us-postal-service-gadsden-flag-case.

7 Rob Walker, "The Shifting Symbolism of the Gadsden Flag," *The New Yorker,* October 2, 2016, https://www.newyorker.com/news/news-desk/the-shifting-symbolism-of-the-gadsden-flag.

8 Mark Fox and Angie Wang, "Trump 24K Gold-Plated," *Communication Arts,* accessed January 1, 2024, https://www.commarts.com/project/25071/trump-24k-gold-plated.

9 Dan Evon, "Did Donald Trump's Campaign Unveil a Swastika-Like Logo?", *Snopes,* November 28, 2015, https://www.snopes.com/fact-check/donald-trump-swastika-logo/.

10 Letterform Archive (@letterformarchive), "Happy 14th birthday to Design is Play!..." Instagram post and comments, September 7, 2021, https://www.instagram.com/p/CTh1YnRh4b1/.

11 Christoph Niemann, "You Are Fluent In This Language and Don't Even Know It," *Ted,* April 2018, https://www.ted.com/talks/christoph_niemann_you_are_fluent_in_this_language_and_don_t_even_know_it?language=en.

12 Christian Leborg, *Visual Grammar.* (New York: Princeton Architectural Press, 2006).

13 Molly Bang, *Picture This: How Pictures Work.* (San Francisco: Chronicle Books, 2016).

14 TO BE UPDATED

15 Christoph Niemann, "You Are Fluent In This Language and Don't Even Know It," *Ted,* April 2018, https://www.ted.com/talks/christoph_niemann_you_are_fluent_in_this_language_and_don_t_even_know_it?language=en.

16 George Lakoff and Mark Johnson, *Metaphors We Live By.* (Chicago: University of Chicago Press,1980).

2

Propaganda:
The Art of the State

Introduction

For thousands of years, governments have used images to either directly or indirectly persuade, compel, and influence their subjects. When these images are attempting to persuade an audience on behalf of a government's agenda, this is called **propaganda.** Oftentimes, the word propaganda has a negative connotation of being images created to mislead or manipulate an audience. In fact, illustrated propaganda uses the same techniques as any other type of visual persuasion and can communicate messages that could be viewed as positive, as well as negative. Symbolism, metaphor, semiology, Gestalt, and other types of visual grammar can be used in persuasive propaganda to save the rainforests just as much as it could be used to elect a dictator.

The root of the word propaganda comes from the Latin root *propagare*, meaning to propagate or to spread, and the first use of the word traces to 1622 when Pope Gregory XV founded the *Congregatio de propaganda fide*, or "Congregation for propagating the faith," formalizing the Catholic church's missionary attempts and countering the spread of the Protestant church.[1] This root that ties the word propaganda to the word propagation provides a unique connection between the term propaganda and the field of illustration. Like propaganda, illustration also exists to propagate a message through a visual medium, serving either the artist's or the client's agenda. Importantly, propaganda and illustration share another important tie: the invention of the **printing press** in the mid 1400s, and its subsequent popularization. The era of the Protestant Reformation indeed heralded a new era for propaganda, spurred on by this new technology. Following the posting of his Ninety-five Theses in 1517, Martin Luther created the first major mass movement and media campaign through utilizing the printing press. Twenty percent of printed material between 1500–1530 were pamphlets created by Luther.[2] Luther also noted the importance of imagery in spreading his message, reproducing engravings by his favorite illustrators Lucas Cranach the Elder and Lucas Cranach the Younger. Undoubtedly, the history of print, propaganda, and illustration are inextricably intertwined.

Illustrated propaganda creates lasting and memorable messages through its use of the **picture superiority effect**. The picture superiority effect, first noted by Allan Paivio, states that images are more easily remembered and recalled than words. This takes place, in part, because of semiotics. While words have to go through two processes to be understood by the brain (reading symbols that need to be converted into the signified), the meaning of pictures is more directly processed. Studies have also shown that visual advertisements take less time to enter long-term memory than verbal ads.[3] Research on memory loss and aging has shown that using pictures can be effective in treating the memory loss of words.[4] The picture superiority effect has a profound influence on the power of images to compel and persuade thought. Visual propaganda can remain in our unconscious mind even when superseded by contradictory verbal information. Effectively using illustrations in a piece of propaganda can create images that will last in a person's mind throughout their lifetime.

Oftentimes we think we know propaganda when we see it, for instance on political posters we see while walking around a city, flyers left in our mailboxes, or a political candidate's latest Instagram post. Many people today, for instance, have been conditioned to associate the term "propaganda" with the limited colors and bold shapes of 20th century posters from the Soviet Union and China. However, propaganda sometimes disguises itself in unexpected styles and doesn't always come in black, white, and red. Frequently, propaganda can show up through unanticipated media and in unexpected places. If you look in your pocket or the cupholder in your car, you might find one of the oldest known examples of propaganda: coins.

GLOBAL POLITICS PERSPECTIVE

Types of Political Systems

This chapter explores how governments can use visual information to influence their people in the form of propaganda. All governments engage in this behavior, regardless of their political system. When we speak of political systems, there are two main categories: authoritarianism and democracy. These two categories can be distinguished in multiple ways, but the most basic way is to use citizen participation and political competition as indicators.[5] In other words, who can vote, and is there competition over political ideas? In a genuine democracy, virtually all adult citizens maintain equal rights, especially the right to vote. Second, meaningful competition between political parties, candidates, or organizations exists in a democracy. If a country has elections, but there are limits on participation or there is virtually no competition, then we would not consider it a democracy; this would be an authoritarian political system (like present-day Russia). The field of Political Science uses additional criteria to determine if a system is democratic, such as open and honest elections, protections for civil liberties, or the alteration of power. The organization Freedom House attempts to measure democracy across the world by classifying each country as free, partly free, or not free, based on the political rights and civil liberties that people hold in that country.[6] (Figure 2.1) It is safe to say that all of those categorized as "Free" are democracies, and all of those categorized as "Not Free" have authoritarian systems. Those in the middle category vary, some might still be considered democracies, while others may not. Finally, these two categories are very broad. Both democracies and authoritarian countries can differ from one another. Some democracies have a parliament, some have a constitutional monarch, and some use **federalism**. Some authoritarian countries have a government run by one party, like China, a government run by the military, like Egypt, or a government that technically has multiparty elections but they are severely restricted, like Russia[7]. One final note on political and economic systems: the two categories, democracy and authoritarianism, can exist with a variety of economic systems. Matters of the economy are often decided by political leaders, but these are separate concepts. In practice, most countries utilize some form of a market economy and capitalism; this is true in both democracies and authoritarian systems. Sometimes, a government may play a guiding role in managing market forces, as in China. As of 2024, virtually no country maintains a completely state-run command-style, or communist, economy that once existed in the Soviet Union. Even North Korea has some private business (although accurate information from North Korea is hard to obtain). While countries may differ in their political systems, governments will still try to shape the attitudes and actions of their people. The distinction between democracy and authoritarianism does relate to whether those people have rights or freedoms to take part in government or to criticize it. It is common to refer to people in democracies as "citizens," as they have the right to influence their governments. In authoritarian countries, the term "subjects" is more commonly used; this reflects the lack of formal opportunities to shape government policies or influence political leaders. Government influence and propaganda may look different when it targets citizens versus subjects, but it occurs in all political settings.

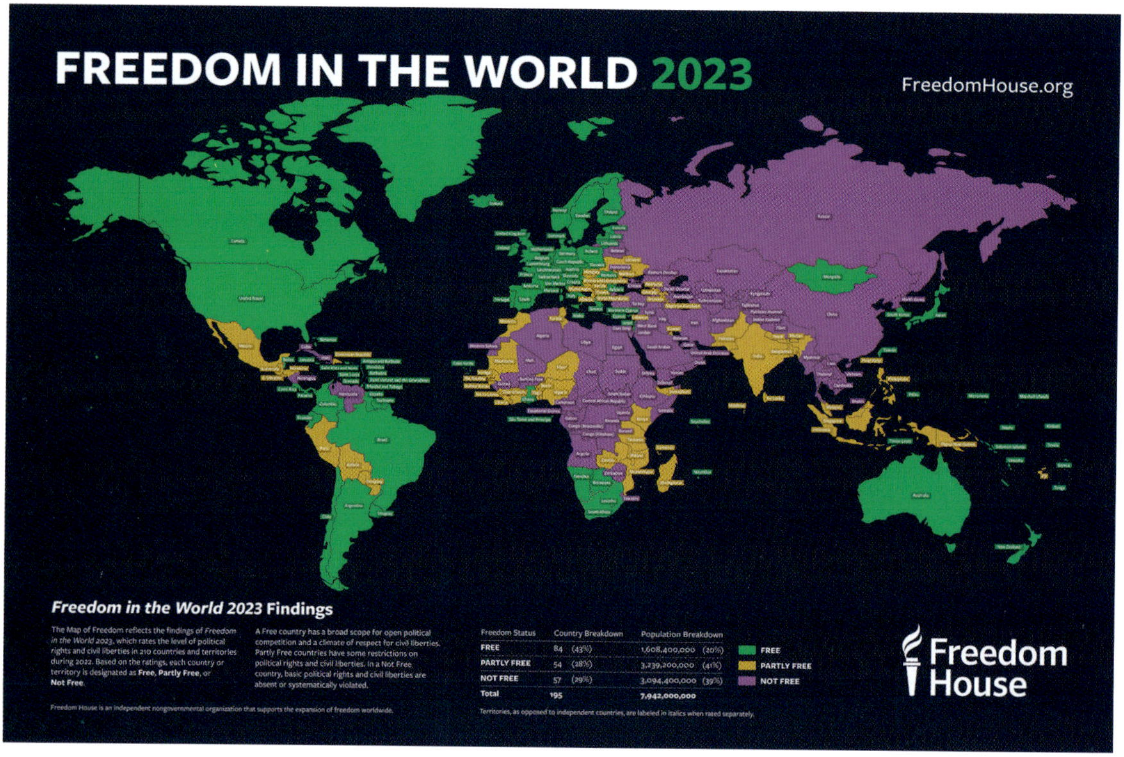

Figure 2.1
The organization Freedom House attempts to measure democracy across the world by classifying each country as free, partly free, or not free, based on the political rights and civil liberties that people hold in that country.
© *Freedom in the World*: Edition 2023 (www.freedomhouse.org)

Everyday Propaganda: Currency, Stamps, and Flags

In 44 BC, Julius Caesar was the first living figure depicted on the face of a coin.[8] (Figure 2.2) Thus began a standard for political and monarchical rulers to be portrayed on coins and currency that continues today. Prior to Caesar's rule, coins often featured a depiction of a god or deity on the front of the coin, and the obverse depicted symbols of the dominion, including animals, plants and resources, or reminders of a key historical event[9]. The symbolism of a political ruler placing their face on a coin is therefore clear: they wish to compare themself to a god. Caesar celebrated his military victories by minting coins, hoping that the repetition and proliferation of his effigy would help solidify his political power and sacred status as emperor.[10]

In the coin depicted in Figure 2.2, Caesar's exaggerated wrinkles were typical of the Roman Republic portraiture style of **verism**, which imbue him with age and authority. The oak leaf wreath on his head, called the "Corona Civica" or Civic Crown, was reserved for a Roman who had saved a fellow soldier in battle. Caesar received the Corona Civica in 79 B.C. and made it an everyday adornment and status symbol when he became emperor.[11] The statement "CAESAR DICT QVART" on the coin states that he has declared himself dictator for the fourth time, although in that same year he declared himself "dictator for life."[12] This absolute power, however, was dependent on Caesar cultivating a cult of personality with the public.

Two millennia later, the street artist Shepard Fairey noted on the creation of his Obey Giant sticker, "I liked the idea of the more stickers that are out there, the more important it seems; the more important it seems, the more people want to know what it is, the more they ask each other, and it gains real power from perceived power."[13] Caesar seized on this timeless idea, multiplying his image on tiny wheels more powerful than those on chariots. By creating such a large quantity of coinage, Caesar changed currency into a method of communication, ensuring the public would encounter his visage on a daily basis. Despite his deposition the same year this coin was issued, Caesar's influence stays with us today in the Julian calendar, the month July, but, most significantly, in his influence on future leaders. The tradition of creating propaganda out of figureheads on currency is used around the world from the United Kingdom to the United States to China to Papua New Guinea, and these portraits convey clear symbolic messages about the structure and basis of these governments.

A notable exception to using portraits on currency is the euro, first introduced in 1999. (Figure 2.3) The front of a euro banknote features, instead of a portrait, pictures of windows and doorways, which symbolize the European Union's commitment to openness and communication. On the back face of the euro, different architectural styles from Europe's history are depicted, without specifically depicting any actual existing structures. Christine Lagarde, President of the European Central Bank, states,

> "Our banknotes reflect a more fundamental development: the decades-long effort to bring Europe closer together. In a union of diverse countries, it is inherently more difficult to foster a common identity and a sense of shared destiny than in a single country. But the euro is one thing we all have in common. It serves as the most tangible symbol of European integration, a process which has brought peace, freedom and prosperity to our continent."[14]

Euro coins also have a unifying design, with a map of Europe printed on the front, but each country independently chooses the design on the reverse. Constitutional monarchies still tend to print a portrait of their monarch on the reverse side, but many countries choose to feature art or architecture from their country. Perhaps this is a sign of more countries moving away from a single figurehead as a national symbol, and moving towards an identity shared by its people. The design of the euro reflects the values of the European Union, creating a shared European identity based on promoting peace, justice, and egalitarianism.

While a country's currency reflects its national values, depicting important symbols and providing identity to its constituents, changes in currency can also affirm changes in governmental structures. After South Africa left the British Commonwealth in 1961, it issued its first currency, but still included a depiction of Dutch trader Jan van Riebeeck, harkening to a time of colonial rule. However, in 1992, when the fall of Apartheid unmasked the lingering damage of colonialism in the country, new currency was released, replacing Riebeeck with symbols that resonated with Black native South Africans, including the elephant, lion, Cape buffalo, leopard, and rhinoceros. In 2012, another critical symbol of South Africa and its independence graced its banknotes: the countenance of former President Nelson Mandela.[15] (Figure 2.4)

In South Africa, not only its currency but also its flag underwent a major change after the fall of the Apartheid government. From 1928 to 1994, the South African flag was in fact four flags combined into one. (Figure 2.5) The former Dutch flag provided the background, and in the center from left to right were images of the British Union Jack as well as two former Dutch colony flags. With the end of Apartheid, the new flag was created, including colors from the flags of the Netherlands, the United Kingdom, and the flag of the anti-apartheid political party in South Africa, the African National Congress. (Figure 2.6) The African National Congress flag had its own history, deriving from the flag of Ethiopia (one of the few African countries not to be formally colonized) and the Pan-African flag. The ANC flag features three horizontal stripes of black, green, and yellow, representing the native Black population of South Africa, the green land, and the yellow minerals and natural resources of the country.[16] After the Sharpeville Massacre in 1960, where 69 people were killed and 180 were injured by the white South African Police, the ANC and their flag were banned by the white South African government until 1990.[17] Incorporating the black, green, and yellow of this flag was a symbol of unity in a reborn South Africa. The Y shape was meant to show the different ethnic groups of South Africa, the British, the Dutch, and the native Black population, separate groups joining together as one towards a unified future. Following its adoption, the new South African flag was embraced as a symbol of harmony as the country moved forward.

With the adoption of the new flag, the old South African flag soon underwent a symbolism shift, becoming a visual embodiment of South Africa's racist past. The Anti-Defamation League lists the old flag as a hate symbol on its website, describing how it has been adopted as a white supremacist symbol.[18] In 2019, South Africa's Equality Court ruled that "gratuitous use" of the former flag constituted hate speech. Judge Phineas Mojapelo wrote in his ruling:

GLOBAL POLITICS PERSPECTIVE

The History of Apartheid South Africa

The system of Apartheid was an institutionalized system of racial segregation that created a strict legally defined hierarchy of power, with white South Africans at the top. This system relied on state-sanctioned political repression and brutal violence to enforce its survival. The Apartheid system officially lasted from 1948 to 1994, but its historical roots stretch back centuries. Like the vast majority of North and Sub-Saharan Africa, South Africa as a country was established through the legacy of European colonialism. First visited by traders from the Dutch East India Company in 1652, South Africa was later colonized by the British Empire. Unlike most other African countries, South Africa had a sizeable settler population: English-speaking British descendants and Afrikaans-speaking Dutch, or Boer, descendants.[19] Of course, prior to the arrival of Europeans, the territory now known as South Africa had been home to a variety of indigenous ethnic groups, including the Zulu and the Xhosa. These groups had established their own varied forms of political organization; most prominently, the Zulu nation had once ruled a sizeable portion of Southern Africa through military conquest, and they continued to fight against British colonial settlers into the 19th century.

The Union of South Africa was internationally recognized as an independent country in 1910. It limited voting rights to property-owning white men and held multi-party elections. Within the white population, Afrikaans-speakers were often poorer and less politically influential than English speakers; this political divide among white South Africans contributed to the staunch nationalist ideology of the Afrikaner-led National Party. Chief among their concerns were worries about their fate given the demographic realities of South Africa: the white population comprised less than a quarter of the overall population, and while non-white people had no voting rights, Afrikaners worried about their long-term survival in such a context. Indeed, the white population had been facing a growing uprising by the Black-led African National Congress (ANC), a movement that pushed back against the lack of voting rights and political representation for the Black majority population. The National Party won national elections in 1948, and implemented their promised vision of strict racial separation known as Apartheid, which means 'Apartness' in Afrikaans.

Under Apartheid, the government racially classified every person into one of four main categories: white, Colored, Indian, and Black (Colored was the term used to describe mixed-race individuals; prior to 1948, some Colored people had the right to vote in South Africa. The Indian category applied to people of Indian descent; Mahatma Gandhi lived for many years in South Africa prior to Apartheid and his experiences with racial segregation influenced his own movement when he returned to India. The South African government denied Black South Africans citizenship and created homelands for each major Black ethnic group; even so, the homelands were never autonomous, nor did they have the resources to function apart from the official South African state. Dissent was strictly punished, the ANC was declared illegal, and prominent activists from the ANC were typically arrested and sentenced to long prison terms. Nelson Mandela, the most famous example of this, was sentenced to 27 years in prison in 1964. Uprisings were often met with brutal violence, as seen in the massacres in Sharpeville in 1960 and Soweto in 1976. Cold War tensions were also important: the ANC's ideology was supportive of communism, winning them support from the Soviet Union. The United States did not want a Soviet-allied government in power, so the US government supported the Apartheid government, both tacitly and explicitly. Anti-Apartheid activism and resistance was especially violent in South Africa in the 1980s, and a global anti-apartheid movement had also gained international attention and support. South Africa's economy began to suffer due to ANC-led work strikes, as well as international sanctions and the global divestment movement. In the face of this pressure, the South African government began a negotiated end to its own power. The regime unbanned the ANC and freed Mandela from prison in 1990, and for the next few years, the white government led by President F. W. de Klerk negotiated with Mandela, the ANC, and other societal groups about the future of South Africa. Ultimately, a new constitution was drafted, a Truth and Reconciliation Commission was established, and elections with universal adult suffrage were held, culminating in the election of Mandela as South Africa's first Black president in 1994.

> "The dominant meaning attributable to the Old Flag, both domestically and internationally, is that it is for the majority of the South African population a symbol that immortalizes the period of a system of racial segregation, racial oppression through apartheid, of a crime against humanity and of South Africa as an international pariah state that dehumanized the black population."[20]

Like the Gadsden flag in the United States, the old South African flag is another example of how the meaning behind symbols is reliant on shifts in culture. While the old flag may have always been associated with a racist government, in just 25 years, this meaning became entrenched in both the culture and the law.

In 1840, a new form of everyday propaganda was introduced in Great Britain: the postal stamp. In response to the complicated and varying postal fees assigned to each letter, based on pages and distance traveled, Sir Rowland Hill proposed a pre-paid, single rate postage stamp.[21] This first stamp was called the Penny Black, which cost one penny and was printed in black ink. (Figure 2.7) (This actually became a problem later on, because the red cancellation mark was difficult to see on the black ink, so the following year it was replaced by the Penny Red.) The stamp depicted a profile of the young Queen Victoria, only 21 years old at the time. The engraving was completed by Charles Heath and his son Frederick, and was based on a drawing by Henry Corbould. The drawing was based on a cameo created by medalist and engraver William Wyon, who also created the Queen Victoria Young Head coin as Chief Engraver at the Royal Mint.[22] In the same tradition as coins, Britain used postage stamps to elevate the Queen to a mythological and religious figure in everyday life.

To this day, Great Britain is the only country that is not required to print the name of their country on their stamp, because of their role in creating the original postage stamp.[23] Instead, the profile of the monarch is the sole distinguisher. It's interesting to think that a face can become so synonymous with the name of a country that it can even supersede it, a great example of the picture superiority effect in play. With the death of Elizabeth II, an iconic symbol of British identity is currently being replaced, with the first banknotes depicting King Charles III entering circulation in 2024, without a crown.[24] After 70 years, Britons will be faced with a depiction of a new leader, a new symbol, and one that carries a very different connotation for the identity of Britons than its predecessor.

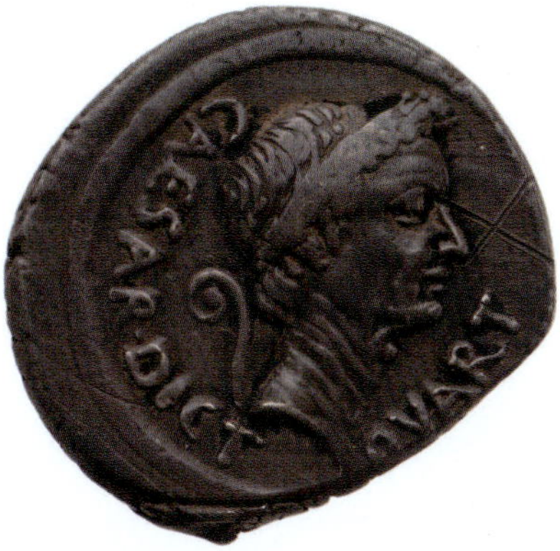

Figure 2.2
In 44 BC, Julius Caesar was the first living figure depicted on the face of a coin.

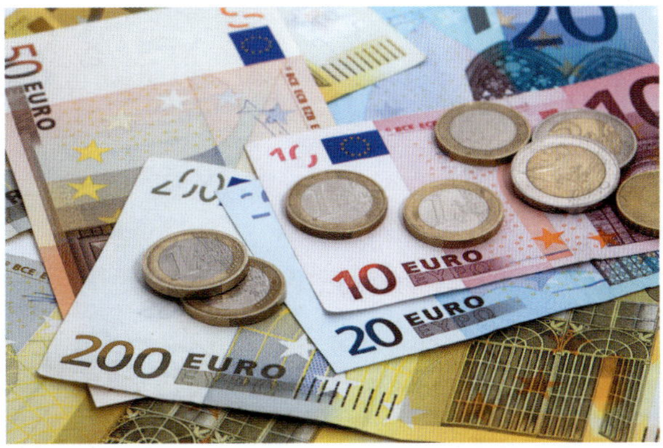

Figure 2.3
The front of a euro banknote features pictures of windows and doorways. On the back face of the euro, different architectural styles from Europe's history are depicted.

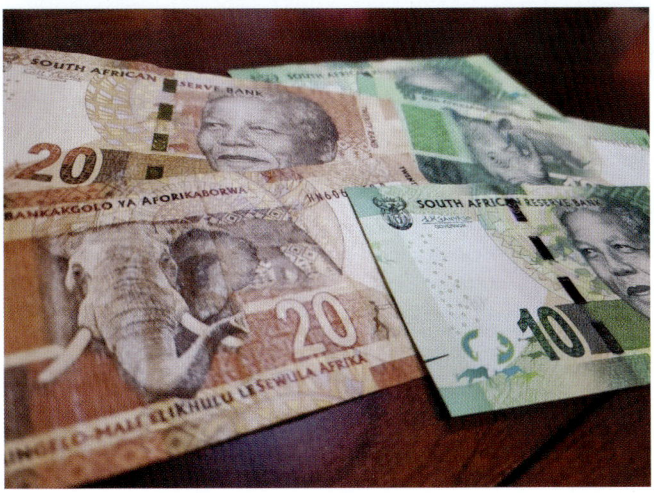

Figure 2.4
South African currency features animal symbols that resonate with Black native South Africans, as well as a portrait of former President Nelson Mandela.
Photo © Julie Bodam Macartney

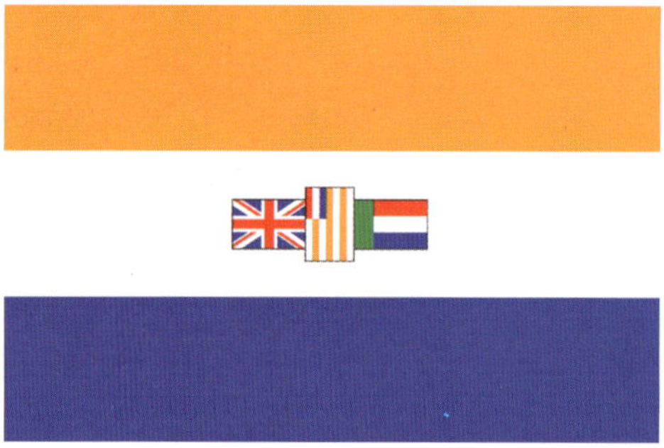

Figure 2.5
From 1928 to 1994, the South African flag was in fact four flags combined into one.

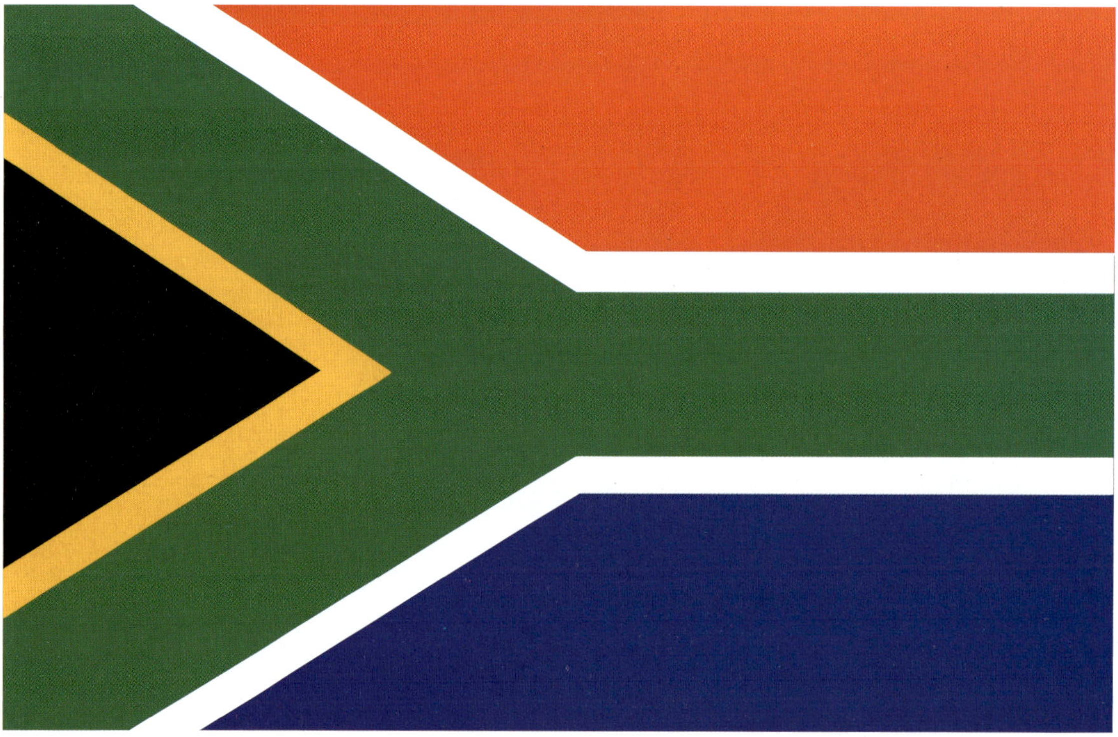

Figure 2.6
The current flag of South Africa includes colors from the flags of the Netherlands, the United Kingdom, and the flag of the anti-apartheid political party in South Africa, the African National Congress. The Y shape was meant to show the different ethnic groups of South Africa, the British, the Dutch, and the native Black population, separate groups joining together as one towards a unified future.

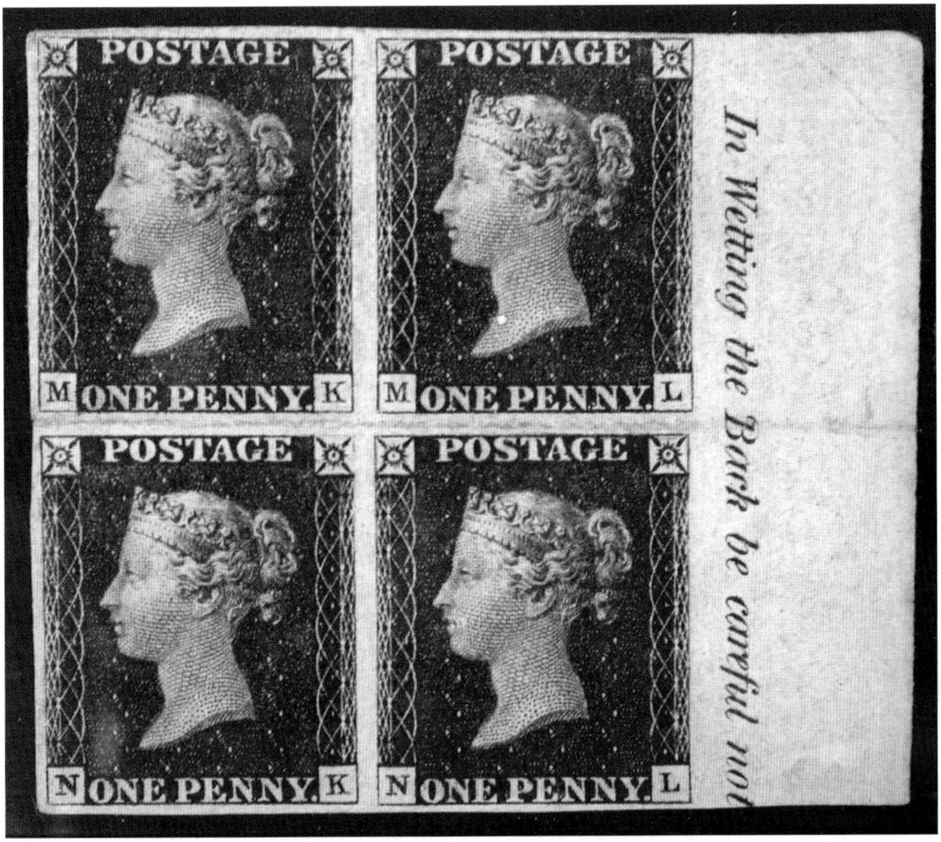

Figure 2.7
The first stamp originated in Great Britain in 1840 and was called the Penny Black, which cost one penny and was printed in black ink.

The Mythos of Political Portraits and the Visual Language of Propaganda

In the introduction of their book on political portraiture, *The Political Portrait: Leadership, Image, and Power*," Luciano Cheles and Pierre Sorlin note the important fact that having one's portrait drawn has historically been a "privilege of the mighty."[25] By default, much portraiture throughout history has been political in that it was created by and of people in power, portraying them in ways that were the most flattering or idealized. Cheles and Sorlin state that with the accessibility of modern recording technology, including snap and shoot cameras and smartphones, now almost anyone can create an image of a political leader, sieving the mythos out of the figure. Technology has played a significant role in stripping this fantasy away from the powerful. Today, in many parts of the world, we have an ability to critique and criticize our political leaders, in part because they have lost the control of being able to mediate their own image. In countries where we still see dictatorships and authoritarian governments in power, we also still see idealized political portraits controlled by the government, and censorship of political art, which we will return to in Chapter 3.

Prior to the 20th century, however, and for most of history, political leaders had the ability to delicately construct the image that they wished to portray to the public. What is it about these political portraits that makes them so effective, beyond just their proliferation? The artists who constructed this propaganda had a working knowledge of how visual grammar can play a role in political portraiture. The art itself contains visual clues that affect human perception about power, influence, and personality. This is where illustration can become a much more effective tool than a photograph. Although photographers have a certain amount of control over how their subject is portrayed, illustration provides more freedom for the creator to take artistic license and control the messaging surrounding the subject. While not every image in this book is a portrait of a political figure, many political illustrations contain portraits and political illustration is a favorite tool amongst government propagandists.

Human development can also give us clues as to why portraits have such an effect over us. Faces are one of the first recognizable visual symbols that humans create as children, and children tend to draw these faces again and again, emphasizing faces over bodies, and especially the eyes within these faces.[26] Eyes have historically been emphasized and enlarged for subjects in power, most famously in the religious and political portraits of the Byzantine empire (c. 395 CE–1453 CE). (Figure 2.8) Recall that in our Principles of Gestalt, size is a significant cue for categorizing items, superseding that of shape. When emphasis and exaggerated size are placed on an item that also contains such significant symbolism, this acts as a strong tool for attracting human attention. Paul Ekman's research on facial expressions has shown that young children receive critical communications from their caretakers by learning to read the messages in their faces, teaching them some of the most important lessons they will learn in early childhood, including empathy and social cues.[27] Ekman's research goes on to show that we are able to universally recognize emotions in facial expressions, including anger, happiness, sadness, fear, surprise, and disgust.[28] Portraits and the facial expressions they contain are therefore one of our most innate methods of communicating and understanding stories, which is in part what makes political portraits so effective and so prolific. Today, minor snapshots of a politician can purportedly reveal the inner machinations of their minds, and, historically, the cool, confident profile of a leader can invoke a sense of trustworthiness.

FOCUS ON TECHNOLOGY

Silhouettes

Ancient portraits from Egypt to Rome often appeared in profile, a viewpoint continued throughout the Renaissance and into the silhouette art of the 1800s. (Figure 2.9) Author Maurizio Bettini writes that, in accordance with ancient cultural beliefs, "the shadow was not only attached to the person: it was also considered to be an expression of that person's most vital and significant characteristics."[29] Tracing a silhouette, commonly used in the 15th century and beyond, and likely earlier, was actually a precursor to photography, and one of the earliest methods of shadow drawing. This technique was later enhanced during the Renaissance using perspectographs and other shadow drawing devices. Therefore, silhouette portraits were more likely to capture critical features of a person.

With this establishing information of how portraits activate our conscious and unconscious minds, we can return to Molly Bang's book, *Picture This*. In the book, Bang demonstrates how the principles of perceptual psychology inform our principles of design and how these work in concert to affect our emotions. The effectiveness of *Picture This* also comes from Bang's ability to translate the human experience of the physical world into the experience of the pictorial world through enlightening verbal and visual metaphors. These principles of visual grammar can be applied to political portraiture. Portrait artists leverage the underlying perceptual psychology of design to inform our interpretation of facial expressions, mood, and narrative within a portrait.

Bang also demonstrates the difference in our emotional perception of horizontal, vertical, and diagonal lines within a composition. Horizontal lines indicate stability, invoking the sense of steadiness the horizon and ground possess, while vertical lines indicate action and energy, such as when we are standing alert. Diagonal lines indicate motion or tension, reminiscent of the motion associated with an object rolling down a hill or a tree falling in the forest. The portraits on the coins we discussed earlier in this chapter portray the subject gazing straight ahead, with an almost perfectly horizontal line, metaphorically indicating the sure, strong, and stable vision the leader has for the country. In *Roosevelt's Guiding Spirit*, created by Thomas Fleming in 1904 for Theodore Roosevelt's campaign for US President, we see the upright, energized figure of Roosevelt balanced by his stable, horizontal gaze, as well as McKinley's horizontal arm. (Figure 2.10) Other political portraits are created to be much more dynamic, with strong vertical and diagonal lines showing an active, engaged political actor moving the country forward. In an earlier image of McKinley, *Prosperity At Home, Prestige Abroad*, diagonal lines project from behind the vertical figure, demonstrating energy and motion, thereby creating a much more dynamic and arresting image. (Figure 2.11) This balance of stability contrasted with dynamism shows up in many examples of political propaganda, with stably grounded figures giving a sense of being grounded or secure with their dynamic vision, often referred to through a dramatic hand gesture or background. These diagonal lines, as the example of horizontal lines mentioned above, can also be applied to the direction of an individual's gaze. When the subject of a portrait gazes in the direction of the upper half of a composition, they are also perceived as being free, happy, triumphant or spiritual, metaphorically leading the gaze of the country to the brightness of the future. This technique was used often in propaganda imagery throughout the 20th century in the USSR and China. For instance, in this 1931 image by Georgy Vladimirovich Kibardin, Vladimir Lenin gazes up into the sky, the diagonal further enhanced by the gesture of his arm. (Figure 2.12) Furthermore, the viewpoint of the audience is situated below Lenin, so the idea that he is above his subjects adds to the ideas of leadership and vision for the country.

Symmetrically aligned figures in portraiture can be portrayed as regal or meditative. In *Portrait of an Old Lady* (1561 or 1621), an example of Chinese ancestor portraiture, symmetry is used to make the subject appear noble and important. (Figure 2.13) Ancestor portraits are painted from memory and descriptions but showed status and power through the clothing and accessories they wore, using striking symmetry.[30] The rank badge with a crane on the woman's belt sash shows the highest rank of a civil official, although because women could not serve in governmental positions, this was a rank that was likely handed down to her from her father.[31] In ancestor portraits of couples, size is also used to indicate the more powerful role of the husband over his wife.

Scale is also a consideration when demonstrating power in a portrait. Throughout history, **hierarchical scale** was used to portray the power of a leader. Seen in artworks from ancient Egypt to ancient Greece to the Middle Ages and beyond, pharaohs, kings, and leaders were shown to be proportionately larger than their insignificant subjects. Even after this practice became less common in art, scale and size still played a role. In the famous portrait of King Henry the VIII painted by Hans Holbein the Younger, the giant scale of the powerful king fills the frame almost to breaking, indicating the power of size to exude confidence and power. (Figure 2.14) In *Plaque: Equestrian Oba and Attendants,* created by the Edo peoples (c. 1550–1680), the king at center is rendered much larger than his attendants to show his rank and power. (Figure 2.15)

A final note on portraiture is the cultural differences of portrait traditions throughout global history. Different cultures have historically placed different value on portraits. For instance, portraiture in China was not used until the Qin and Tang dynasties, c. 221 BC, which already showed Western influence (this could also be connected to changes in governmental structure, since the Qin dynasty was the first imperial dynasty of China).[32] Global portraits also vary in terms of style and emphasis. While full-body portraits are common worldwide, many examples of Western portraiture, starting in ancient Rome and revived during the Renaissance, emphasize the head and shoulders of the subject. This is rarer in global art without Western influence, with notable exceptions of sculpture, including the giant Olmec heads, Mayan sculptures, and Benin bronzes. While the full body portrait promotes status through clothing, accessories, and pose, head and shoulders portraits can influence the viewer's view of the subject's intellectual and personality attributes.[33]

One example of Western influence on Eastern portraiture comes from the Deccan sultanates of India in the 1500s and 1600s, where art flourished especially in the Bijapur sultanate during the reign of the sultan Ibrahim Adil Shah II. Adil Shah was famous for his patronage of the arts, and he himself was a skilled poet, calligrapher, musician, and artist.[34] Much of Mughal and Deccan painting was done in miniature, including the *Portrait of Sultan Ibrahim Adil Shah II of Bijapur* (c. 1590 AD), which is only about 10" × 6". (Figure 2.16) At this time, portraiture in India was in its infancy, and portraits of this time show a European influence, including the modeling techniques on the face and a crop of the head and shoulders.[35] The painting of this time was also influenced by the art of Persia, which had a strong relationship with this part of India. The art of this era is notable because of the combination of flat patterning and realistic modeling, allowing the sitter to be part of a modeled earthly world but also a colorful, divine one that does not have to adhere to the rules of light and shadow. The Deccan sultanates were Sunni Muslim, and the inscription on the decorative turban compares Shah to Abraham and King Solomon.[36] These portraits show political influence and power and are some of the oldest known political portraits from the region.

Now that we understand more about the tools propagandists can use in their artwork, we'll turn to the story of one of the most influential purveyors of propaganda in history, and the story of the artist who illustrated him into infamy.

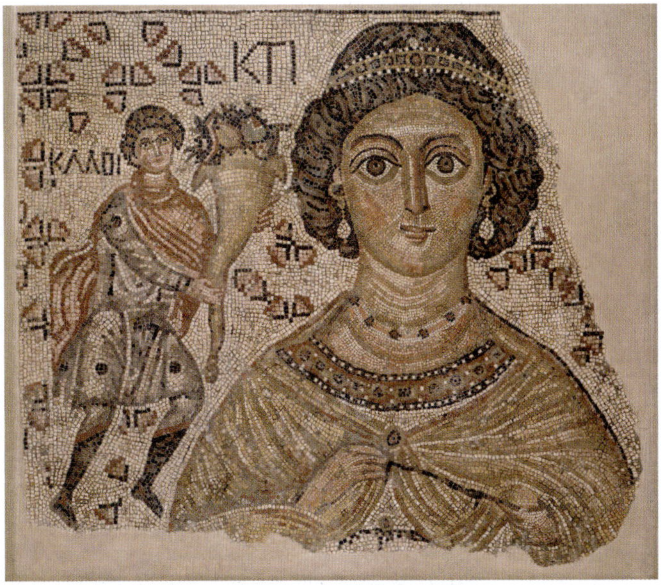

Figure 2.8
Eyes have historically been emphasized and enlarged for subjects in power, most famously in the religious and political portraits of the Byzantine empire.

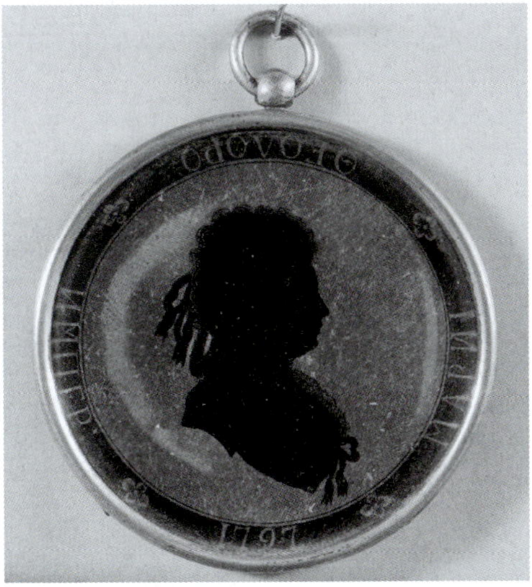

Figure 2.9
Ancient portraits from Egypt to Rome often appeared in profile, a viewpoint continued throughout the Renaissance and into the silhouette art of the 1800s.

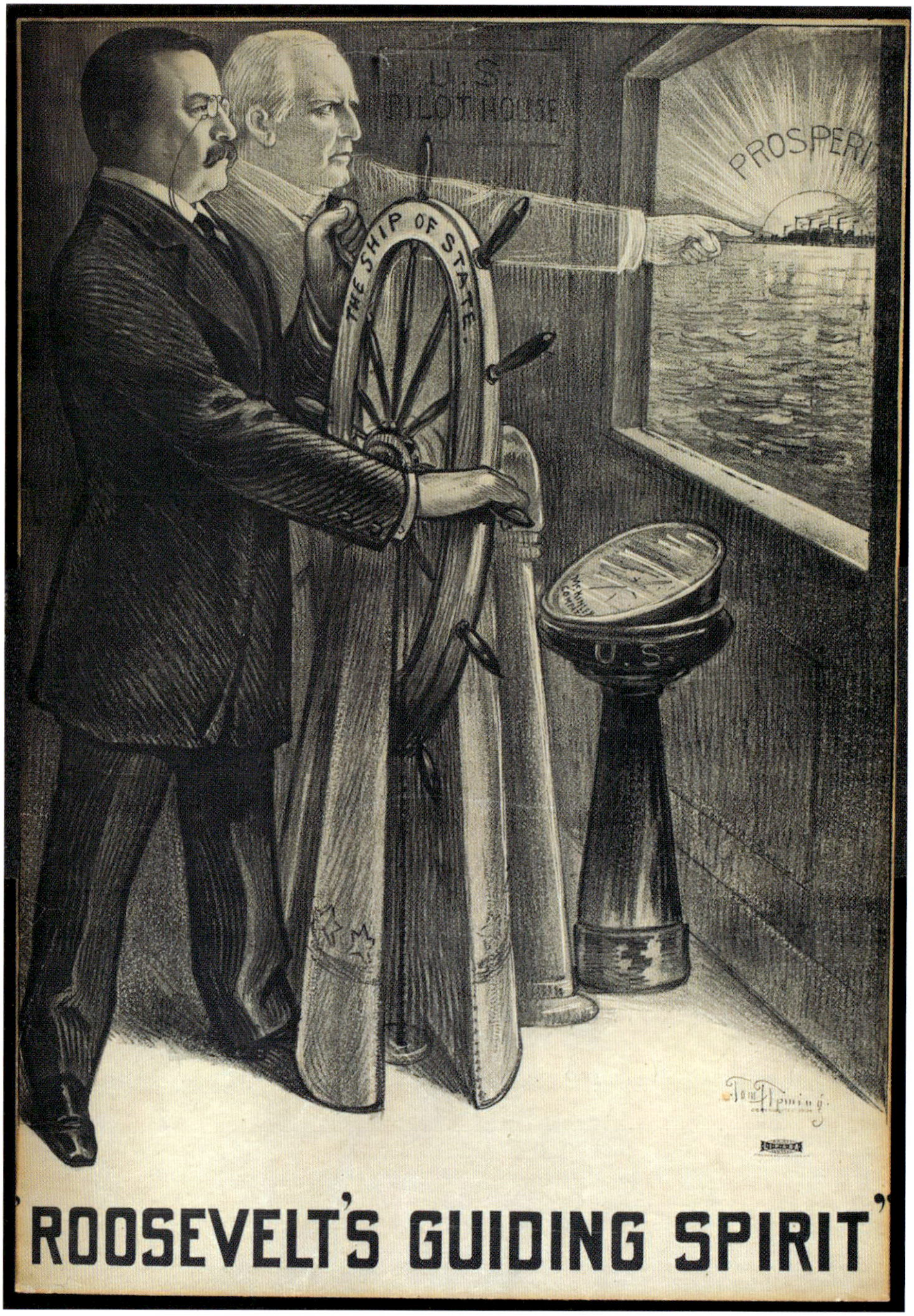

Figure 2.10
In this example of *Roosevelt's Guiding Spirit*, created by Thomas Fleming in 1904 for Theodore Roosevelt's campaign for US President, we see the upright, energized figure of Roosevelt balanced by his stable, horizontal gaze, as well as McKinley's horizontal arm.

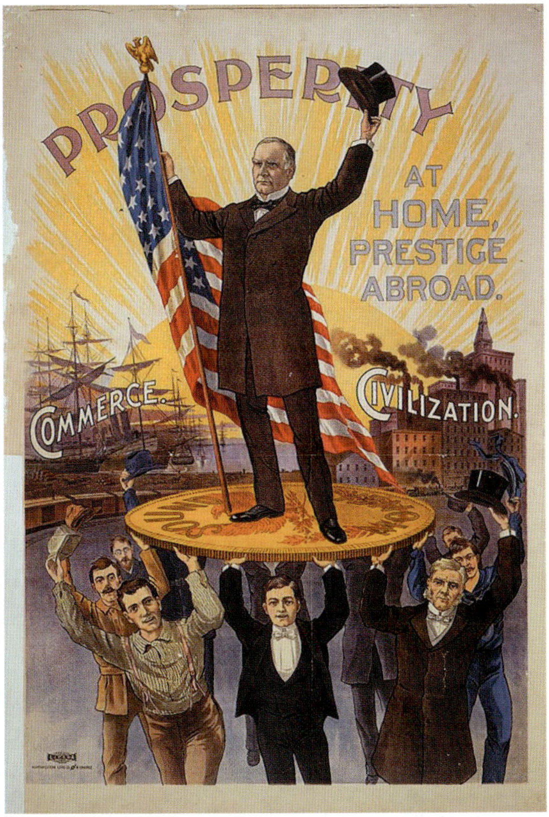

Figure 2.11
In *Prosperity At Home, Prestige Abroad*, circa 1895–1900, a color lithograph by Northwestern Litho. Co., Milwaukee, diagonal lines project from behind the vertical figure, demonstrating energy and motion, thereby creating a much more dynamic and arresting image.

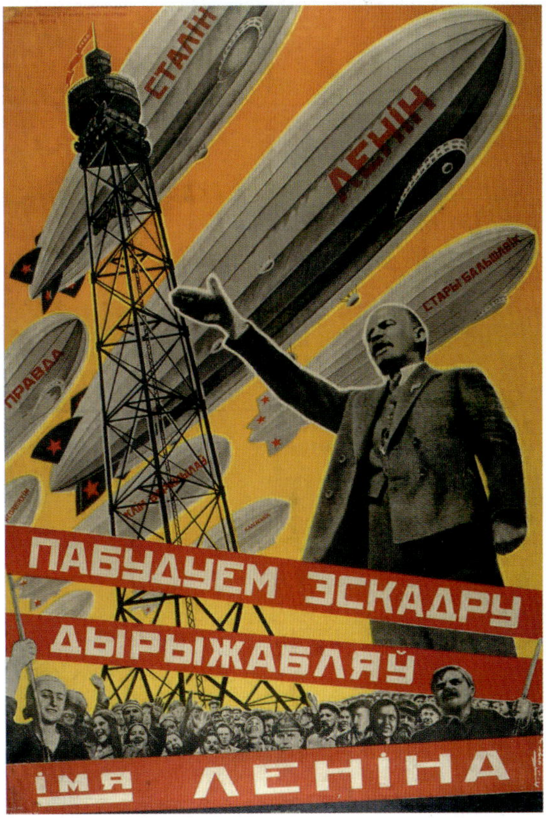

Figure 2.12
In the 1931 image *We Will Build Lenin's Squadron of Airships* by Georgy Vladimirovich Kibardin, Vladimir Lenin gazes up into the sky, the diagonal further enhanced by the gesture of his arm.

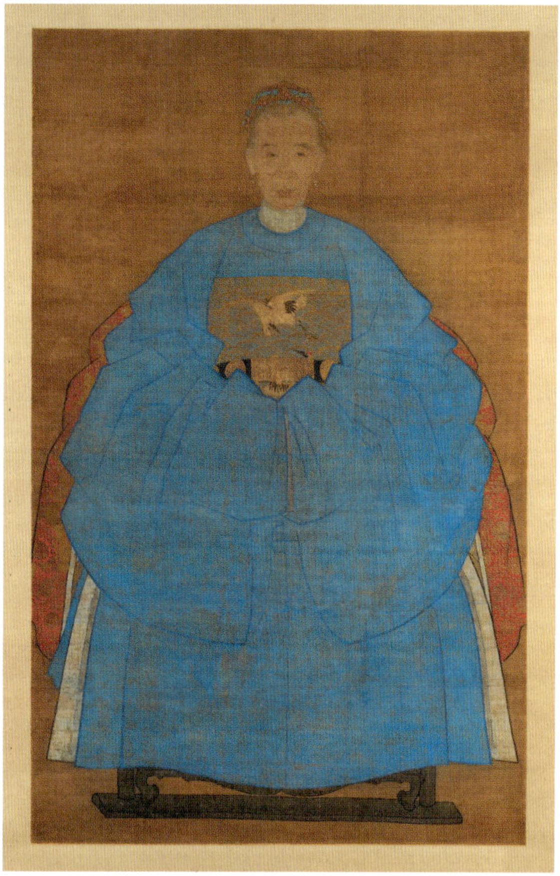

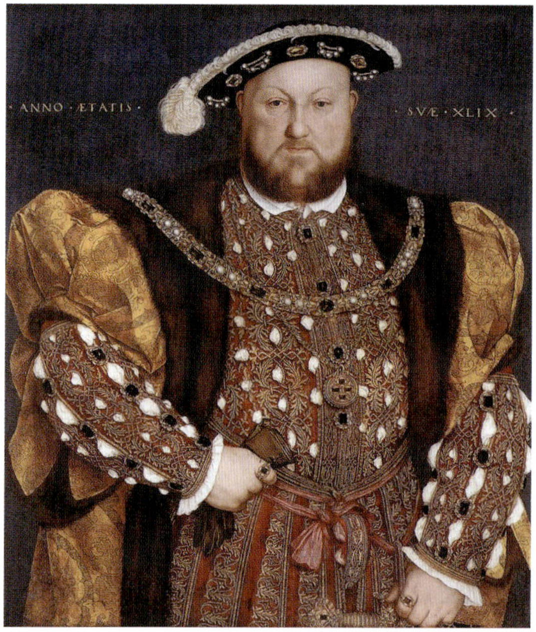

Figure 2.14
In the famous portrait of King Henry the VIII painted by Hans Holbein the Younger, the giant scale of the powerful king fills the frame almost to breaking, indicating the power of size to exude confidence and power.

Figure 2.13
Portrait of an Old Lady (1561 or 1621), painted by Ruan Zude in the Ming Dynasty, is an example of Chinese ancestor portraiture. Here, symmetry is used to make the subject appear noble and important.

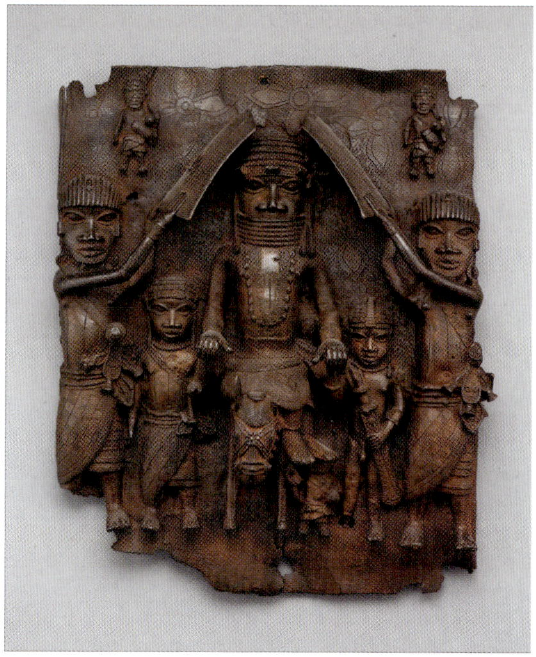

Figure 2.15
In *Plaque: Equestrian Oba and Attendants*, created by the Edo peoples (c. 1550-1680), the king at center is rendered much larger than his attendants to show his rank and power.

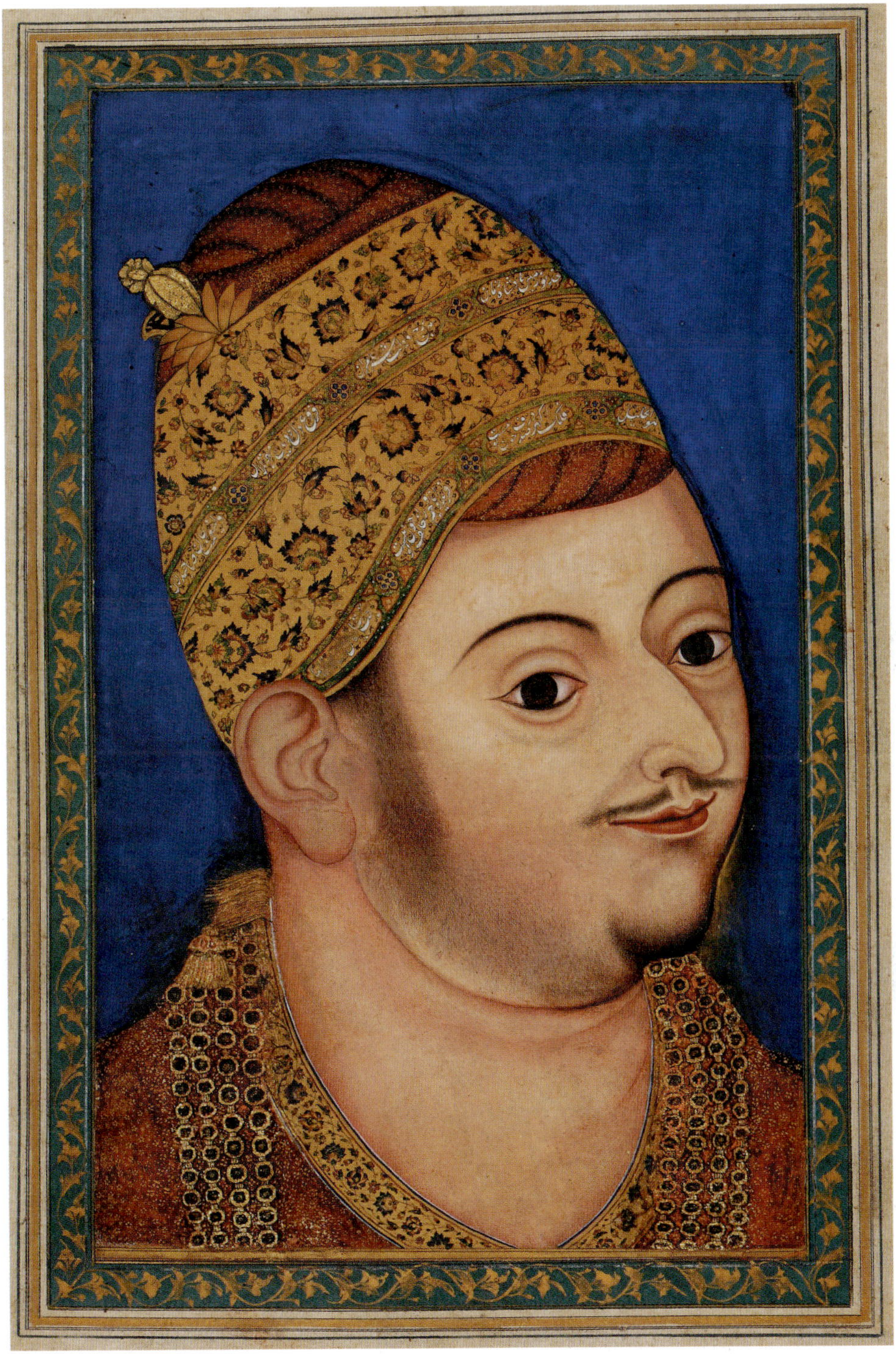

Figure 2.16 *Portrait of Sultan Ibrahim Adil Shah II of Bijapur* (c. 1590 AD), attributed to the Bikaner Painter, shows the influence of Western portraiture on Deccan painting.

Napoleon: The Forefather of Propaganda

Caesar created a foundation for propaganda that Napoleon Bonaparte would later perfect. Like Caesar, Napoleon rose to power through military successes, becoming the first de facto leader of the French Republic and later the Emperor of France in 1804 after the French Revolution.[37] Napoleon saw Caesar as an influence, and similarly saw the potential for art to exaggerate and proliferate his successes amongst the masses. On his conquests across the European continent, Napoleon pilfered, or as he called it "liberated," the art of the conquered, parading it through Paris and eventually collecting it at the Louvre, which he renamed the "Musée Napoléon." Napoleon saw the exceptional value of art, hiring artists to document the cultural assets of his conquered lands, and producing books to distribute the greatness he had "discovered." In addition, Napoleon used a variety of media to create propaganda, including sculptures, music, theater, newspapers, and leaflets.[38] Paintings of Napoleon were often adapted into engravings and printed for the public, along with verbal descriptions of the bravura of the original.[39] Napoleon keenly understood the power art could have and how he could use it to manipulate the people who viewed it.

One of Napoleon's favorite commissioned painters, Jacques-Louis David, was likewise savvy in shaping his own image for success and has a story just as compelling as Napoleon's. Inspired by the grandeur of ancient Greece and Rome and influenced by the light contrast of Caravaggio, David was one of the founders of the style of **neoclassicism**.[40] Neoclassicism shared ancient Greece and Rome's fondness for mathematical simplicity and symmetry, echoing their ideals of order and civilization. Neoclassicism was not only a style of painting, but a set of beliefs that art was based on a set of moral values, and that an artist could communicate these values to their audience. Throughout David's early career, he became increasingly aligned with the political ideals of the French Revolution, creating famous works of propaganda for the revolution, including the incomplete *Oath of the Tennis Court* (1790 and 1794) and *Death of Marat* (which he preferred to be called *Marat Breathing his Last*, 1793). David's political mentor, Maximilien Robespierre, was guillotined following the Revolutionary Tribunal and subsequent Reign of Terror, in which 27,000 Frenchmen who did not actively support the revolution were executed or died in prison. David narrowly avoided this fate, in part because of his renown as a painter, and subsequently aligned himself with Napoleon's new regime.[41] Arguably David's most famous painting, *Napoleon Crossing the Alps*, depicts Napoleon's legendary crossing in May 1800, but certainly with more bravado than the actual journey. (Figure 2.17) David made five versions of this painting; the one depicted here is the first, completed in 1801. When David asked Napoleon to sit for the painting so he could capture his resemblance, Napoleon refused, saying, "A resemblance? It isn't the exactness of the features, a wart on the nose which gives the resemblance. It is the character that dictates what must be painted... Nobody knows if the portraits of the great men resemble them, it is enough that their genius lives there."[42] This opened up a floodgate for David to take additional artistic license to increase the bravado in the painting. In his actual crossing, Napoleon rode a mule instead of a horse, and he didn't lead his troops but followed a few days after. Also, reportedly, the weather was just fine, not the stormy clouds depicted in David's paintings. And as in most of Napoleon's propaganda, he is depicted as tall and athletic (Napoleon was reportedly 5'6" tall, average for the time, and "so thin as to have a sickly air").[43] However, viewers of David's famed painting saw just one thing: a steady, strong, and heroic leader reining in the tempestuous situation in the country and showing his subjects a path forward.

GLOBAL POLITICS PERSPECTIVE

So, What Actually Was the French Revolution?

It is almost impossible to state just how significant the French Revolution was. It has been referenced in pop culture countless times, with phrases like, "let them eat cake" and the use of guillotines, and it set in motion events that eventually inspired the famous novel *Les Misérables* (and its musical adaptation). And it saw the dramatic rise and even more tumultuous fall of Napoleon Bonaparte. To understand these events, we need to start with France prior to the revolution. Like most of Europe, France had been ruled by a hereditary monarch from the House of Bourbon since the 16th century. France engaged in fierce military competition with its European neighbors and it conquered land in the Americas, Caribbean, and West Africa. These activities helped enrich the royal family and a small group of elite nobles. At home, ordinary French citizens lived in squalid conditions, paid significant taxes, and were often drafted into never-ending military campaigns. This led to lavish palaces like Versailles but kept most people in dire poverty. The king was accountable to only himself. In 1789, small protests emerged over the rising costs of bread, but these eventually morphed into a full-scale revolution that saw people storm the Bastille armory in Paris, and promoted the slogan, "Liberty, Equality, Fraternity!".[44] Over the next few years, revolutionaries sought to tear down the old government, culminating in the arrest, and eventual execution of King Louis XVI and Queen Marie Antoinette in 1793. These revolutionaries agreed that France must reject monarchy and become a republic, but this group was extremely varied in their goals and interests. As the new parliamentary government form was debated, in-fighting grew among the revolutionaries, as one group, the Jacobins, wanted even more radical changes to the class system and distribution of power. The Jacobins, led by figures like Maximilien Robespierre, focused on rooting out enemies and perceived counter-revolutionaries. History has shown that a focus on terror in a post-revolutionary setting is quite common, as seen in the revolutions in Russia, China, Cuba, and Iran. By 1799, General Napoleon Bonaparte maneuvered himself into power given the disorder and in-fighting. He was determined to reestablish a strong central ruler in France and was declared Emperor in 1804. Over the course of the next eleven years, Napoleon led a French invasion of Europe, as he sought to conquer territory ranging from Great Britain to as far east as Russia. This war ended in defeat for Napoleon in 1815. This was not the end of the revolutionary change in France, as its government oscillated between monarchy and representative democracy over the next sixty years. Revolutionaries continued to pushback on attempts to reestablish an empire and monarchy, with two more revolutions taking place in 1830 and 1848. By the end of the century, the monarchy had been rejected for good, but France would continue to experience changes to its political system through World War II. Even today, protests, strikes, and demonstrations are seen as normal and necessary aspects of French politics and society; the Yellow Vest Movement is one contemporary example.[45] The French Revolution was also the first modern example of a population revolting against their own leaders, toppling their own government, and seeking to establish a new political system while keeping the same borders and national identity.[46]

David continued to chronicle the events of Napoleon's reign with a revisionist's lens, and was awarded the title of "First Painter of the Emperor."[47] Another painting by David that positively influenced Napoleon's image within the empire was *The Consecration of the Emperor Napoleon and the Coronation of Empress Joséphine in Notre Dame Cathedral on 2 December 1804,* completed in 1807 and displayed in 1808. (Figure 2.18) Inspired by Emperor Constantine, whom Napoleon greatly admired, Napoleon's consecration was a political act, and he wished for the pomp of the ceremony to help justify to the public his goal in legitimizing himself as Emperor. During the French Revolution, Catholicism had been banned and the former Pope had been imprisoned, so Napoleon sought to help repair this rift by inviting the new Pope Pius VII to perform the consecration. What Napoleon was actually doing, however, was declaring his power over the Catholic church. After creating an elaborate ceremony, Napoleon was not crowned by the Pope, but made the unprecedented move of crowning himself (with a crown of laurel leaves, reminiscent of Napoleon's beloved Caesar and other Roman emperors), and then, as pictured in David's painting, he crowned Empress Joséphine.[48]

The painting utilizes scale in order to gain power, standing at 10 meters × 6 meters, and at the time David wanted it to be the largest painting in France. The scale was so tremendous that Napoleon stated that "This is not painting; you walk in this work."[49] It also takes plenty of creative liberties. First, Napoleon's brother Joseph Bonaparte, who had conflict with his brother, and Napoleon's mother, in part to protest these conflicts, were not present in real life but are depicted in the painting. While the Pope's hands were initially crossed, Napoleon requested the edit that he be seen anointing the proceedings instead. Napoleon's arms are raised in a gesture of power, while he looks condescendingly down at Joséphine and his subjects. While he is not the highest point of the image, David uses the combination of light and shadow to show Napoleon as the highest point of the *lit* image, while other subjects fall into shadow. The gaze of all the subjects' eyes are brought to Napoleon, with the exception of Joséphine, whose gaze brings us humbly to Napoleon's feet. (Speaking of Joséphine, she was 41 when the event took place, but David took a few years off.)

FOCUS ON TECHNOLOGY

Paintings

Wait, aren't paintings considered to be fine art? Firstly, we return to the introduction of Chapter 1 on the definition of illustration. Illustration is meant to spread an idea or message, which often, but not always, includes reproducibility. However, reproducibility is reliant on technology, and illustration has still existed for longer than printing methods have been popular. Ancient cultures used public art, sculpture, and architecture to convey political messages and to gain power. Many oil paintings from the 1800s or earlier were displayed publicly and meant to serve the same purpose as a political poster or work of street art would today: to get as many eyes on them as possible. Portraits of Napoleon were displayed publicly, such as at the Paris Salon, and he was depicted in public statues. Paintings were also created as templates for engravings, which Napoleon embraced as a method of propaganda, accessing a larger audience through engravings that could be reproduced, sold, and displayed. Napoleon intentionally capitalized on the power of print reproductions to distribute his likeness across Europe, often impatient with the amount of time it took to create them.[50] He also employed artists to create paintings of his battle victories for the direct purpose of turning into engravings. Napoleon even employed Raphael Morghen to etch Jacques-Louis David's famous *Napoleon Crossing the Alps*, although Napoleon fell from power before it was completed. Therefore, paintings could, and continue to be used as the basis for many works that we would more popularly define as illustration, and their inclusion in the illustration canon should not be limited by its medium.

After the fall of Napoleon in 1814, David was spared from exile by the new Bourbon government again because of his renown as a painter, but refused the pardon, putting himself into self-exile in Brussels, where he lived the remainder of his life as a successful painter. The style and methods of propaganda that he and Napoleon created together, however, would live on into the 19th century.

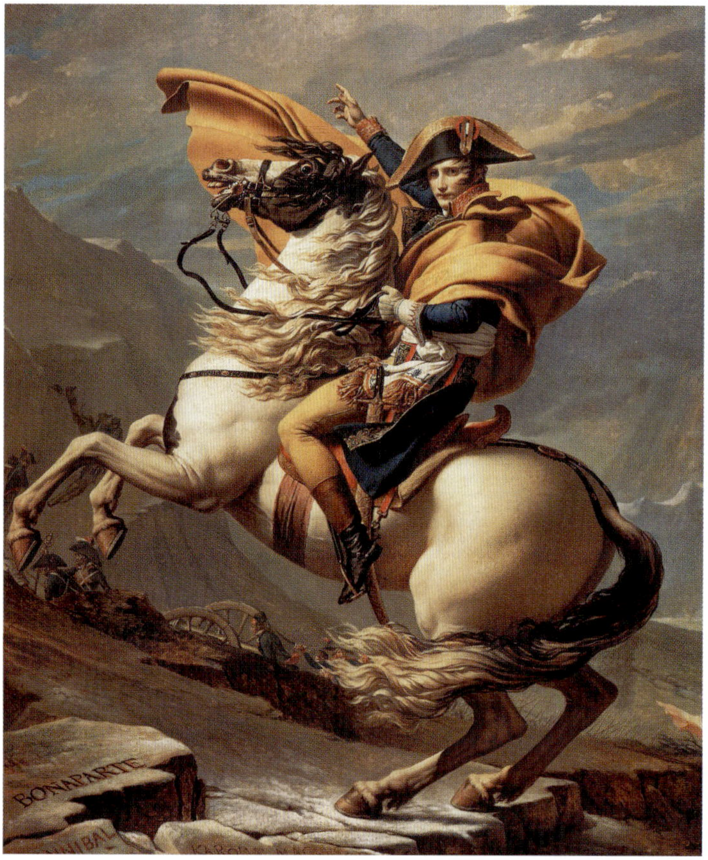

Figure 2.17
Jacques Louis David's famous painting, *Napoleon Crossing the Alps*, depicts Napoleon's legendary crossing in May 1800, but certainly with more bravado than the actual journey.

Figure 2.18
In his painting *The Consecration of the Emperor Napoleon and the Coronation of Empress Joséphine in Notre Dame Cathedral on 2 December 1804*, Jacques-Louis David made significant alterations from the actual event that occurred.

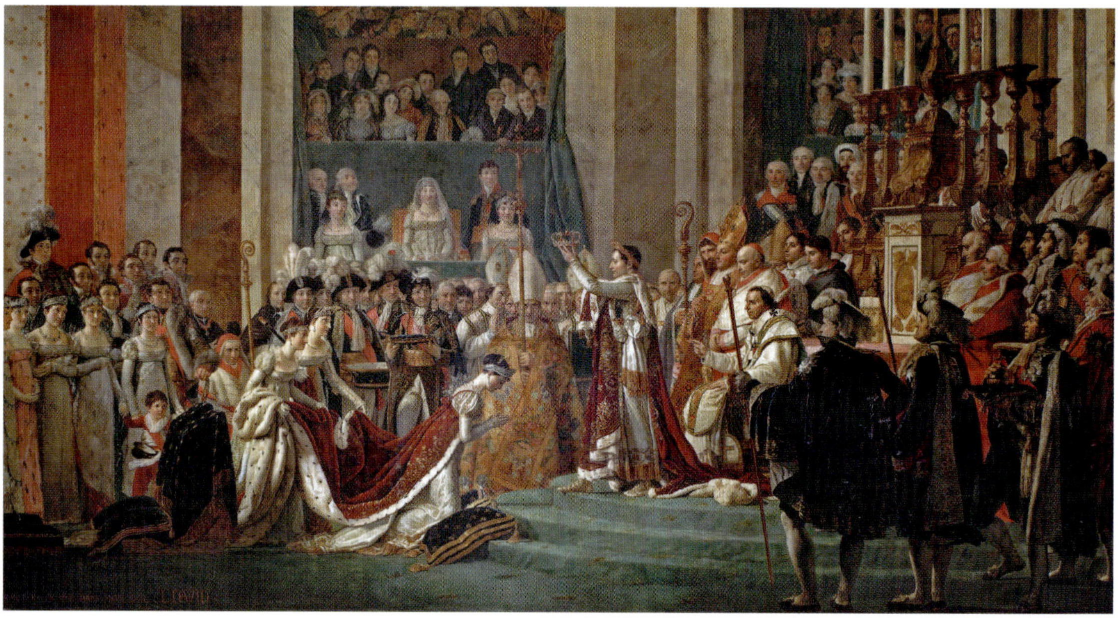

Global Imperialist Propaganda

Napoleon's admiration of the Romans was also echoed through his ambition to create a vast empire. Prior to Napoleon, the Roman Empire once stretched from Western Europe to the Middle East in the 2nd century, and in the 13th century, the Mongols ruled an empire that stretched across the Eurasian continent. However, beginning in the 16th century, Europeans began exploration and colonization that by World War I spanned the majority of the globe. (In fact, only 11 countries have never been formally colonized by a European power, although even some of those have been partially colonized).[51] There were plenty of advantages and incentives for Europeans to practice colonization, including spreading Christianity and gaining influence over their neighboring European countries, but most of the motivation was economic. Extracting raw materials from colonized countries and controlling economic regulations in these countries brought the colonizers great wealth and power over their subjects. But it was also to their advantage to keep the populations of these countries satisfied and happy under the ruling power, and therefore, massive propaganda campaigns were released throughout the colonized world.

The Australian continent was first inhabited by humans 50,000–65,000 years ago[52,53], with the oldest human remains dating from 32,000 years ago.[54] At that time, land bridges existed between Papua New Guinea, the Australian continent, and the island of Tasmania, but around 12,000–14,000 years ago seawaters rose and created the Bass Strait, separating Tasmania from the mainland.[55] Thus formed the indigenous Palawa culture of the island, whose indigenous name was *lutruwita*, which was cut off from the mainland and any other outside culture for almost 12,000 years. Iain Davidson and David Roberts write that, "They [aboriginal Tasmanians] were alone for five hundred generations, knowing no other people in the world, living with the knowledge and beliefs derived from those they had known before the sea surrounded them."[56] But in 1772, this all changed. Although a Dutchman named Abel Tasman first spotted the island nearly 130 years earlier in 1642, a subsequent voyage by Frenchman Marion Dufresne made the first contact with native Tasmanians.[57] By 1803, after a couple of other expeditions establishing contact, the British settled their first colonies in Tasmania (then named Van Diemen's Land), staking a claim to the land to prevent Napoleon's French Empire from establishing control.[58] Over the following 20–30 years, the population of indigenous Tasmanians was cut from somewhere between 4000–15,000 to less than 2000.[59] Disease, warfare, and destruction of their homes contributed to the great losses amongst the Palawans. Eager to capture the most valuable of the Tasmanian lands for sheep grazing and farming, by 1824, the British began the Black War against the Palawans, and even greater fighting broke out. Eventually, Lieutenant Governor George Arthur declared martial law in the settlements, labeling Tasmanian Aboriginals as "open enemies," with no legal protections.[60]

By 1830, the Governor was ready to attempt a different approach, creating an infamous piece of propaganda entitled his *Proclamation to the Aborigines*. (Figure 2.19) In order to quell the growing violence on the island, he oversaw the creation of a four paneled illustration to communicate an equal rights policy to the indigenous Tasmanians.

In order to communicate with Aboriginals, most of whom did not speak or write English, the story told in the proclamation is entirely in pictures. In the pictured example (many versions of these so-called "proclamation boards" were created), the top two panels exhibit the Europeans and Aboriginals living in harmony, standing arm in arm, caring for each other's children, and greeting each other by shaking hands. The bottom two panels, however, are much more foreboding, picturing an Aboriginal javelining a white man, and being hung for the crime, and the final panel picturing a white man javelining an Aboriginal, and receiving the same fate.[61] The method of communication for the proclamation boards is worth noting. The Aboriginals had a practice of drawing and carving on trees to tell stories, and thus the colony's Surveyor-General George Frankland recommended to Arthur that the proclamations be painted on the bark of trees.[62] Over 100 boards were originally produced, as well as lithographs, copied via a method borrowed from the Italian Renaissance called **pouncing**. In pouncing, a sketch is laid over the surface, with small holes poked around the contours of the image. After the holes are created, a charcoal dust is brushed over the top of the drawing so that a stencil is created for the painter.[63] Often the boards were created by convict artists.[64] Notably, the boards are also an early example of sequential art used as political illustration, a topic we'll return to in Chapter 4.

The boards, not surprisingly, did not achieve peace between the British colonists and the Tasmanian Aboriginals. British colonists brutally murdered Aboriginal Tasmanians, and, over time, the unpleasantness and danger of living near the British settlements became too much for the indigenous Tasmanians.[65] They retreated further from the settled districts and surrendered to the British, and, by 1847, only 40 known full-blooded Aboriginals lived in the British districts. The last, reportedly, was a woman named Truganini born circa 1812, passing away in 1876.

The proclamation boards remain as an example of propaganda distributed by the state, which failed to deliver on its promise, and serve as visual reminders of the genocide of the indigenous Tasmanians. Nevertheless, despite this violence, over 23,000 people of Tasmanian Aboriginal descent still survive today, many of whom actively pass down the traditions and culture of their ancestors. Traditions such as necklace making, mutton birding, kelp basket weaving, rope making, and shell-stringing continue, and the first indigenous style canoe built in over 170 years was constructed in 2007. There has also been a reclamation of the few recorded *palawa kani* names for places across the state. From the small surviving community, this reclamation of culture has become a political act of its own.[66]

The influence of the pattern of European imperialism would inspire and influence other countries in the period leading up to the world wars. Japan had become increasingly industrialized and wished to establish itself as the major power in East Asia, clashing with the Qing Dynasty in China to solidify its power over the Korean Peninsula. Following a weakening of China's power, a regime change in Korea, and a peasant revolt, Japan saw its chance to overthrow the Chinese. During the First Sino-Japanese War (1894–1895), *ukiyo-e* printmaking experienced a late revival when artists such as Mizuno Toshikata and Kobayashi Kiyochika created woodblock print triptychs of war scenes.[67] While war scenes are traditionally a topic covered by ukiyo-e printing, often they would depict historical wars fought with katanas, not modern warfare fought with guns and cannons. At the turn of the 20th century, color **woodblock printing** began to compete with lithography and photography for popularity, and so creating colorful, dramatic propaganda of the war was a commercially beneficial endeavor for artists. Around 3,000 woodblock prints were created during the one-year war, informing the Japanese public about the war and dramatizing Japan's victories. Kiyochika studied western style painting and integrated this into his woodblock prints, creating the first *kōsen-ga*, or "light ray pictures," which used a Western style of light and tone.[68] The use of the triptych (or *sammaitsuzuki*) creates a vastness of the scene being portrayed, especially effective in the dramatic Kiyochika print *Our Great Victory in the Battle of the Yellow Sea* from 1894.[69] (Figure 2.20) Use of value contrast, color, and directional forces are shown in *Attacking Pyongyang: Our Soldiers Conquer the Enemy Fortress* by Mizuno Toshikata (1895). (Figure 2.21) Following China's humiliating defeat in the war, Taiwan was annexed to Japan as a colony, establishing the first non-Western imperial power. Russia attempted to quell Japan's growing power in the region, which led to the subsequent Russo-Japanese War of 1904–05 and an even greater explosion of propaganda from both sides. In 1910, Japan formally annexed Korea as a colony, expanding its imperial power as many forces in Europe were also doing.[70] Thus set the stage for World War I and the greatest eruption of propaganda the world had ever known.

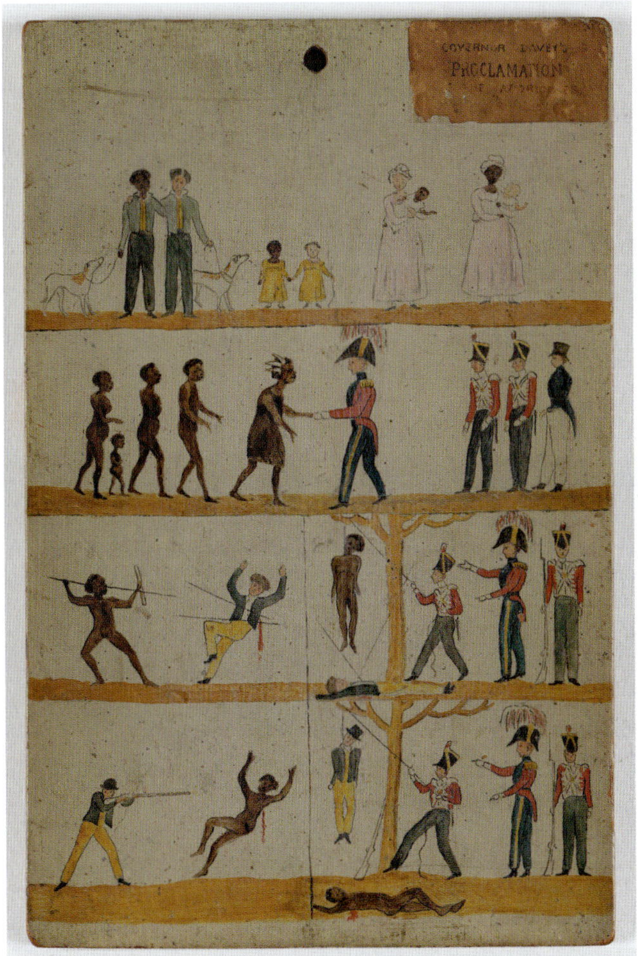

Figure 2.19
Governor Arthur's *Proclamation to the Aborigines* (1828–1830) is an example of early British colonialist propaganda. The proclamation boards were painted on tree bark and copied using a method calling pouncing.

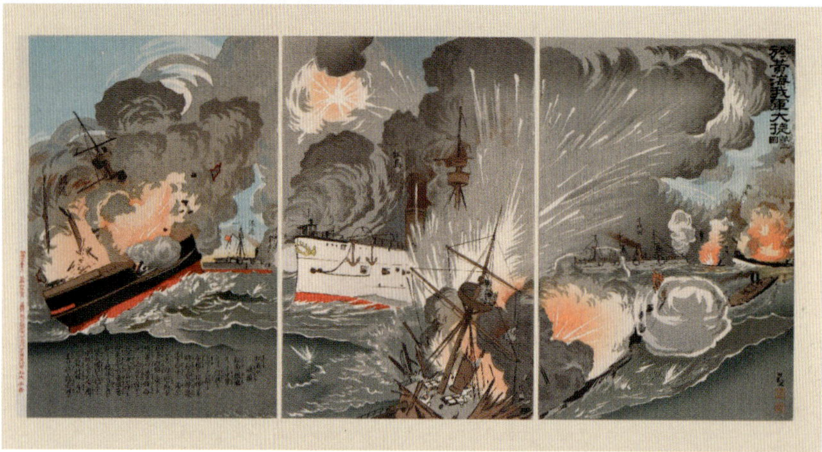

Figure 2.20
Kobayashi Kiyochika's *Our Great Victory in the Battle of the Yellow Sea* from 1894 is an example of Japanese wartime propaganda from the turn of the 20th century that melds modern themes with traditional style.

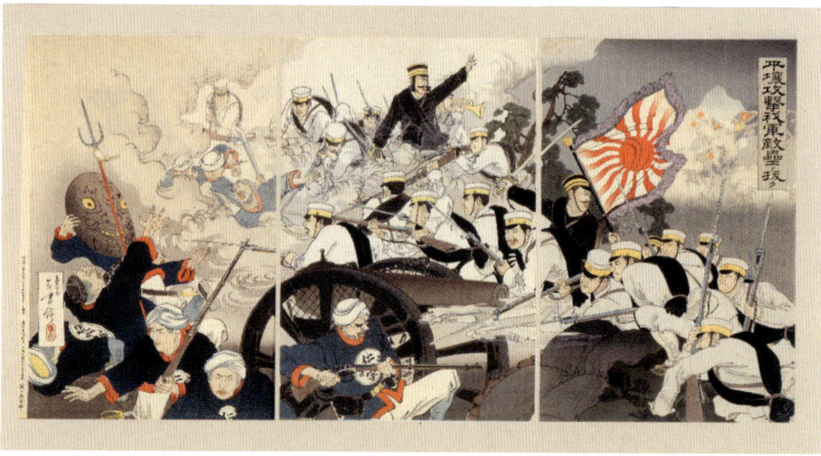

Figure 2.21
Use of value contrast, color, and directional forces are shown in *Attacking Pyongyang: Our Soldiers Conquer the Enemy Fortress* by Mizuno Toshikata (1895).

GLOBAL POLITICS PERSPECTIVE

Imperial Enlistments and the Soldiers of World Wars I and II

World War I was primarily fought in Europe, while World War II was fought throughout Europe as well as East Asia and the Pacific. This alone helped give each conflict the monikers of "world wars." Yet, beyond this, those fighting in the wars represented an even wider scope of the globe. It is estimated that hundreds of thousands of soldiers joined the wars from what is now India, Pakistan, Kenya, and Sudan, as well as from Western and Southern Africa, the Middle East, and Northern Africa.[71] During both wars, these areas were still under British, French, or other European colonial rule, which meant that the indigenous peoples living in these colonies did not have control over their own laws, economies, or foreign affairs. While military recruitment posters suggest that there was a choice for Indians or Kenyans to fight, it is important to remember that there was a massive power imbalance in place in these colonial territories. Colonialism and Imperialism themselves were built upon ideas of racism and white supremacy, and the institutions of colonialism served the economic and political priorities of the European powers.[72] Moreover, colonial rule fundamentally transformed the cultures, societies, and economic activities in almost every non-European corner of the globe. While men were not always overtly forced to take part, they were expected by society to participate, and these individuals also did not have full autonomy or self-determination over their own lives. Cooperating with their imperial British rulers, for example, could make life easier for their families and could pave a way for personal economic advancement.[73] In the case of the Indian army, officer positions were almost exclusively held by British individuals, while the lower ranks were composed of Indian nationals.[74] The world wars, especially World War II, were unpopular among the indigenous peoples of the British and French colonies, and they spurred greater resentment toward their European rulers. In India, the deaths of Indian soldiers in far-away conflicts fueled the independence movements that were already underway at home, led by leaders like Mahatma Gandhi, Jawaharlal Nehru, and Mohammed Jinnah, and their organizations, the Indian National Congress and the Muslim League. In some cases, soldiers themselves became politicized while fighting in Europe, and joined independence movements when they returned to Asia or Africa.[75] Ultimately, colonial involvement in the two world wars helped fuel the end of European colonization, beginning with the independence of India in 1947 and its partition into India and Pakistan. All told, more than 80 new countries came into existence as European colonization came to an end.

Propaganda of the World Wars

This wave of imperialist opportunism throughout the globe was one of the many factors contributing to the conflict of World War I, and, as part of this, countries became increasingly defensive and sought to grow their militaries at an unprecedented rate. Countries also drew up mutual defense agreements in order to further protect their imperialist holdings and used propaganda to foster feelings of growing **nationalism** amongst their people. While the assassination of Archduke Franz Ferdinand in 1914 may have been the direct catalyst for World War I, the world had already become a powder keg waiting to be lit. Following the assassination, a domino effect of activated alliances caused dozens of countries to enter the war within a month, each utilizing nationalist propaganda to recruit soldiers to step up and defend their homeland.

Understanding these motivations for World War I is key to understanding how propagandists utilized their craft in order to successfully achieve their primary goals:

recruiting soldiers to the fight and fostering popular public support for the war. Propaganda efficacy is also reliant on image reception theory; assuring most readers adopt a dominant reading of the message is necessary for the propaganda to be successful. Understanding and being able to manipulate their audiences was critical. Enthusing the audience about the growing nationalism across Europe and the globe, and inviting them to buy into that message, was key to tapping into their motivations and spurring them to action. Thus, the tone of much propaganda distributed from imperialist Europe to its colonies had to take a drastic shift.

The British Raj, or period of British rule in India, began in 1858, although the East India Company, a powerful British joint-stock company, had effectively maintained control on the Indian subcontinent since 1757. The beginning of the British Raj followed the violent Indian Rebellion of 1857, and Britain was able to propagandize stories to justify its "civilizing force" in the area and finally acquire it as a colony with popular support. One such piece of propaganda followed the Siege of Cawnpore, in which British colonists surrendered to rebel forces in exchange for safe evacuation, but when additional British forces approached, the rebels killed many of the remaining settlers.[76] This piece of propaganda, distributed by the London Printing and Publishing Company, pictures Margaret, the daughter of the British General Hugh Wheeler. (Figure 2.24) Margaret was actually part Indian, since General Wheeler had married an Anglo-Indian woman, but the print depicts her as a white, Anglicized figure, highlighted against the dark background and attacked by racist caricatures of the Sepoy forces. If the message of British superiority and purity was not clear enough, a Holy Bible is pictured in the front of the scene. While this piece of propaganda certainly served its purpose of justifying British occupation of India at the time, it was not as useful when Britain hoped to recruit Indian forces to fight its battles.

At the onset of World War I, British propaganda in India took a dramatically different tone. Earlier stereotypes were pared down and replaced with messages of patriotism, loyalty, and equality. In the poster *This Soldier is Defending India*, the Indian soldier is front and center, standing nobly clad in a British military uniform and turban (or pagri), an accoutrement of many Indian soldiers' uniforms in World War I and World War II. (Figure 2.25) The soldier is also dressed in shorts, as many Indian fighters were deployed to warmer regions the British were less keen on traveling to. The bold color red symbolizes the passion of the fight and pride of country (also note the expanded borders at the time to include modern day Pakistan, Bangladesh, and Burma). The upward gaze of optimism, discussed previously, is also in play here, as well as symmetry creating a sense of nobility. The text at the bottom reads with an intent to be inspiring, but also comes off as somewhat menacing, "This soldier is defending India. He is protecting his home and family. The best way to help your family is to join the army." Unlike the racist caricatures of the Indian Rebellion, this new propaganda created to meet new goals was met with some success. From 1914 to 1918, the British Indian Army grew from 215,000 to 573,000 soldiers.[77]

Not all stereotypes and caricatures were eliminated from European propaganda by World War I. The French continued to exhibit racist caricatures of Senegalese and African soldiers fighting for the French army in their propaganda. Called *tirailleurs sénégalais*, regardless of their nationality, these soldiers were often portrayed as immature, harmless, and naïve in French propaganda. Here, the goal of the propaganda was not to recruit soldiers, but to distribute among the French public to gain support for the African troops and create the impression that they were not threatening to the French people. Often, a pidgin French was used in this propaganda to further infantilize the African soldiers.

During World War I, the advertisement for a chocolate banana drink “Banania” was changed to include a Senegalese recruit with a wide, innocent grin, including the pidgin phrase “Y’a bon” for “It’s good.”[78] (Figure 2.26) (The first President of the Republic of Senegal, a former French recruit, famously stated “I will tear off the banania grins from all the walls of France.”[79]) This naïve and child-like stereotype was called a *grand enfant*.[80]

Over the course of World War I, France recruited around 175,000 soldiers from North and West Africa, and 17 percent of them, approximately 30,000, were killed in action.[81] Most of these soldiers were conscripted, and some resisted by fleeing or even committing suicide to avoid fighting for the French.[82] The poster *Journée de l’Armée d’Afrique et des Troupes Coloniales* (*African Army and Colonial Troops Day*), was created by Lucien Jonas to raise money for recruiting African soldiers, and depicts a different type of stereotype of African soldiers. (Figure 2.27) Instead of infantilizing the *tirailleurs sénégalais*, the artist has shown the African soldier as a bloodthirsty savage, mouth open wide in a yell, the whites of his eyes showing, and his tattered clothes furthering the sense of chaos.[83] The soldier breaks through the barbed wire without hesitation, the red headscarf attracts the viewer’s eye to the soldier, his black skin silhouetted against the white cloud background. The cherry blossoms are an interesting addition to the composition, leading the eye to the subject, and symbolizing optimism, rebirth, and renewal, sometimes through violence. This type of propaganda, however, was arguably more effective on German soldiers than the French public, and provides a reminder of the very tangible consequences of promoting racist stereotypes. The French also propagated cartoons further barbarizing African soldiers, depicting them carrying and displaying severed German heads to their officers.[84,85] During World War I and World War II, these rumors of the savagery of African colonial soldiers spread amongst the Germans. German General Heinz Guderian’s Chief of Staff Walther Nehring stated, “It has been established that French colonial soldiers have mutilated in bestial fashion our German wounded. Towards these native soldiers, all kindness would be an error.” As a consequence, both African officers and soldiers taken as prisoners of war were executed by the Nazis without mercy.[86]

Recruitment posters had not been used in Britain since the Napoleonic Wars, and a variety of British offices spun into action to fulfill the need for soldiers in the war. Connection with an audience’s needs and values, or in this case, confrontation, came to a forefront with what is now Britain’s most iconic World War I image, “Lord Kitchener Wants You,” created in 1914 by Alfred Leete. (Figure 2.28) In this image, the British Secretary of State for War points directly at the viewer, confronting them with an inescapable gaze and finger point, along with the bold address to their national identity, “BRITONS!” Recalling how arresting a direct human gaze can be to our psyche, here Leete broke the fourth wall of the picture plane, using the design storytelling effect of **invisibility**, inviting the decoder of the image as a direct participant. In invisibility, one becomes so immersed in the storytelling experience that the existence of the medium fades.[87] Leete’s image also speaks to the communication advantages of illustration and the picture superiority effect. One of the first British recruitment posters of the war featured a Union Jack in the background, with type reading “Your King and Country Need You: Enlist Now” centered over the flag. While the design of the *King and Country* poster is strong, the psychology of the illustration in the Lord Kitchener image proved to be much more effective. The image, mostly printed as a postcard and not a poster, was not the most popular or influential propaganda image at the time in Britain, but gained its later fame from the imitations and lasting quality of its design. The image has stuck in the public’s consciousness so strongly that dozens of imitations were created around the world, from Armenia, to Canada, to Russia, the Weimar Republic, and even Smokey the Bear in America.

The most recognized imitation of the Lord Kitchener poster was the American *Uncle Sam Wants You* poster from 1917, which pictured the same design, but with the iconic symbol of Uncle Sam, a personified symbol for the US government. (Figure 2.29) James Montgomery Flagg used his own face for the design, and arguably the illustration is even more effective here than in the Lord Kitchener poster. Flagg's gaze is much sterner, and he took a symbol associated with political cartoons and made it serious and foreboding, adding some wrinkles and gray hair for added dignity. Flagg boasted his own poster was "the most famous poster in the world," and over four million copies were printed between 1917 and 1918.[88]

Flagg's fame was also not limited to this poster. Working under the US Government's Committee on Public Information (also called the Creel Committee or CPI) Division of Pictorial Publicity, Flagg created 46 posters during World War I.[89] Creel famously lobbied for the committee with President Woodrow Wilson by stating he wanted to create a government agency to make, "not propaganda as the Germans defined it, but propaganda in the true sense of the word, meaning the 'propagation of faith.'"[90] Other famed illustrators who created posters for the CPI included N.C. Wyeth, Charles Dana Gibson, Howard Chandler Christy, Joseph Pennell, and Laura Brey, one of the few women to work with the organization, amongst 300 other famous designers and illustrators of the time.[91]

As Europeans created propaganda to recruit Black Africans to fight in the war, Americans created propaganda to recruit African Americans. In the illustration *True Sons of Freedom*, created in 1918 by Charles Gustrine, a white Swedish-American artist, Gustrine evokes Abraham Lincoln and the fight for freedom in the Civil War as a bid for African Americans to join the war effort. (Figure 2.30) In the foreground, steady, determined African American soldiers wage attack against the surrendering Germans, although in the background, Gustrine includes undertones of the barbarity from the European posters, such as soldiers brutally stabbing downwards with their bayonets. E.G. Renesch was another white illustrator and publisher who also made a number of African American recruitment illustrations during World War I. In *The Colored Man is No Slacker*, Renesch shows the metaphor of fidelity to love as fidelity to country. (Figure 2.31) Here, the word "slacker" was used as a World War I era term for draft dodging. Francis Xavier Luca, Chief Librarian of the Wolfsonian Library, notes that in *Colored Man*, Renesch attempted to de-racialize the characters portrayed, and furthermore attempted to blend the soldier's black skin with the khaki of their uniforms. This could be seen as showing them as equal members of the army, but only by erasing their racial identity. More than 350,000 African Americans served in the US military in segregated units during World War I and 42,000 saw action in Europe.[92] However, upon returning from the war, many Black soldiers experienced renewed discrimination and hostility, including the "Red Summer" race riots of 1919.[93] Kelli Morgan, a curatorial fellow with the Pennsylvania Museum of Arts, describes this discrimination: "Because there was a sense that African-American men, particularly veterans, had kind of gotten out of their place, so this idea of bravery and subjectivity and autonomy in particular couldn't stand."[94] Notably, although few, if any, Black Americans were involved in the creation of the recruitment propaganda that brought them into the war, many of the soldiers who fought went on to create reportage art of the war, and the newfound freedom and proud self-ethos of African American veterans ushered in the artistic revolution of the Harlem Renaissance.

GLOBAL POLITICS PERSPECTIVE

How Did the World's First Communist Country Come About?

The Soviet Union was officially established in 1922, and its founding remains one of the most significant historical events of the 20th century. As with most enormous events, this did not happen overnight. Much of the territory of the Soviet Union had been ruled by the Romanov Dynasty of the Russian Empire since the 17th century. The final Tsar of the Russian Empire, Nicholas II, was overthrown in a coup in March of 1917, in the height of World War I. The coup leaders were not communists, but supporters of parliamentary democracy who had grown weary of the Tsar's autocratic and haphazard leadership. These individuals deposed the Tsar and his family, abolished the monarchy, and set up a provisional government, led by Alexander Kerensky; they hoped to create a republic like they had seen in France or Germany. During this transition period, many former critics, and former political opponents of the Tsar, like Vladimir Lenin, Leon Trotsky, and Joseph Stalin, began to return to Russia from exile. They represented a broader ideological interest in Communism, which had been gaining traction in Europe since the publication of the *Communist Manifesto* by Karl Marx and Friedrich Engels in 1848. Marxists like Lenin were deeply inspired by the notion that workers would inevitably rise up and lead a revolution against the bourgeois elites. While Lenin and his colleagues were not laborers, and had familial ties to the wealthy elite themselves, they took advantage of the new, young provisional government in Russia.[95] In November of 1917[96], Lenin and his followers, known as the Bolsheviks, led an uprising against the provisional government, and ousted Kerensky and the other leaders. At this point, there were multiple factions within Russia that all wanted different types of governments, including a return of the Tsar, a new communist system or a parliamentary democracy. A civil war broke out, between the pro-communist Bolshevik Red Army, the pro-monarchist White Army, and other factions. By the war's end in 1923, the Bolsheviks had defeated the other noncommunist forces, the Tsar and his family had been executed, and Lenin was firmly in control of the country. He established the Soviet Union as a federal republic that included present-day Russia, as well as Ukraine, Georgia, Kazakhstan, and eventually, eleven other now-independent states. This tumultuous start also contributed to Lenin's, and subsequently Stalin's, rejection of any criticism, and fueled a post-revolutionary campaign of terror to root out any potential opponents or threats to their rule, just as we saw in Revolutionary France. The first secret police, the Cheka, was created in 1917, and this would eventually transform into the KGB.[97] The official name of the Soviet Union was the Union of Soviet Socialist Republics, which reflected Lenin's view that a government could not exist in Marx's utopian communism. Therefore, the Soviet Union would practice what Lenin termed 'socialism', but that this was a temporary transition that would eventually lead to the end of all governments, complete communal living, peace, and communism.

Statues, murals, and images of Lenin proliferated throughout the Soviet Union; his name was often included on prominent streets and buildings. While statues and public imagery of Lenin still stand today throughout Russia, his likeness has been viewed as a relic of Soviet imperialism and failed communism in other post-Soviet countries. This has been most clearly observed in Ukraine, where over 500 statues have been dismantled since 2014. This targeted removal of Soviet imagery and Lenin statues began in response to the Russian annexation of the Crimean Peninsula and to Russian support for Ukrainian separatists in the eastern regions of Donetsk and Luhansk. It accelerated after the full-scale Russian invasion of Ukraine in 2022. This process occurred earlier in many other post-Soviet countries, as they gained independence following the collapse of the Soviet Union in 1991. Since then, Lenin statues have been removed and then often replaced with monuments connected to their national history, such as the Independence Monument in Tashkent, Uzbekistan and the statue of Ismoili Somoni in Dushanbe, Tajikistan.

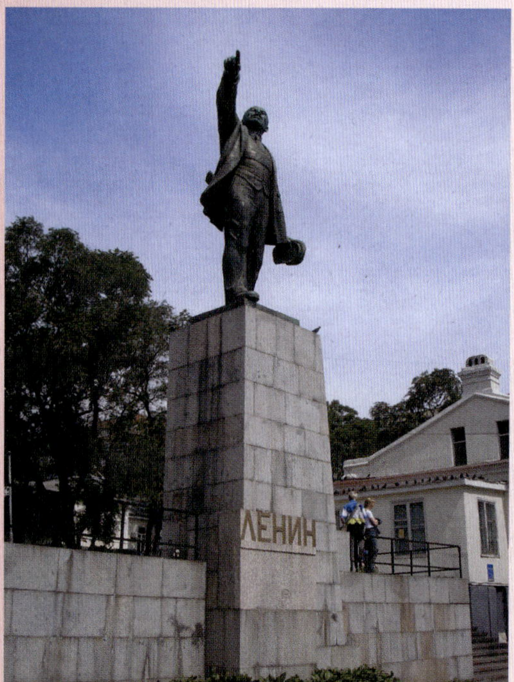

Figure 2.22
Statues, murals, and images of Lenin proliferated throughout the Soviet Union and his name was often included on prominent streets and buildings. This statue is from Vladivostok, Russia.
Photo © Megan Hauser, 2007

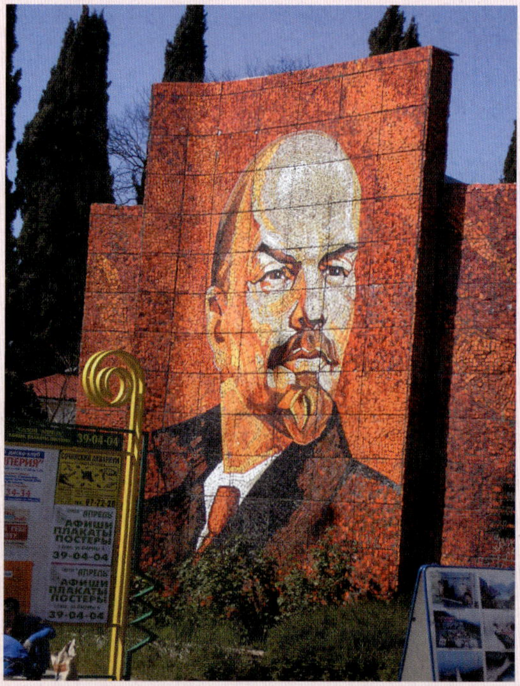

Figure 2.23
This mural of Lenin is from Sochi, Russia. Many post-Soviet countries have removed monuments to Lenin.
Photo © Megan Hauser, 2007

World War I had a significant impact on the creation of future propagandists, leaving a treasure trove of information to study with a critical eye. Some pacifists made condemning statements about propaganda, such as "There must have been more deliberate lying in the world from 1914 to 1918 than in any other period of the world's history" (British pacifist MP Arthur Ponsonby) and "A really efficient propaganda could reduce most human beings to the condition of abject slavery" (Aldous Huxley).[98] The Soviet Union, however, embraced the power of propaganda. Following the Bolshevik overthrow of the provisional Russian government, the interwar period saw a flood of propaganda emanating from the newly formed Soviet Republic. The Department for Agitation and Propaganda created numerous works of propaganda in multiple media, dubbed **agitprop**. The Soviet censorship organization Glavlit, formed in 1922, inspected propaganda to make sure it contained the correct messaging and ideology and had the final word over its publication.

Constructivism and **photomontage** played a large influence on the style of these early propaganda posters from the Soviet Union. Artists such as Germans Hannah Höch and John Heartfield popularized the technique of the collage as they experimented with photo juxtaposition and created new ideas out of the rearrangement of preexisting material. Meanwhile, artists such as El Lissitzky, a protégé of **Suprematist** Kasimir Malevich, began developing Constructivism, simplifying shapes and forms to their basics, which imitated the industrial and urban age of geometric architecture and spaces.[99]

Gustav Klutsis was inspired by all of these artists when he began creating posters for the Soviet Union in the 1920s. Klutsis is primarily known for his photomontages, creating dramatic compositions full of angles and dynamic shapes. In *The USSR is the Shock Brigade of the World's Proletariat* from 1931, Klutsis shows a working comrade, clad in overalls, hoisting a Soviet flag, simplified into a dramatic red angle that bisects the page. (Figure 2.32) To further the drama in the composition, Klutsis plays with three-dimensional space, making the man's hand unusually large so that it seems to jump out towards the audience. The figure plants the flag into the planet earth, surrounded by men of different races gazing admiringly at their Soviet leader. Klutsis was an ardent admirer and supporter of the Soviet Union, creating dozens of these innovative posters over his short lifetime. However, Klutsis' passion for the Soviet Union did not save him from its purge of native Latvians, and he was executed in 1938.[100]

Another notable style of the Soviet interwar period were the mostly hand-painted postcards created by the Russian State Telegraph Agency, known as the ROSTA windows. (Figure 2.33) These flat, graphic images, inspired by the German **Plakatstil** movement and **Futurism**, were posted in shop windows, and shared political, economic, and military messages with the Russian public. Many of these posters used illustration to describe the messages, due to the high illiteracy rate amongst the public. ROSTA artist Vladimir Mayakovski was born in Georgia and moved to Moscow as a teenager, where he became enthralled by Marxist literature and became a Bolshevik activist. Mayakovski devoted himself to creating Socialist arts, mostly writing poetry until he became employed by ROSTA and began creating posters. The text on this poster reads: "Hurry to join shock brigades! – *Do you want it? Then join. 1. Want to defeat cold? 2. Want to defeat hunger? 3. Want to eat? 4. Want to drink? Hurry, join the advanced exemplary labor group.*" (The phrase rhymes in Russian.) The shock brigades were groups of enthusiastic, super-productive workers that were used as a propaganda tool to inspire others, although in reality they lacked safety regulations, sleep, and concern for personal health. After his time creating ROSTA posters, Mayakovski continued to write poetry, defying form and becoming one of the Soviet Union's most famous propaganda poets, with Stalin declaring him, the "best and most talented poet of our Soviet epoch." Accused of being a "false leftist" and facing increasing smear campaigns from the Soviet press, Mayakovski committed suicide in 1930 at the age of 36. Like Klutsis and Mayakovski, many artists devoted to the Soviet cause did not survive to see their full ideals actualized.

Towards the end of World War I, Britain created its Ministry of Information, which was dissolved between the world wars, but renewed at the onset of World War II to create national propaganda and "to promote the national case to the public at home and abroad in time of war."[101] With the onset of World War II, colonized persons found themselves in a propaganda tug of war between the Axis and Allied forces. Germany and the Axis powers were keen on stealing Allied colonial support by convincing their colonies that this was their chance for independence. Some of these attempts were successful. One Indian independence leader, Subhas Chandra Bose, sought Axis support of Indian independence and arranged an army of Indian soldiers to fight with the Japanese. The Japanese occupation of the Dutch West Indies during World War II supported nationalist movements, which eventually led to Indonesia declaring their independence. Britain and the Allies, in turn, countered with their own propaganda. One British pamphlet attempted to make West Africans scared of the German government, noting the advantages of supporting a British government and the dangers of supporting a German government. The pamphlet used simple, sequential illustrations, similar to the ROSTA windows, to spell out the consequences without requiring the audience to be literate. In the pamphlet, cooperation with the British shows happy citizens engaging in trade, while claiming West Africans would be subject to violence and slavery under Nazi rule. Britain also released a series of, perhaps ill-conceived, *Thank You!* posters in countries including Nigeria and Sierra Leone, focusing on the value of the raw materials Britain extracted from these countries for the war effort. (Figure 2.34) The irony of these posters that framed West Africa as a source for raw goods but did not mention the contributions of the native people themselves became apparent after the war, when there was a lack of war pensions, jobs, or improvements to their countries. Not surprisingly, following World War II, many African nations began mounting their independence from colonial rule, the first being Ghana in 1957.

Britain continued with its push towards a unified warfront, distributing its famed *Together* posters, including this one by William Little depicting marching rows of all of the Allied countries and colonies, entitled *Freedom Shall Prevail!* (Figure 2.35) The faces and uniforms of the soldiers are saturated with color, emulating the V for victory formation of flags, and a tone of optimism rings throughout the piece. Similarly, in America, calls to its citizens to join the war effort echoed these bright colors, full shapes, and encouraging messaging, including J. Howard Miller's *We Can Do It!* poster showing a woman factory worker flexing a muscle while sporting bold feminine makeup. (Figure 2.36) This theme of optimism and patriotism echoed through much of the American propaganda of World War II.

The inaugural address of Franklin D. Roosevelt invoked America's Good Neighbor policy, a foreign policy statement of non-intervention of the United States in the politics of Central and South America. Roosevelt stated in his 1933 speech: "In the field of world policy I would dedicate this Nation to the policy of the good neighbor – the neighbor who resolutely respects himself and, because he does so, respects the rights of others – the neighbor who respects his obligations and respects the sanctity of his agreements in and with a world of neighbors."[102] Following America's military interventions in Latin

America in the early 20th century, the policy attempted to support good relations with Latin American countries through economic and commercial means, but its real goal was to pave the way for the United States to have access to their resources. Metals, oil, and rubber, all valuable resources for war efforts in the United States, were abundant in Latin America.[103] In addition, the US needed workers. Through the Bracero program of 1942, millions of Mexican men were brought to the US during the labor shortage of World War II.[104] When World War II began, the US needed to counter the influence of the Axis powers through unity in the Western Hemisphere, and hired many artists from Mexico and other Latin American countries to create pro-US propaganda through The Office of War Information (OWI).[105]

One of these artists was Leon Helguera, who immigrated to the United States at age 17 and became a naturalized US citizen. Helguera spent 35 years in the US before returning to Mexico, during which he worked for OWI through a Manhattan design agency, designing posters and postage stamps.[106] Helguera also designed the first portrait of Uncle Sam by a Mexican American, used through a war information security campaign.[107] Helguera was not critical of the Good Neighbor policy, but wrote to Roosevelt in 1943: "As one who shares the admiration most Latin Americans have for your sincere pursuit of the Good Neighbor Policy, I suscribe [sic] myself as your faithful admirer."[108] Helguera's posters use strong directional forces to add drama to his compositions. His bold use of colors and the "sunshine" motif present in many propaganda posters from around the world gives a sense of hope and optimism. (Figures 2.37 and 2.38)

Contrarily, in Germany, the propaganda took on a more somber tone with darker colors and more hard-edged shapes. In contrast to Britain's *Together* posters, a German poster recruiting French citizens to join the SS uses a similar layout, but the image conveys a very different message. (Figure 2.39) Rows of German soldiers, instead of showing diversity, have the same face and serious expression, and a dark shadow falls upon their faces. Instead of warmly inviting the French to comply, the message becomes a dark demand. Throughout the 1930s and into World War II, Nazi propaganda idealized their figures describing Hitler's obsession with "faultless, sports-trained bodies" and his vision of the blond haired, blue-eyed superior "master race." Much of their art borrowed from the Socialist Realism style of the Soviets, which promoted an optimistic view of hard-working and united citizens.

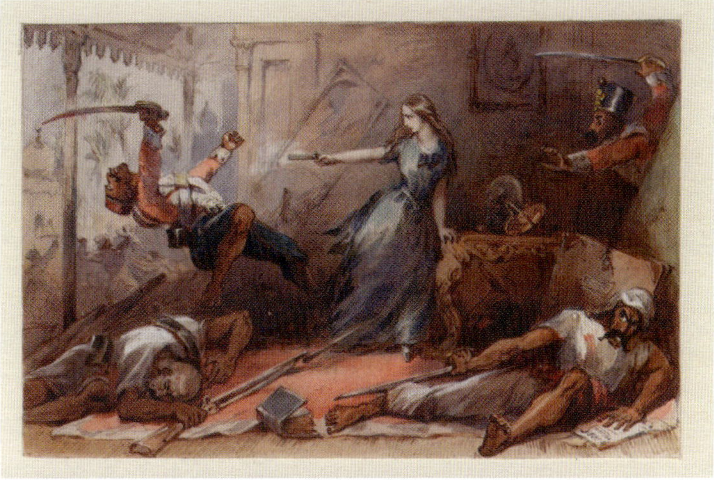

Figure 2.24
A colorized version of *Miss Wheeler Defending Herself Against the Sepoys* at Cawnpore (1857), distributed by the London Printing and Publishing Company, shows how the British used racist stereotypes to promote their agenda in India.

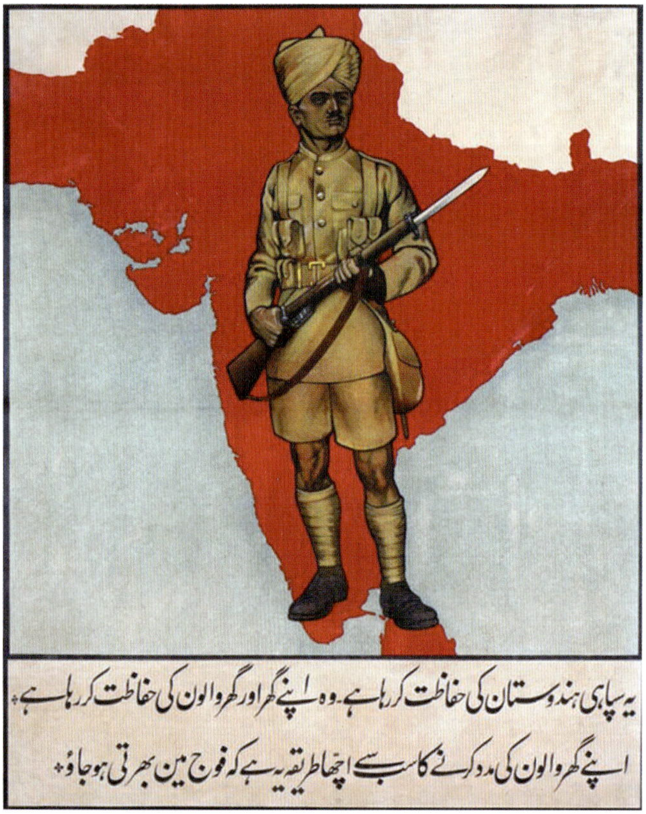

Figure 2.25
In the British poster *This Soldier is Defending India* from World War I, earlier stereotypes were pared down and replaced with messages of patriotism, loyalty, and equality.

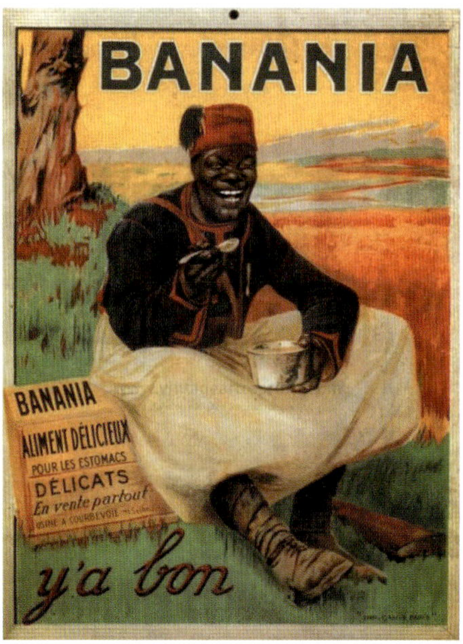

Figure 2.26
During World War I, the advertisement for a chocolate banana drink "Banania" (1915) infantilized African recruits through a wide smiling facial expression and the use of a pidgin French. Similar techniques were used in French recruitment propaganda.

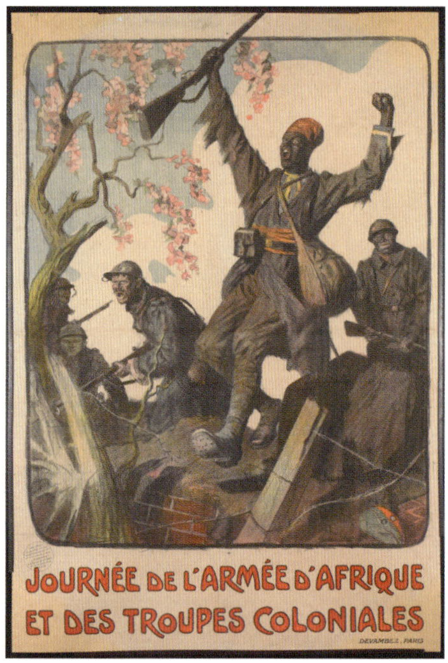

Figure 2.27
The poster *Journée de l'Armée d'Afrique et des Troupes Coloniales (African Army and Colonial Troops Day)*, created by Lucien Jonas in 1917, depicts a racist stereotype of African soldiers as bloodthirsty and violent.

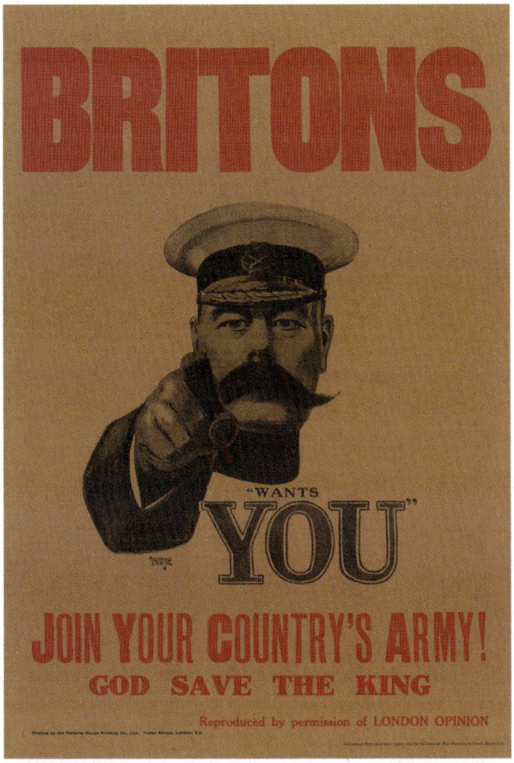

Figure 2.28
Britain's most iconic World War I image, *Lord Kitchener Wants You*, created in 1914 by Alfred Leete, was parodied by many artists over the following century.

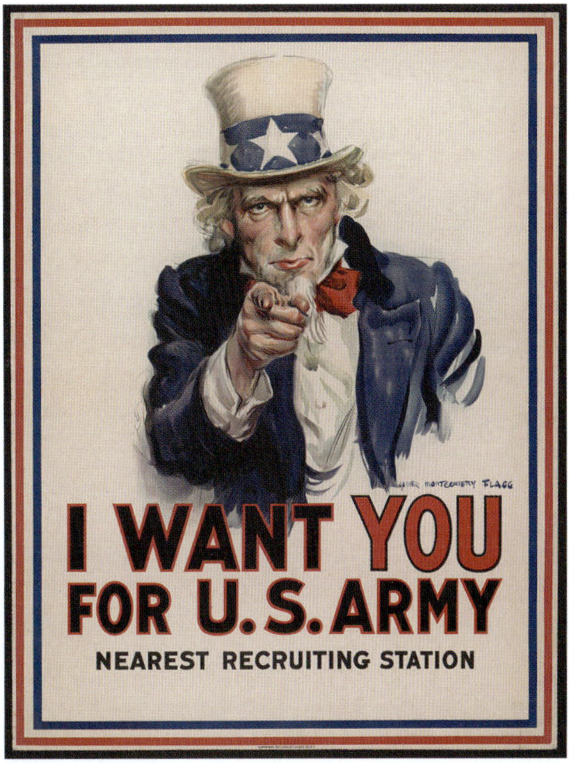

Figure 2.29
The most recognized imitation of the Lord Kitchener poster was James Montgomery Flagg's *Uncle Sam Wants You* poster from 1917, which pictured the same design, but with the iconic symbol of Uncle Sam, a personified symbol for the US government.

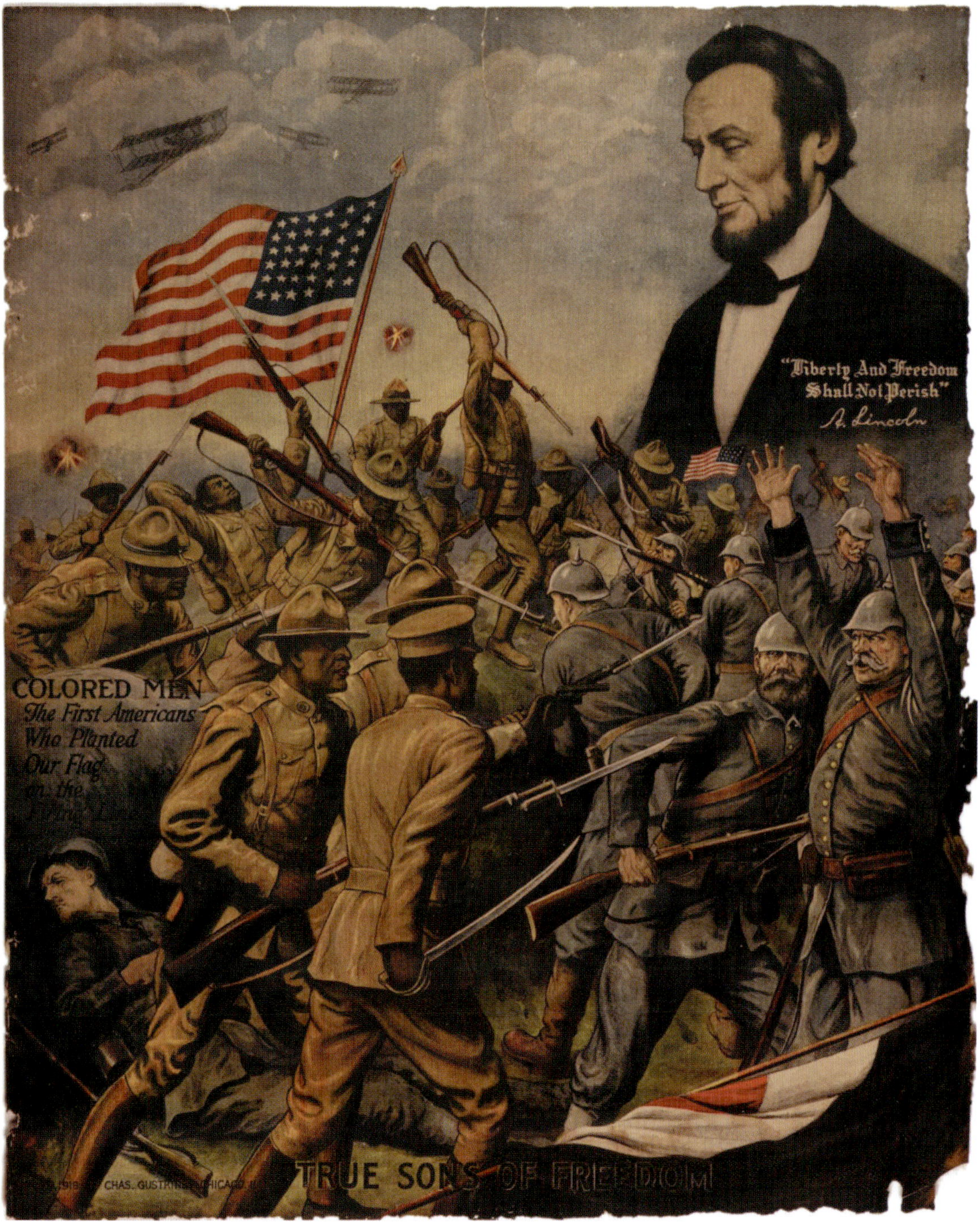

Figure 2.30
The illustration *True Sons of Freedom*, created in 1918 by Charles Gustrine, a white Swedish-American artist, encouraged African Americans to join the war effort during World War I.

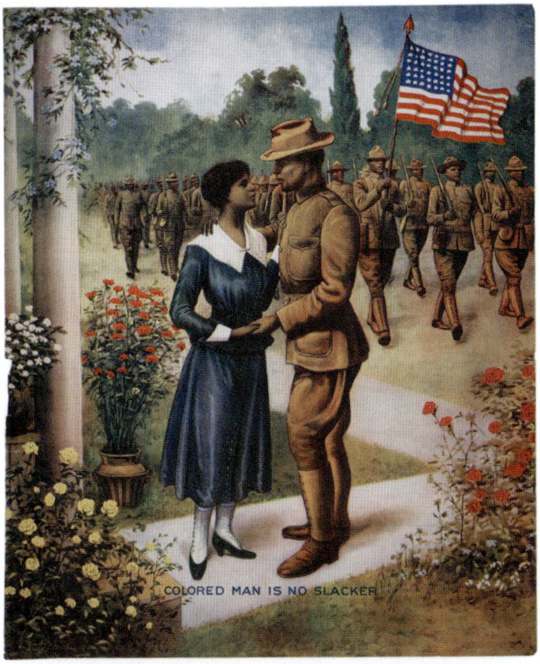

Figure 2.31
E.G. Renesch was another white illustrator and publisher who also made a number of African American recruitment illustrations during World War I. In *The Colored Man is No Slacker* (1918), Renesch shows the metaphor of fidelity to love as fidelity to country.

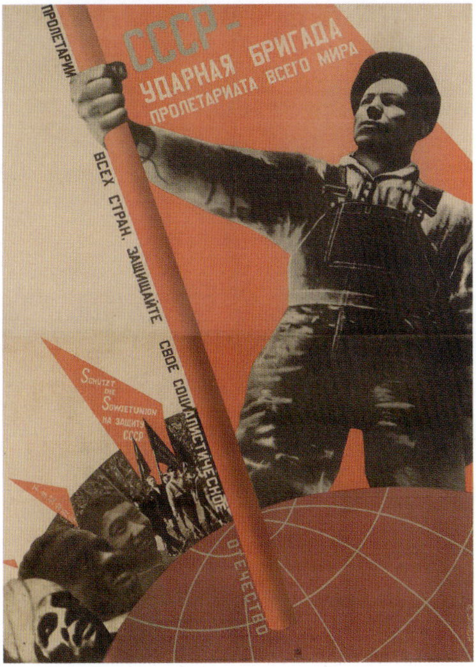

Figure 2.32
Gustav Klutsis' *The USSR is the Shock Brigade of the World's Proletariat* from 1931 is an excellent example of his photomontages, in which he would create dramatic compositions full of angles and dynamic shapes.

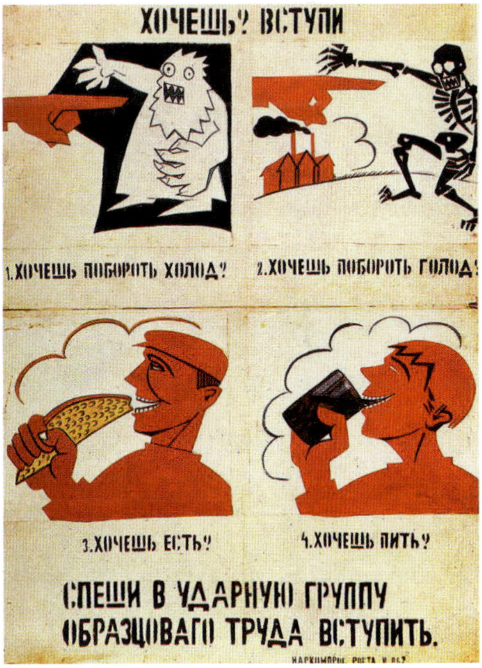

Figure 2.33
The ROSTA windows, created by the Russian State Telegraph Agency between 1919 and 1921, were flat, graphic images posted in shop windows, and shared political, economic, and military messages with the Russian public.

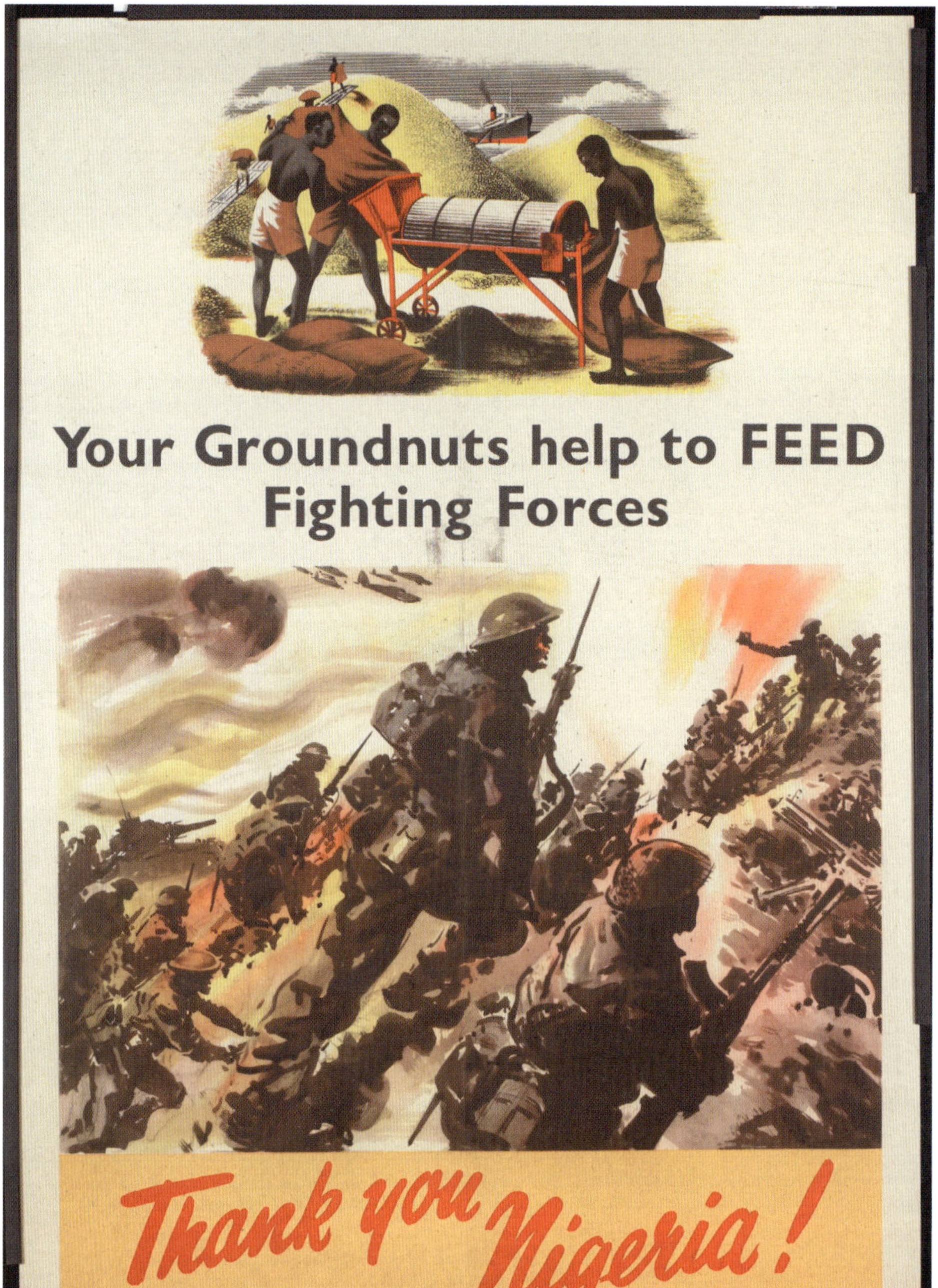

Figure 2.34
The British *Thank You!* Posters during World War I framed West Africa as a source for raw goods but did not mention the contributions of the continents' native people.

Figure 2.35 The British *Together* posters from World War II, including this one by William Little entitled *Freedom Shall Prevail!*, were optimistic, colorful examples of propaganda which have remained in the cultural zeitgeist.

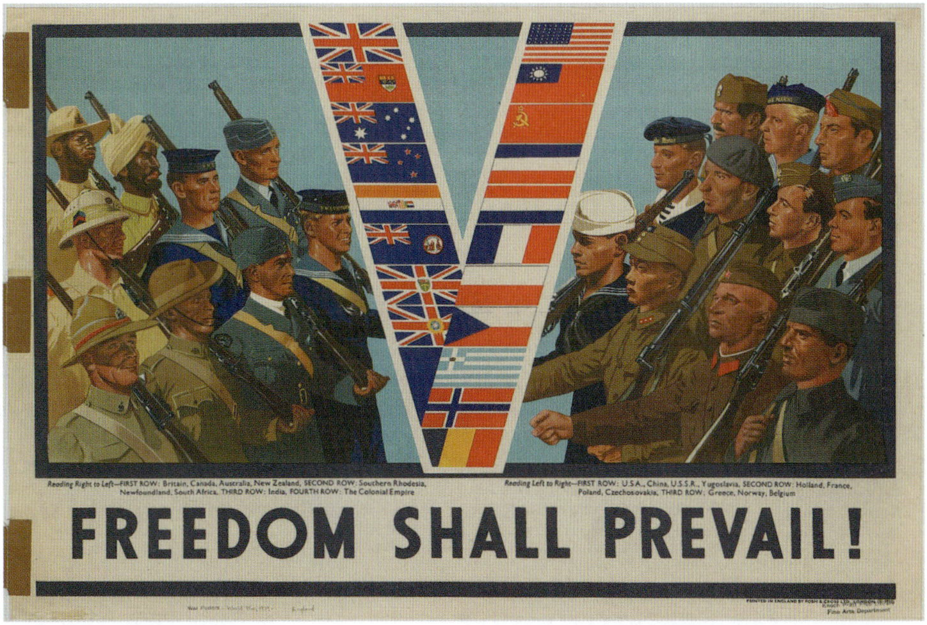

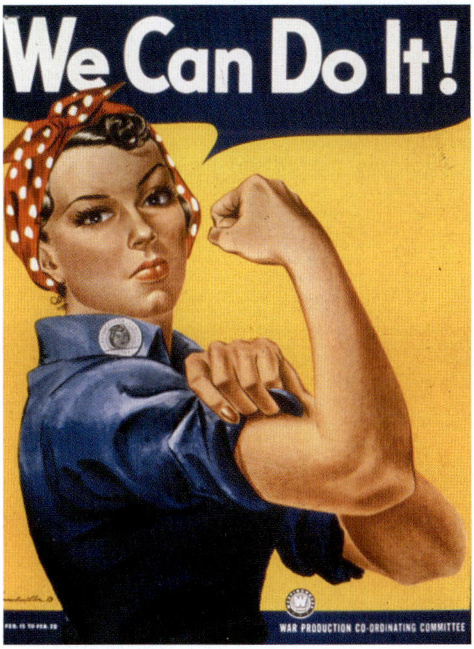

Figure 2.36
J. Howard Miller's *We Can Do It!* poster (1943) is another example of how optimism and patriotism echoed through much of the Allied propaganda of World War II.

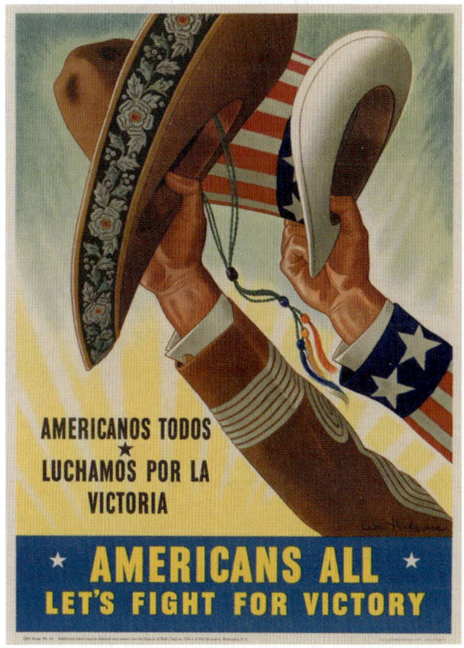

Figure 2.37
In his 1943 poster *Americans All: Let's Fight for Victory!* for the Office of War Information, Leon Helguera used bright colors and dramatic lines to convey unity between Latin Americans and the American war effort.

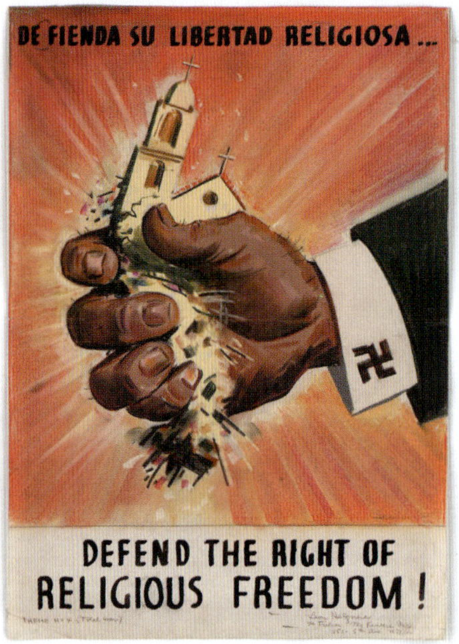

Figure 2.38
Leon Helguera's *Defend the Right of Religious Freedom* (1943) also used his characteristic visual drama to convey an anti-Nazi message.

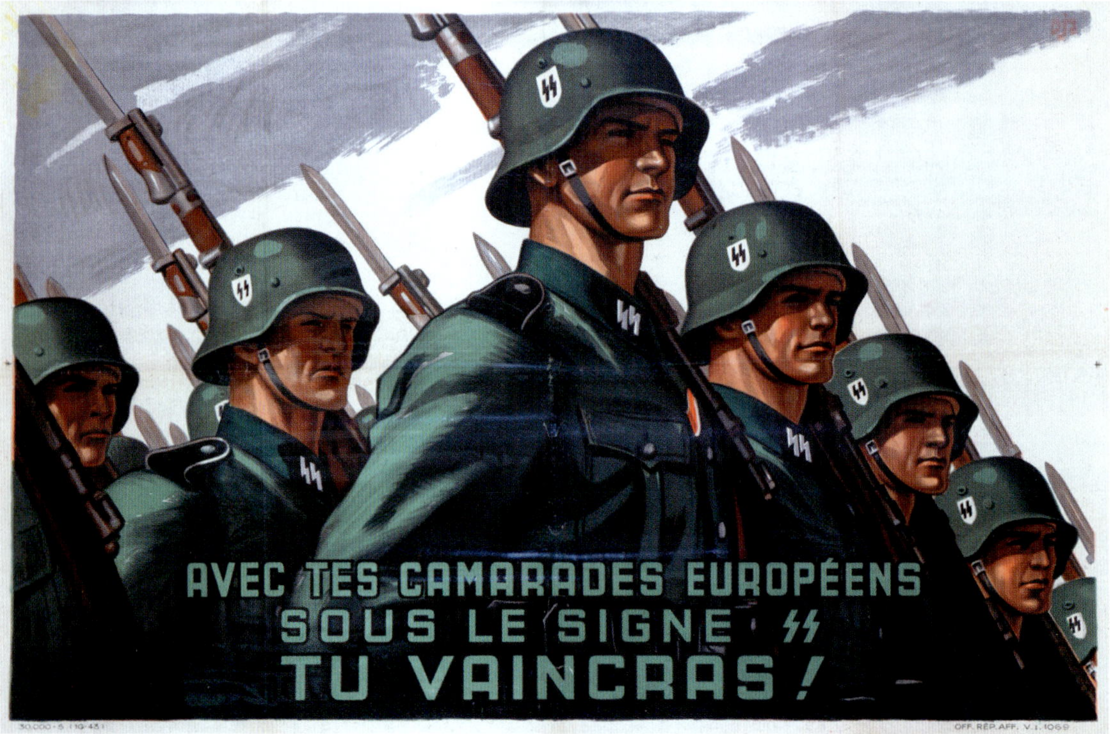

Figure 2.39
German World War II propaganda, including this example from occupied France from 1943, took on a somber tone with darker colors and more hard-edged shapes.

Socialist Realism in the Soviet Union and China

Socialist Realism emerged in Russia following the communist revolution and Josef Stalin's rise to power, during a time when the avant-garde art movement was still tolerated by the government. By the 1930s, however, Socialist Realism had become state policy, turning public favor against experimental artists such as Klutsis and Mayakovski. Stalin rejected this avant-garde art as elitist, and believed that art should serve a functional purpose and provide depictions of an idealized Soviet Union that could be appreciated and admired by the public. Stalin declared art ought to be "national in form, socialist in content," and called artists "engineers of the soul." A number of Socialist Realism art groups formed in Soviet Russia in the 1920s and 1930s that later disbanded, unable to continue the façade of an idealized and equal society. This included the Association of Artists of Revolutionary Russia and the Society of Easel Painters. Maxim Gorky, a Realist writer, gave a speech in 1934 which solidified the principles of Socialist Realism, stating art should be proletarian (for the workers), typical (showing regular people, and not the elite bourgeoise), stylistically Realist, and partisan (supporting the Communist Party). During this time, purges of avant-garde and experimental art occurred throughout the Soviet Union, with art being removed from galleries and museums. This removal also attacked the elitism that Socialist Realism sought to avoid, and art was placed more into public spaces for the everyday worker to admire and enjoy. Publicly displayed sculpture became a favorite medium of Socialist Realism, grabbing the attention of the public and creating a symbol of permanence and strength.[109]

One female painter who gained success as a Socialist Realist was Tetiana Yablonska. During the years of World War II, Yablonska found it inconceivable to paint under the circumstances, and was evacuated from German-occupied Kyiv to work as a collective farm worker. Once the city was liberated, she returned to painting, teaching at the Kyiv Art Institute. Yablonska had been criticized for being influenced by the style of Impressionism, especially in response to her painting *Before the Start* (1947), of a snowy skiing race, but refuted this with her most famous painting, the 1949 *Grain* (also translated as *Bread*). (Figure 2.40) The painting was conceived when her students visited a famous collective farm in Letava, and wrote her that the farm was "awfully dreary, with nothing beautiful, interesting or picturesque; the landscape is unvaried, and the people are working all the time, and refuse to pose. Why don't we go to the collective farm next door – it is located on a picturesque river bank..." Yablonska replied that "It is impossible for a place where so many good people work to be boring."

The painting depicts a mass of joyful Soviet women workers, heads encased by gleaming white headscarves. The white of the headscarves creates similarity and connection between the workers, and three directional lines lead to the hero woman, one of the few faces depicted in the image. The other workers are seemingly too busy to pay attention to the viewer. The woman beams at the viewer, extending her right arm to roll up her sleeve (reminiscent of J. Howard Miller's *We Can Do It* poster), her tucked skirt showing a traditional Ukrainian design. A pattern of red and blue create a triadic color scheme against the yellow tones of the background and the massive pile of grain in the foreground. A tone of optimism and purity overlays the sun-drenched painting. Yablonska wrote extensively of her process of creating the painting, publishing her article stating how she was "astonished" by the "vast scope of work performed by the united, happy workers at the collective farm." She goes on to say, "The way I saw art changed entirely after my visit to the collective farm. Formalism and naturalism both find foundation in the artist's estrangement from our Socialist reality."[110]

Yablonska's Socialist Realism conviction expressed in her article and letters following *Grain* come into question with her later work, inspired by folk art and other art traditions, which liberally shows vast experiments with form, simplification, impressionism, and color. The fate of her esteemed teacher and mentor Fedir Krychevsky also bring this single-minded loyalty into question. Krychevsky, himself a student of Vienna Secessionist Gustav Klimt, used a variety of artistic styles, from avant-garde to impressionism. Krychevsky, despite having a Jewish background, was able to stay in Kyiv during the German occupation and became an Honored Artist of the Ukrainian SSR. When Ukraine was retaken by the Soviets, he was arrested by the NKVD as a possible collaborator, interrogated and tortured, and stripped of his titles. He died in exile in 1947. Although Krychevsky was later "rehabilitated" by the Soviet government, with retrospectives of his work reemerging in 1959, this incident raises doubt that Yablonska would have been so devoted to a government and a style that destroyed her valued and influential teacher.[111] Before her death in 2005, Yablonska went on to gain the highest state award of Ukraine, the title Hero of Ukraine. Her most famous work *Grain*, a celebrated example of Socialist Realism, was printed on a postage stamp in 1967.

The last Chinese dynasty, the Qing, lost power in 1911 with the Xinhai Revolution and the abdication of the final Chinese emperor in 1912. In place of the imperial system in China, the Republic of China was established, after which followed a tumultuous period of power exchange and conflict. The Communist Party of China (CCP) was established in 1921, and in 1924 briefly formed an alliance with the nationalist Kuomintang (KMT) party, partly in order to receive support from the Soviet Union. The two parties subsequently entered a decades long civil war, and during World War II, China established its independence from Soviet communism when its own communist party continued to gain power in the country. In 1942, the Yan'an Conference on Literature and Art sought to determine art's role in Mao Zedong's communist government, specifically how it would be propagated, and what content it would contain. At this Conference, Mao declared his policy for Socialist Realism,

"All our literature and art are for the masses of the people, and in the first place for the workers, peasants and soldiers; they are created for the workers, peasants and soldiers... If everyone agrees on the fundamental policy, it should be adhered to by all our workers, all our schools, publications and organisations in the field of literature and art and in all our literary and artistic activities. It is wrong to depart from this policy and anything at variance with it must be duly corrected."[112]

Like the Soviet Union, Mao's plan for art as part of the CCP was to focus on peasants and working people by incorporating Western realism as an art technique, part of the CCP's goal to modernize China. However, unlike the initial art guidelines of the Soviet Union, Mao also encouraged artists to incorporate folk traditions of the countryside into their work. Part of Mao's Yan'an program included a Rectification Campaign to seek loyalty to the party, in which Mao quashed his rivals through a campaign of terror by forcing them to criticize themselves and each other, confess to crimes, and turn others in. Reminiscent of Tetiana Yablonska's farm work for the Soviet Union, many intellectuals and party elites were brought to villages to reconnect with China's agrarian economy.[113] The campaign is estimated to have resulted in the deaths of over 10,000 people.[114]

Socialist Realism in China was also significantly influenced through revolutionary romanticism. In 1953, at the Second China Conference of Writers and Artists, Zhou Yang encouraged artists to "imbue the people with a sense of the loftiness of patriotism and socialism so that the people will be able to advance towards the socialist society."[115] Artist Dong Xiwen studied at a French art academy in Vietnam, and produced one of the most recognized pieces of early Chinese Socialist Realism in 1953, *The Founding of a Nation*. (Figure 2.41) Xiwen hoped to blend his knowledge of Western oil painting with the traditional art of China, to, as Wan Shaojun writes, "consciously infuse oil painting with the forms and spirit of Chinese art, giving oil painting a Chinese style and artistic spirit."[116] The painting depicts the inauguration of the People's Republic of China at Tiananmen Square on October 1, 1949. Chairman Mao stands at the center of the painting, gazing upon his subjects, with prominent officials in the background. Unlike the muted colors in examples of Soviet Socialist Realism, including Tetiana Yablonska's painting *Grain*, the colors in Chinese Socialist Realism tend to be bright and saturated, while maintaining a triadic color scheme. The directional lines of the ground, columns, and skyline bring your eye to Mao (along with the yellow tail of a balloon), complimented by the psychic gaze lines of the officials in the background. Interestingly, due to Mao's consistent loyalty purges, Xiwen was compelled to remove officials from the painting the following year in 1954, and again in 1967. A reproduction was created and later modified to show other deletions and readditions and previously purged officials were rehabilitated.

One of the most famous examples of Mao propaganda is his giant portrait, which hangs in Tiananmen Square at almost two stories tall at 15'×20'.[117] (Figure 2.42) Portraits of Mao, like the monarch's portrait in Britain, proliferated in China following the Cultural Revolution of 1966, gaining monumental status and making the portrait more like a Greek **icon** or religious figure. The symbolism of the portrait is also fluid depending on the decoder of the image, and can be a symbol of old government, or of the spirit of China. The Tiananmen Square portrait was the culmination of this symbolism and importance. Initially the portrait in Tiananmen square was merely a sketch, then a portrait of Mao in uniform, but in the 1950s, 30 artists were asked to create a new image and Zhang Zhenshi was named official portrait maker and created the model for the current Tiananmen Square portrait. The design of the portrait was adjusted over time to include additional symbolism and communicative elements. Mao's gaze is always direct, showing he is looking over his people, and in 1967, the portrait was changed to show both of his ears to show he was always listening to the people.[118] The color used in the portrait is also key to its visual communication. Artist Liu Yang says, "Mao's face must be painted extra red to show his robust spirit," Liu said. "It can never be too yellow, which would seem sickly, like he hadn't eaten in days. You could be accused of being a counterrevolutionary." The famous portrait is actually two portraits, which are taken down and replaced by one another while the other is refreshed from weather damage by a team of artists. These artists, however, remain anonymous, sometimes dying without their identities being revealed. Mao portrait artist Wang Guodong, 76, who once received an infraction for painting Mao with only one ear showing, says, "Nobody is allowed to put their names on that painting. It's that way before, and it's that way now."[119] Liu Yang said of working on the Mao portrait, "We were told not to think of ourselves as artists. That's a stinky idea of the bourgeoisie. We are 'art workers.' We don't paint for ourselves. We serve the revolution." Interestingly, this idea is reminiscent of the field of illustration, where most jobs are done to serve another person, company, or group's idea and goal, sometimes fully selling their right to that illustration. Illustration itself, printed in popular and easily accessible media, can often be thought of as the "art of the people."

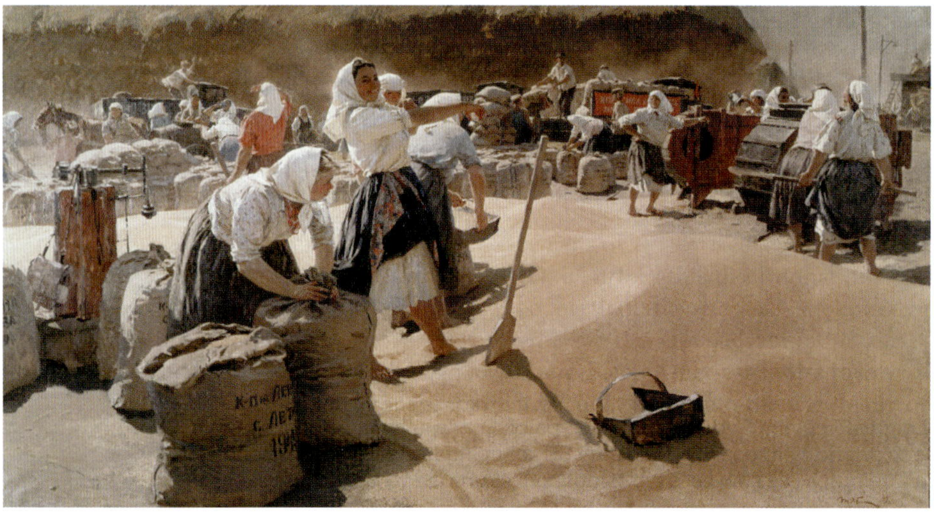

Figure 2.40 Tetiana Yablonska's *Grain* (1949) is a quintessential example of Socialist Realism's optimism and purity.

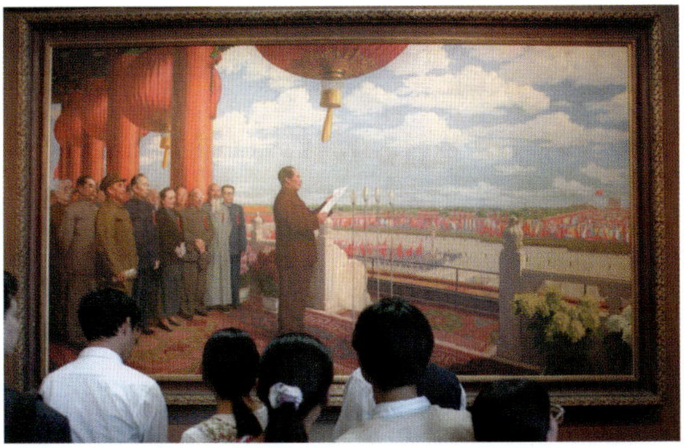

Figure 2.41
Dong Xiwen's *The Founding of a Nation* (1953) is an example of Chinese Socialist Realism, but has been altered many times since it was originally painted.

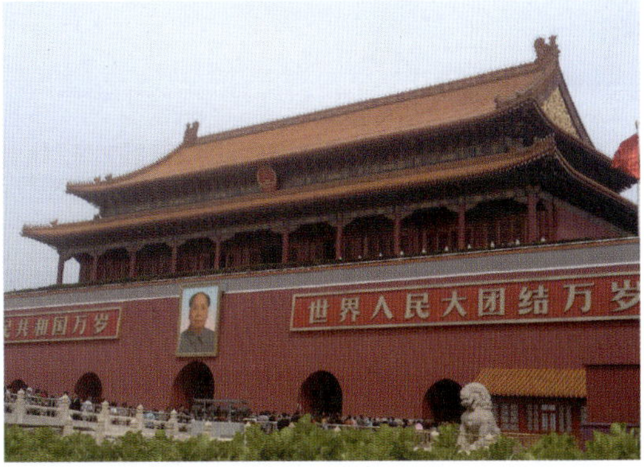

Figure 2.42
The portrait of Mao on Tiananmen Square has become an iconic tourist destination, but is actually a set of different portraits. Each portrait is periodically traded out for cleaning, restoration, and changes by a team of anonymous artists. Photo © Amanda Plumb, 2016

A Cult of Personality: Colonialism and Dictatorships in Africa and South America

The close of World War II also signaled the beginning of the end of imperialism, with the defeat of Nazi Germany's imperialist ambitions leading nations to question their own imperialist ambitions. After the war, many former colonized nations began the process of decolonization, declaring independence. Germany and Italy lost their African territories following the war, and although they were under the control of the British and/or French for a number of years following, this opened the door for independence. Multiple reasons contributed to this relatively sudden end to imperialism after it dominated for centuries as the primary form of government. One was economic; after World War II, the global imperialist powers did not have as much funding or resources to control numerous colonies. The second was political; European countries realized that they could not hold onto their colonies forever. In 1941, Roosevelt and Churchill met to discuss what the post-war world would look like, writing the Atlantic Charter. African colonies were encouraged to hear that the third clause in the charter sought a restoration of self-government. Although Churchill was concerned of the effects this would have on decolonization, he understood creating a joint declaration was necessary.[120] The third was social; during the war, European powers focused less on their colonies, and therefore independence movements among native people flourished. A small number of African elites who had been educated at European universities and became familiar with politics and ideas such as self-determination, led the way for education and literacy amongst the African people and a collective call for independence.

This newfound independence did not come without problems, however. Firstly, when the European colonialist powers divided Africa at the Berlin Conference of 1884–85, many of the borders were arbitrary or pernicious, and grouped together very different groups, religions, and tribes, leading to future civil wars and conflicts. In addition, many of the previous leaders during colonialism were ousted as collaborators with the colonialists, and these voids left caused conflicts between different groups that hoped to attain power. Individual European powers also treated decolonization differently. After brief conflicts in Ghana, Britain saw the "winds of change" in Africa and proceeded with peaceful decolonization. France, however, fought a number of bloody conflicts, especially in Madagascar and Algeria, with up to 100,000 Malagasy and possibly 1.5 million native Algerians losing their life to the conflict.[121,122]

All of these factors contributed to the rise of dictatorships in postwar Africa. One of the most infamous of these dictators was Idi Amin of Uganda. A former British Lieutenant, Amin became the commander of the Ugandan Army following its independence in 1962. Amin went on to seize power through a coup in 1971, ousting current president Milton Obote and declaring himself President of Uganda. During his subsequent brutal rule, Amin oversaw the deaths of 100,000–500,000 Ugandans, who were arrested, tortured, and killed for suspected disloyalty, including many ethnic minorities such as Christians and Asians, as well as journalists. Amin's rule was successful in part for establishing a cult of personality, with massive media campaigns showing the dictator interacting with the people with a huge smile and what Dr. Richard Vokes calls "a kind of manic energy." Dr. Vokes was quoted by *The Guardian* as saying, "We see how [Amin] embraced the media and understood its power ... How he had a great sense of how media could amplify his ego and his political will."[123] Like Mao Zedong in China, Amin created large scale portraits of himself to elevate his status, and also limited freedom of expression in Uganda, with government sanctioned art the only art that proliferated during his rule.[124] One example from 1975 shows a multi-story portrait in a stadium in Kampala and a group of people standing in various colors, creating a mosaic portrait of Amin. (Figure 2.43) Scale is used to amplify Amin's presence, and also closure in order to view the full portrait on the many pieces of fabric. Amin's portrait was also featured on Ugandan currency from 1973–79, further establishing his status.[125] Artists today continue to paint images of a smiling Amin, continuing his legacy of covering up brutality through personality.[126] Uganda has never officially addressed the violence that occurred under Amin's rule, and Amin died in exile in 2003.

Muammar Gaddafi began his career as an idealistic and enterprising military officer, who admired President Gamal Abdel Nasser of Egypt and his fight against European powers in Africa. In 1969, Gaddafi led a military coup in Libya, and managed to secure greater revenues from Libyan oil that had been controlled by foreign powers. Gaddafi went on to explore political philosophy in his *The Green Book*," which gave the illusion of power to the people while maintaining Gaddafi's absolute power. Libya's oil money and Gaddafi's unchecked power caused him to fund anti-imperialist groups and movements, including terrorism movements, throughout the world. Socialist Realism was employed by many postage stamps in Libya featuring Gaddafi, including many showing him as a young leader of the socialist 1969 coup. (Figure 2.44) Other stamps showed him as a hero against American aggression. Gaddafi's visage appeared on numerous billboards and street portraits, as well as a gilded portrait outside the Ras Lanuf Oil and Gas plant, often sporting his signature sunglasses and turban. (Figure 2.45) The multitude of portraiture allowed Gaddafi to claim popularity from his subjects that was not necessarily true. Libya maintained a cautious relationship with Western powers that endured for years, but in 2010, the Libyan people rebelled against Gaddafi's dictatorship, and, with the aid of NATO air strikes, Gaddafi was captured and killed in 2011.

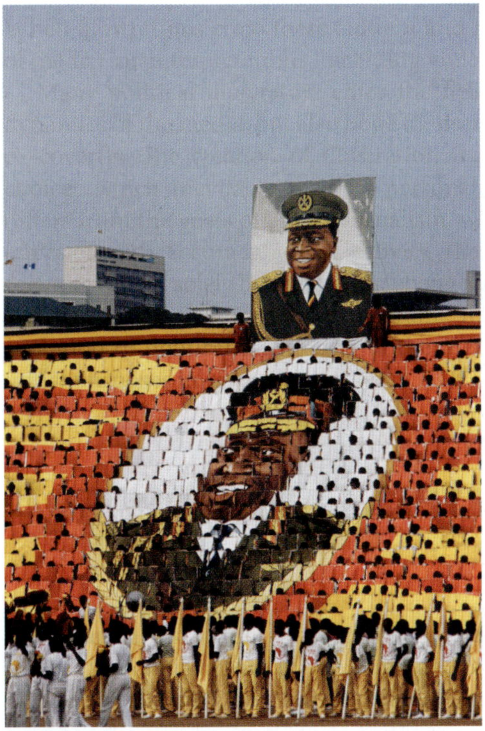

Figure 2.43
Ugandan dictator Idi Amin is depicted in mosaic in a multi-story portrait (1975) in a stadium in Kampala, created by a group of people standing in various colors. Amin propaganda proliferated in Uganda during his rule.

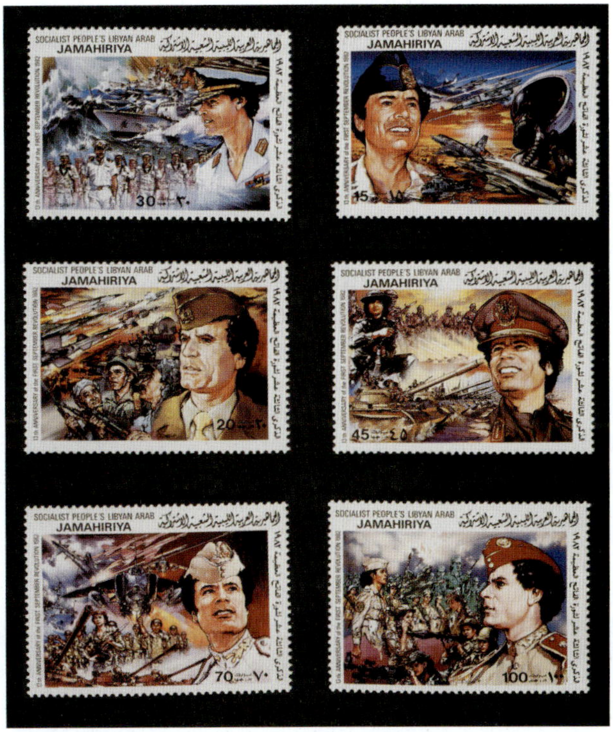

Figure 2.44
Libyan dictator Muammar Gaddafi's portrait was ubiquitous in Libya following his socialist 1969 coup. Many postage stamps in Libya featuring Gaddafi in a Socialist Realist style.

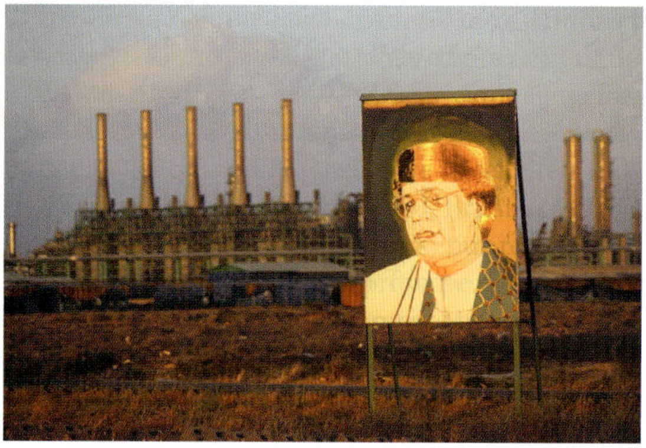

Figure 2.45
Gaddafi's visage appeared on numerous billboards and street portraits, as well as a gilded portrait outside the Ras Lanuf Oil and Gas plant (2000), where he sported his signature sunglasses and turban.

Post-War American Propaganda

Campaign materials are a formative part of how a democratically elected government comes to be, functioning as propaganda even if they are not created by the state. Candidates that won their campaigns often found themselves beholden to the image they created once they took office and would continue to benefit from the ethos of these images through a reelection campaign. Creating a cult of personality in the second half of the 20th century was not limited to dictatorships. After World War II, a shift in the focus of campaign materials in the US became evident. Previously, campaign materials and posters had focused on policies, and used metaphorical imagery to communicate character. One example was the use of hickory trees to represent Andrew Jackson, who had earned the nickname "Old Hickory," from his troops for being determined and for suffering alongside his men as a Major General. Another example is how William Henry Harrison and the Whig party used log cabins and hard cider in their campaign materials to show that he was a man of the people and not an elitist.[127] (Figure 2.46) After World War II, however, portraits and personalities dominated campaign materials.

Part of this change was due to shifts in media technology, which experienced significant changes throughout the 20th century. By the turn of the 20th century, **color lithography** was an established printing method, and 1903 brought about the invention of **offset lithography**, which made the process of lithography more efficient and cheaper. By the end of World War II, stone lithography had become a thing of the past, except for art printers. **Xerography**, a dry photocopying technique, was developed in the 1930s and automated into today's copy machines in the 1960s. **Screenprinting,** as we'll discuss in Chapter 4, also experienced technology changes and popularity in the 1960s and 1970s. Overall, creating printed materials became cheaper, quicker, and easier.

In addition to printing technology, television created a significant change in the focus on politics from issues to personalities. In 1950, only 9 percent of households owned a television set, but by 1960, this number had risen to 90 percent.[128] Now most of the communication received from political candidates was via television instead of radio.

The first televised presidential debate in the United States was between John F. Kennedy and Richard Nixon in September of 1960, and showed the newfound importance of cultivating a personality among the populace. In the debate, John F. Kennedy comfortably spoke to the camera, never breaking eye contact with the camera, and wore a dark suit that provided strong value contrast with the light colored wall in the background. Nixon refused to wear makeup and can be seen visibly sweating during the debate, appearing to be nervous. In addition, he wore a light-colored suit which caused him to blend into the background. Following the debate, Chicago mayor Richard J. Daley said of Nixon, "My God, they've embalmed him even before he died." While substantiated evidence of who "won" the debate is mostly anecdotal, the contrast between the two candidates showed how a new era was being issued in, one where aesthetic principles and personal appearance mattered more than any issue being discussed.

Consequently, throughout the remainder of the 20th century and into the 21st, stylized portraits of candidates dominated the campaign materials surrounding them. Dwight D. Eisenhower's face, paired with the catchy phrase "I Like Ike" was displayed on his campaign merchandise in 1952 and 1956. A 1968 poster of Robert Kennedy reading "Bobby is My Choice for '68" used psychedelic lettering and colors and a cartooned face of Bobby Kennedy, probably inadvertently reminiscent of Mad Magazine's Alfred E. Neuman, but nevertheless unique, eye-catching, and of the times. (Figure 2.47) In 1976, Jimmy Carter's campaign created an eye-catching and humorous peanut with a broad smile, alluding to his past as a peanut farmer (and, ergo, an everyman) and his trademark big white teeth. (Figure 2.48) A 1980 poster of Ronald Reagan reads like an 1980s era movie poster, with realistically illustrated faces of Reagan and his vice presidential candidate George H.W. Bush. (Figure 2.49) Jesse Jackson's campaign poster in 1988 featured a two-tone screenprint of his face in a 2/3rds profile, highlighting his blackness and creating strong contrast with the bright yellow of the background. These posters all portray arresting portraits though unique experimentations in technique and style never before seen in presidential campaigns. Overall, as the 20th century turned into the 21st, the style and marketing of a candidate via illustrated campaign materials was emphasized more than it ever had been before.

Another significant example of an American campaign poster is that of Shepard Fairey's *HOPE* poster for Barack Obama's 2008 campaign. (Figure 2.50) Inspired by Obama's speech at the Democratic National Convention in 2004, Fairey approached the Obama campaign in hopes of making a poster to highlight Obama's 2008 presidential campaign. In January 2008, the Obama campaign gave Fairey permission to move forward. At this time the Obama campaign was faltering, with Hillary Clinton holding the most polls leading into Super Tuesday.[129] With only two weeks before the fateful primary day, Fairey worked quickly, creating the image from a reference photo taken by Mannie Garcia, with the intent of creating an iconic Obama. Originally, the *HOPE* poster instead used the word PROGRESS, and the word was a last minute change after the Obama campaign disapproved of the connotation of the word "progress."[130] During Obama's campaign, approximately 700 Progress posters and over 350,000 *HOPE* posters were produced and distributed, along with stickers and countless copies printed from Fairey's website that were available for free to the public.[131] As Fairey intended, the poster not only became an icon of Obama, America's first Black president, but also of a generation of young American voters. After the creation of the poster, Obama himself wrote of Shepard's work, "The political messages involved in your work have encouraged Americans to believe they can help change the status quo. Your images have a profound effect on people, whether seen in a gallery or on a stop sign."[132]

The poster combines the bold shapes and colors of early Soviet Suprematism and Constructivism and the detail and realism of Socialist Realism. Fairey used many of the techniques we've discussed previously to create an effective poster. He placed Obama's head at a diagonal, and turned the direction of his gaze also upwards and at a diagonal, again metaphorically creating a vision of future through optimism and dynamism. Obama's determined countenance contrasts with this action, giving the impression of steadfastness. The colors in the background, combining the Democratic blue and Republican red, indicate patriotism and unity between the parties. The change of the word at the bottom of the poster to the powerful HOPE created additional efficacy. Fairey chose a Futura font for the letters, and made the O perfectly round and the same width as the other letters. The perfectly round O created a visual analogy with the O logo of the Obama campaign, and incorporated symbolism of a circle meaning unity. The shorter, single syllable word created additional punch and power. While experimentation and innovation in campaign posters had been occurring in American campaign posters throughout the past 50 years, the Fairey poster transformed a dull photograph into a cultural revolution and symbol of a generation. Peter Schjeldahl, an art critic for *The New Yorker*, stated that the poster is "the most efficacious American political illustration since 'Uncle Sam Wants You.'"[133]

All of these propaganda illustrations have used the techniques of semiotics, Gestalt, metaphor, symbolism, and visual grammar, and have used the power and intention of governments to propagate these images. The distribution of political illustration, however, is not limited to the art of the state, and is not limited to dominant interpretations of the images. Throughout history, governments and religious institutions have maintained power over messaging, but with the invention of the printing press, increasing literacy, and increasing visual literacy, more actors were introduced to political illustration and, with it, the dynamics of propagation and visual communication. Our next chapter will address the role of the media and popular press in political illustration.

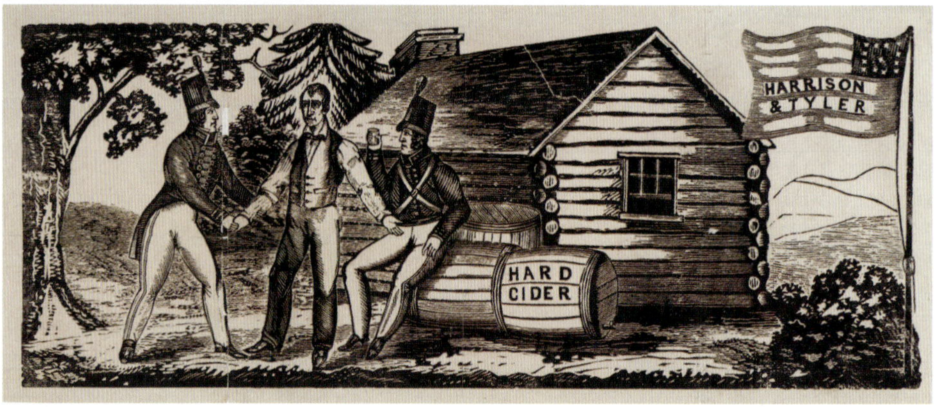

Figure 2.46
William Henry Harrison and the Whig party used log cabins and hard cider in their campaign materials for the 1840 election to show that he was a man of the people and not an elitist.

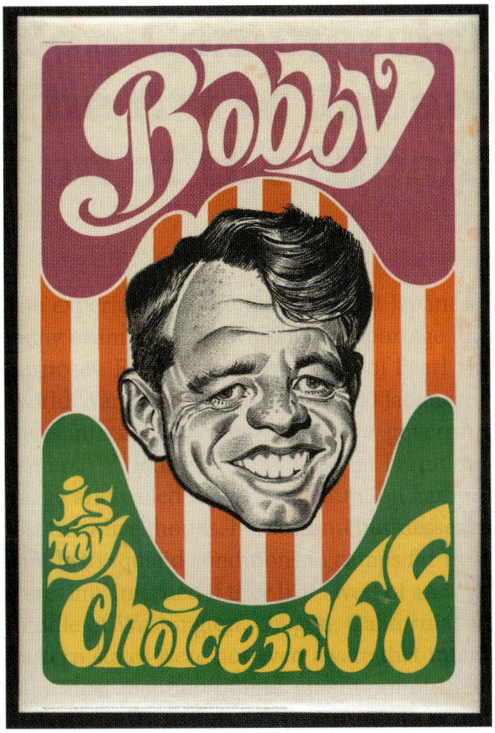

Figure 2.47
This 1968 poster of Robert Kennedy, *Bobby is My Choice for '68*, used psychedelic lettering and colors to create an image that was unique, eye-catching, and of the times.

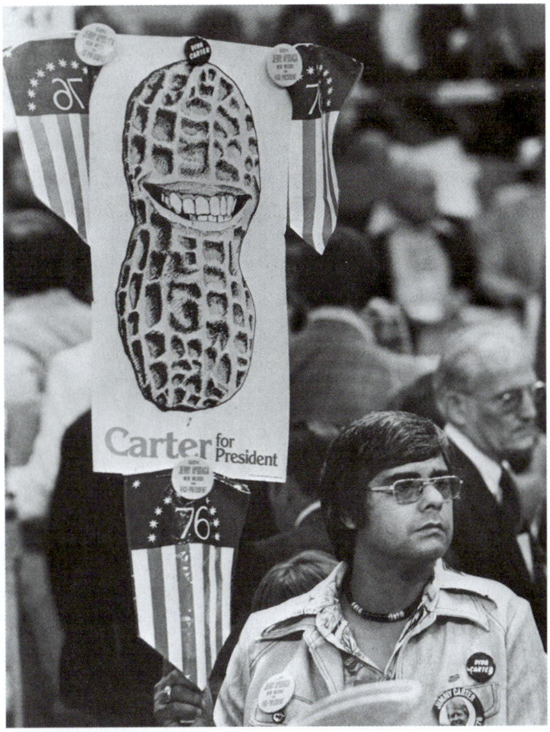

Figure 2.48
In 1976, Jimmy Carter's campaign created an eye-catching and humorous peanut with a broad smile, alluding to his past as a peanut farmer (and, ergo, an everyman) and his trademark big white teeth.

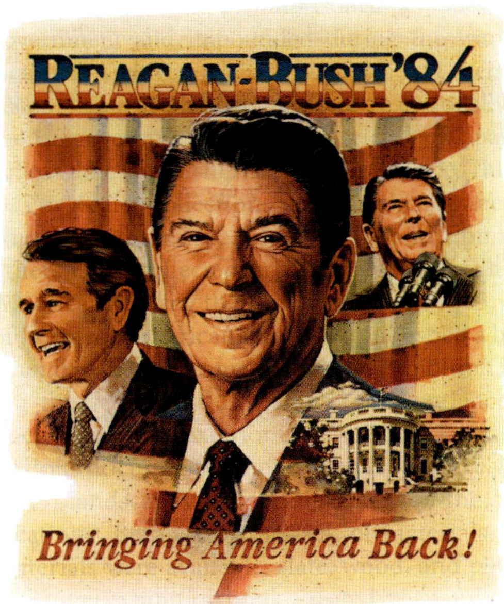

Figure 2.49
This 1980 poster of Ronald Reagan reads like an 1980s era movie poster, with realistically illustrated faces of Reagan and his vice presidential candidate George H.W. Bush.

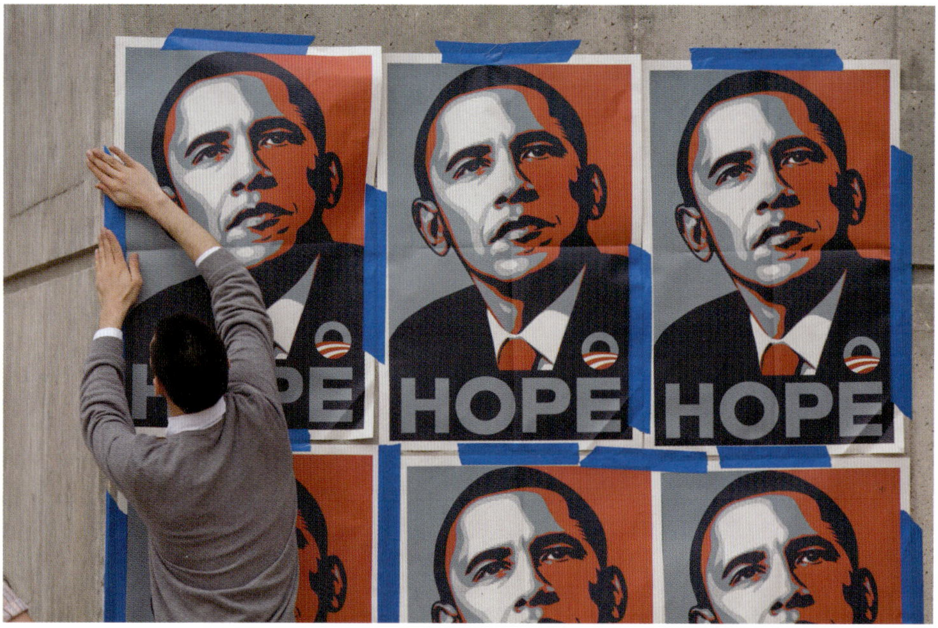

Figure 2.50 Shepard Fairey's *HOPE* poster for Barack Obama's 2008 campaign reinvigorated his campaign and became an icon of American culture.

Group Activities/Discussion Questions

- Form a small group and choose one of the periods of political history mentioned in this chapter. Discuss the goals of the government at this time, who their audience was, and what art techniques and movements were influencing the culture. With your group, design a piece of propaganda that communicates these goals to an audience. Create a sketch of your work, but also determine the medium in which your work of propaganda would be created. Present your idea to the class, discussing how the principles of Gestalt, semiotics, metaphor, and other techniques of visual grammar are used.
- The beginning of this chapter discusses examples of "everyday propaganda," or possibly overlooked items in our everyday life that are perpetuating a government or a political idea. Are there any other examples of "everyday propaganda" that you can think of?
- This chapter discusses many examples of the styles of two or more cultures coming together to create new styles and innovations in art, including in Deccan and Mughal India, as well as Socialist Realism in China. Research and discuss other examples of how the interaction of cultures has produced new transformations in illustration techniques.
- Clearly, the scope of this book cannot accommodate every piece of illustrated propaganda. Choose an example of political propaganda you have encountered in the past and analyze the visual grammar of the piece, including Gestalt, semiotics, and metaphor.

Endnotes

1 "Propaganda," *Merriam-Webster Dictionary*, accessed January 17, 2024, https://www.merriam-webster.com/dictionary/propaganda#:~:text=The%20word%20propaganda%20is%20from,reference%20to%20this%20Catholic%20organization.

2 Marc U. Edwards, Jr, *Printing, Propaganda, and Martin Luther* (Berkeley: University of California Press, 1994).

3 Pearson, Hilary C., and Jonathan M. P. Wilbiks. 2021. "Effects of Audiovisual Memory Cues on Working Memory Recall." *Vision* 5 (1): 14. https://doi.org/10.3390/vision5010014.

4 Ally, Brandon A., Jill D. Waring, Ellen H. Beth, Joshua D. McKeever, William P. Milberg, and Andrew E. Budson. 2008. "Aging Memory for Pictures: Using High-Density Event-Related Potentials to Understand the Effect of Aging on the Picture Superiority Effect." *Neuropsychologia* 46 (2): 679–89. https://doi.org/10.1016/j.neuropsychologia.2007.09.011.

5 Robert Dahl, *Polyarchy: Participation and Opposition* (New Haven: Yale University Press, 1971).

6 "Freedom House: Freedom in the World 2023", *Freedom House,* accessed January 18, 2024, https://freedomhouse.org/report/freedom-world.

7 Juan Linz, *Totalitarian and Authoritarian Regimes* (Boulder: Lynne Rienner Publishers, 2000).

8 "Denarius (Coin) Portraying Julius Caesar," *Art Institute of Chicago*, accessed January 17, 2024, https://www.artic.edu/artworks/5588/denarius-coin-portraying-julius-caesar.

9 "Denarius (Coin)."

10 "Silver denarius of Julius Caesar, Spain 46–45 BC," *University of Leeds Library*, accessed January 19, 2024, https://library.leeds.ac.uk/special-collections/view/2199.

11 "Julius Caesar and Marcus Mettius, AR denarius, 44 B.C.," *Lawrence University*, accessed January 19, 2024. https://www2.lawrence.edu/dept/art/BUERGER/CATALOGUE/060.HTML.

12 Clare Rowan, *From Caesar to Augustus (c. 49 BC–AD 14): Using Coins as Sources* (Cambridge: University Printing House, 2019).

13 Banksy, dir., *Exit Through the Gift Shop*. London: Revolver Entertainment, 2010, Film.

14 "Welcome address," European Central Bank, November 27, 2019, https://www.ecb.europa.eu/press/key/date/2019/html/ecb.sp191127~3ad384365f.en.html.

15 "What the faces on its currency tell us about a country?" *National Geographic*, accessed January 19, 2024, https://www.nationalgeographic.com/history/article/what-can-faces-on-currency-tell-us-about-country.

16 "The Logo, Colours and Flag of the African National Congress," *African National Congress,* archived from the original on 24 March 2017, *accessed 10 January 2023,* https://web.archive.org/web/20170324052027/http:/www.anc.org.za/content/anc-logo-colours-and-flag.

17 Stephen Ellis, "The ANC in Exile," *African Affairs*, Vol. 90, No. 360 (1991): 439–47.

18 "South African Flag (Apartheid Era)," Anti-Defamation League, accessed January 19, 2024, https://www.adl.org/resources/hate-symbol/south-african-flag-apartheid-era.

19 Timothy D. Sisk, "South Africa: Enabling Liberation" in *Transitions to Democracy: A Comparative Perspective*, ed. Kathryn Stoner and Michael McFaul (Baltimore: Johns Hopkins University Press, 2013), 168–91.

20 Katie Mettler, "South Africa bans most displays of the apartheid flag, a symbol of 'a crime against humanity,'" *The Washington Post,* August 21, 2019, https://www.washingtonpost.com/world/2019/08/22/south-africa-bans-most-displays-apartheid-flag-symbol-crime-against-humanity/.

21 Douglas N Muir, *Postal Reform and the Penny Black: a New Appreciation* (London: National Postal Museum, 1990), 42.

22 H. W. Hill, *The Fight for the Penny Post* (London: Warne, 1940), 75–7.

23 Simon Garfield, *The Error World: An Affair with Stamps* (Boston: Houghton Mifflin Harcourt, 2009), 118.

24 Hannah Ward-Glenton, "New British banknotes featuring portrait of King Charles III revealed," CNBC.com, December 20, 2022, https://www.cnbc.com/2022/12/20/new-british-banknotes-featuring-portrait-of-king-charles-iii-revealed.html#:~:text=Bank%20of%20England-,The%20Bank%20of%20England%20released%20images%20of%20the%20first%20bank,'%20see%2Dthrough%20security%20panel.

25 Luciano Cheles and Alessandro Giacone, ed, *The Political Portrait: Leadership, Image and Power*, (New York: Routledge, 2020).

26 Betty Edwards, *The New Drawing on the Right Side of the Brain* (Los Angeles: Tarcher, 1999), 71.

27 Paul Ekman, *Emotions Revealed* (New York: Owl Books, 2003), 34.

28 Ekman, *Emotions*, 6–10.

29 Bettini, *Portrait*, 43.
30 "Portraits of Shi Wenying and Lady Guan," *National Museum of Asian Art*, accessed January 19, 2024, https://asia.si.edu/learn/for-educators/teaching-china-with-the-smithsonian/explore-by-object/portraits-of-shi-wenying-and-lady-guan/.
31 "Portrait of an Old Lady," *The Met*, accessed January 19, 2024, https://www.metmuseum.org/art/collection/search/36082.
32 Dietrich Seckel, "The Rise of Portraiture in Chinese Art," *Artibus Asiae* 53, no. 1/2 (1993): 7–26, https://doi.org/10.2307/3250505.
33 Lidwell, William, Kritina Holden, and Jill Butler, *Universal Principles of Design, Revised and Updated: 125 Ways to Enhance Usability, Influence Perception, Increase Appeal, Make Better Design Decisions, and Teach through Design*, (Beverly, MA: Rockport Publishers, 2010), 88.
34 Navina Najat Haidar and Marika Sardar, *Sultans of Deccan India, 1500–1700: Opulence and Fantasy* (New York: The Metropolitan Museum of Art, 2015), 79.
35 "Miniature opklaebet pa et albumblad. ' Portraet af sultan Ibrahim Adil Shah 2. Af Bijapur,'" Davids Samling, Accessed January 19, 2024, https://www.davidmus.dk/islamic-art/the-indian-sultanates/item/1410.
36 Haidar and Sardar, *Sultans*, 27.
37 Sheila O'Connell and Tim Clayton, *Bonaparte and the British* (London: The British Museum, 2015), 11.
38 Phillipe Bordes, *Jacques Louis-David: Empire to Exile* (Williamstown, MA, The Clark Art Institute, 2005), 21.
39 Bordes, *Jacques Louis-David*, 22.
40 "David: Great Artists (Series 2)," Films On Demand, 2003, accessed January 19, 2023, https://fod.infobase.com/PortalPlaylists.aspx?wID=96309&xtid=59675.
41 "Jacques-Louis David," National Gallery of Art, accessed January 19, 2024, https://www.nga.gov/collection/artist-info.1212.html.
42 Ben Pollitt, "Jacques-Louis David, *Napoleon Crossing the Alps*," Smarthistory, January 7, 2016, accessed December 8, 2022, https://smarthistory.org/jacques-louis-david-napoleon-crossing-the-alps/.
43 Ben Pollitt, "Jacques-Louis David, *Napoleon Crossing the Alps*," *Smarthistory*, January 7, 2016, accessed December 8, 2022, https://smarthistory.org/jacques-louis-david-napoleon-crossing-the-alps/.
44 Theda Skocpol, *States and Social Revolutions*, (Cambridge: Cambridge University Press 1979).
45 Ingeborg Misje Bergem, "When the revolution did not look like you thought it would: the Yellow Vest Movement through radical-left activists' imaginaries," *Modern & Contemporary France* 30, no. 3 (2022): 295–312.
46 This is in contrast to the American Revolutionary war, where the goal was independence from British rule and the creation of a completely new country.
47 "David," Films On Demand.
48 "The 'Sacre' or Consecration of Napoleon I," Foundation Napoleon, accessed January 19, 2024, https://www.napoleon.org/en/young-historians/napodoc/the-sacre-of-napoleon-i/.
49 "The Sacre or Consecration," Foundation Napoleon.
50 O'Connell and Clayton, *Bonaparte and the British*, 38.
51 Arhan Ertain, Martin Fiszbein, and Louis Putterman, "Who Was Colonized and When? A Cross-Country Analysis of Determinants," *European Economic Review* 83 (2016): 165–84.
52 James F. O'Connell, Jim Allen, Martin A. J. Williams, and Alan Cooper, "When did Homo sapiens first reach Southeast Asia and Sahul?" *PNAS* 115, no. 34 (2018): 8482–90.
53 Chris Clarkson and Lee J. Arnold, "Human Occupation of Northern Australia by 65,000 years Ago," *Nature* 547, no. 7663 (2017): 306–10.
54 J.M. Bowler and A. G. Thorne, "Human remains from Lake Mungo: discovery and excavation of Lake Mungo III" in *The Origin of the Australians*, eds. R. L. Kirk and A. G. Thorne (Canberra: Australian Institute of Aboriginal Studies, 1976), 127–38.
55 "Separation of Tasmania," National Museum Australia, accessed January 19, 2024, https://www.nma.gov.au/defining-moments/resources/separation-of-tasmania.
56 Iain Davidson and David Roberts, "14,000 BP—on being alone: the isolation of Tasmania," in *Turning Points in Australian History*, eds. Martin Crotty and David Roberts (Sydney: UNSW Press, 2008): 20.
57 Davidson and Roberts, "14,000 BP," 20.
58 "The Black Line," National Museum Australia, accessed January 22, 2024, https://www.nma.gov.au/defining-moments/resources/the-black-line#:~:text=European%20settlement,and%20Europeans%20occurred%20in%201772.
59 "Black Line," National Museum Australia.
60 "Black Line," National Museum Australia.

61 "Governor Arthur's Proclamation to the Aborigines," State Library New South Wales, accessed January 22, 2024, https://www.sl.nsw.gov.au/stories/governor-arthurs-proclamation-aborigines.

62 "Proclamation board, Tasmanian frontier era," Australian War Memorial, accessed January 22, 2024, https://www.awm.gov.au/articles/blog/governer-daveys-proclamation.

63 "Governor Arthur's Proclamation," State Library New South Wales.

64 Khadija von Zinnenburg Carroll, *Art in the Time of Colony*, (Farnham, UK: Ashgate Publishing, 2014).

65 Benjamin Madley, "Patterns of frontier genocide 1803–1910: the Aboriginal Tasmanians, the Yuki of California, and the Herero of Namibia," *Journal of Genocide Research* 6, 2 (2004): 169.

66 Andrew Bain, "The rebirth of Tasmanian indigenous culture," BBC, Last modified October 25, 2021, https://www.bbc.com/travel/article/20211024-the-rebirth-of-tasmanian-indigenous-culture.

67 "The Sino-Japanese War Woodblock Prints," *Naval History and Heritage Command*, September 3, 2019, https://www.history.navy.mil/browse-by-topic/exploration-and-innovation/steam-navy/sino-japanese-war/sino-japanese-prints.html.

68 "Fireworks at Ikenohata," The Met, accessed January 22, 2024, https://www.metmuseum.org/art/collection/search/712976.

69 "The Triptych Format in Japanese Woodblock Prints," RISD Museum, accessed January 22, 2024, https://risdmuseum.org/exhibitions-events/exhibitions/triptych-format-japanese-woodblock-prints.

70 "Sino-Japanese War," *Naval History.*

71 Marika Sherwood, "Colonies, Colonials, and World War Two," BBC, accessed December 29, 2022, https://www.bbc.co.uk/history/worldwars/wwtwo/colonies_colonials_01.shtml#five.

72 L.H. Gann and Peter Duignan, *Colonialism in Africa 1870–1960: The History and Politics and Colonialism 1870–1914, Volume 1,* (Cambridge: Cambridge University Press, 1969).

73 Hal Brands, "Wartime Recruiting Practices, Martial Identity and Post-World War II Demobilization in Colonial Kenya", *The Journal of African History* 46, no. 1 (2005): 103–25.

74 Kaushik Roy, "Military Loyalty in the Colonial Context: A Case Study of the India Army during World War II," *The Journal of Military History* 73, no. 2 (2009): 497–529.

75 Adrienne Israel, "Ex-Servicemen as the Crossroads: Protest and Politics in Post-War Ghana," *The Journal of Modern African Studies* 30, no. 2 (1992): 359–68.

76 Rajmohan Gandhi, *Revenge and Reconciliation*, (India: Penguin Books, 1999), 175–6.

77 Indian Army in World War I. n.d. Obo. Accessed June 19, 2024. https://www.oxfordbibliographies.com/display/document/obo-9780199791279/obo-9780199791279-0039.xml.

78 Stephan Likosky, *With a Weapon and a Grin: Postcard Images of France's Black Colonial Troops in WWI*, (Atglen, PA: Schiffer, 2017), 49–50.

79 Claire Voon, "The Racist Caricatures of African Soldiers that Soothed French Colonial Anxieties," Hyperallergic, Last modified June 2, 2017, https://hyperallergic.com/380053/the-racist-caricatures-of-african-soldiers-that-soothed-french-colonial-anxieties/.

80 Likosky, *Weapon and a Grin*, 11.

81 Myron Echenberg, "'Morts Pour la France'; The African Soldier in France During the Second World War," *The Journal of African History* 26, no. 4 (1985): 363–80.

82 Claire Voon, "The Racist Caricatures of African Soldiers that Soothed French Colonial Anxieties," Hypoallergic, Last modified June 2, 2017, https://hyperallergic.com/380053/the-racist-caricatures-of-african-soldiers-that-soothed-french-colonial-anxieties/.

83 Lucien Jonas, "Journee de l'Armee d'Afrique et des Troupes Coloniales," Boston Athenaeum Digital Collections, accessed January 22, 2024, https://cdm.bostonathenaeum.org/digital/collection/p16057coll34/id/31/.

84 Kenneth J. Orosz, "Propaganda in the Colonies (Africa)," International Encyclopedia of the First World War, Last modified February 21, 2017, https://encyclopedia.1914-1918-online.net/article/propaganda_in_the_colonies_africa.

85 Likosky, *Weapon and a Grin*, 69–73

86 Echenberg, "'Morts Pour la France,'" 363–80.

87 William Lidwell, *Universal Principles of Design, 230.*

88 "I want you for U.S. Army: nearest recruiting station," Penn State University Libraries, accessed on January 24, 2024, https://digital.libraries.psu.edu/digital/collection/warposters/id/299/.

89 "Domestic Propaganda in World War I," Lynchburg Museum, accessed January 22, 2024, https://www.lynchburgmuseum.org/blog/2014/12/8/domestic-propaganda-in-world-war-1#:~:text=The%20Most%20Famous%20Poster%20in%20the%20World&text=As%20one%20of%20America's%20leading,war%20Flagg%20designed%2046%20posters.

90 George Creel, *Rebel at Large: Recollections of Fifty Crowded Years* (New York: G.P. Putnam's Son's, 1947), 158.

91 "World War I Poster Art," U.S. Army Heritage and Education Center, accessed January 22, 2024, https://ahec.armywarcollege.edu/exhibits/constitution_center.cfm#:~:text=Under%20the%20leadership%20of%20Charles,sacrifice%20on%20the%20home%20front.

92 "Recruiting posters for African American soldiers, 1918," The Gilder Lehrman Institute of American History, accessed January 22, 2024, https://www.gilderlehrman.org/history-resources/spotlight-primary-source/recruiting-posters-african-american-soldiers-1918.

93 Elizabeth West, "How WWI Sparked an Artistic Movement that Transformed Black America," *JSTOR Daily*, Last modified April 10, 2017, https://daily.jstor.org/how-wwi-sparked-an-artistic-movement-that-transformed-black-america/.

94 "How American artists captured the Great War up close," *PBS News Hour,* March 2, 2017, https://www.pbs.org/newshour/show/american-artists-captured-great-war-close#:~:text=KELLI%20MORGAN%3A,in%20particular%20couldn't%20stand.

95 Richard Pipes, *Three "Whys" of the Russian Revolution*, (Toronto, Canada: Vintage Books, 1995).

96 At the time, Russia still used the Julian calendar, which was 13 days behind the Gregorian calendar used throughout Europe and North America. Therefore, this revolution was coined the "October Revolution" in the Soviet Union, even though it took place in November, according to the Gregorian calendar.

97 Archie Brown, *The Rise and Fall of Communism*, (New York: Harper Collins, 2009).

98 "The Legacy of World War One Propaganda," *British Library,* accessed November 1, 2023, https://www.bl.uk/world-war-one/articles/the-legacy-of-world-war-one-propaganda.

99 Ellen Lupton, "Cut, Paste, Action: How Photomontage Keeps Revolutionizing Graphic Design," (Lecture at the High Museum of Art, Atlanta, GA, March 31, 2022).

100 "Gustav Klutsis (Latvian 1895–1938)," The Art Institute of Chicago, accessed January 22, 2024, https://archive.artic.edu/avant-garde/klutsis/.

101 Hirving, "The Ministry's Launch," *Ministry of Information Digital,* June 23, 2014, https://moidigital.ac.uk/blog/ministrys-launch/.

102 Franklin Delano Roosevelt, "Address at Chautauqua August 14, 1936," The American Presidency Project, accessed January 22, 2024, https://www.presidency.ucsb.edu/documents/address-chautauqua-ny.

103 Daniel Dancis, "Researching WWII Spanish Posters at the National Archives," *National Archives*, accessed January 22, 2024, https://www.archives.gov/files/calendar/know-your-records/handouts-presentations/2020-09-16-dancis-presentation.pdf, 8.

104 "1942: Bracero Program," Library of Congress, accessed January 22, 2024, https://guides.loc.gov/latinx-civil-rights/bracero-program.

105 Dancis, "Researching WWII Spanish Posters," 10.

106 "Helguera, Leon, 1899–1970," *National Archives Catalog,* Accessed January 22, 2024, https://catalog.archives.gov/id/10601387.

107 Dancis, "Researching WWII Spanish Posters."

108 OF 101-a: Box 6, Folder 5, Use of the President's name for Advertising, 1943. Series: Franklin D. Roosevelt President's Official Files, 1933 – 1945 (NAID 567634). Image courtesy of the Franklin D. Roosevelt Presidential Library, Hyde Park, NY.

109 "Summary of Socialist Realism," *The Art Story*, accessed January 22, 2024, https://www.theartstory.org/movement/socialist-realism/.

110 Olga Polyanskaya, "Tatiana Yablonskaya. 1949, The artist's 'true heart,'" *The Tretyakov Gallery Magazine*, accessed January 22, 2024, https://www.tretyakovgallerymagazine.com/articles/4-2014-45/tatiana-yablonskaya-1949-artists-true-heart.

111 "Krychevsky, Fedir," *Internet Encyclopedia of Ukraine*, accessed January 22, 2024, http://www.encyclopediaofukraine.com/display.asp?linkPath=pages\K\R\KrychevskyFedir.htm.

112 Liu Ding and Carol Yinghua Lu, "From the Issue of Art to the Issue of Position: The Echoes of Socialist Realism," *Tate*, accessed January 22, 2024, https://www.tate.org.uk/research/research-centres/tate-research-centre-asia/socialist-realism#:~:text=The%20Introduction%20of%20Socialist%20Realism,typical%20characters%20under%20typical%20circumstances.

113 Frederick C. Teiwes, "The Origins of Rectification: Inner-Party Purges and Education before Liberation," *The China Quarterly*, no. 65 (1976): 15–53: 27.

114 US Joint Publication research service. (1979). *China Report: Political, Sociological and Military Affairs.* Foreign Broadcast information Service. No ISBN digitized text March 5, 2007.

115 Walter J. Meserve, and Ruth I. Meserve, "REVOLUTIONARY REALISM: CHINA'S PATH TO THE FUTURE," *Journal of South Asian Literature* 27, no. 2 (1992): 29–39, 33.

116 Wan Shaojun, 'Youhua Zhongguo Feng – Dong Xiwen Yishu Sixiang yu Chuangzuo Shijian Tixi de Zai Renshi' ('Oil Paintings Chinese Style: Reappraising Dong Xiwen's System of Artistic Ideas and Creative

Practices') in Beijing Academy of Painting, *Dong Xiwen Yanjiu Wenji* (*Collected Research Writings on Dong Xiwen*), originally published in *Meishu Yanjiu* (Fine Art Research), Beijing 2 (1958): 168.

117 David Barboza, "Chameleon Mao, the Face of Tiananmen Square," *The New York Times*, Last modified May 28, 2006, https://www.nytimes.com/2006/05/28/weekinreview/chameleon-mao-the-face-of-tiananmen-square.html.

118 Barboza, "Chameleon Mao."

119 Ching-Ching Ni, "Mao is their Canvas," *Banderas News*, September 2006, http://www.banderasnews.com/0609/art-maoart.htm.

120 "The Atlantic Conference & Charter, 1941," *Office of the Historian US Department of State*, accessed January 22, 2024, https://history.state.gov/milestones/1937-1945/atlantic-conf.

121 "The Algerian War of Independence," *Britannica*, accessed January 22, 2024, https://www.britannica.com/place/Algeria/The-Algerian-War-of-Independence.

122 R.T. Howard, "Revolt in Madagascar," *History Today*, Last modified March 29, 2017, https://www.historytoday.com/history-matters/revolt-madagascar.

123 Jason Burke, "Idi Amin's mastery of media revealed in newly published photos," *The Guardian*, Last modified October 7, 2019, https://www.theguardian.com/world/2019/oct/07/idi-amins-mastery-of-media-revealed-in-newly-published-photos.

124 Aurora Harwood, Olivia Crellin, Connie Scozzaro, Debbie Farquhar, Andrew Spyrou, Jessica King and Paul Merchant, "The artist's manifesto," *Varsity*, accessed January 22, 2024, https://www.varsity.co.uk/culture/2110.

125 "History of Ugandan Currency," *Central Bank of Uganda,* accessed January 31, 2024, https://archive.bou.or.ug/bou/currency/history_of_the_currency.html#:~:text=Uganda%20Currency%20has%20changed%20seven,and%20ease%20transactions%20as%20well.

126 Maria Alawua, "Different But One 16: A Story without End," *Start Journal Contemporary Art on the African Continent*, Last modified March 30, 2012, https://startjournal.org/2012/03/different-but-one-16-a-story-without-end/.

127 S.A. Seidman, "Election Posters in the United States After World War II" in *Election Posters Around the Globe*, eds. C. Holtz-Bacha and B. Johansson, (Springer, Cham 2017), https://doi.org/10.1007/978-3-319-32498-2_18.

128 "American Women: Resources from the Moving Image Collections," *Library of Congress*, Accessed January 22, 2024, https://guides.loc.gov/american-women-moving-image/television#:~:text=In%201950%20only%209%20percent,figure%20had%20reached%2090%20percent.

129 "New Super Tuesday Polls Favor Hillary (AZ, NJ, CA, NY)," *DAILY KOS*, Last modified January 23, 2008, http://www.dailykos.com/story/2008/01/23/441706/-NewSuper-Tuesday-Polls-Favor-Hillary-(AZ,-NJ,-CA,-NY).

130 William W. Fisher III, Frank Cost, Shepard Fairey, Meir Feder, Edwin Fountain, Geoffrey Stewart & Marita Sturken, "Reflections on the Hope Poster Case," *Harvard Journal of Law and Technology* 25, no. 2 (Spring 2012): 243.

131 Fisher, et. al., "Reflections," 253.

132 Terry Gross, "Spreading the Hope: Street Artist Shepard Fairey," *Fresh Air,* January 20, 2009, https://www.npr.org/transcripts/99466584.

133 "Barack Obama 'Hope' Poster," *Art Institute of Chicago*, Accessed January 22, 2024, https://www.artic.edu/artworks/229396/barack-obama-hope-poster.

3

Media, Censorship, & Taboo

Introduction

As a form of visual communication, the distribution and reception of illustration is key to its impact. The type of media used to distribute propaganda varies, from posters to postcards to magazines, but the intentions are the same. The intent by the coder is that the image is decoded dominantly, literally, and directly. The creators of propaganda imagery continue to hope that the decoders of the image play a limited role in interacting with it, and take the message at its denotative face value. Clearly, however, decoders do not always accept a dominant interpretation of an image. For example, the British proclamation boards from the previous chapter did not create peace with indigenous Tasmanians. Instead, many resisted or fled attempts at British assimilation. Many examples of dissident art play off of propaganda art to create **parody**, showing that many decoders saw the irony in these images and processed them with an oppositional view. This serves as a reminder to us that the coder of a message, even when it is a powerful government, does not always hold the full command of the messages communicated through their images.

In his book *Editorial Illustration*, Andrew Selby describes the "performance" of an illustration, quoting Stuart Hall that an illustration's engagement "is the ability to use visual impact and rhetorical means to arrest the reader's attention and to create an ideological bond."[1] In any performance, the audience is just as active of a participant as the performer, but there is also a third actor in the scenario, the producer that presents the performance, advertises it, and provides the resources for its creation. In illustration, this role is fulfilled by the **media**, which plays just as important of a role in negotiating the performance of an illustration as the coder or decoder. From newspapers to social media platforms, the media serves to give context to an illustration and dictate the circumstances as to how and what it communicates. Selby notes this as the "constellation theory" of Dr. Nanette Hoogslag, in which there is "a clear communication between producer and consumer of information in a harmonious, symbiotic relationship supported by *the environment of published matter* [emphasis added]."[2] This environment will be the focus of the following chapter, in which we will explore how individual voices interacted and interact with the media in order to successfully distribute their message.

It is difficult to separate the field of illustration from its lifelong relationship with the media. The term "media" encompasses the relationship between the encoder, the mediator, and the decoder. It can include the editing of an image, the distribution of an image, and/or the reception of an image. For a non-traditional illustration example, the media can include the dynamics of ownership behind the wall that a work of street art is painted on, or the traffic flow of people walking past it. When decoding an image dominantly, the decoder risks lacking acknowledgement of the role of media in the formation of the image and media's contributions in creating and communicating its message. Even when it is not acknowledged, almost every illustration we see has gone through the filter of the media, creating a **mediated image**. A mediated image is an image that has been intervened by the media in which it was presented, which could be a government's public relations committee, a newspaper's editorial staff, a magazine's art director, or an illustration annual's jury. A mediated image could also refer to the media or context in which it is presented, for instance a newspaper, website, social media post, billboard advertisement, or other source. In negotiated or oppositional decoding, a critical eye is turned to the illustration and the media through which it is presented is taken into account when interpreting an image. For instance, in the poster *This Soldier Is Defending India* from the previous chapter, one's understanding of the image changes when considering how and why the mediated force (in this case, the British Ministry of Information) created this image, its goals behind creating the image, and the visual techniques utilized in successfully marketing the image.

In 1964, communication theorist Marshall McLuhan stated in his book *Understanding Media: The Extensions of Man*, that the "medium is the message." Through this statement, McLuhan proposed that communication mediums are just as important, if not more important, as the messages they carry, if not more important. Illustration is uniquely situated to be an exemplar of this theory. Not only does illustration span a variety of types of media, from magazines to posters to digital publications and beyond, but it can also be created with a huge variety of mediums. Encased in an illustrator's style, technique, and medium is a message in and of itself. Shepard Fairey's use of bold diagonals, limited color palette, and naturalistic portraits, inspired by Russian Constructivism and Socialist Realism, communicates the message of political action regardless of the subject matter. Currency design likewise becomes a symbol of a nation's values and elevates the importance of commercialism and its connection to the success of a nation. When filtered through McLuhan's theory, political illustration shows a vast ability to communicate different messages depending on the media through which it is produced and the mediums that contribute to its creation.

As discussed in Chapter 1, illustration has long been associated with the misnomer "commercial art," although much illustration, as explored in this book, lacks a commercial basis. However, this does not mean that non-commercial illustration lacks mediation. A protest poster exists in the media context of the protest event and ideals, an illustration for a non-profit still exists in a media context, and a reportage illustration could change in meaning depending on the media through which it is presented. In turn, any art, including fine art, also exists as a mediated image. A gallery or art museum chooses artwork based on business and curation goals. A fine artist selling a piece to independent collectors is subjected to their choices in where and how to display the work. In almost every example of art and visual communication, it is impossible to weed out the art from the context in which it exists and is presented.

The commercialization of illustration, however, has ballooned the role of media in the image communication process, and distorted the power shift between illustrators and the media. Most of the traditional venues for political illustration are commercial ventures including newspapers, magazines, and websites, that are regulated by successful business models and economic shifts to produce profit. In the mid-20th century, Neil Borden popularized the term "marketing mix," which delineated the key ingredients to marketing products and services, and by the 1980s, equations to weight these ingredients in the marketing process were established. While some media outlets, including non-profit entities, may purport to advance a noble, or ignoble, outlook or goal, they are only able to hold up this goal if their profit margins allow it. Corporate and advertising bias remain issues in journalistic ethics. Therefore, when being commissioned for or licensing a political illustration, illustrators may be asked to create or alter an image not based on editorial intent so much as profit intent.

A significant example of this is the windfall of media coverage on Donald Trump leading up to and during his presidency. During Trump's 2016 campaign, he enjoyed a mutually beneficial relationship with media outlets. Trump's brash and often offensive statements, bombastic personality, and easily lampoon-able appearance led to great media interest among the public, both positive and negative. Although many were created as parodies, illustrations of Trump still perpetuated his image in the media, attracting attention to his campaign and presidency. Through this method of attracting attention and his knowledge of the media, Trump was successfully able to exercise the idea that "any publicity is good publicity." During Trump's campaign and subsequent time in office, profit margins for all types of media outlets skyrocketed, including newspapers that frequently hired illustrators to portray Donald Trump. From early 2017 to November 2020, subscriptions of *The New York Times* grew from 2 million to over 7 million.[3] *The Washington Post* grew from 100,000–200,000 subscribers in early 2016 to 1 million by the end of 2017, and then again grew to 3 million by the end of 2020.[4] Cable news viewership grew as well, more than doubling from 3.1 million in 2015 to 7.2 in 2020.[5] With this media attention came profits for media networks, deemed the "Trump Effect" or the "Trump Bump." After the first quarter of Trump's presidency, Twitter's profits grew 28 percent.[6] *The New York Times* stock climbed 22 percent between 2018–2019.[7] While many liberal-leaning news sources benefited financially from the Trump presidency, only later did they realize Trump's spread of mis- and disinformation was damaging to their reputations and the trustworthiness of a free press. Trump's statements, including banning some news sources from his events, increased public distrust of journalists and the mainstream media. A 2020 Gallup poll stated, "the percentage [of Americans] with no [media] trust at all is a record high, up five points since 2019."[8] Journalist Margaret Sullivan wrote, "Too many times, we acted as his stenographers or megaphones. Too often, we failed to refer to his many falsehoods as lies… And it took too long to moderate our instinct to give equal weight to both sides, even when one side was using misinformation for political gain."[9]

Peer review helps to balance a media outlet's profit goals with journalistic integrity. National and international organizations set standards of journalistic integrity, most of which value truth, objectivity, and accuracy when presenting what they report. In addition, an educated public is more likely to challenge the images presented to them and demand diverse and critical viewpoints on current issues. When viewing any image in the media, audiences need to be aware of the mediating factors contributing to why the illustration was printed, what viewpoint the illustration purports, and the roles of the publisher, editor, and author in the creation of the image. Political illustrations, like editorials, are often used as a way for a journalistic outlet to insert a more editorial viewpoint. Like editorials, by nature, illustration inserts the opinion and beliefs of the author, sometimes subtly or sometimes boldly; this can especially be seen in political cartoons.

Importantly, when referring to the mediator of an image, this can and does include **censorship** of images. Censorship needs to be distinguished from art direction, although sometimes the latter can incorporate the former. The goal of art direction is to participate in a shared encoding of a specified message, but the goal of censorship is to limit this message. Much of the propaganda we discussed in Chapter 2 was not censored, because a message is only censored when mediating forces interrupt its passage on the way to the decoder. Censorship can also include censorship of *who* the creators of published or presented illustrations are. For centuries, the illustration of people of color, women, and other underrepresented populations has been limited or eliminated in the media, either intentionally or unintentionally.

Censorship can often incorporate editorial elimination of societal, cultural, and religious **taboos**, which vastly differ from country to country and culture to culture. For instance, while sex is a taboo topic in much of the American media sphere, it is much more openly addressed in European outlets. Meanwhile, extreme violence is often accepted in American media but is more limited in Europe. Feet remain a taboo in many parts of Asia and the Middle East, and people from most parts of the world, except in Anglo countries, remove their shoes before entering a room. Dress and what can be eaten is regulated by many social norms across the world. However, more serious issues can be taboo in different parts of the world, while being culturally accepted in others, including abortion, adultery, public nudity, and interfaith marriage, among others. When illustrations cross these cultural and religious barriers through the globalization of media, misinterpretations, including violent retaliations, can occur.

Many political illustrators enter the field in hopes of being good actors in these dynamics of the media, but also hope to insert their own political opinions either overtly or covertly. The creation of illustration incorporates design, color, and other visual choices which inevitably insert a personal, editorial opinion. Therefore, illustration differs from the goals of photojournalism, which align with the goals of the journalistic ethics of truth, accuracy, and objectivity. The introduction of photography into an arena previously held solely by illustration changed the nature, purpose, and dynamic of political illustration as an editorial medium. To understand this historic change and the evolution of political illustration in the media, we can go back to one of illustration's initial purposes in media: reportage.

Reportage Illustration

Reportage illustration can be seen as the precursor to photojournalism. However, unlike photojournalism, it has a unique ability for artists to insert their message and perspective through their drawing style. Visual documentation that could be categorized under reportage has existed for thousands of years in the form of science and nature illustration, visual descriptions of wars and historical events, and sketchbook art. Much of this work was created on a non-commercial basis, such as the ledger art created by Plains American Indians and Egyptian wall painting. However, in the early to mid-1800s, newspapers began to seize on illustration as a way to market their product. In 1842, Herbert Ingram founded *The Illustrated London News*, which was marketed based on his observation that sales increased when newspapers included illustrations. The paper was significantly influenced by art director and illustrator Henry Vizetelly, who pushed the paper to report factual versus sensational news, employing professional illustrators to accurately depict events. Vizetelly's vision helped to establish newspapers' enduring reputation as devices to educate and inform the public.[10]

Prior to the early 1800s and the introduction of periodical illustration, newspapers tried to pack as much text and information onto the page as possible, partially as a cost-saving method. This created a product that placed no emphasis on the relative importance of certain articles, save for the larger headline for the paper at the top.[11] Introducing illustration created **visual hierarchy** on the page, giving the viewer's eye a place to rest on the page and emphasizing the importance of certain issues within the paper by providing them with an illustration. These early illustrated periodicals had a significant impact on the newly evolving field of graphic design. By the early 1800s, newspapers had just begun to realize the marketing potential of images, which were often created as woodcuts in boxwood, which had a dense grain that was especially durable for printing.[12] With the introduction of the type-revolving rotary "lightning presses" in the mid-1800s, these engravings were cast in metal and then cooled as a curved stereotype for faster production.[13]

By 1842, *The Illustrated London News* had a circulation of 60,000, and dozens of other illustrated periodicals emerged during the 1840s. (Figure 3.1) These included *L'Illustration* in Paris, *Illustrirte Zeitung* in Leipzig, *La Illustración de Madrid,* and later, in the 1850s and 1860s, *Frank Leslie's Illustrated Newspaper* and *Harper's Weekly* in New York, *Le Monde illustré* in Paris, *Vsemirnaya Illyustratsiya* in St. Petersburg, and *Graphic* in London. With the invention of the electric telegraph in 1844 and the first submarine telegraph cables in the 1850s, news could now suddenly travel quickly around the world, contributing to the boom in newspapers and the public's demand not only to read the news but also to *see* the news. In 1848, *L'Illustration* printed the first news "photograph," which was actually an engraving created from a photograph. While photographs were sometimes used as engravings by newspapers over the following decades, illustrations were still favored for a couple of reasons. Printers could only print in black ink on white paper, they could not reproduce the graytones found in photographs. In addition, the collodion method cameras used from 1851–1867 required a 3–5-minute exposure time and portable darkrooms to produce the photograph. Furthermore, illustrators were able to capture action, drama, and composition in a way photographs were unable to do at the time. Illustrators could work from their own sketches as well as multiple **photo references** to combine events into a scene, capturing the emotion of a situation through composition, design, and style, as well as the actual event. These illustrated papers enjoyed about 50 years of dominance before the halftone process was introduced in the 1890s, making the reproduction of printed photographs possible.

This coevolution of illustration journalism and photojournalism was also spurred by world events, especially the Mexican American War from 1846–48, the Crimean War from 1853–56, and the American Civil War from 1861–65. As it remains today, war sells, and visuals of these events spurred newspaper sales. After newspapers were able to amass finances through their popularity, they were able to build up a cadre of news-illustrators called **Special Artists**, whose primary subject matter was wars.[14] (Figure 3.2) Special Artists were valued for their speed, ability to quickly choose subject matter, and, much like photojournalists today, "being in the right place at the right time." In addition, however, they had to make drawings under any possible circumstances, even if bullets were flying past their heads. Also, similar to today's photojournalists, Special Artists often put themselves into significant danger in order to do their reporting, and were sometimes captured as spies, wounded, or killed. Unlike photojournalists, however, the process of creating an image was not a solo endeavor. If an artist was able to return their incomplete and quickly created sketches back to their editor, often after a long horseback ride, they were then handed over to a team of artists who would complete the drawings based on their specializations. For instance, one completed the buildings, another the portraits, or another the landscape. Newspaper editors took multiple liberties with composition, often adopting a signature editorial style for their publication. Therefore, once the drawing was converted to a woodblock print, it bore small resemblance to the original sketches. This process also highlights the various ways that photography and illustration were collectively utilized in newspapers for many years. Photographic images often served as references for the illustration, and the final illustrated images were often photographed onto a woodblock before being engraved. Photography did not immediately serve as a threat or a rival to editorial illustration; on the contrary, it often was used as a tool in the process.[15]

By the late 1800s, however, photography began to gain the upper hand as a tool for visual communication in periodicals. In 1880, the first photograph (of a shantytown in New York) was printed as a halftone image in *The Daily Graphic*.[16] By 1888, the Kodak box-camera was readily available to the public, issuing in the era of amateur photography, and a decade later, over 1.5 million box cameras had been sold.[17] By 1905, most major news stories were covered in the press by photography, not illustration.[18] Nevertheless, illustration retained a role in the press by providing a means for social critique and storytelling in a way photography was unable to do. Instead of following reportage practices that began earlier in the century as being solely a means to report the news, illustration could finally allow artists to produce visual content that considered larger social issues, rather than constantly "chasing the story." Thus, the first visual essays began to emerge. Most importantly, illustrators became freed to explore topics and stories of personal interest for them, and many art-focused journals emerged, including *Der Sturm, The Masses,* and *L'Assiette au Beurre* during the 1910s. Many artists we may recognize as fine artists provided illustration during this time, including Toulouse Lautrec, Marc Chagall, Ernst Ludwig Kirchner, and John Sloan.[19]

Another saving grace of illustrators was their ability to use design and artistic principles to dramatize their subjects, an ability still developing in photography at the time. The beginning of World War I made this advantage particularly apparent, when it became clear that static photographs of war-ravaged landscapes lacked the historic drama and heroic mythology of war. At this time, many papers returned to illustrators to depict the news, in part for their ability to paint a picture of victory for their readers, despite the reality of the war's progression. Artist-soldiers who experienced the war therefore had the ability to cement the evolution of illustration. Often, contrary to the wishes of their publishers, illustrators were also able to provide a social critique in their illustrations instead of merely depicting dramatizations of war. Many artists used their harrowing experiences to depict war's death, destruction, and desperation, including Germans Otto Dix, Max Beckmann, Käthe Kollwitz, and George Grosz, and Frenchmen Luc Albert Moreau and André Dunoyer de Segonzac. Although some newspapers on both sides seized and printed many collections of these dramatic illustrations, others were censored until long after the war in a move to maintain morale. As the century progressed and World War II loomed on the horizon, the separation of reportage illustration from commercial practice and its evolution into personal, social, and political critique became particularly important in creating the foundations of political and editorial illustration today.

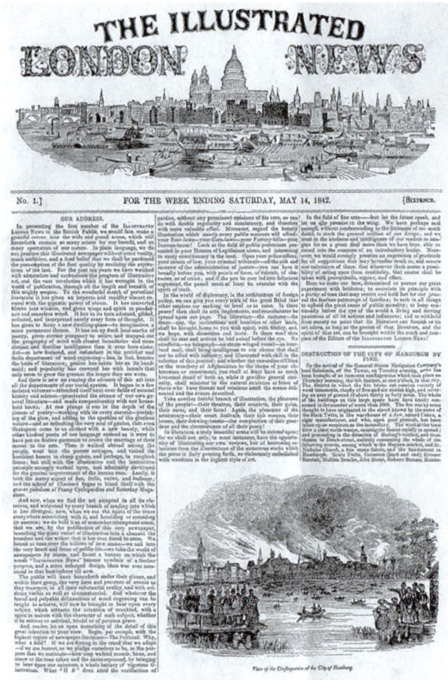

THE ILLUSTRATED LONDON NEWS

No. 1.] FOR THE WEEK ENDING SATURDAY, MAY 14, 1842. [SIXPENCE.

Figure 3.1
By 1842, *The Illustrated London News* had a circulation of 60,000. Dozens of other illustrated periodicals emerged during the 1840s.

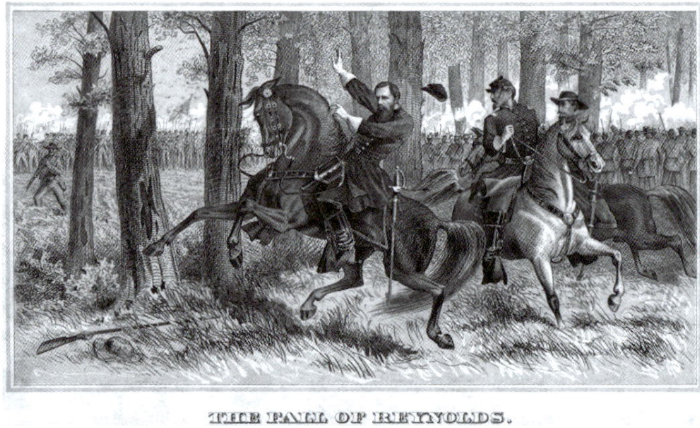

Figure 3.2
Special Artists such as Alfred Waud, who drew *The Fall of Reynolds* in 1863, were valued for their speed, ability to quickly choose subject matter, and, much like photojournalists today, "being in the right place at the right time."

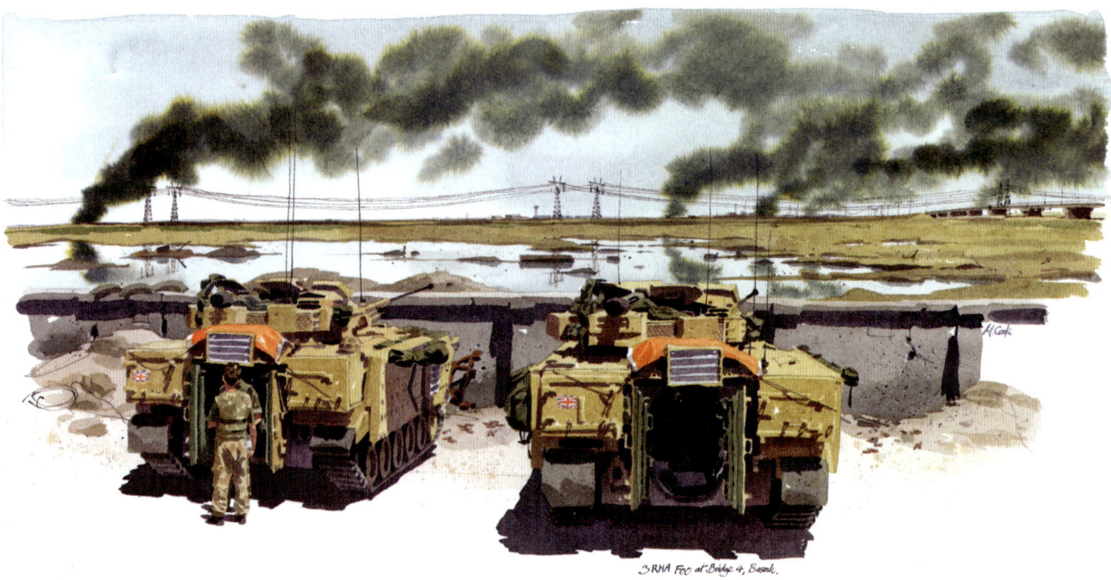

Figure 3.3
British illustrator Matt Cook is one example of how traditional reportage illustration continues to be practiced today. Cook records soldiers in the field, as well as political figures at work. This illustration depicts "Fighting near Bridge 4 and the technical college" in Basra, Iraq in 2003.

Non-Commercial Reportage: The Art of Japanese Internment and of the *Hibakusha*

The experience of the Japanese and Japanese Americans during World War II provided many examples of how political reportage illustration could be used for non-commercial purposes. Following the bombing of Pearl Harbor, which ushered in US participation in World War II, approximately 12,000 Japanese Canadians and 120,000 Japanese Americans were interned by their respective governments in "relocation camps" or "relocation centers."[20,21] However, US President Franklin Roosevelt did not use this sugarcoated language and called them "concentration camps." Most of these people of Japanese heritage lost their livelihoods, homes, and businesses as part of the process, and were sent to live in simple to squalid conditions in camps far from their homes. Because Japanese Americans were only interned if they lived west of an invisible "exclusion line," which ran through the middle of Washington, Oregon, California, and Arizona, many people in the Midwest or Eastern states were not even aware that internment was happening, and the government kept most mention of internment out of the media. (Figure 3.4) Photographer Dorothea Lange was hired by the US government to document the relocation of Japanese Americans, in order to show that the US government was treating Japanese American internees humanely, should the greater public learn what was occurring.[22] Despite this intention, the reality of the camps was that US citizens and their families were imprisoned behind barbed wire, forced to live with multiple families in uninsulated barracks in the desert, where temperatures reached extremes, and had little to no privacy.[23] Lange's photographs showed great sympathy with the imprisoned persons, and were subsequently censored by the US government and impounded during the war. They were then quietly housed by the National Archives, where few people saw them until 2006, when they were finally published.[24] Lange's photographs were exceptionally important in documenting the actions of the US government and the experience of Japanese Americans, but were nevertheless an act of white authorship over the experience. This is where illustration comes into play.

For years, collections such as the Japanese American National Museum in Los Angeles and the Japanese Cultural and Community Center of San Francisco, among others, had collected art and reportage illustration that was created by Japanese Americans during their internment. In 2005, author Delphine Hirasuna, the daughter of Japanese American internees, published a book of these artworks entitled *The Art of Gaman*, which became a traveling exhibition. *Gaman* is the Japanese word for "enduring the seemingly unbearable with patience and dignity." As Lange's photographs documented the exterior experience of Japanese Americans, these artworks and illustrations documented their inner experience. Many of the illustrations are of the bleak desert landscapes surrounding many of the camps, highlighting the isolation of these locations. Because of the lack of materials, artworks were created out of whatever materials were available: slate, wood, and pieces of wire. The cover image for *The Art of Gaman* exhibition book, created by an unknown artist at Heart Mountain, Wyoming, featured the camp's landscapes carved into wood. (Figure 3.5) A 1943 drawing by Chiura Obata documents the moment a man named James Hatsuaki Wakasa was shot by a guard when he attempted to pet a dog at the perimeter fence. The subjects are surrounded by a backdrop of barbed wire, comparing the experience of the internees to that of a hunted animal.[25] (Figure 3.6) Mikisaburo Izui, a pharmacist, was separated from his family and, unlike others, imprisoned at a P.O.W. camp in Louisiana due to his status of what the US considered to be a "leadership role" in the Japanese American community. Each of his letters home featured a tiny painting on the envelope, recording the small pieces of imperfect and impermanent beauty in the camp, such as a winter snowfall or small flowers. Many of these works fit within the Japanese tradition of *wabi-sabi*, or the imperfection and transience of beauty. Reportage illustrations created by interned Japanese artists were also able to capture parts of the camp Lange was not allowed to photograph. For instance, Lange was prohibited from photographing the barbed wire fences or armed watchtowers surrounding the camps. In contrast, a dark illustration by George T. Tamura features the ominous watchtower surveilling over the Tule Lake War Relocation Center in Northern California.

The works featured in *The Art of Gaman* are not the only examples of using reportage illustration documenting the internments. Internee Miné Okubo was a university-trained artist who was completing a fellowship in Paris with Fernand Léger when the war broke out. Even though Okubo worked for the Works Progress Administration upon her return to the US, as well as curating and completing other major art projects, she was still separated from her family and interned at Tanforan Assembly Center, and later at Topaz Internment Camp in Utah. While in the camps, she taught art, illustrated and art directed a literary magazine, and founded two art schools. In 1946, she compiled 206 of the over 2,000 drawings she made while at the camps into a book about her experience.[26]

Actor George Takei recorded his experience of being a young boy in his 2019 graphic novel *They Called Us Enemy*, illustrated by Harmony Becker, a Japanese American illustrator. (Figure 3.7) Takei shared his vivid memories with Becker, remembering "the details of the exact layout of the barracks they were forced to stay in."[27] Describing these memories also came with great purpose for Takei, who stated, "It's been my mission in life to raise the awareness of my childhood imprisonment—with no charges, no trial, and no due process—to other Americans because I'm always shocked to learn how unknown this is."[28] Here too the photography of Lange, the art of the interns, and illustrated visual memoirs such as Takei's did not work at odds, but with one another to paint a full picture of the events that took place.

By May of 1945, the Allies finally declared victory in Europe, but the war ravaged on in the Pacific Theater. The US was hoping to find a solution to avoid a costly invasion of Japan, and to save the lives of its own soldiers. Over the previous six years, the US, determined to create an atomic weapon before Germany did, embarked on what was called the Manhattan Project to create the first nuclear weapon. On July 16th, 1945, the first successful test of an atomic bomb took place near Los Alamos, New Mexico, and the US quickly put plans in place to drop atomic bombs on Japan. On August 6th, 1945, the US dropped its first atomic bomb on Hiroshima, killing 90,000–166,000 Japanese civilians. Three days later on August 9th, the US dropped a second bomb on Nagasaki, killing 60,000–80,000 people.[29,30] Over the following decades, thousands of more Japanese people died of radiation poisoning and cancer due to their exposure.

Here too, where photographs document the exterior effects of an important political event, illustrations revealed the interior effects on the people who experienced it. In Japan, the term *pica-don*, or "flash bang," was used to describe the stunning bright light of the bombs, followed by the deafening sound of the explosion. Sumako Yamada, who was 10 years old at the time of the blast, recorded the echoing reverberations of the explosion. (Figure 3.8) Survivors of the blast visually recorded the hell-like scene surrounding the cities: bodies burning and bloated corpses floating on the water, when people had jumped into rivers in attempts to save themselves. Some of the drawings, accompanied by writing, become a twisted version of the ukiyo-e prints that the country had become beloved for over the past century. Artist Akiko Takakura, who was 19 years old in 1945, drew a picture of a mouth raised upwards, attempting to catch the "black rain" that fell from the sky to quench her thirst. (Figure 3.9) (Takakura's illustrations and memoirs have been adapted into a powerful animation by Andre Hörmann and Anna Samo, published in *The New York Times*.)[31] These reportage illustrations, not created for commercial intent, remind us of the very human consequences of political actions, and are as much of an important part of the political illustration record as newspapers' constructed narratives of the previous century.

What is also revealed in both of these examples is how much easier government censorship can be when illustration is not paired with a media source to advocate for and distribute it. Following the atomic bombings of Hiroshima and Nagasaki, the US occupation authorities in Japan restricted public criticism of the US bombings, and also denied the existence of the radiation sickness which killed thousands more Japanese citizens.[32] The Civil Censorship Detachment of the Supreme Commander for the Allied Partners (SCAP) censored and suppressed any personal accounts or information about the bombing, criticism of it, and even the mention of the censorship itself. In 1951, SCAP eased their censorship restrictions, and the occupation ended in 1952. By this point, the damage had been done, with survivors suffering from radiation sickness still not receiving medical care, and many perishing by this time. However, it was not solely the government dictating censorship of the testimonies of *hibakusha*, or "bomb survivors." By the 1980s in Japan, many of these testimonies, including art, novels, and poetry, were available to the public, but very few had been translated to English or shared in Western media.[33] The few

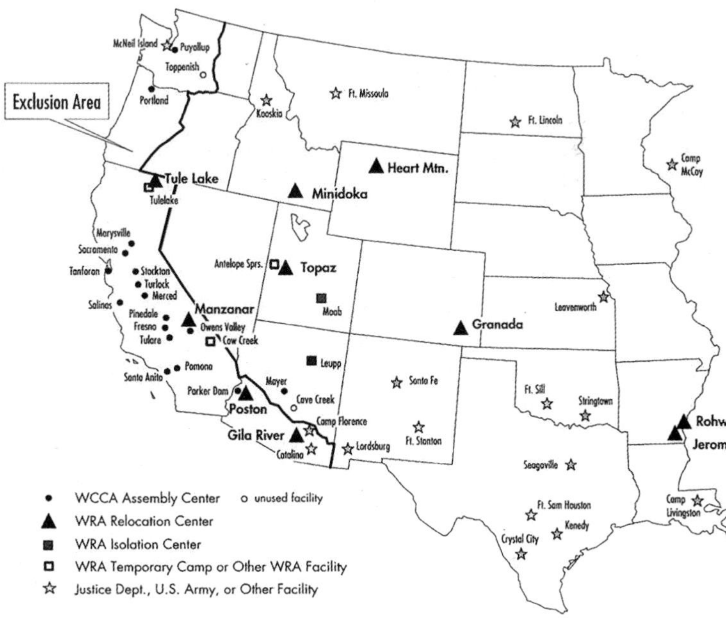

Figure 3.4
Japanese Americans were only interned if they lived west of an invisible "exclusion line," which ran through the middle of Washington, Oregon, California, and Arizona.

photographs taken by Yamahata Yōsuke and other photographers of Nagasaki and Hiroshima were filtered by the media to show only the least dramatic images. Thankfully, due to the efforts of collections and efforts such as the Hiroshima Peace Memorial Museum and the Nagasaki National Peace Memorial Hall for the Atomic Bomb Victims, these illustrations and personal memoirs have been preserved to remind future generations of the dangerous and tragic consequences of nuclear warfare. Political illustration can be at its most powerful when created for non-commercial purposes.

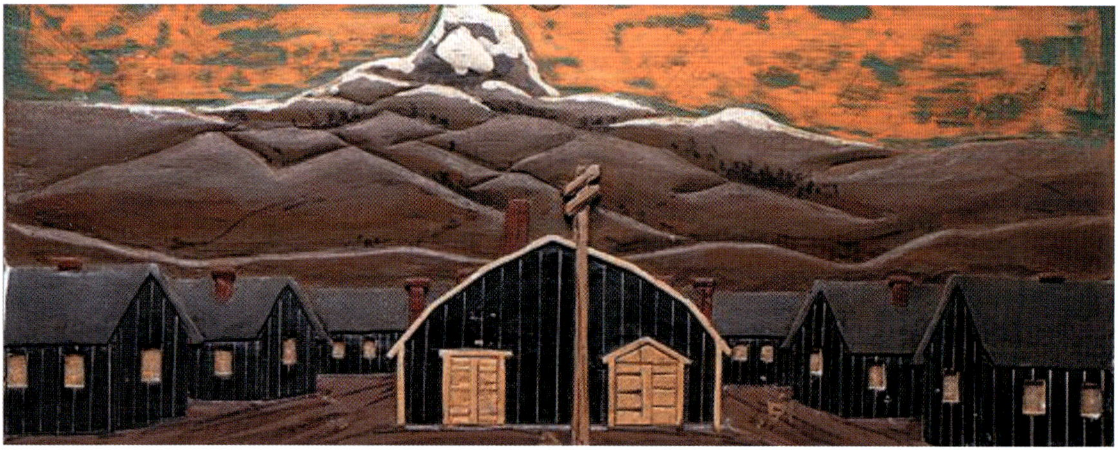

Figure 3.5
The cover image for *The Art of Gaman* exhibition book, created by an unknown artist interned at Heart Mountain, Wyoming, featured the camp's landscapes carved into wood. © Photo by Delphine Hirasuna

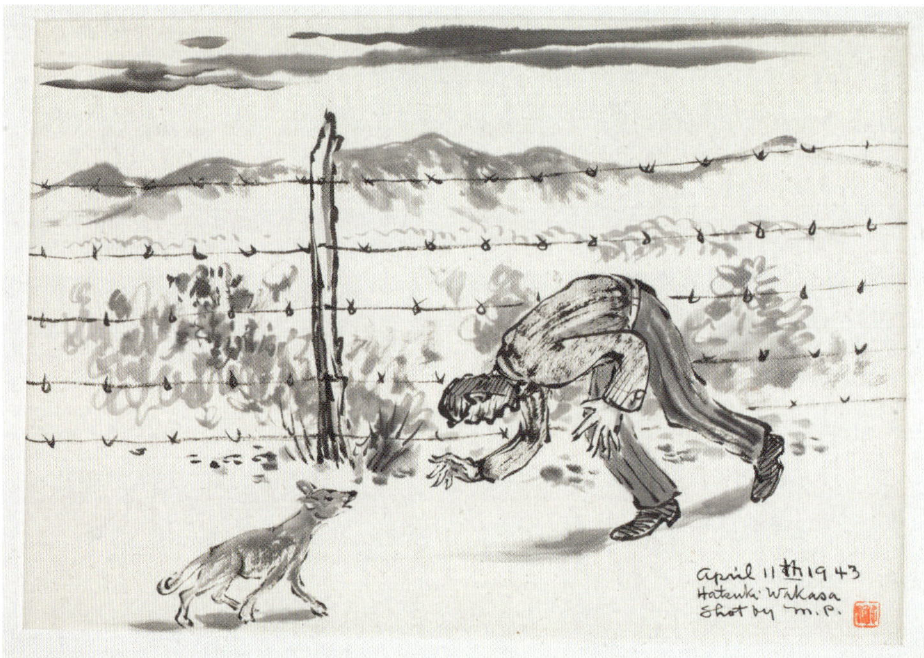

Figure 3.6
A 1943 drawing by Chiura Obata documents the moment a man named Hatsuaki Wakasa was shot by a guard when he attempted to pet a dog at the perimeter fence of an internment camp.

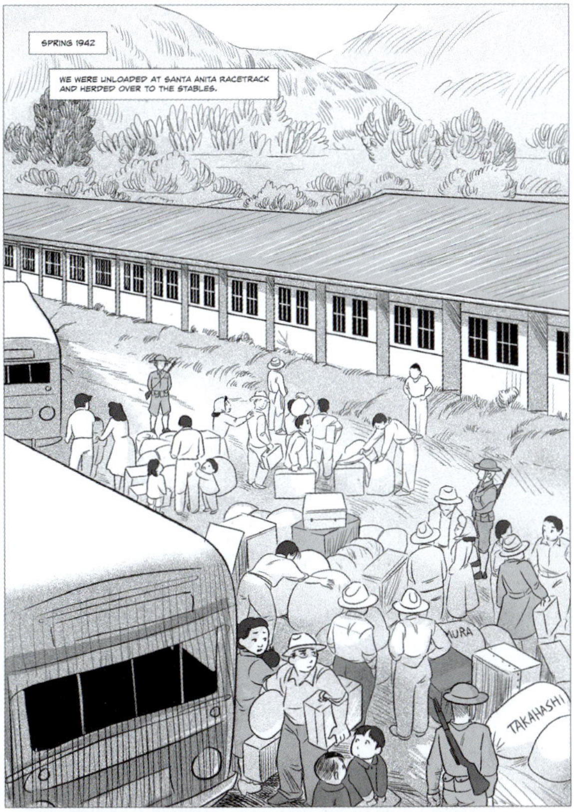

Figure 3.7
Actor George Takei recorded his experience of being a young boy in his 2019 graphic novel *They Called Us Enemy*, illustrated by Harmony Becker, a Japanese American illustrator.

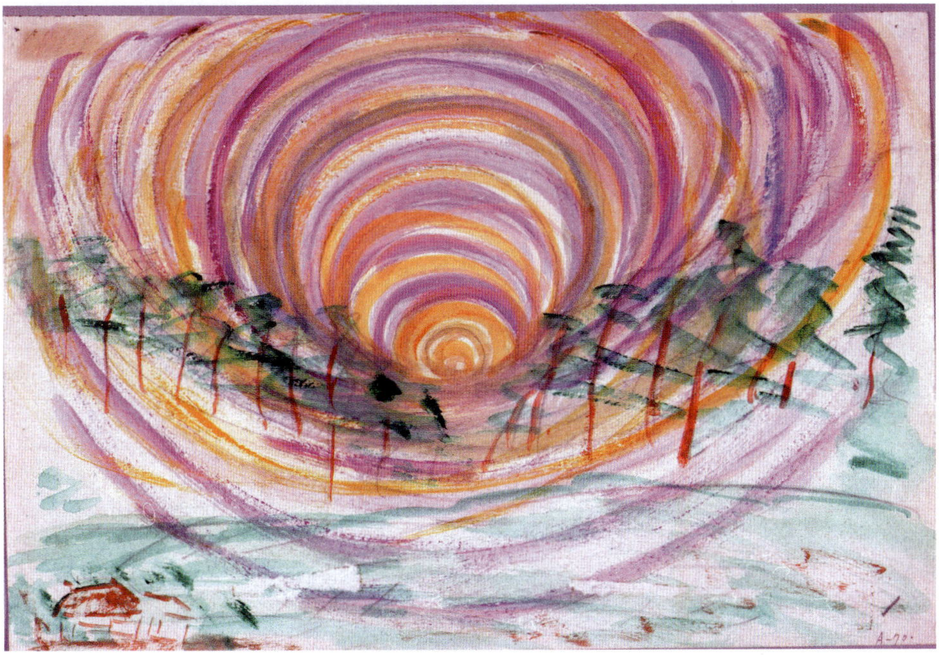

Figure 3.8
Sumako Yamada, who was 10 years old at the time of the nuclear blast in Hiroshima, recorded the echoing reverberations of the explosion.

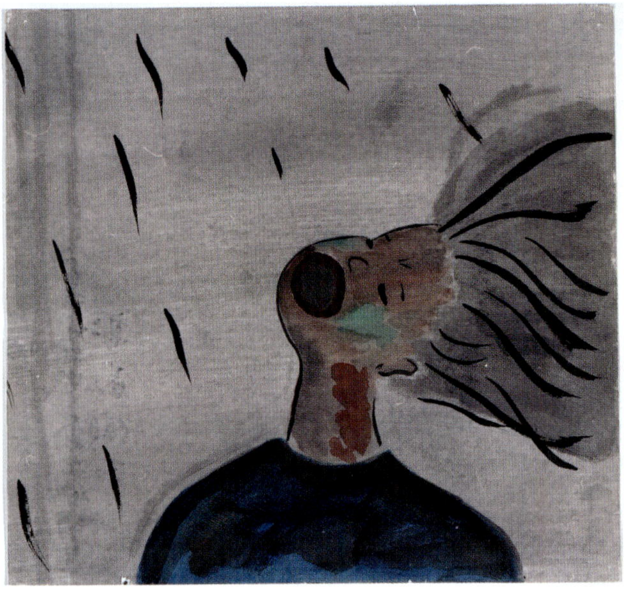

Figure 3.9
Artist Akiko Takakura, who was 19 years old in 1945, drew a picture of a mouth raised upwards, attempting to catch the "black rain" that fell from the sky to quench her thirst.

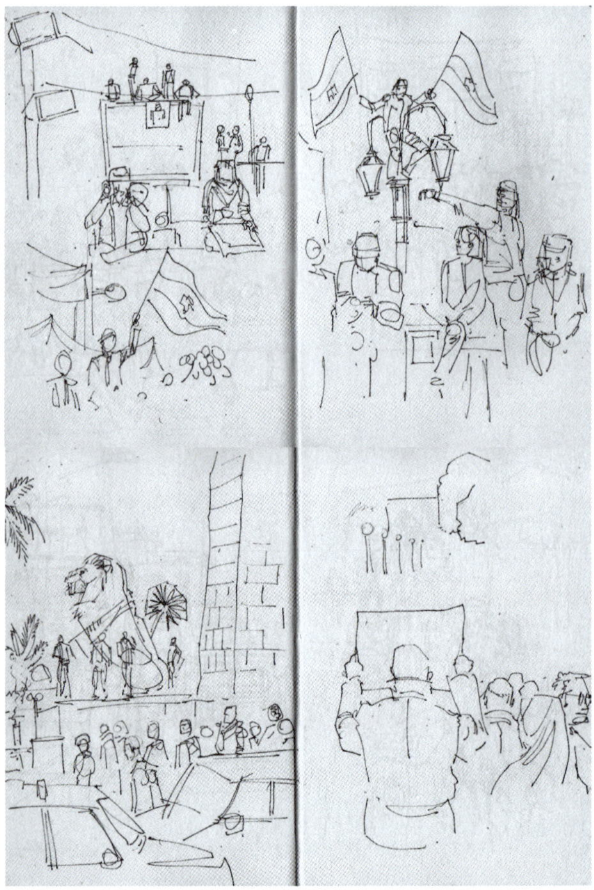

Figure 3.10
Many illustrators today continue the practice of non-commercial reportage illustration through their sketchbooks. These illustrations were completed by Yamen Elgamal during the 2011 Egyptian Revolution protests in Cairo. In the sketches you can see one of the ever-watchful Lions of Qasr al-Nil, as well as protestors displaying the Egyptian flag.

The History of Political Satire

Political satire is another important illustration genre in the historic record of illustration's relationship to printed media, and one that continues to exist today. Political satire has existed for essentially as long as humans have had politics, but in the 18th century, the relationship of political satire and illustration resulted in a new form of media, the **political cartoon**. Political cartoons are perhaps the most familiar and most analyzed type of political illustration. While many political cartoons are also used as a method of dissent, because of their long-standing relationship with print media, censorship, and taboo, we have chosen to include their history in this chapter. The popularity of political cartoons grew along with the growth of printing and newspapers, which gave the opportunity for social critique to be proliferated among the public. The history of political cartooning is vast, and there are many publications that detail different political cartoonists and movements. The content covered in this chapter is meant as an abridged introduction to the field.

As early as the 1500s, as mentioned in Chapter 2, Martin Luther worked with Lucas Cranach the Elder and Lucas Cranach the Younger to create political satires critiquing the Catholic Church. In the 1600s, Italian artists such as Annibale Carracci and Pier Leone Ghezzi began developing the art of **caricature**, exaggerating facial features of public figures to reveal aspects of their personality (perhaps inspired by even earlier Italian caricature artists such as Leonardo da Vinci). (Figure 3.11) Caricatures can also lampoon a particular archetype of a person, such as a nobleman or a beggar. Carracci valued the ability of caricatures to both strike a likeness, while offering an amusing critique, saying, "Good caricature, like every work of art, is more true to life than reality itself."[34] By the 1700s, artists such as William Hogarth and Arthur Pond were inspired by the earlier Italian illustrators to popularize caricature, and Hogarth expanded these caricatures into social critiques through developed political illustrations. Many of these early political cartoons were either self-published, sometimes shared amongst friends or posted publicly on walls, or printed as pamphlets or prints by popular print sellers and distributors.

This was the case for many of Hogarth's earlier political critiques, including *Emblematic Print on the South Sea Scheme*. (Figure 3.12) Many considered this illustration to be one of the first political cartoons, including John J. Richetti, who stated that, "English graphic satire really begins with Hogarth's *Emblematical Print on the South Sea Scheme*."[35] In this print, Hogarth critiques a stock market crash in 1720, caused by the South Sea Company, which sold stocks irresponsibly and eventually collapsed, causing its shareholders to lose a lot of money. Following the crash, fraud and corruption within the company were revealed. In the print, only the base of a giant unseen monument is seen, a symbol of London's greed, bearing the engraving: "This monument was erected in memory of the destruction of the city by the South Sea in 1720." In the background, St. Paul's Cathedral, a symbol of purity, is dwarfed in comparison. The center of the print features a wheel of fortune or merry-go-round, on which caricatures of different classes and members of society all ride, including prostitutes, priests, and noblemen. The goat at the top of the wheel, a symbol of demonic forces, asks of the greedy public, "Who'l ride?" Hogarth's rhyme printed underneath the engraving uses letters to identify further allegories in the illustration. On the left side of the image, a priest, rabbi, and Puritan play a game of chance ("Pitch and Hustle"). In the foreground the figure of Honesty is tortured on a wheel by Self-Interest, and Honor is whipped by Villainy. On the left, the Devil slices apart Fortune. In engravings, using value contrast is a critical visual tool to effective communication and visual focus. The value contrast within the image helps bring focus to the wheel and specific characters within the image, aiding in the storytelling. For instance, Hogarth purposely hides the forgotten figure of Trade in the shadows on the bottom right. The darkness on each side of the image, along with compositional directional lines pointing you at the wheel in the center, helps emphasize it as a focal point. This exceptional storytelling and attention to detail was summarized by English essayist Charles Lamb, who rightfully said of Hogarth's works, "Other pictures we look at, his prints we read."[36]

Hogarth also made another important contribution to illustration following the publication of his prints *A Harlot's Progress* and *A Rake's Progress,* both of which attempted to send a message about morality. Both prints were pirated and reproduced by less talented artists, and sold for a cheaper price. Hogarth took this issue to parliament and demanded laws be enacted to protect artists over reproduction of their work. This resulted in the 1735 Engraver's Copyright Act, also known as Hogarth's Act. Historically, this was the first law to protect the authorship of visual artists.

Following Hogarth's death in 1764, caricatures and political cartoons thrived in England in the late 1700s, and strongly influenced both the style of political illustration and political thought across Europe.[37] Caricature shops were popular locations where the public could go to view and purchase the latest satirical commentary, sometimes paying a fee to view a special exhibition. While the caricatures themselves were sometimes the equivalent of a week's wage to buy, anyone from any class could view the images in the window of the shop, and, for an evening's entertainment, one could rent a folio of caricatures to take home.[38] Many print sellers had successful businesses during this era, setting up shops in fashionable neighborhoods, and popularizing themselves by printing their name on the cartoons they sold to advertise their business.[39] Taverns, businesses, and individuals would also prominently display their purchases in their windows for public view. Proprietors Matthew and Mary Darly had a successful print shop business where they also offered caricature lessons for individuals and published a "book of instruction" in 1762, aiming their services at amateur artists and holding exhibitions for amateur caricatures. George Townshend, a member of the House of Commons, was one of the first amateur cartoonists to have his work published, although because of his noble status, he used the pseudonym "Leonardo da Vinci."[40] Henry William Bunbury, son of a Baronet, was also a prominent caricaturist of the time, being called the "second Hogarth" by author Horace Walpole.[41] Many other lower-class amateurs threw their hats in the ring, providing a great variety of style and content to early political cartooning. While many aristocrats took up caricature, all of these aforementioned examples show how caricature and cartooning became "an art of the people," allowing the opinions of the public a forum for discussion and debate in the media. Cartoons that came from aristocrats, however, also gave the public a newfound accessibility to the inner machinations of the British government.

James Gillray ushered in a new era of combining caricature with sharp political commentary. In the spirit of Hogarth, his work was often moralizing, but also issued nuanced political views of the political parties of the time, as well as Napoleon and the French Revolution. Gillray made bold choices, such as satirizing the Royal family, which had historically been a taboo topic for satire. In a portrait of the Prince of Wales, Gillray portrayed him as lazy and gluttonous, a critique on the lavish spending of the royal family. (Figure 3.13) Gillray also made stylistic choices that helped to support the ideas he was communicating; instead of using the usual bold hatch lines of engraving, he used a soft stipple, mimicking the style of royal portraits of the time, further mocking the aristocracy. A final jab was showing the Prince's coat of arms as a crossed knife and fork.[42] Twentieth century cartoonist David Lowe stated that while Hogarth was considered the grandfather of the political cartoon, Gillray was the father of the political cartoon, learning how to use the medium itself to help convey his biting messages. Gillray, unlike Bunbury and Townshend, was not a member of the aristocracy, and took chances on taboo topics and scatological humor more than his contemporaries. In *The French Invasion: ... or... John Bull, bombarding the Bum-Boats*, Gillray combined both by showing one of his favorite subjects, King George III, defecating "The British Declaration" onto the coast of France. (Figure 3.14) Gillray is also given credit for the persistent myth of Napoleon's height, often portraying the French imperialist as tiny, nicknamed "Little Boney".[43] Perhaps the most famous of Gillray's political cartoons, as well as one of the most famous of his time, was his 1805 cartoon *The Plum Pudding in Danger*, which portrays the spindly English Prime Minister William Pitt and tiny Napoleon Bonaparte carving up the globe to assert their spheres of influence. This cartoon shows Gillray's masterful skill and effectiveness at creating caricatures. (Figure 3.15)

Throughout his career, Gillray became associated with his printer and publisher Miss Hannah Humphrey, sometimes sneakily portraying her and her shop in the background of his prints. Johann Christian Hüttner, a German translator and journalist living in the United Kingdom, said that "Caricature shops are always besieged by the public, but it is only in Mrs. Humphrey's shop, where Gillray's works are sold, that you will find people of high rank, good taste and intelligence."[44] Humphrey and Gillray's association continued up until his early death. By 1807, Gillray's eyesight was failing, and, frustrated he could not create work up to his previous standards, by some accounts, he began, by some accounts, to drink heavily.[45] Sickened by rheumatism, depression, and possibly gout, Gillray had periods of insanity during which he was cared for by Miss Humphries, especially after an attempted suicide by defenestration in 1811, which was the year of his last created work.[46] When he died at age 58 in 1815, leaving his estate to Humphries, it left the window open for new political satirists to fill the gap left by Gillray.[47,48]

Even the famed Gillray was not free of censorship during his career, and government officials looked for ways to direct his work away from themselves. He was once arrested for blasphemy for creating a print showing politicians kissing the bottom of a new royal baby. Prime Minister William Pitt's administration gave Gillray a £200 annual fee between 1797 and 1801 for not satirizing the government in his illustrations.[49] Often, however, illustrators would mock censorship and call out its injustice, such as in George Cruikshank's *Free Born Englishman (Gagging Acts)* cartoon in which he called out the government for enacting a series of "Six Acts" which suppressed protest and criticism of a protestor massacre in Manchester. (Figure 3.16) The print accompanied a poem, whose author, like Cruikshank, chose to remain anonymous for fear of retribution.[50] Upon Gillray's death, George Cruikshank was ready to step into Gillray's shoes, creating his first major work in 1821, and continued to dish out commentary on Britain's political parties. Cruikshank's father Isaac was also a political cartoonist and contemporary of Gillray's, and George Cruikshank had a strong education and background in cartooning. The younger Cruikshank was able to use his skills to, like Gillray, boldly lampoon the Royal family in his cartoons, with King George IV once paying Cruikshank £100 in 1820 "in consideration of a pledge not to caricature His Majesty in any immoral situation," and issued thousands of pounds more in bribes.[51] In fact, when George IV was the Prince of Wales, an artist could assume if they made something libelous enough, they could guarantee the Prince would buy its copyright to protect his reputation, so their salacious prints would almost always be good earners for either the popularity or the payout.[52]

Unlike Gillray and his predecessors who mostly utilized print shops for their publications, Cruikshank's work found a new medium for publication: illustrated newspapers and magazines. Along with *The Illustrated London News* and the other aforementioned publications, satirical magazines began to make their debut in the early to mid-1800s. George Cruikshank made many illustrations for *The Scourge*, first published from 1811. The famed *Punch*, named after the Punch and Judy puppet act, debuted in Britain in 1841 and ran for over 150 years. In fact, the term "cartoon" was not used to describe the caricatures and satirical illustration that these magazines exhibited until *Punch* appropriated the term from its previous connotation of "a preliminary sketch or drawing." George Cruikshank's own comic newspaper *Cruikshank's Comic Almanack* was driven out of business by the popularity of *Punch* (although Cruikshank continued to succeed as a book illustrator and contributor to *Punch*). John Tenniel, *Punch's* principal cartoonist, rose to fame through the publication, although we also remember him today mainly as a book illustrator of the 1865 publication of *Alice's Adventures in Wonderland. Punch* succeeded in gaining a reputation as the most sophisticated of the humor magazines, and gained further notoriety when some of its articles were published in mainstream news publications such as *The Times* and *News of the World.*

Although the British royalty and government engaged in some non-codified attempts at censorship, the amount of freedom in the British press at this time was unusual in contrast to most of Europe. France had especially strict censorship laws that political satirists had to work around. An engraver could not own their own printing press in France between 1586 to 1734, and, starting in 1685, anyone who did own a press was required to get permission, or a *permission tacite*, from the government for any of their publications, which was a lucrative method of both income and propaganda for the king.[53] Some printers were able to collaborate with police who offered *permission clandestines*, where they would take a bribe to ignore printers who printed secret editions, and warn them if there would be a raid. As France approached the time of the Revolution, this broken censorship system, which was disorganized and not centrally controlled, became challenged by illegally self-published journals, flyers, and pamphlets. The 1789 publication of the *Declaration of the Rights of Man and the Citizen*, a human rights document that stated the core values of the French Revolution, proclaimed that freedom of speech and publication were key to the revolution's goals. During the Revolution, **reverse censorship** was enacted upon Royalist journals by the revolutionaries, and although censorship was not absent, from 1789 to 1792 French citizens briefly enjoyed a greater freedom of the press. When Napoleon seized the government, he initially embraced freedom of the press, and during the first two months of his rule allowed the greatest freedom of the press France had seen in decades. Soon, however, Napoleon's propaganda campaign began, and with it, France returned to strict censorship, with Napoleon declaring *Le Moniteur* as the only official journal, while discrediting all other journals. In 1800, the Law of 27 Nivôse stated that only thirteen newspapers would be allowed during the duration of the war, down from the previous seventy-three.[54] By 1811, this number was down to four. Following Napoleon's regime, censorship laws continued to limit the French press. Because of British illustrations making their way to France, however, more artists were inspired to lampoon the regimes following Napoleon's. In 1830, King Louis-Phillipe I enacted a ban on illustrative attacks on the monarchy, inadvertently ushering in one of the most creative periods of French political cartooning.

In 1830, Charles Philipon introduced *La Caricature* in France, followed by *Le Charivari* in 1832. In his publications, Philipon, a caricaturist himself, learned the art of lithography and printed his newspapers with lithography as a way of saving money on hiring engravers to translate cartoonists' art to the paper. With lithography, the drawing could be placed directly onto the stone of the lithography plate, therefore eliminating a step most papers had to expense. Lithography could also be printed on a cheaper paper. Philipon, who associated with leftists, anti-monarchists, and satirists, was eager to print cartoons in his papers that satirized the new monarch Louis-Phillipe. One, *Le Replâtrage,* however, took it too far and landed Philipon in court for the first of many times. (Figure 3.17) The cartoon depicted Louis-Phillipe as a mason plastering over his promises. During this trial, for which Philipon was accused of the crime of *lèse-majesté* or dishonoring the king, he defended himself through an ingenious method: describing the nature of drawing. Philipon said that a picture of the king was merely a symbol or a figurehead of the government, a metonym, and was therefore not lampooning the king himself. (Likewise, a hundred years later, Henri Matisse famously claimed a picture of a pipe is not a pipe itself.) Philipon went on to defend the resemblance of the figure in his drawing of the king, saying that "anything can resemble the king," and he could not be held liable for the resemblance. Then, in court, he drew a four-step illustration metamorphosing the king's head into the shape of a pear. (The connection of a pear and the king had a further meaning, however, because *poire* in French means both *pear* and *fool.*) Philipon's argument was to break down the steps of the caricature and ask at which step is the resemblance to the king too obscure to be considered a resemblance? Philipon argued if they were to ban a caricature at one step, they must ban all images of pears. Not buying his argument, the judges gave Philipon a 2000 franc fine and six months of jail time.

However, Philipon could not be silenced and later commissioned illustrator Honoré Daumier to reproduce his drawing for *Le Charivari.* (Figure 3.18) Upon its publication and the public's reaction, Philipon wrote, "What I had foreseen happened. People seized by a mocking image, an image with a simple design and a very simple shape, started to reproduce this image everywhere they found a way to draw with coal, to sketch, to scratch a pear. Pears soon covered and spread across all the walls of Paris and of France."[55] The profits from the publication of *Les Poires* more than covered his fine. Other artists started depicting images of people drawing pears on walls, creating an early version of a **meme.** (Figure 3.19) The government furiously tried to repress the drawings of pears, without full success. When they banned the image of the pear from *Le Charivari,*

FOCUS ON TECHNOLOGY

Lithography

Lithography was invented in the late 18th century, and was popularized in part by Charles Philipon's early 19th century publications. Lithography is now a multistep process that uses many different chemical materials, and can be quite confusing to learn for a novice, but is based on a simple scientific idea: water repels oil. At the close of the 18th century, a Bavarian playwright named Alois Senefelder discovered a process to make copies of his scripts. Instead of creating engravings on costly copper plates, Senefelder used a material readily and cheaply available in Bavaria: limestone. The word lithography comes from the Greek word *lithos* for "stone".[56] Through experimentation, Senefelder learned that drawing with a greasy crayon (called a *tusche*) on the limestone would cause the text or image to repel water. When the limestone was wetted with water and then inked, the repulsion of the water to the limestone surface would cause the ink to only stick to the greasy image. Therefore, a limestone plate could be inked and reused over and over to create prints. Key to this process, however, was creating a method so that images and words did not have to be written backwards. In 1853, John Strather patented the method of *offset lithography*, in which one could write or draw the original work on paper and then transfer it to a stone, so that the stone image for reproduction is backwards. Another benefit to this method is that the drawing retains the original texture of the paper. By the 1870s, a rubber cylinder was used as the intermediary, flipping the image twice so it could be printed without having to invert it.

Lithography had many advantages compared to previous printing methods, including the fact it could be reproduced an almost limitless amount of times, unlike copperplate etching, and could be printed on inexpensive paper. Therefore, lithography soon became a favored illustration printing method around the world. Zinc plates replaced stone around 1830, and aluminum replaced zinc around 1890.[57] Lithography grew in popularity throughout the 19th century, commonly used by political cartoonists and caricaturists. In France, the "golden age" of French caricature was born through lithography, despite heavy censorship of the press by King Louis-Philippe. Cartoonists such as Cham and Honoré Daumier used lithography to quickly communicate their commentaries on the Napoleonic reign to the public. *Color lithography* (also called chromolithographs or oleographs) became popularized in the 1860s, when artists such as Henri de Toulouse-Lautrec and the firm Currier and Ives created beautiful, bold, colorful prints. Prior to this time, commercial illustration presses such as Currier and Ives would print in black and white and hire an assembly line of women to hand paint the lithographs.[58] Other technologies such as the steam-driven lithographic press helped popularize the medium. By the late 1800s, lithography became one of the most popular methods of printing illustration, and the technology was even able to be used to print photographs.[59] Today, lithography remains a popular medium for posters, flyers, and other forms of political illustration. Many political illustrators around the world used lithography, including Käthe Kollwitz of Germany, Diego Rivera of Mexico, and Emory Douglas of the US.

Philipon, who had to announce the court order against the publication in the publication itself, arranged the typography so that it looked like a pear. In 1835, however, after a failed assassination attempt of Louis-Philippe, the government passed the "September Laws," fully outlawing any discussion or criticism of the king, and effectively banned political caricature in France until the Revolution of 1848.[60]

The publication success of political cartoons in America followed a slightly different tone and timeline. Although caricature shops were able to be popular in large cities such as London, which sported a population of 1 million in 1800, the population of the largest US city at the time was New York at approximately 61,000. Therefore, the market for cartoon prints was much smaller and less viable.[61] America was also slightly behind in the technologies sweeping through Europe, including lithography and wood engraving. Although wood engraving had been around for centuries, significant improvements in the practice such as the type of wood and tools used were developed at the end of the 18th century in England.[62] Prior to this, most illustrations were created using copperplate etching, and each plate could only be printed about 200 times before it deteriorated.[63]

FOCUS ON TECHNOLOGY

Copperplate Etching

During the golden age of caricature in Britain, copperplate etching was the primary method of mass-producing political cartoons. The ideation of these cartoons came as a collaboration between the artist and the printmaker in order to maximize profit, and sometimes the printer would even publish customers' and "Gentlemen's" designs and ideas.[64] Profit was always the primary motivator behind which ideas were published, and the printing process was also utilized to maximize profit. In copperplate etching, a copper plate was covered with a wax ground and drawn into by the printmaker. The printmaker then gave the plate an acid bath, so that any area where the wax was carved away by the needle would be engraved into the plate by the acid. This made the process quick and easy, in comparison to engraving, in which the artist carves directly into the copper itself. The plates were then printed with a rolling press, and, by 1790, printed onto newly invented "wove" paper, which was better able to hold a watercolor wash than the previously used ridged "laid" paper. The dried prints were then hand colored by women who could be hired as cheap labor.[65] Usually first editions of a print were about 500 copies, which is when etched plates began to wear down and needed to be recarved.[66] Because this supply could not always meet demand, forgeries and copyright infringement of previously published caricatures was rampant.

Many notable examples of early American cartooning came from the time surrounding the American Revolution and the War of 1812. Benjamin Franklin can be credited with publishing one of the first American cartoons in 1754, *Join, or Die,* which was created during the French and Indian War to unite the colonies against the French and their Native American recruits and mercenaries (not, as commonly believed, an illustration about the colonies uniting against the British). (Figure 3.20) Franklin created a strong visual metaphor of a snake split into pieces that cannot live alone, but can deliver a sharp bite when joined together. Another memorable example of early American cartooning came in 1813 when Massachusetts Governor Elbridge Gerry signed the infamous bill creating the first gerrymandered legislative district. This district was so misshapen that political cartoonist Elkanah Tisdale saw it as inspiration for a clawed, salamander-like, nefarious creature.[67] (Figure 3.21) Tisdale's friend, poet Richard Alsop deemed the creature the "Gerry-mander," taking from the name of the governor. (Gerry was at the time actually pronounced "Gary," a pronunciation that did not stick over time.) Tisdale's cartoon was first printed in the Boston Gazette in 1812, with a quote underneath stating the monster had been born from the "many fiery ebullitions of party spirit, many explosions of democratic wrath and fulminations of gubernatorial vengeance within the year past."[68] Despite the media scrutiny, the distorted district lines had their intended effect: the Democratic-Republicans won more seats, even though the opposing Federalists won the most votes statewide. However, Elbridge Gerry, whose name will forever be associated with gerrymandering, lost his reelection in a popular vote against his opponent.

Even so, it wasn't until newspapers became popular in the US that cartoons took off in the country. Much of this success was due to the work of Thomas Nast, often referred to as the Father of the American Political Cartoon, who shaped the media standard for political cartoons as we know it today. Nast began his career by creating his political cartoons with ink brushwork, but his style was later influenced by Englishman John Tenniel, and he eventually adopted Tenniel's distinctive cross-hatching style from an illustration he saw in *Punch* magazine. This style then became Nast's signature as he created political cartoons on a variety of topics.[69] Another appeal of Nast's work was his ability to create a caricature not based solely on someone's physical features, as Philipon and Daumier did of King Louis-Phillipe, but was able to use caricature to show aspects of the subject's personality. Unlike the British and French caricature artists, Nast also used costuming and dress to show the character of the caricatured person.[70] Nast's cartoons heavily relied on commonly understood symbols in order to interpret their work, including the Bible, Shakespearean plays, fables and folktales, and myths, and was, as quoted by political cartoonist Steve Brodner, "very well-versed [in his subject matter], the way a sophisticated politico would be."[71,72] Today some of these symbols are clear, although others, becoming less popular throughout time, need context in order for the illustration to be fully understood. Nast also created symbols of his own and was the first illustrator to use an elephant to represent the Republican party, commenting on how the party was strong, but lumbering and inarticulate. Nast also popularized the preexisting symbols of America, Uncle Sam and Columbia,[73] and the use of the donkey to represent the Democratic party by converting it into a jack-ass, which was inspired by the character Bottom from Shakespeare's Midsummer Night's Dream. Nast innovated the political cartoon through his work at *Harper's Weekly*, where he began creating cartoons at the age of only 18. Because the magazine published weekly, Nast was able to create cartoons that commented on the minutiae of up-to-date political events, and was therefore able to move away from the broader political or social themes necessary for cartoonists of the past to make their living. This is another excellent example of the media affecting the medium.

Nast's work became especially popular during and after the American Civil War, when he drew a number of popular sentimental illustrations. Nast aligned with the Republicans and Abraham Lincoln, and created a cartoon celebrating the Emancipation Proclamation. In September of 1864, Nast created his political cartoon *Compromise with the South--Dedicated to the Chicago Convention* at a time when the fate of the war was still unclear, and Northern Democrats, critical of Lincoln, had a faction called the Copperheads who wished for an immediate peace with the South. (Figure 3.22) Nast sought to show the folly of this thought by showing the results of a compromise with the South: a wounded Northern soldier with his head hung in shame, the Confederate president Jefferson Davis breaking the sword (labeled "Northern Power") of the deceased Union soldier on his grave, with Lady Columbia weeping over it. In the background, the North is shown on fire while in the South, an enslaved family is returned to servitude. Each corner has a flag, on the left, the American flag turned upside down, while on the right, the Confederate flag lists all of the sins of the South. Nast used symmetry and value contrast to bring the viewer's eye to the grave and the inequality of the handshake deal, emphasizing the unfairness and waste of a compromise. Fortunately, the Democratic candidate was healthily defeated by Lincoln in the election, and soon after the Democratic convention, the tide of the war turned to favor the Union.[74]

Following the end of the war and Lincoln's assassination, Nast continued to lambast any compromise with the Confederacy, especially during the Johnson administration and Reconstruction. Nast's post-war cartoons elevated the voices of Black Americans and criticized the Johnson administration. In his 1866 cartoon *The Georgetown Election – The Negro at the Ballot Box,* Nast depicts a Black man voting for the mayor of the District of Columbia, the first US election open to all adult male citizens, with General Ulysses S Grant standing staunchly beside him, defending his vote. (Figure 3.23) On the left, President Johnson glowers at the voter, clutching to his recently overridden suffrage veto and accompanied by a former Confederate soldier.[75] After the Fourteenth Amendment passed in 1868, which established equal protections under the law for all people, regardless of race, Nast made a number of cartoons calling out the racism and Black lynchings within the country. In *This is a White Man's Government,* Nast depicts three men stepping on the back of a Black soldier who clutches the American flag in one hand and reaches for the ballot box with the other. (Figure 3.24) The three men include a Southerner with CSA (Confederate States of America) on his belt, holding a knife labeled "The Lost Vote," a stereotyped Irishman to the left holding a club labeled "a vote," and a capitalist wearing a pin that says "5th Avenue" and a wallet that says "capital for votes." In the background, Nast depicts a burning Black orphanage, and a lynched man hanging from a lamppost.[76] This illustration brings up an important fact about Nast. Although he advocated against segregation and slavery, and also for the rights of Chinese Americans and American Indians, he was not immune to depicting **visual stereotypes**. Nast often illustrated Irish-Americans as drunk and violent, associating them with Northern Democrats and racists. In his illustration *Colored Rule in a Reconstructed State,* Nast buys into the popular narrative of the time that state governments during Reconstruction were corrupt, although they were not necessarily more corrupt than any other state government at the time. Because the Black legislators were new to holding office, they became scapegoats for this stereotype. Here Nast created a racist depiction of an imaginary exchange of Black legislators from South Carolina, the only state government to have a majority Black legislature. (Figure 3.25)[77]

In the second half of the 19th century, publications featuring political illustration continued to abound. In the tradition of *Punch* in England, America's *Puck* emerged as an illustrated humor magazine in 1877, its title another Midsummer Night's Dream reference to the mischievous character Puck. Unlike Nast's cartoons, which were serious in tone and style, *Puck* was the first magazine to print full-color lithographs, and its cofounder, Austrian-born Joseph Keppler, introduced the humorous tone of European satire to American audiences. Similarly, a competing satirical magazine *Judge* began in 1881, and by the end of the 1880s, many, if not most, American newspapers began employing political cartoonists full-time, including Fred Opper of the *New York Journal*, John McCutcheon of the *Chicago Tribune*, and Clifford Berryman of *The Washington Post* and *Evening Star*.[78]

African American newspapers also flourished in the first half of the 20th century, and, with them, so did illustration by Black illustrators for Black causes. Although Southern states attempted to ban Black newspapers during World War I so that Black sharecroppers wouldn't leave their exploitative employment, by the eve of World War II, there were almost 150 Black newspapers in print.[79,80] Many Black citizens were discontent with their participation in World War II, such as C.L.R. James, who stated: "Why should I shed my blood for Roosevelt's America, for Cotton Ed Smith and Senator Bilbo, for the whole Jim Crow, negro-hating South, for the low-paid, dirty jobs for which negroes have to fight, for the few dollars of relief and the insults, discrimination, police brutality, and perpetual poverty to which negroes are condemned even in the more liberal North?" In 1942, *The Pittsburgh Courier* began it's "Double V Campaign" or Double Victory Campaign, bringing attention to the fact that Black citizens were limited by racial discrimination and Jim Crow laws at home, while being drafted to fight a foreign war for their country.[81] The campaign hoped to win on both fronts, and is thought to have been a significant contributor to the Civil Rights Movement following the war. United States Vice President Henry Wallace put his support behind the movement, stating: "We cannot fight to crush Nazi brutality abroad and condone race riots at home. Those who fan the fires of racial clashes for the purpose of making political capital here at home are taking the first step toward Nazism."[82] Illustrators and writers for the Black newspaper *The Chicago Defender* were vocal in their anger against discrimination against Black troops during World War I and II. Illustrator Jay Jackson (1905–1954) created many comics for *The Chicago Defender* that addressed racial issues and discrimination, including the irony of African Americans defending a country that abused them. Jackson's cartoon *We'll Be Back* shows American soldiers rushing to save an enslaved Europe, while leaving Black Americans in the metaphorical chains of Jim Crow and the Ku Klux Klan. (Figure 3.26) The title clarifies the priorities of the US government in regards to the Double V Campaign: war first, then civil rights. His cartoon *The Blind Leading the Blind*, shows two figures blinded by their racist hate, the US leading Nazi Germany. (Figure 3.27) Knowing Nazi Germany based much of their Anti-Jewish legislation on the Jim Crow laws of the US makes the metaphor even more chilling.

World War II also offered an opportunity for another overlooked group to take up a role in political cartooning: women. Prior to this era, few women were able to break into the industry, with exceptions including Mrs. Mary Darly from 18th century Britain and women such as Rose O'Neill and Nell Brinkley, who created cartoons on the topic of suffrage. This iniquitous tradition was finally broken when *The Miami Daily News* published Anne Mergen's first political cartoon and hired her as a full-time cartoonist in 1936. Mergen continued to hold the status as the only female political cartoonist in America until she retired in the late 1950s. At the beginning of World War II, many Americans took an isolationist stance towards the war. Mergen chose to lampoon this in her cartoon *Isolationist, huh?*, in which a plane circles around the globe to confront a man about globalization and the impossibility of the United States to ignore the consequences of the war. By late 1941, on the eve of the Pearl Harbor bombing, most Americans believed defeating Germany was more important than maintaining isolation. Another cartoon, *The Master of Jet Propulsion*, depicts a Nazi war plane flying high, with Joseph Goebbels, Hitler's propaganda minister, spouting the fiery rhetoric and "hot air" that helped the Nazis propel their war. However, Mergen was best known for her cartoons that depicted optimism. In *The Golden Gate of Opportunity,* created after VE Day in 1945, the globe, holding the newly ratified United Nations security charter, walks through the gates of World Unity to A Better Future.[83] Although a Pulitzer Prize for Editorial Cartooning was first issued in 1922, it was not until 1992 that a woman, Signe Wilkinson, won the award. As of 2017, there still has never been a full-time female cartoonist for a national newspaper in the UK.[84] It is important to remember the most striking form of omission in political illustration, which continues today: silencing and excluding the voices of women and people of color.

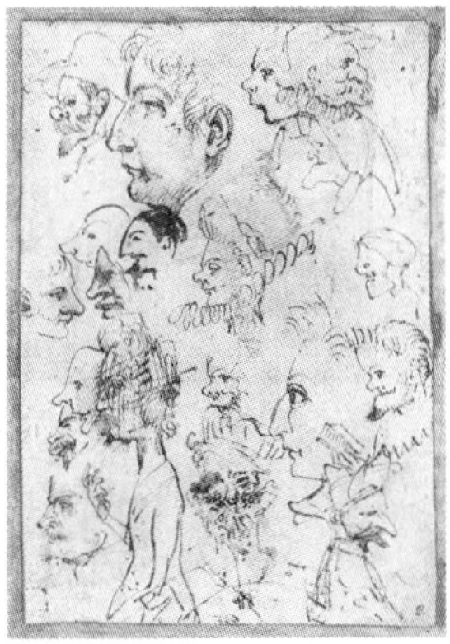

Figure 3.11
In the 1600s, Italian artists such as Annibale Carracci began developing the art of caricature, exaggerating facial features of public figures to reveal aspects of their personality. (*Sheet of Caricatures*, 1595)

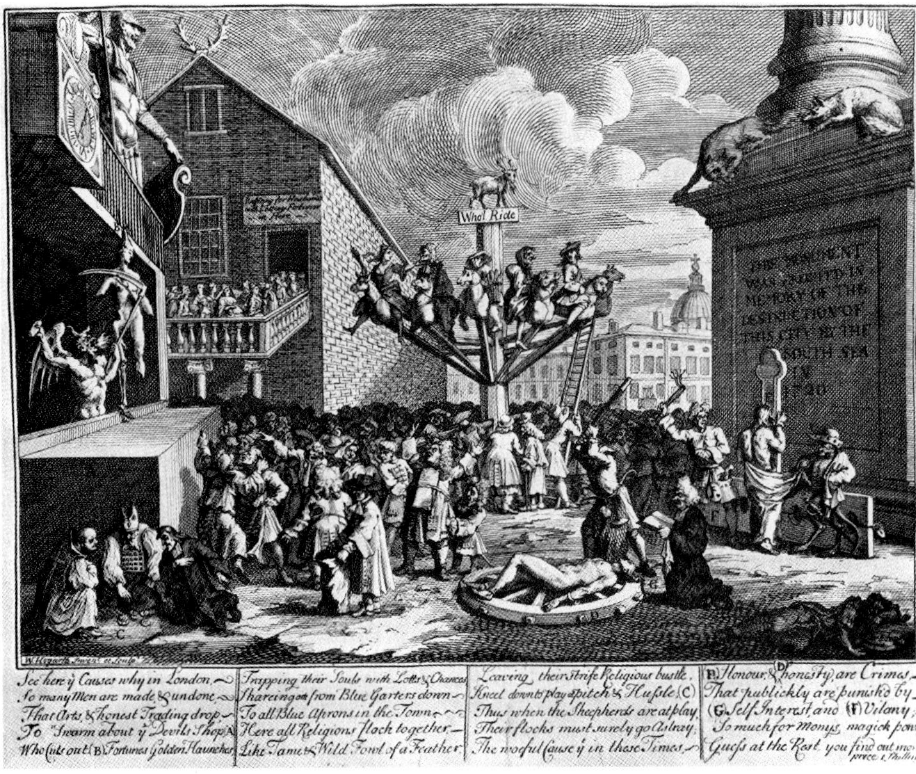

Figure 3.12
Emblematic Print on the South Sea Scheme (1721) by William Hogarth is considered by many to be one of the first political cartoons.

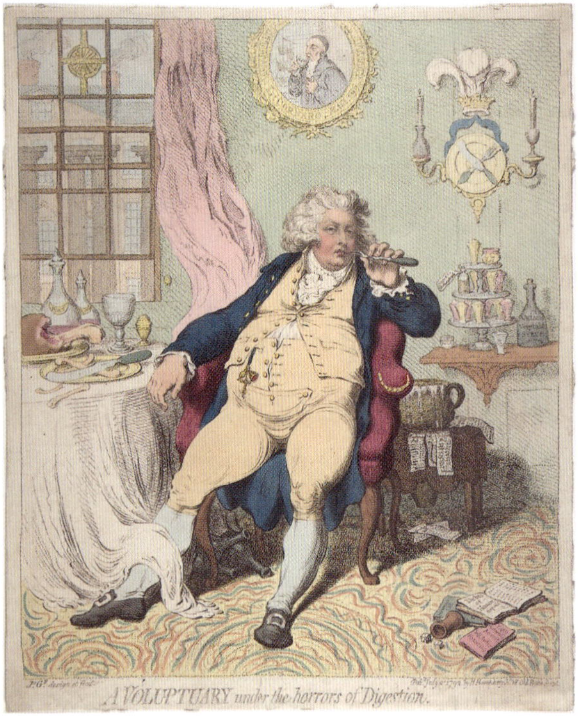

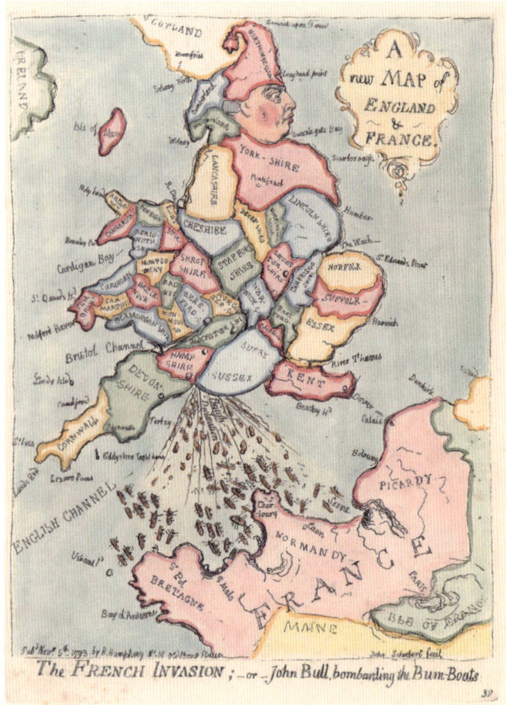

Figure 3.13
In *A Voluptuary Under the Horrors of Digestion* (1792), James Gillray portrayed the Prince of Wales as lazy and gluttonous, a critique on the lavish spending of the royal family.

Figure 3.14
In *The French Invasion: … or… John Bull, bombarding the Bum-Boats* (1793), James Gillray portrayed one of his favorite subjects, King George III, defecating "The British Declaration" onto the coast of France.

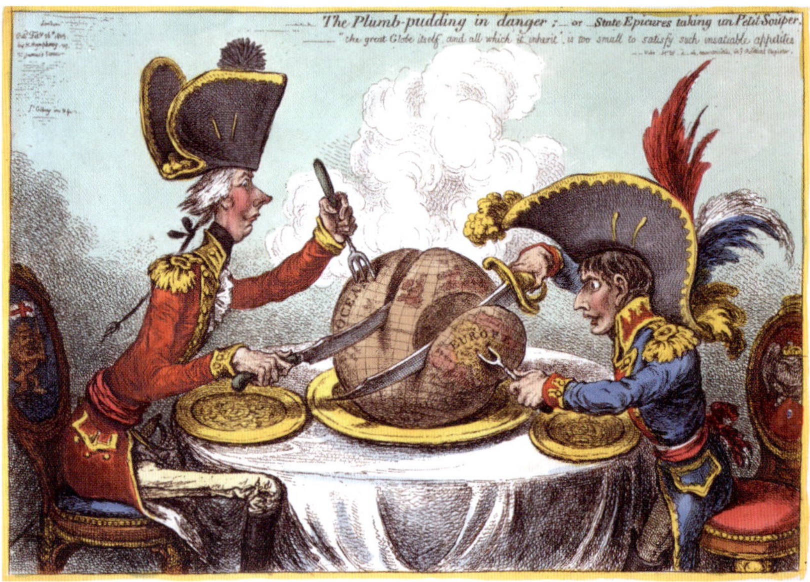

Figure 3.15
In his 1805 cartoon *The Plum Pudding in Danger*, Gillray portrays the spindly English Prime Minister William Pitt and tiny Napoleon Bonaparte carving up the globe to assert their spheres of influence.

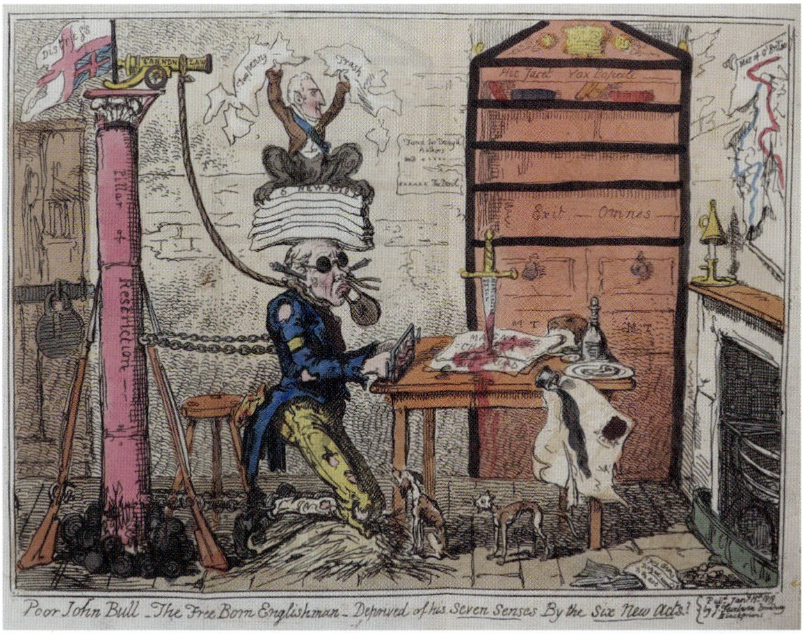

Figure 3.16 *left*
In his cartoon *Free Born Englishman (Gagging Acts)* (1819), George Cruikshank called out the government for enacting a series of "Six Acts" which suppressed protest and criticism of a protestor massacre in Manchester.

Figure 3.18 *below*
Honoré Daumier's 1834 etching *Les Poires*, based on Philipon's four-step illustration metamorphosing the king's head into the shape of a pear, created a public sensation in France.

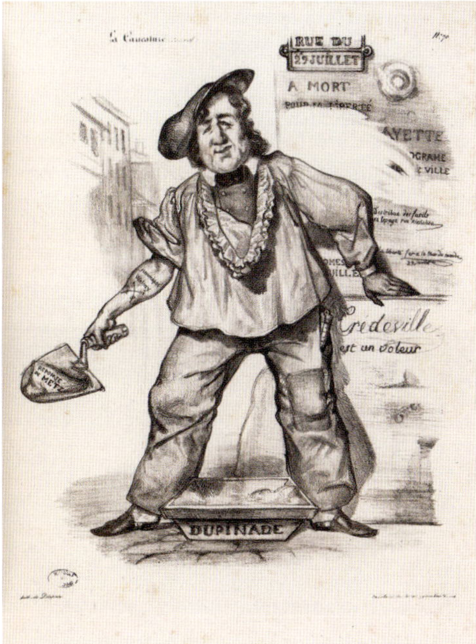

Figure 3.17
Charles Philipon's cartoon *Le Replâtrage* (1831), depicting Louis-Phillipe as a mason plastering over his promises, landed him in court for the first of many times.

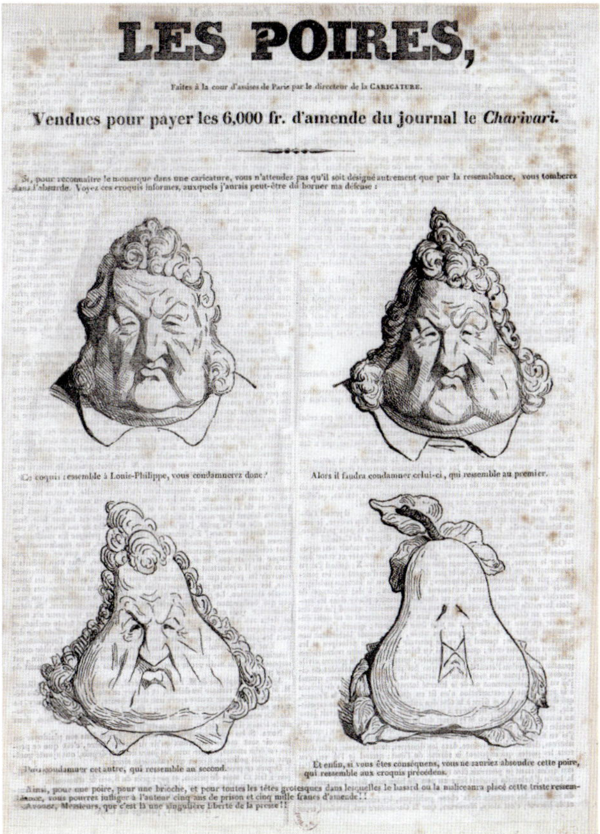

LES POIRES,

Faites à la cour d'assises de Paris par le directeur de la CARICATURE.

Vendues pour payer les 6,000 fr. d'amende du journal le *Charivari*.

Si, pour reconnaître le monarque dans une caricature, vous n'attendez pas qu'il soit désigné autrement que par la ressemblance, vous tomberez dans l'absurde. Voyez ces croquis informes, auxquels j'aurais peut-être dû borner ma défense :

Ce croquis ressemble à Louis-Philippe, vous condamnerez donc?

Alors il faudra condamner celui-ci, qui ressemble au premier.

Puis condamner cet autre, qui ressemble au second.

Et enfin, si vous êtes conséquens, vous ne sauriez absoudre cette poire, qui ressemble aux croquis précédens.

Ainsi, pour une poire, pour une brioche, et pour toutes les têtes grotesques dans lesquelles le hasard ou la malice aura placé cette triste ressemblance, vous pourrez infliger à l'auteur cinq ans de prison et cinq mille francs d'amende!!

Avouez, Messieurs, que c'est là une singulière liberté de la presse!!

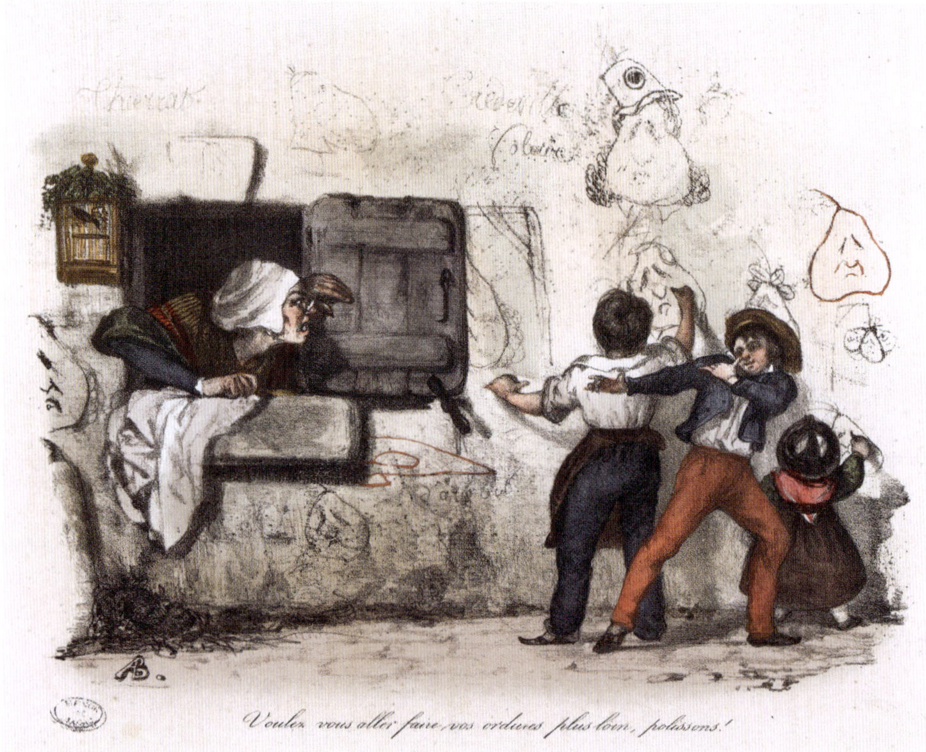

Figure 3.19 After the publication of Daumier's *Les Poires* in *Le Charivari*, artists started depicting images of people drawing pears on walls, creating an early version of a meme.

Figure 3.20 Benjamin Franklin can be credited with publishing one of the first American cartoons in 1754, *Join, or Die*, which was created during the French and Indian War to unite the colonies against the French and their Native American recruits and mercenaries.

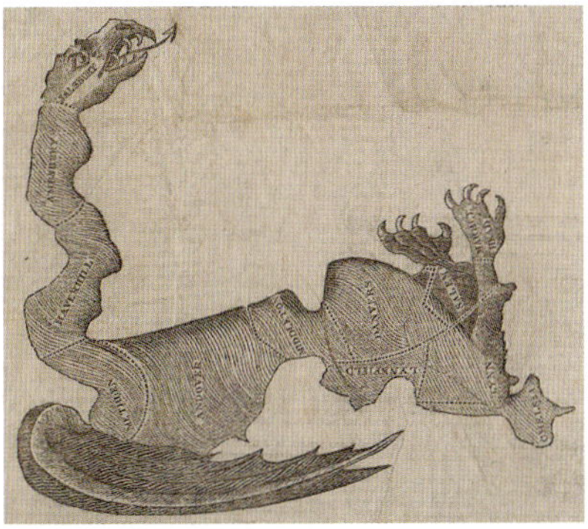

Figure 3.21
A misshapen district created by Massachusetts Governor Elbridge Gerry inspired political cartoonist Elkanah Tisdale to create *The Gerry-Mander* in 1813.

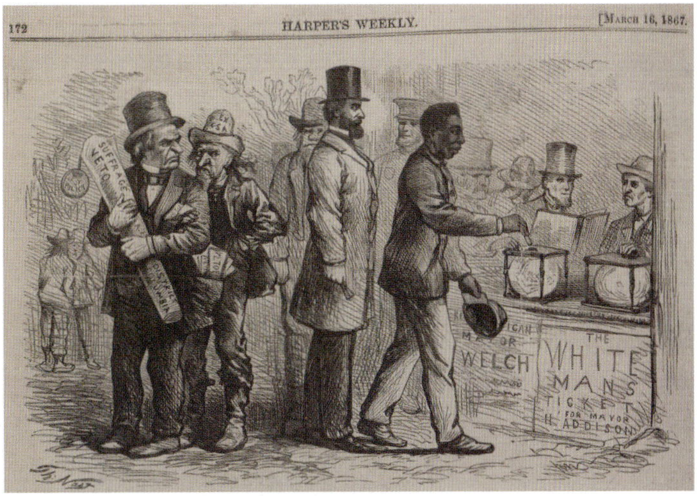

Figure 3.23
In his 1867 cartoon *The Georgetown Election – The Negro at the Ballot Box*, Nast depicts a Black man voting for the mayor of the District of Columbia, the first US election open to all adult male citizens, with General Ulysses S Grant standing staunchly beside him, defending his vote.

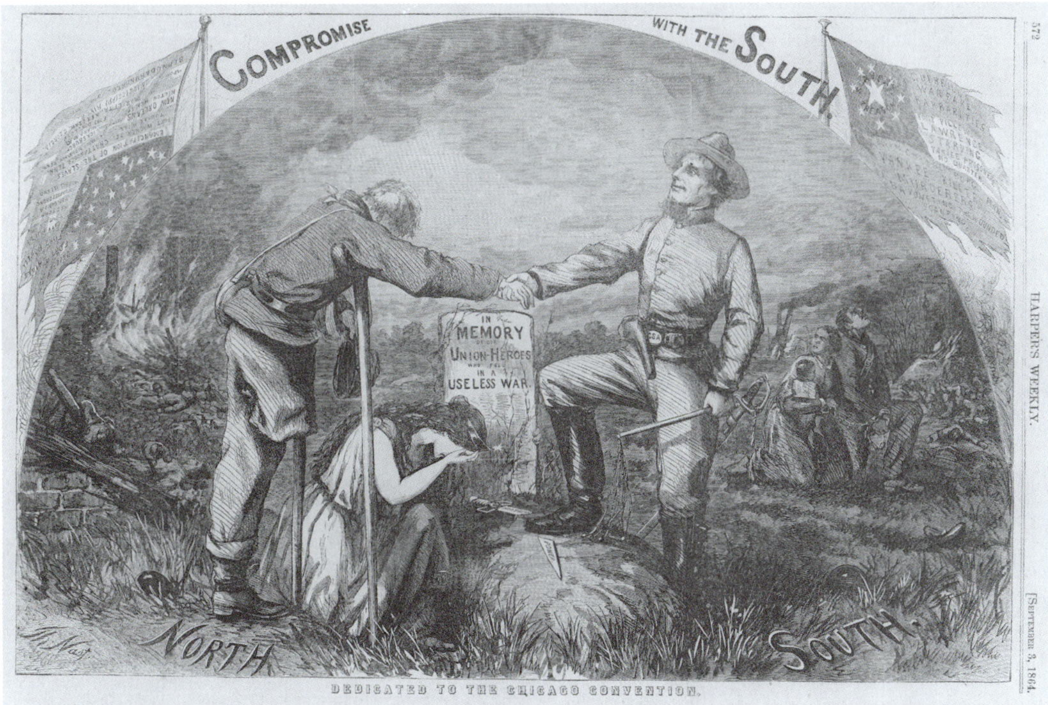

Figure 3.22
In September of 1864, Nast created his political cartoon *Compromise with the South--Dedicated to the Chicago Convention*.

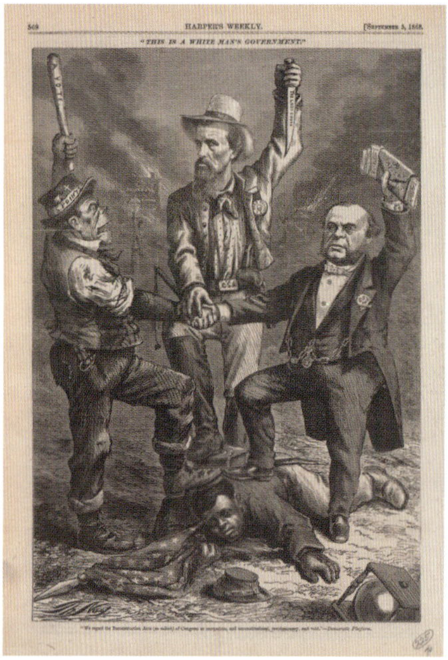

Figure 3.24
In *This is a White Man's Government* (1868), Nast depicts three men stepping on the back of Black soldier who clutches the American flag in one hand and reaches for the ballot box with the other.

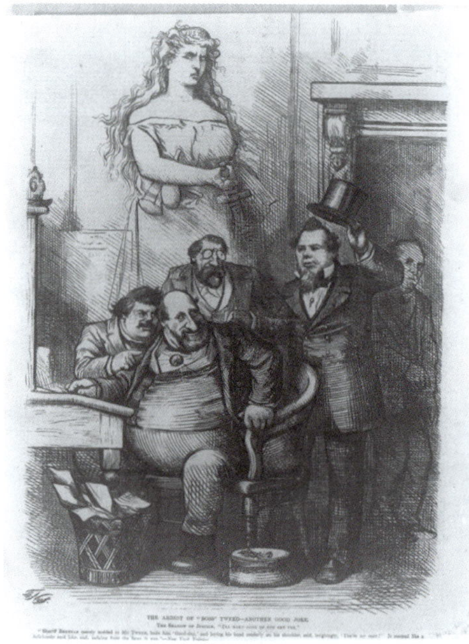

Figure 3.25
Nast became widely known for depicting the corrupt politician Boss Tweed. After Tweed was finally arrested, he escaped jail and fled to Spain, where the Spanish authorities were able to catch him due in part to recognizing his likeness from Thomas Nast's cartoons. (*The Arrest of Boss Tweed*, 1871)

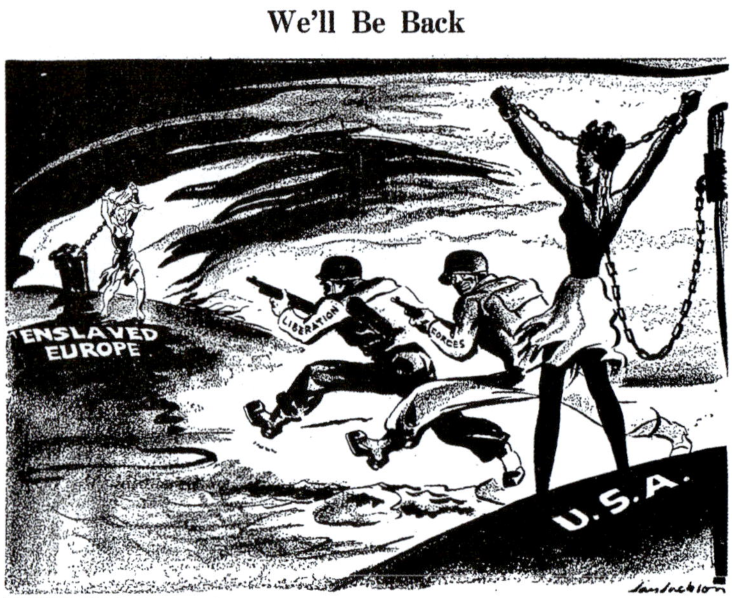

Figure 3.26
Jay Jackson's cartoon *We'll Be Back* from World War II, shows American soldiers rushing to save an enslaved Europe, while leaving Black Americans in the metaphorical chains of Jim Crow and the Ku Klux Klan.

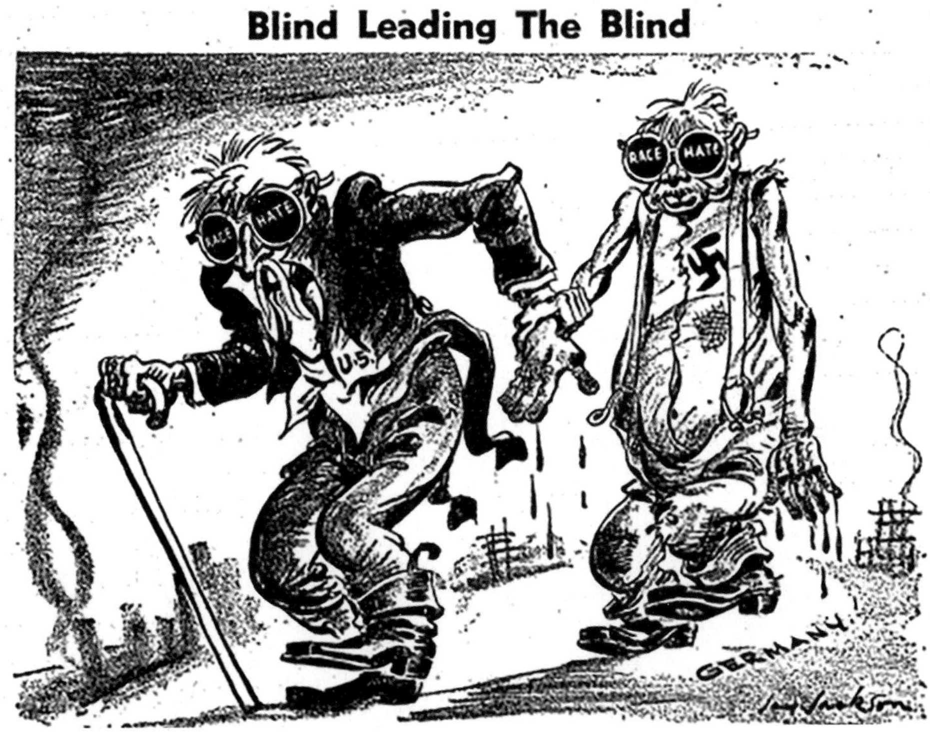

Figure 3.27 Jay Jackson's cartoon *The Blind Leading the Blind* from World War II, shows two figures blinded by their racist hate, the US leading Nazi Germany.

Censorship in Democracies vs. Authoritarian Governments: Violent Censorship, Self-Censorship, and Market Censorship

Censorship is situated at the intersection of propaganda and dissent, and used as a tool of government or media control, and, therefore, we have situated this chapter as a mediator between our chapters on propaganda and dissent. Although we often associate media censorship with authoritarian governments, such as the censorship efforts of China and the Soviet Union introduced in Chapter 2, the amount of censorship enacted in democracies can also be an indicator of democratic decline. The propaganda of China and the Soviet Union was successful because of a deliberate and measured campaign of censorship in both of these countries following World War II that repressed any contradictory or dissenting opinions. Propaganda and censorship both serve to maintain the power of the ruling regime and manipulate public opinion to their advantage using the media.

GLOBAL POLITICS PERSPECTIVE

Media Censorship and Political Systems

Government treatment of the media is one of the defining differences between democracies and authoritarian governments. Earlier in this book, we distinguished between these two political systems in terms of participation and competition, but the treatment of the media can also be very telling. Many researchers will use the relative freedom or restriction of the media as an indicator of the quality of democracy in that country. Laws that partially or severely limit media content, shut down critical media outlets, or curtail truthful coverage of the government signal that a country likely is not a genuine democracy or that a democratic country is experiencing a deterioration in democracy, known as **democratic backsliding**.[85] Media ownership and editorial decision making are also indicators of whether a country is a democracy, or not. When the government itself owns major media outlets and sets the agenda in terms of coverage, this usually limits the range of issues that can be covered; it would be impossible for a country to be a democracy in this case. The nongovernmental organization Freedom House, discussed earlier in this book, has released a Press Freedom Index (PFI) to globally rank and compare countries based on their media freedom and media restrictions.[86] (Figure 3.28) There is definitely a large overlap between democracy and media freedom, based on these rankings. Even so, press freedom has declined globally in most regions of the world, including both democracies and authoritarian countries.[87] As Figure 3.28 shows, media freedom varies even among the 27 countries of the European Union; the media are constrained by the government in Hungary, for example, which has also experienced democratic backsliding.

Post-Soviet Russia offers a clear example of this. After the fall of the Soviet Union, many private and independent media outlets emerged, both in print media and in television, but by the early 2000s, all three major television news channels in Russia, NTV, RTR and Channel 1, were all fully owned and directed by the Russian government; this produced a highly censored media environment. Some private newspapers and cable news channels like Novaya Gazeta and TV Rain continued to exist, but they reached very limited audiences due to their independence, and their journalists often faced harassment, pressure, or worse, after reporting on sensitive topics like national security or government corruption. Multiple Russian journalists, such as Anna Politkovskaya, were murdered in extremely suspicious circumstances. Still, these remaining independent media outlets persisted despite such conditions. Novaya Gazeta editor Dmitri Muratov jointly won the Nobel Peace prize in 2021, along with Maria Ressa of the Filipino media outlet Rappler; the Nobel Prize committee explained that this was to recognize "their efforts to safeguard freedom of expression, which is a precondition for democracy and lasting peace".[88] The full-scale Russian invasion of Ukraine in 2022 led to new and extreme restrictions on those remaining independent media outlets in Russia. The Russian government passed laws restricting coverage, saying that it cannot even be referred to as a "war," but instead as a "special military operation." Laws like these have severely restricted both domestic and foreign media operations in Russia, causing many international outlets to pull their correspondents out of the country. TV Rain and Novaya Gazeta were forced to suspend their operations and move their coverage fully online outside of Russia, after having their media licenses revoked for not complying with the new laws.

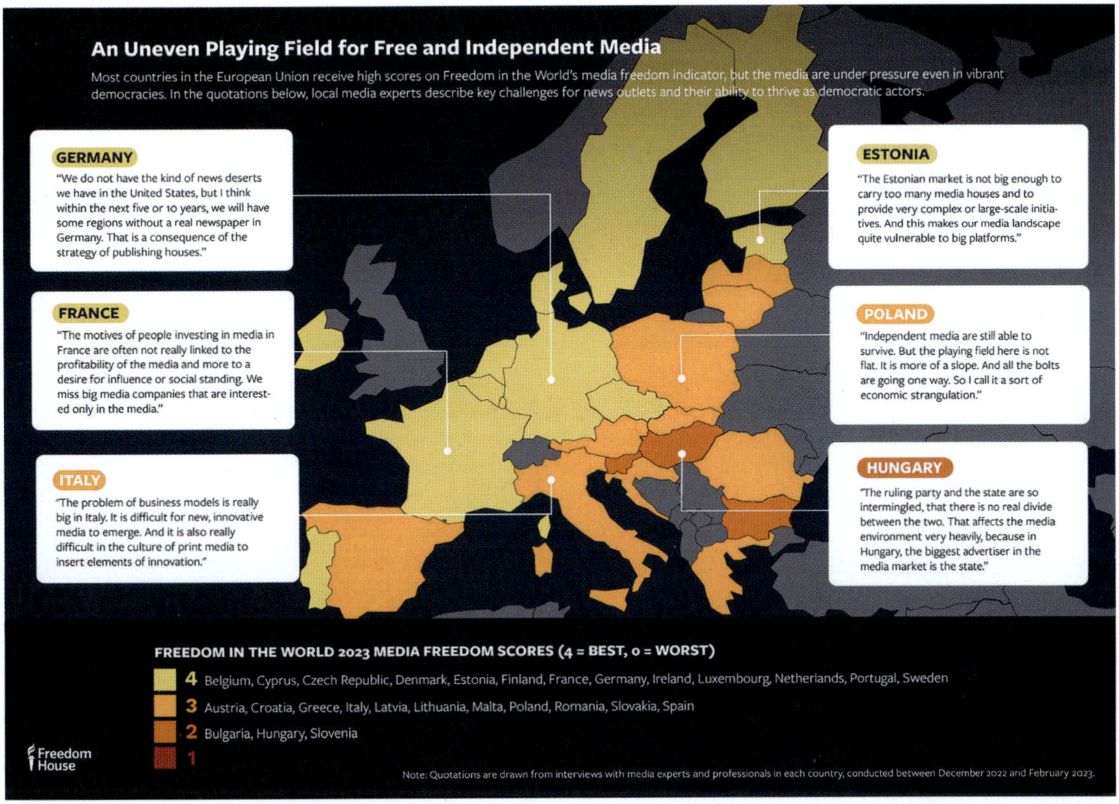

Figure 3.28
This image shows the variation in media independence and freedom across the European Union.
© Freedom House, 2023
(www.freedomhouse.org)

In the most extreme authoritarian governments, however, the *only* media is the government. Following the Korean War, the Democratic People's Republic of Korea (DPRK), or North Korea, became the most censored country in the world. North Korea's censorship laws are based on the same policies of the country's first ruler, Kim Il Sung, who incorporated the Korean Central News Agency (KCNA) in 1946, which continues to be solely responsible for any news coming from North Korea.[89] All televisions and radios broadcast solely censored and regulated North Korean content, and all books and publications are subject to the same censorship. Very few examples of foreign media are allowed into the country, and although the country allows a minimal number of foreign media visitors for certain holidays and events, these visits are fastidiously controlled.[90]

Similar to other dictatorships discussed earlier in this book, North Korea developed its cult of personality around its leader, Kim Il Sung, and, subsequently, around his descendants Kim Jong Il and Kim Jong Un. Due to the influence of China and the Soviet Union on the country, North Korean propaganda adopted a similar style of Socialist Realism. Because of the lack of foreign influence in the country, North Korea continues to create propaganda in this style and has been called "the last vestige of socialist realism."[91] (Figure 3.29) However, North Korean propaganda also incorporates **chosonhwa**, a type of Asian ink painting on rice paper, which differentiates itself from other examples of Socialist Realism. Georgetown professor B.G. Muhn states, "DPRK art attempts to show the reality by expressing the subtlety of a person's inner emotion."[92] The North Korean government operates the Mansudae Art Studio in Pyongyang, one of the largest art studios in the world. It is the only studio allowed to create images of the Kim family. The studio also produces other forms of propaganda, even creating beer steins and greeting cards that feature patriotic imagery. The studio has also been employed outside of the country, including projects in Senegal and Germany, because of the high level of craftsmanship and low prices.

In the 1990s, an economic collapse and subsequent famine in North Korea began forcing people into illegal trade to acquire food. However, not just food crossed the border with China, but also media and technology such as sim cards, USB drives, and flyers began leaking through. As more defectors and refugees flee North Korea, the outside world can learn more about the extent of the strict censorship in the country. Organizations such as the North Korean People's Liberation Front in Seoul, South Korea, attempt to subvert censorship through information balloon drops and information smuggling. Song Byeok is an artist who was born in North Korea and, at age 24, was chosen to become an official propaganda artist.[93] When the famine in North Korea resulted in the deaths of his father, mother, and sister, Byeok became determined to escape the country.[94] Byeok was tortured for his attempts to enter China to find food, but finally escaped to South Korea in 2002.[95] Now he creates artworks that work towards the ideals of peace and freedom, including works that mock Kim Jong Un's regime and show the plight of the North Korean people.[96] In 2018, he was awarded the Global Artist Award for his work about the human rights crisis in North Korea.[97]

So far in this book, we have focused on government censorship and media restrictions in authoritarian countries. Yet, censorship and media restrictions exist in democracies as well. Within the United States, even the First Amendment does not offer a blanket protection for media freedom; media outlets can face legal challenges for defamation and libel if their media content damages the reputation of a person or entity. In 2023, the American media outlet Fox News settled a defamation lawsuit with Dominion Voting Systems for $787.5 million after some of their anchors made false claims about Dominion-made voting machines used in the 2020 Presidential elections. Therefore, media activities in democracies are typically shaped by government regulations and they are affected by the media ownership environment.[98] Media censorship in democracies can take shape in different ways, from journalists choosing to refrain from covering controversial or dangerous topics due to safety concerns, as has been the case in Mexico and coverage of drug trafficking, to the implementation of laws and regulations that may limit media coverage on negative or controversial topics. Commercial media coverage can also provoke censorship and government restrictions if the priorities of the media clash with those of elected leaders. In Latin America, for example, many media outlets have historically been owned by conservative-leaning conglomerates that typically criticize the policies of left-leaning politicians; in response to this, left-leaning presidents in some of these countries, such as in Ecuador, have used confrontational language towards the media and have pushed for greater media regulations and restrictions.[99]

Satirical media typically has greater legal protections in democracies, but it can still face outcry by offended groups. In 2006, the French magazine *Charlie Hebdo* (*Charlie Weekly*) republished a series of cartoons depicting the Muslim prophet Muhammed which had originally run in a Danish publication called *Jyllands-Posten*. Subsequently,

Islamic organizations in France unsuccessfully sued the magazine over French hate speech laws, since Muhammed's depiction is forbidden in most types of Islam. *Charlie Hebdo* has a reputation of depicting anti-religious, left-wing cartoons, and has often been criticized for printing offensive content. In 2011, the newspaper again printed a cartoon of Muhammed on its cover, mocking Sharia law by changing the title of the issue to *Charia Hebdo*, and in 2012 ran another series of Muhammed cartoons. As a result of the cartoons, the director of *Charlie Hebdo*, Stéphane "Charb" Charbonnier, along with three Danish journalists and cartoonists, were added to Al-Qaeda's most-wanted list. While many planned attacks on *Jyllands-Posten* were thwarted, on January 7th, 2015, two terrorists stormed the offices of *Charlie Hebdo* and murdered Charb, his bodyguard, seven of his colleagues, and three other people in the building.

Although the *Charlie Hebdo* attack was certainly the most widely known attack based on political cartoons, there are many other instances of cartoonists facing persecution and violence, especially in authoritarian settings. In 1987, Palestinian cartoonist Naji Al-Ali, who at the time was one of the best-known cartoonists in the Arab world, was assassinated. Al-Ali created cartoons criticizing leaders on both sides of the Israeli-Palestinian conflict, and was best known for creating Handala, a cartoon of a 10-year-old boy with his hands clasped behind his back. Since 1973, Handala has always been depicted facing backwards, a symbol for how the world had turned on the Palestinians after they were forced from Palestine. The name Handala came from the Arabic name for a bitter-tasting fruit symbolizing the embittered Palestinian people. Al-Ali's murder remains unsolved.[100][101] In 2013, Syrian cartoonist Akram Raslan died in custody, after being abducted by military officers at the offices of the newspaper *Al-Fida'a,* for drawing cartoons criticizing the government of Bashar Al-Assad.[102] In 2011, Ali Ferzat, another Syrian cartoonist critical of the Assad government, was beaten and had his hands broken. After Ferzat recovered, he (satisfyingly) drew a self-portrait with his middle finger raised, and went on to be named one of *Time* magazine's most influential people of 2012.[103] In 2020, Bangladeshi cartoonist Ahmed Kabir Kishore, who criticized the government and its response to the COVID-19 pandemic, was held for ten months in government detention and tortured.[104] Upon release, Kishore had to undergo numerous surgeries for his injuries. Numerous other cartoonists have faced threats, lawsuits, abductions, and imprisonment over their work. Due to this persecution of political cartoonists, numerous agencies have been established to celebrate and reward cartoonists who challenge authority by practicing free speech, including *Cartoonists Rights Network International, Cartooning for Peace,* and the *Freedom Cartoonists Foundation* (formerly the *Swiss Foundation Cartooning for Peace*).

However, as outlined in the book *Red Lines: Political Cartoons and the Struggle Against Censorship,* violent censorship by authoritarian countries is not the only type of censorship that affects which political cartoons are propagated by the media. Fear of violent retribution has caused many political illustrators to practice a less commonly recognized type of censorship: **self-censorship**. Self-censorship can be enacted either by an author or an editor of a publication. When self-censorship occurs, it is a sign that the censoring party, often a powerful ruler, has truly enacted control over a populace by taking control of the population's ideology. Self-censorship also makes the job of a censoring party easier, because people are willing to enact censorship themselves to avoid reprisal. Self-censorship also helps make a censor immune to criticism, because their role in the censorship has been masked. As Hannah Arendt writes in her book *On Violence*, "power needs legitimacy," and violent retaliations can undermine that legitimacy. While we might associate this ideology shift with authoritarian rulers such as Vladimir Putin and Xi Jinping, this shift can also affect democracies in more subtle ways. In his talk for the School of Visual Arts' The Masters Series, Steve Brodner recalls an illustration that was rejected by *The New Yorker* about soldiers arriving in Iraq to begin combat during the 2003 American invasion of Iraq. Many more controversial ideas were rejected, and although the final sketch for the idea was approved, of picturing soldiers looking at a smoking landscape in disbelief, the final image was not. Brodner says,

> "It was a time of censorship – self-censorship – where anyone who opposed the war was liable to be punished. If you remember Phil Donahue and the well-known Dixie Chicks... were all punished for speaking out. It was only until later you could tell the truth, but during this period of 2003 or so, even just showing that the soldiers are arriving with a doubt in their mind, looking up at burning oil wells, and remnants of cities and bombings, was too much. You could not say in imagery what you could say in text."[105]

Ideological shifts that occur partially through self-censorship can lead to **market censorship**. In market censorship, a certain type of communication becomes more financially beneficial than another, and publications fail to publish opposing viewpoints that hurt their earnings. For-profit media companies may set the tone of their coverage based on what may be profitable and what may be perceived as "good for business." This can result in media coverage that favors controversy, but also the maintenance of the status quo in a business sense; radical or unpredictable change may be implicitly or explicitly censored or negatively covered as a result. Market censorship commonly occurs in capitalist democracies, and exposes the power that media moguls have in controlling a narrative. Rob Rogers created political cartoons for the *Pittsburgh Post-Gazette* for 25 years until he was fired in 2018 for being too critical of Donald Trump. The paper's publisher, John Robinson Block, was later documented intimidating and threatening the jobs of his employees if they engaged in union activity.[106]

Another example of the results of market censorship occurred in 2023, when protestors fought against a police training facility, dubbed "Cop City," to be built in a forest outside of Atlanta, Georgia, and demanded an investigation into the police killing of protestor Manuel "Tortuguita" Terán. While the protestors were fighting for popular causes such as environmentalism and against police killings, local media printed stories that elevated the violence of protests, conducting a narrative that the protestors were violent, out-of-town radicals. Many national news sources mimicked the ideology of the local news, downplaying the concerns of local residents regarding the police facility and elevating the role of violent protests. This occurred in part because it was financially beneficial for the media to print a narrative that supported the police force and the training facility. The facility was primarily funded by the Atlanta Police Foundation, which accepted money from many major private business donors and private equity firms in the area, including Cox Enterprises, which owns the local Atlanta paper, the *Atlanta Journal Constitution*. While the paper's coverage showed bias, international media coverage of the police facility was more balanced and some political cartoonists were able to freely address the issue. In this case, many stake-holders in the local market, such as advertisers, investors, distributors, and customers, accepted this ideology and influenced the market censorship of the issue.[107] Much of the illustration surrounding the issue of Cop City was limited to outsider and folk art, or independent cartoonists publishing on social media, such as the anonymous 9mmballpoint. (Figures 3.30 and 3.31) While market censorship and self-censorship are not as morally egregious as torture, they are nevertheless forms of censorship decoders of images need to be aware of.

A populace's ideology can often affect the market choices made by a publication. One example of this comes from the famed German artist Käthe Kollwitz. Kollwitz was born in 1867 in the former kingdom of Prussia to a socially radical father who was a committed Social Democrat. Kollwitz' upbringing strongly influenced the work she would later create advocating for peace and unveiling the horrors of poverty and war. Unable to gain entrance into all-male art academies, Kollwitz studied at the Union of Women Artists, before meeting her husband, Karl, a doctor who worked with economically downtrodden patients.[108] These patients often became the subjects of Kollwitz' work and reinforced her social justice views. Kollwitz contributed illustrations to the German magazine AIZ, the *Arbeiter-Illustrierte-Zeitung*, and also created her own posters. One image Kollwitz created in 1931 of workers rallying together, shown here, was rejected by the pro-communist and anti-fascist AIZ. (Figure 3.32) Instead, they printed her initial, softer version, featuring a child. (Figure 3.33) They also printed a Karl Marx quote with the piece, "We have a world to win," instead of Kollwitz' preferred quote, "We are marching with the new times." Kollwitz embraced the ideals of communism but is quoted as saying in 1920, "I think that the world has seen enough killing, lies, corruption, distortion, in short everything diabolical. The communist empire built on all this cannot be the work of God."[109]

Market censorship has long held sway over the "free" democratic press. *Time* magazine was co-founded by Henry Luce in 1923, and soon became one of the most popular publications in the nation. Luce transformed mass communication in the 20th century, also founding *Life* and *Fortune* magazines. Luce was a strongly opinionated and influential member of the Republican party, devoted businessman and capitalist, and anti-communist. Luce, who remained editor-in-chief of *Time,* wanted the magazine to educate poorly informed Americans about world events, including what their opinion should be about them.[110] *Time* thrived in part because of its devotion to illustration, especially their impressive array of cover portraits telling the stories of the world through people, which grabbed attention and focused the reader's attention to particular issues. American artist Bernard Safran was one of *Time* magazine's most popular cover artists who painted over 73 *Time* covers during the span of his career.[111] In August 1960, Safran was commissioned by *Time* magazine to paint a portrait of the newly independent Democratic Republic of Congo (DRC)'s Prime Minister, Patrice Lumumba. (Figure 3.34)

Lumumba was born in Congo while it was under oppressive Belgian colonial rule of Congo, and founded the first nationwide political party in Congo, the Congolese National

Movement, thus becoming a figurehead for anti-imperialism and the Pan-African movement. Immediately after the country declared its independence in June 1960, the Belgian government supported a secessionist rebellion led by a Congolese rival to Lumumba, Moise Tshombe, in the mineral rich state of Katanga. The United States also had an interest in controlling this part of the country, in part because they had used uranium from this region to create the atomic bombs dropped in Japan. When United Nations forces, including the United States and France, refused to help Lumumba quell the rebellion, Lumumba turned to the United States' Cold War enemy, the Soviet Union, for support. After only three short months in office, the DRC's pro-Western president ousted and jailed Prime Minister Lumumba. Safran's commission from *Time* occurred during this tenuous period between Lumumba's election and his ouster, during which the United States was carefully negotiating their relationship with the UN, Belgium, and the Democratic Republic of the Congo. The article which accompanied Safran's portrait reported on the rebellion within the DRC, and on Lumumba's request that the UN send in troops to restore peace and order within the nation. The portrait never ran. Instead, Luce, in typical fashion, inserted his take on foreign policy by replacing the cover with a photograph of UN Secretary Dag Hammerskjöld, superimposed over Safran's background. According to Safran's daughter Elizabeth Malyon, Luce was "often contacted by the US government, and the President personally, to manage images both in print and cover art."[112] Here, governmental interests led to censorship, even within a democracy, and Luce also protected his market interests. As for Lumumba, his story ended tragically. A year after he was deposed, he was executed by the secessionists in collaboration with the Belgium government. Malcolm X called Lumumba, "the greatest black man who ever walked the African continent."[113]

Importantly, when we think of art history and illustration history as a whole, market censorship has long existed. The history of art has favored the privileged, those who have the financial means to commission art and convey their messages. We can see a clear example of this with Napoleon's propaganda machine as described in Chapter 2. Those without the financial means to afford to create and perpetuate their visual messages, or those whose messages have not been profitable or popular to reproduce through the media, have had their voices silenced. With the rise of the internet and social media, a larger range of voices have the opportunity to voice their opinions and share their illustrations unedited by traditional censorship and market censorship. This is why equitable internet access remains an important democratic goal. In summary, the media landscape is greatly shaped by both government and private factors, which means that media censorship is possible in all political systems.

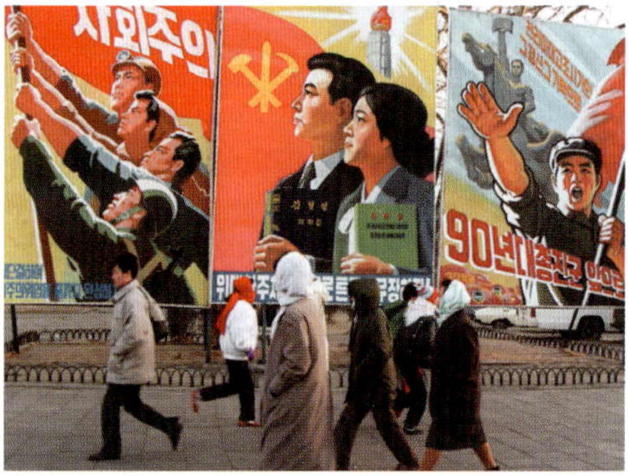

Figure 3.29
Due to the influence of China and the Soviet Union on the country, North Korean propaganda adopted a similar style of Socialist Realism.

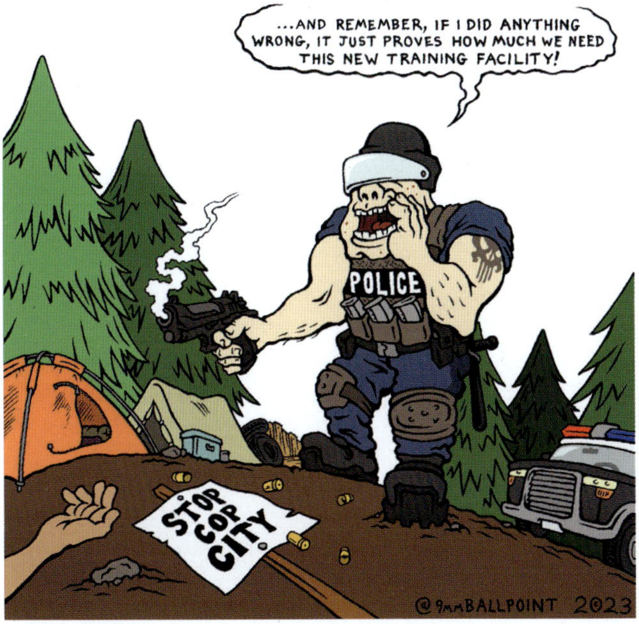

Figure 3.30
Remedial Killology (2023)
© @99mmBallpoint

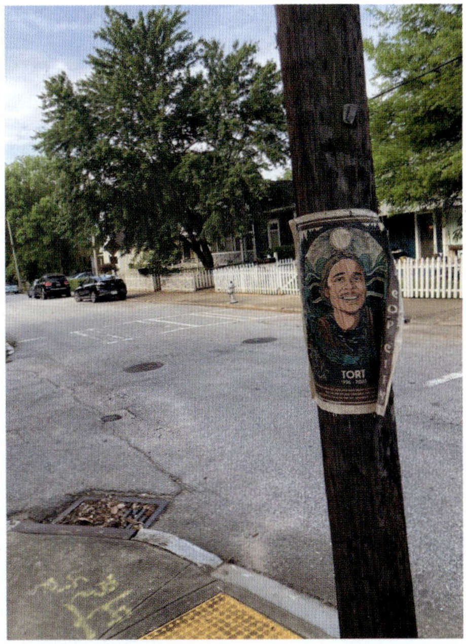

Figure 3.31
Following the police killing of Manuel "Tortuguita" Terán, many artists from Atlanta and around the world created art and illustration to honor him and protest the building of Cop City.
Photo © Catherine A. Moore, 2023

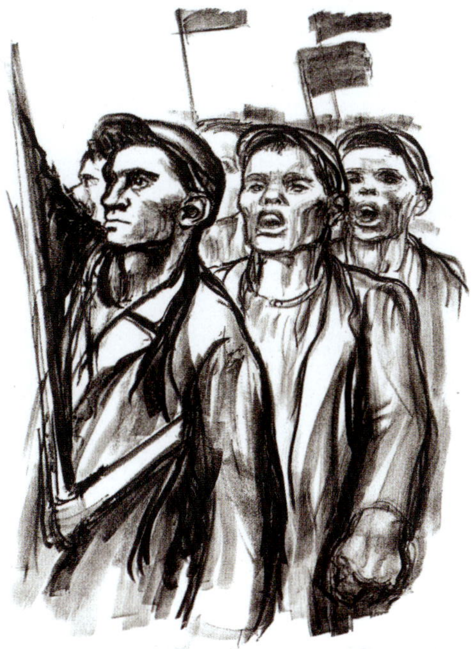

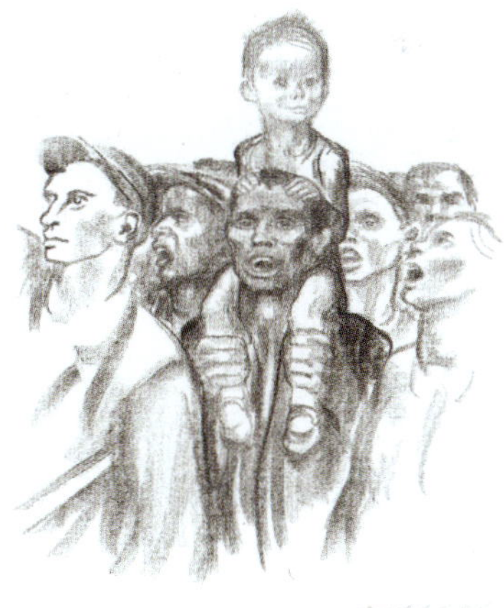

Figure 3.32 & 3.33
In 1931, Käthe Kollwitz created an illustration of workers rallying together, which was rejected by the pro-communist and anti-fascist AIZ. Instead, they printed her initial, softer version, featuring a child.

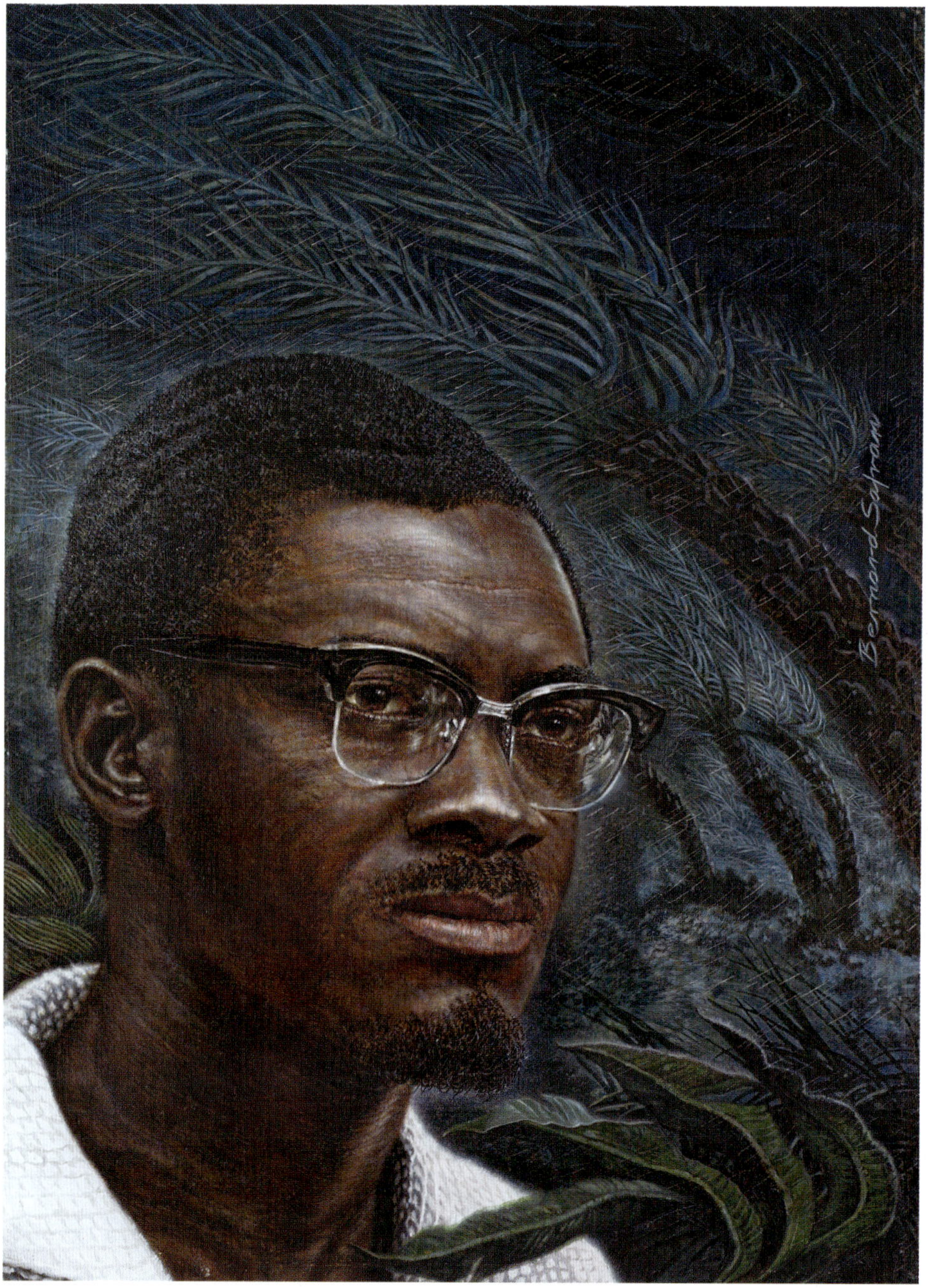

Figure 3.34

Bernard Safran's 1960 cover portrait for *TIME* of Democratic Republic of Congo (DRC)'s Prime Minister, Patrice Lumumba, was never printed. Instead, it was replaced with a photograph of UN Secretary Dag Hammerskjöld, superimposed over Safran's background.

Contemporary Editorial Illustration

Political illustration is not limited in the media to reportage illustration and political cartoons, but thrives today with visual commentary by means of editorial illustration. One of the US's most prominent daily papers, *The New York Times*, no longer prints political cartoons, but continues to serve more regulated and art-directed messages through editorial illustrations with political themes. In addition, print magazines such as *Time*, *Der Spiegel*, and *The New Yorker* continue to thrive because of the power of strong editorial illustrations as cover design. Editorial illustrations differ from political cartoons in a number of ways. Firstly, they tend to be more intentionally designed through the work of art directors and editors, instead of solely being the authorship of one cartoonist. Secondly, editorial illustrations tend to accompany an article, instead of existing independently of outside text. However, some editorial illustrations, especially those constructed as illustrative infographics or sequential art, can exist as a stand-alone work. Illustrators such as Steve Brodner also propose their own stand-alone editorial illustrations. Sometimes illustrators such as Edel Rodriguez create personal or portfolio work that later on get licensed for editorial contexts. These personal projects can also show art directors the types of work or projects an illustrator would like to take on. (Figure 3.35) Finally, the style of editorial

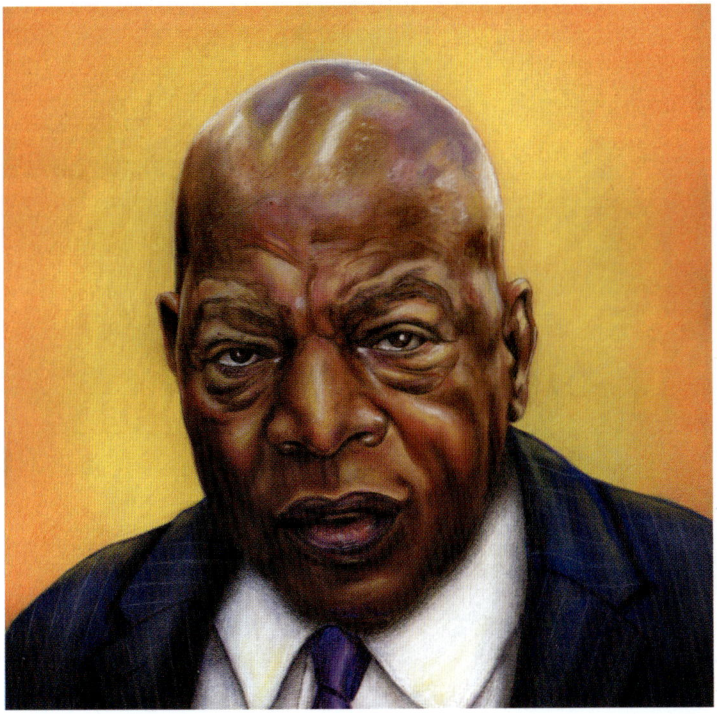

Figure 3.35
Catherine A. Moore's illustration of Congressman John Lewis was initially created as a personal portfolio piece, but was later licensed by *The Washington Post* for publication.

illustrations tends to be more fully developed, using materials, techniques, and technology beyond simple line drawings. However, it is important to note that the distinctions between political cartooning and editorial illustration are not black and white, but significantly overlap. Newspapers and other publications have recently embraced how new technology can be used to create marketable and eye-catching illustrations, including photo-illustration, digital collage, three-dimensional illustration, and animation. Contemporary illustrators have pushed new horizons of style and technique and use them to deliver strong and clear visual messages.

One illustrator who explores digital collage in new ways is American illustrator Doug Chayka, who was influenced by the Dada montage artists including Kurt Schwitters, John Heartfield, and Hannah Hoch. Chayka's illustration leads with an idea, and his mastery of a variety of techniques including painting, drawing, lettering, and seamless digital collage allows him to execute a variety of illustrations while maintaining stylistic consistency. Chayka's strong use of visual metaphor is key to expressing his ideas clearly. For his illustration *Head On* for *Politico Europe,* Chayka uses "founding fathers" of the US and China (Benjamin Franklin and Mao Zedong, respectively), as metaphors for the countries. (Figure 3.36) Chayka plays with the media by crumpling the paper when the two heads smash into each other, and abstracts the European Union flag into exploding shapes in the background (as if the leaders are "seeing stars"). The illustration accompanied an article entitled "Missing in Action: Europe's China Plan," and intended to show how European nations were caught between the US and China. In *America 2050* for the *New Republic,* Chayka shows a fractured United States, again using the element of **texture** inherent in collage to evoke broken glass, while also using color metaphors of blue and red to indicate the left and right fracturing. (Figure 3.37) In his illustration *Irish Unity* for *Politico Europe*, Chayka shows the Irish and the North Irish flags stitched together by green thread, symbolizing how the controversial Sinn Féin party has gained political power in both countries and provides a way forward for uniting them. (Figure 3.38)

INTERVIEW

Doug Chayka

Something that stands out to me about your work is its unique style. Can you tell me about how your style and technique influence the messaging in your work, and about any influences on your style? How much of your final work is traditional vs. digital?
I think modern conceptual illustration owes a huge debt to Dada and collage movements. John Heartfield's political work is a big influence, but as the pioneer of photomontage his influence is just part of the visual fabric today. I think collage works so well for editorial because you can use diverse material and diverse reference points in terms of source material, so it creates this tension in the art where seemingly conflicting elements are

forced into a dialogue. And, in my mind, editorial is very much about conflict and exposing the pressure points related to a given issue. But in a modern sense I see collage not just as a 2D cut and paste thing, it's more about creating narrative by putting any element against another, not just in a DIY kind of way but also in a more 3D/photographic space. In my work I use a combination of tactile elements, such as paper cut or drawing or assemblage and usually combine it with some kind of photography– either my own or via a stock source. The final art is completely digital and there is no physical "original" other than the props left over from the process.

A strong concept seems to drive your work, and you are able to adjust and fit your style to best fit the idea. Can you describe the process of deciding which aesthetic to use for each visual problem you're solving?

Yes the idea is everything for me when approaching an assignment and what I love about this work is being able to react to a specific topic and be open about how the art might be executed. When I read the text I'm usually looking for opportunities to visually manipulate some kind of object or situation. I think over time the consistency in the work just becomes apparent. When I'm working I try not to think about something like "is this me," it's more about fully engaging with the issue and trying to understand what's at stake.

How do you identify and develop the metaphors and symbols you use in your work? How do you make sure that the symbolism is successfully communicated to your audience?

I look for keywords or sentences that might encapsulate a big part of the text, but there needs to be zero space between the quality of the visual and the metaphor. We need to see the elements and understand immediately what they represent in the context of the image. There's usually a combination of metaphors, where A+B+C= something unexpected. So I find simple images where the visual is as condensed as possible helps make the message clear. I try to be as objective as possible about how the ideas communicate and of course having a great art director involved is also a big part of the process. Ultimately the editors and art directors will decide if it communicates or not. Over time I've really come to appreciate that process. Fairly often though a sketch will get chosen with no edits and I'm trusted to do what I think works best. Still, there are checks along the way to make sure the image works, and that's necessary.

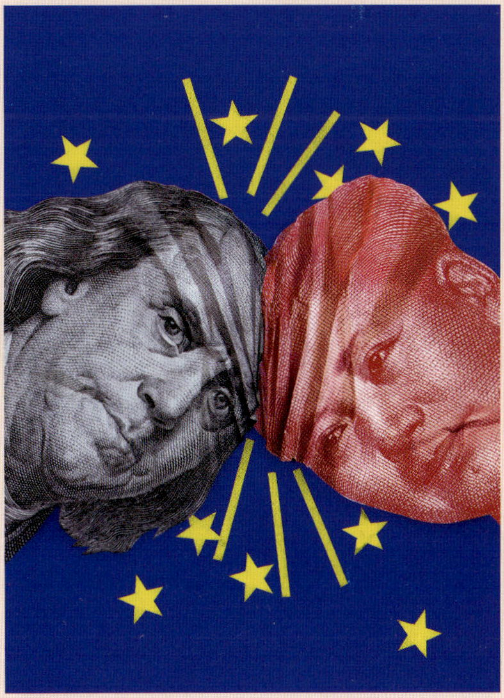

Figure 3.36
Head On
© Doug Chayka, 2021

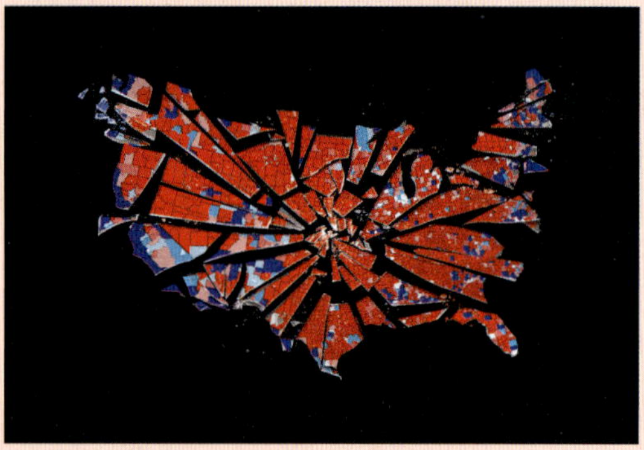

Figure 3.37
America 2050
© Doug Chayka, 2022

Much of your work focuses on political themes in an editorial context. How did you come to focus on this type of illustration and this sector of the illustration industry?
It happened gradually. As I experimented more, and later travelled and studied abroad with a focus on painting and printmaking, I started to play with mixed media and applied that to assignments and self-directed work. I showed that work around and had an early break working on a lot of projects for *The Nation*. I was assigned a big range of topics and they were very open to different aesthetics. I was inspired by that work and pursued it with other outlets. It's the diversity of subjects that keeps me focused on this sector and feeling like it has purpose. I think political art can be anything that shows how we relate to everyday life, whether it's some social or personal issue, or related to technology or culture or entertainment. It's a huge field and more than just the horse race of elections or government officials.

In a 2016 AI-AP, you stated the election of Trump were really good for the illustration industry and picture making and "less good for anything else." I think of that in relation to the media's relationship to Trump and how, especially early on, there was a symbiotic relationship between them. What do you think an illustrator's role is in the media's focus on certain political topics or figures? What responsibility do illustrators have to approaching certain topics or an editor's chosen stance on a topic? Have you ever turned down a job because it did not productively add to the political discourse on a topic?
We're still in this media crisis moment. Yes, there was/is this symbiotic relationship between Trump and the media, but it's cynical to think that covering Trump is purely profit driven. It's more complicated and it's also a crisis of journalism when it's perceived that covering events and discussing them is just fanning the flames. As I mentioned before, there's an institutional process at work in these media outlets and I try to trust that. In my experience I've never had a project where I felt I was illustrating some editor's "take" or stance on the issue. The task of the art has always been, in my approach, exposing the tensions within a given problem. One difficulty now is that a hyper-polarized audience can't agree on what the "problems" are and I think there's maybe less appetite for discussion. But I think

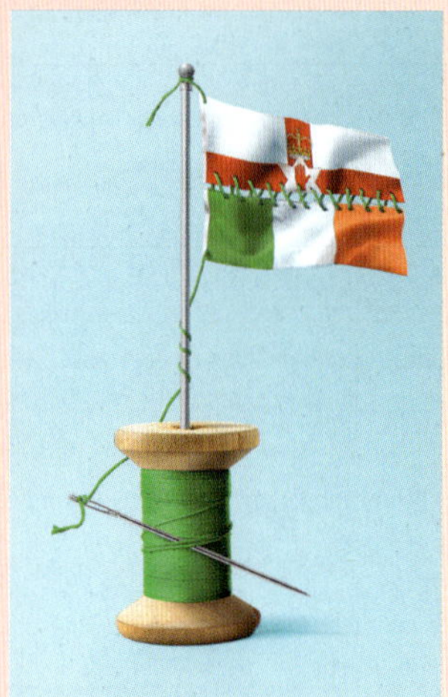

Figure 3.38
Irish Unity
© Doug Chayka, 2022

art needs to push our buttons, not to inflame but with the intention of sorting through the noise and communication something coherent and on-point.

You incorporate animation into many of your illustrations and embraced animated illustration early on. How do you think animation is contributing to change in the illustration industry and what can it contribute to a message that static illustration cannot?

I like to use motion when it used as a loop, where there's not a beginning and end and we get the sense of some ongoing problem. Again, it's about tension, so I think something subtle works best. I first started experimenting with motion when I was hired to illustrate a weekly technology column for the *New York Times*, and so exploring a digital-animated aesthetic seemed to create a more connection between the art and the text.

Another illustrator who has broken boundaries in style through technology is digital illustrator Miriam Martincic. Martincic studied as a stone carver and holds an MFA in the field, and this experience influenced the three-dimensionality of her work, which is reminiscent of the sculpture of Fernando Botero. Martincic devotes a lot of thought to her process of sketches, iterations on an idea, and the communication between her and an art director. The composition, metaphor, and use of design in her work result in striking and unique visual solutions. In her illustration *Afghan Women Denied Education* for *Al Majalla*, Martincic creates a conceptual connection between chalkboards in a classroom and the idea that Afghan women are being erased from schools. (Figure 3.39) A dark Taliban figure is in the foreground and holds the eraser, but because of the dark values on the figure, it becomes a secondary focal point after the strong contrast and gaze of the faces on the board captures our attention. For her portfolio piece *Box*, which won a gold medal at the Society of Illustrators NY, Martincic uses compressed space to heighten the feelings of confinement and misery experienced by children being held on the US-Mexico border. (Figure 3.40)

INTERVIEW

Miriam Martincic

Something striking about your work is the three-dimensionality of your shapes and figures. It reminds me of Fernando Botero. Your background as a stone sculptor clearly shows its influence. Could you describe your process in translating the forms and textures from sculpture skills to two-dimensional digital illustrations?

Botero's approach to bodies is significant as a counter to the predominance of thin culture in visual representation. I choose to draw thicker bodies because the world has enough images of skinny people.

The medium of my work is experience—experience stone carving, experience drawing in pencil and charcoal, experience living in a female body, experience living in a culture filled with images that suggest that my appearance is my main value. I filter this experience though memory and digital drawing.

Digital drawing is interesting because it can look like anything. Many of Gérard DuBois' digital illustrations look like oil paintings because he spent years working with oils. His intention is grounded in experience; he *thinks* in the medium of oil.

15 years of stone carving has given me a strong understanding of volume. I *think* with volume. Working as a sculptor has given me a library of volume that allows me to work from memory. My aim is to draw in a way that feels personal. My memory is imperfect. This is not a bug, but a feature. No one else in the world will remember or misremember things the same way I do.

Do you still do stone sculpting?

I no longer carve stone, but I rely on my understanding of volume every time I draw. I also rely on my understanding of light, learned from setting up gallery shows. When I exhibited my sculpture, I noticed that poor lighting flattened volume and good lighting heightened volume. It works the same in a drawing. Light informs volume.

Yet your lighting is so consistent, like a 3D program with a set light source.

My lighting isn't *actually* consistent, it's just consistent *enough*. In addition to informing volume, I make lighting choices for design reasons. I'm happy to sacrifice lighting consistency in favor of activating space and directing the eye with light and shadow. The imperfection of drawing from memory affords me creative license in lighting design. Compositional balance creates the illusion of a consistent light source.

Can you speak to the role that composition and framing plays to communicating an idea? How do you create a visual emphasis so that the idea you want to communicate is highlighted?

I like to say things loud and clear. Value contrast and clear silhouette are the visual equivalent of loudness. Emphasis comes from a combination of scale, value contrast, and control of density. I like to balance my pictures, to make sure that no one area feels too congested or too open. Playing with these beginner design tools never gets old. If a picture is a car, visual balance is the thing that makes the car go.

Getting the right concept seems to happen flawlessly in your illustrations, but you have a sketch process that leads to each successful visual idea. Could you describe your ideation and sketch process? How does the role of metaphor come into play in your illustrations? Do you lead with a verbal or visual idea when you begin an illustration?

My basic process is wordlists/doodles, thumbnails, value sketches, black and white, color studies, and final art. I bounce back and forth between visual and verbal ideation and am deeply guided by my feelings. What words or images *feel* most important or have creative energy? Sometimes I write a word, make a doodle of that word, and it's the doodle—the image—that has power. Sometimes I make a thumbnail sketch and it's the act of putting that image into writing—the words—that resonate. A good solution can range from symbolic, to metaphorical, to literal, to narrative. In ideation I try anything, pay attention to when I feel a spark, and move from spark to spark. Christoph Niemann talks about process as a series of timid choices, the end of which feels inevitable. I think that's perfect. I rely on process, not eureka moments.

Could you describe the process of communication between yourself and the art director? Do you ever have ideas you like edited or shut down?
The process is simple but not easy: work your butt off to provide good sketch options, be responsive to feedback, and follow through on what you promised in your sketches. Providing good options is the key to approval, a form of creative fitness, and a point of pride. It's my job to make options; it's the AD's job to define communication needs and to choose. Conflict in a work relationship is often the result of two people trying to do the same job.

I don't care if an AD picks my "favorite" sketch because I *only* give options for things I want to make and that solve the problem. I love it when an AD picks my least favorite option and I realize, after completing the final, that they were right!

I have ideas edited and rejected all the time. It doesn't feel personal. We're all professionals, we all care about our work, we're all doing our best. Sharing these larger goals feels more important than agreeing on every detail.

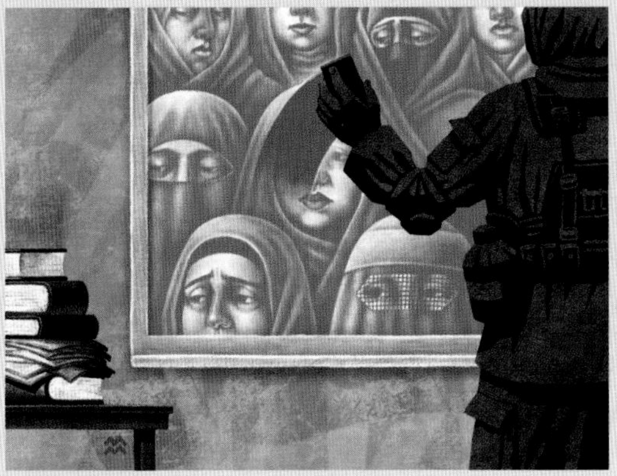

Figure 3.39
Afghan Women Denied Education
© Miriam Martincic, 2023

Political illustration reemerges periodically throughout your canon of work. What role does creating illustration about political subjects and causes have in your career?
My values drive my choices in *all* my work, whether a project is explicitly political or not. An assignment doesn't have to be about race for me to aim for diversity. An assignment doesn't have to be about fat-shaming for me to celebrate larger bodies. An assignment doesn't have to be about patriarchy for me draw women as primary actors. Every illustrator I admire integrates their values and work in some way—from embracing their heritage to giving voice to LGBTQIA experience. Political art happens organically when an artist has clarity about their values and the courage to be authentic.

Can you talk about your art influences?
I love the work of UK wood engraver and stone carver, Harry Brockway. His command of volume is so immediate in his wood engravings. His work is informed, but never slavish and he beautifully balances representation, mark making, and design. I also admire Armando Veve and Marc Burckhardt for their distinct personal voices. Historically, I have an affinity for the Mexican muralists, Diego Rivera specifically. As mentioned earlier, Fernando Botero is on my list. My influences are not people I try to copy, but artists who help me recognize what matters to me, with whom I feel kinship and shared creative DNA.

I know you're an educator as well as an illustrator. What advice would you give to students who want to pursue political and editorial illustration?
Being an illustrator takes tremendous love and dedication. You have to ask, "What am I willing to give up to do this?" If you love illustration, it will

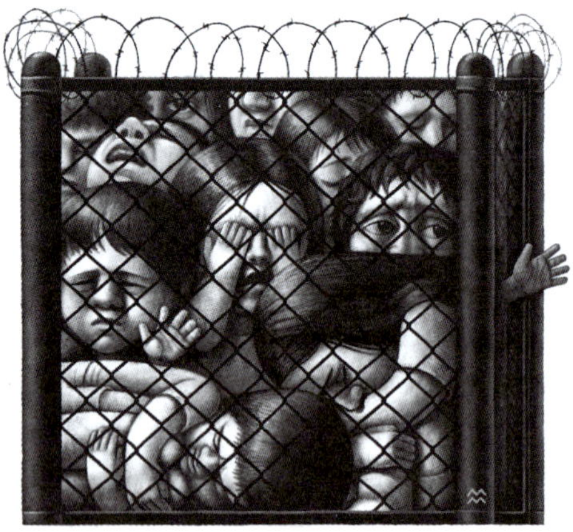

Figure 3.40
Box

feel worth it. If illustration is your idea of a good time, you will find a way to survive the rejection and the not-good-times. If illustration is a good fit, you will find community with others who love to make pictures as much as you do.

You never know how your past experiences—especially your failures—will come together in the future, so don't censor yourself. When I quit making sculpture because I couldn't make a living, I felt like a failure. I would never have guessed that stone carving would later define me as an illustrator. I applied for over 200 teaching jobs as a fine artist and didn't get one. Because I failed at getting a teaching job, I became a graphic designer. Graphic design sustained and grounded me. Years later, graphic design led to me be an illustrator, lead me back to teaching, and shapes my illustration process today. After I became an illustrator, I learned that fine art taught me how to have a voice.

Fail as often as possible. If there's something you want to do—do it. The sum of your experiences will inform you and shape your heart in ways you cannot imagine. Your heart matters; it is the compass that guides your choices. Illustration is the art of making choices. Life is the art of making choices. Take good care of your heart.

Armando Veve believes that an illustrator's style is the first step in how they communicate the metaphors in their work. Veve works in graphite and adds layers with watercolor, gouache, and colored pencil, evoking the layers of meaning in his highly conceptual works. Reminiscent of scientific illustrations, with a high level of realism and detail, Veve uses surrealism to expand on the conceptual possibilities of an issue, looking at both the big picture and the microscopic details. In 10 Theses on Russia for Global Brief in 2017, Veve uses the metaphor of the Russian bear performing a highly intricate balancing act. (Figure 3.41) Veve incorporates Russian symbolism while indicating the complexity and precarity of the government, which illustrates the points of the article to show the country was balancing between extremes. In Operation Valkyrie for VICE, Veve explores the historical politics of drug use in the Third Reich, unmasking Hitler as a metaphor to show the previously untold story of madness. (Figure 3.42) In A Disconnected World for The New Republic, Veve's scientific illustration metaphors shine, as he creates separate glass vitrines to display different countries like scientific specimens, indicating the isolation of the nations. (Figure 3.43)

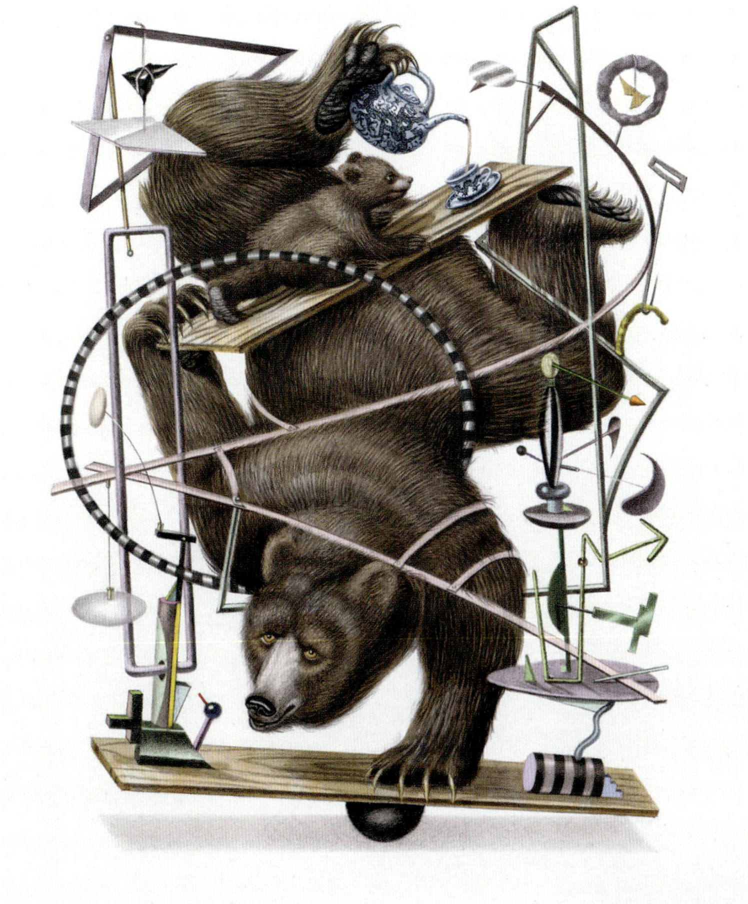

Figure 3.41
10 Theses on Russia, Global Brief, Winter 2018

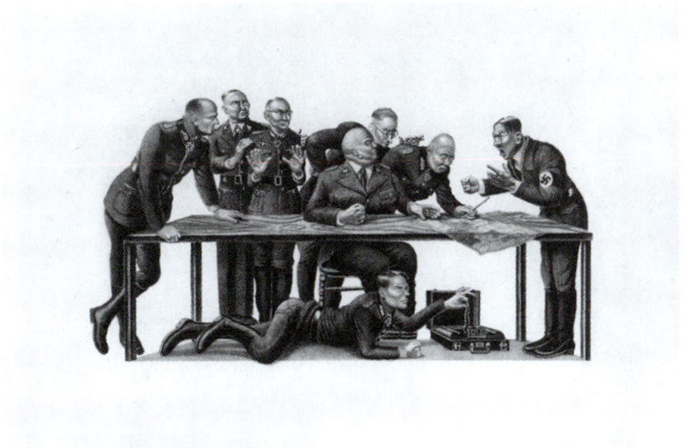

Figure 3.42
Operation Valkyrie, VICE Magazine, April 2017

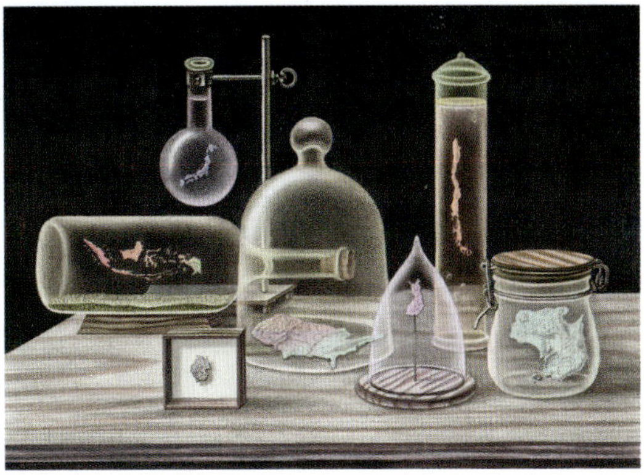

Figure 3.43
A Disconnected World, The New Republic, June 2019

INTERVIEW

Armando Veve

How does the role of metaphor come into play in your illustrations? Do you lead with a verbal or visual idea when you begin an illustration?

I use visual metaphor as a strategy to distill abstract concepts. I particularly rely on metaphorical thinking when working with scientific or medical content, which often involves visualizing invisible and complex subject matter. When it comes to sensitive and polarizing themes like the body, political or religious differences, or even the existence of extraterrestrial life, I am cautious to rely too heavily on metaphorical thinking as it can erase nuance and complexity surrounding an issue, and can even reinforce problematic stereotypes or social biases. However, I find power in metaphorical thinking – the process of seeing something through the lens of something else. Through the use of metaphor in my works, I aim to create new visual relationships that can reframe our understanding of our bodies, systems, and physical and natural environments.

My drawings usually begin with a concise verbal idea, which I then expand upon through a mind map in my sketchbook. This allows me to explore the issue or topic from various perspectives. Composing an image becomes delicate choreography, often involving weaving multiple metaphors within a single piece. When creating illustrations, I always consider the audience, constructing a complete world that still allows room for the viewer to interpret and complete the story, fusing new connections along the way.

Your style is very distinct and consistent throughout your portfolio, and works well for clearly communicating your visual messages. What role does your style and technique play in your messaging process?

I typically work on paper, as I love its association with writing, and often think of my work as a process of writing with pictures. But I have recently ventured beyond the page and into sculpture and installation. I employ traditional drawing strategies and utilize traditional drafting tools to articulate my concepts with surgical precision. My works are conceived in the urgency of a present moment: the news cycle, things I observe, my dreams. But they emerge slowly through layers of graphite, watercolor, colored pencil, and gouache, like the formation of sedimentary layers. My final pieces function as a record of this unfolding process supported by a deep well of personal and collective mythos.

My drawings are often paired with sensitive, nuanced, and layered topics from fragile ecosystems to government surveillance. The clarity and physicality of my drawings forces viewers to really confront the subject matter. This tactile quality in my drawings pulls directly from the microscopic clarity found in botanical and anatomical diagrams and the architectural language of blueprints, among other things. There is a rawness, honesty, and accessibility to drawing on paper that lends itself well to sculpting layered stories for a viewer.

I also think there is something to be said about working slowly and methodically with traditional media in a visual culture that prioritizes moving images and is now saturated by images made instantaneously by AI. By working slowly and methodically, I am consciously embedding the work with an energy that inspires careful and slow looking. There is something beautiful and peculiar about the stillness of a layered and delicately constructed drawing.

Could you describe your ideation and sketch process? What is your process of communication between yourself and the art director? Do you ever have ideas you like edited or shut down?

My process usually involves an absorption period—reading a manuscript, observing the world on walks, research, reading, etc., followed by a period of regurgitation—thumbnailing, iterating on concepts in a sketchbook or iPad, hybridizing drawn and collected fragments in search of odd juxtapositions, and studies that lead to a final work.

I view the world through both microscopic and macroscopic lenses. Zooming out, I construct intricate, labyrinthine compositions that mirror the absurdity of our systems and networks. But I also enjoy focusing my lens on singular cultural specimens, like a Sonoran desert toad applying lipstick or a detailed study of a queer hand gesture. I pointedly and playfully bend my lens to show that what we think of as so-called objectivity is actually a deeply particular way of seeing the world, and aim to draw out alternative perspectives.

Communication with an art director really depends on who I am working with. Some art directors prefer to be more hands off, while others are more open and eager to iterate on concepts. The number of sketches I present for each project can vary, but I usually try to pitch at least three concepts that communicate a variety of possible directions for a project. There have been MANY instances when an art director selects a sketch I am less excited about. However, more often than not, it is these images that surprise me, push me beyond my comfort zone, and become my favorites in retrospect. Any unused sketches go to my "sketch graveyard" to be resurrected on another day.

Does creating a work with a political theme differ from other types of editorial illustration? What role does creating illustration about political subjects and causes have in your career?

Whether I'm working with an endangered species or a political clown, my process is similar. But format and scale can change how I decide to frame and dissect my subject.

In the past, I actively avoided accepting any jobs involving Trump because I was worried I would get stuck drawing him (I did illustrate one article about writing jokes about Trump, but it didn't involve having to draw and stare at his face). However, this election cycle, I want to be more engaged and visually responsive to the election.

Can you talk about your art influences? Either people, styles, or anything else.

Although I can create clean lines between my work and key moments in the history of illustration, my work is animated by a web of artistic traditions. I mine the histories of art and design, searching for images and ideas that resonate: Northern Mannerist Dutch engravings, anatomical models, cartography, botanical illustration, postmodern furniture design, political cartoons, surrealist objects, and Dada-esque appropriation. I may draw cues from the way a contemporary artist like Sarah Sze grapples with entropy, or find comfort in a grotesque pile of entangled legs in a painting by Philip Guston, or intellectual stimulation in a scientific illustration. I enjoy fantasy, as a world building tool to propose new structures and relationships, but always try to remain firmly grounded like a WPA mural. I love the intricate language of maps, with their hybrid creatures and terra incognita; the way they can inspire a sense of discovery, but also streamline complex information. I look to medieval pictorial construction, specifically the awkward way space is created through stacking, and appreciate how this lack of perspective gives the viewer freedom to create their own pathways in an image (but also never underestimate the power of a vanishing point to turn a head.) As my library of references expands, so does the richness of my illustrated worlds.

What advice would you give to students who want to pursue political and editorial illustration?
Whatever sets you apart, makes you unique, strange, complicated, or vulnerable – embrace those qualities and incorporate them into your work.

Zina Saunders was an early adopter of digital illustration and has created editorial illustrations for a number of US publications including *The Wall Street Journal*, *Los Angeles Times*, and *The New Republic*, as well as working in reportage illustration, book illustration, and poster illustration. Saunders' style stands out for its rich colors, vibrant shadows, and her ability for a likeness, and pushed the boundaries of what digital painting could look like. In 2008, she began creating an iconic series of illustrations of the Republican vice-presidential candidate Sarah Palin, which were published by *The Nation*, *Mother Jones Magazine*, and other publications, and were eventually compiled into a book. (Figures 3.8 and 3.81) She says about her work:

> "My Palin paintings were my first foray into political illustration. What prompted me was the NY Society of Illustrators show of political illustration that featured only one woman artist out of the whole bunch. It burned me up that women weren't on those walls, so I set out to do something about it!
>
> It was the Fall of 2008, at just the same time that John McCain, the Republican candidate for President, chose the ludicrously ignorant right-wing buffoon, Sarah Palin, as his running mate. She provided me the perfect vehicle for satirizing the right-wing politics of the Republican Party.

I did many Palin satires over the course of the 2008 Presidential campaign, as well as many other lampoons of pols, plutocrats and assorted miscreants. Over time my political art expanded to include more serious commentary and subjects for magazines and newspapers, as well as animations for websites and online media."

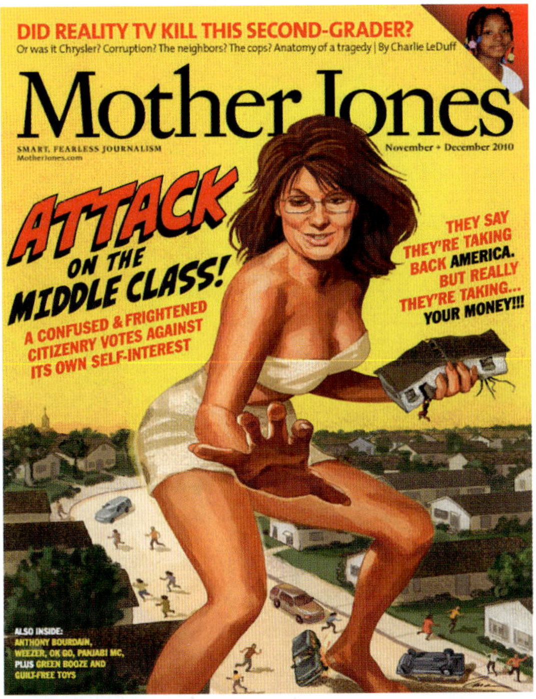

Figure 3.44
Sarah Palin, Mother Jones
© Zina Saunders, 2010

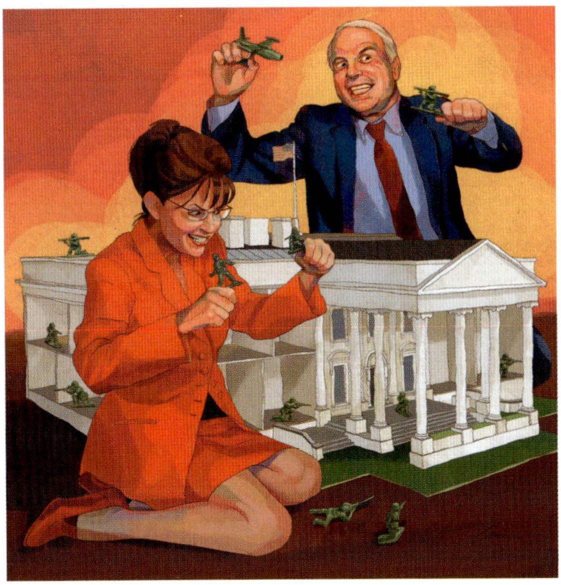

Figure 3.45
Playing White House, The Nation
© Zina Saunders, 2008

Edel Rodriguez is a Cuban-American illustrator and artist who was born in Havana and raised in El Gabriel, a small farm town. In 1980 his family immigrated to the United States as part of the Mariel boatlift, a mass emigration of Cuban refugees. From 1994 to 2008, he worked as an art director for *TIME* magazine, before he devoted himself full time to art and illustration. During this time and after Edel made a number of notable TIME magazine covers, but gained further fame when Donald Trump announced his run for presidency in 2015. From his experience growing up in Cuba, Edel was compelled to begin using his skills in illustration to create work criticizing Donald Trump, including an image of Trump cutting off the head of the Statue of Liberty and an image of Trump, simplified into a melting orange and yellow face. Edel hoped his illustrations would be picked up, and over the course of the following years *Der Spiegel* and *TIME* published a number of his Trump illustrations.[114] Beyond his commercial editorial work, Edel creates self-generated work, including a graphic novel *Worm* about his childhood in Cuba.

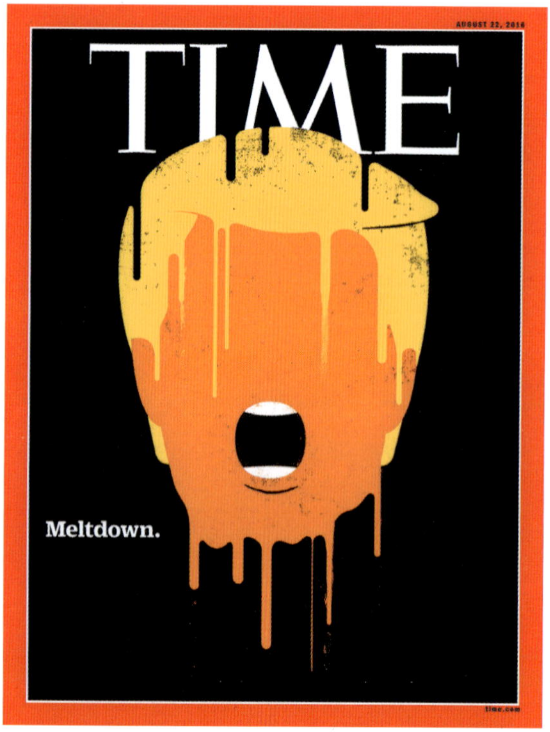

Figure 3.46
Trump Meltdown for *TIME*
© Edel Rodriguez, 2016

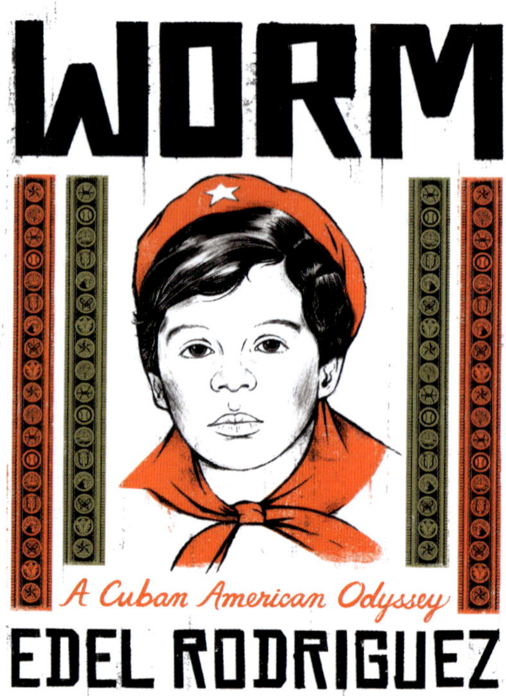

Figure 3.47
Cover of *Worm*
© Edel Rodriguez, 2024

INTERVIEW

Edel Rodriguez

Something I find notable about your work is the vast variety of styles you work in. How does style play into visual messaging in your work? Does the idea inform the style, or does the style inform the idea?
The most important thing to me is the idea, that's where the key to clear communication is. Style to me is secondary. I follow the idea wherever it goes. There are times where something visual, a color, or combination of colors, is intrinsic to the concept. If that works, then I'll head in that direction.

Are there any specific influences on the different styles you work in? (either people or art movements)
I love so many different kinds of work, from self-taught to Cubism, Surrealism, and Pop art. I always gravitated to political art from the beginning, from Goya and Picasso to many of the German expressionists like Max Beckman, George Grosz and Käthe Kollwitz. The German artists dealt with many of the issues that were on my mind at a young age.

You use a lot of visual metaphor in your work, which especially comes into play with your series of abstracted Trump portraits. Could you explain your ideation process of how you come up with your metaphors? With your Trump portraits, do you ever find yourself struggling for ideas and visual metaphors when you've drawn the same figure so many times?
I haven't struggled much with this series of works, the ideas just kind of flow naturally. From the beginning, I wanted to set a certain set of parameters that dealt with the design of the images. I decided to use the same colors, usually on a white or black background, so that the viewer would recognize that this was all part of an ongoing project. Once I had those rules, the pieces just kept falling into place. I could just spend my time bouncing ideas in my head and on paper, knowing that the look and format of the series was in place. Placing limits sometimes helps with creativity.

Your Cuban-American identity informs much of your illustration work and perspective. Could you tell us a little about your background and how it inspired you to pursue illustration as a method of communicating your worldview?
As a child, I was very upset about leaving my extended family behind in Cuba. I spent many years trying to figure out why we had to leave. I became interested in history and the imagery associated with politics and propaganda, with artists that dealt with issues surrounding war, refugees, and detention. Many of these artists were painters and printmakers who also illustrated stories and books. They inspired me to put my ideas down and tell my own stories.

Your new memoir *Worm* explores a new visual format for you, a graphic memoir. Did you experience challenges creating illustration in this new format? What about this format made it the best method to communicate your story?
There are many challenges in creating a graphic novel. The main challenge is maintaining one's stamina over so many pages.

Another is organizational. It takes a while to figure out the balance between text and image, how to create flow, and how to create a narrative that keeps the reader engaged. I've had these images and experiences on my mind for much of my life. The graphic novel format felt to me like the best way to get all of these images out into the world.

Have you ever experienced censorship of your art or art direction that felt like censorship? If so, how did you handle those experiences? When you were an art director, did you see examples of work being edited or censored for content? How does this compare to what you saw in Cuba?
Most of the art direction that happens in this country is about being accurate or sensitive to the subject matter being portrayed, to be true to the story one is illustrating. I usually work back and forth with the art director and eventually figure it out when there is an issue. The censorship in Cuba is more about banning speech or material that is critical of the dictatorship. The two cases are very different.

What do you think is the most powerful or memorable form that political illustration can take? (e.g. magazines, street art, political cartoons, posters) Why do you think that form is so powerful?
I think magazine covers are the most powerful because they usually get the most eyes. You are more likely to impact a higher number of people. Posters and street art are very powerful in person, why I love them as well.

Do you have any advice for students who are interested in pursuing political illustration?
Study history, civics, social justice movements, current events, and be involved in what is happening in the world. All ideas flow from knowledge.

Steve Brodner's illustrations defy categorization between editorial illustration, political cartoon, self-generated work, and commissioned work, which is why we've placed him at the conclusion of this chapter. Since the 1970s, Brodner has worked for almost every major publication in the US and Canada, and many international publications as well, including partnering with *The New Yorker* in 2009 to create a political animation series called *The Naked Campaign*. Brodner has stretched the boundaries of what it means to be an illustrator/author, cartoonist, and content creator, continuing to create self-generated work for major publications such as *The Washington Post*, sending content to his SubStack subscribers, and creating immediate, up to date commentary on political issues on social media.

INTERVIEW

Steve Brodner

I assume you've always been drawing and always been into politics... which came first? Or did they evolve together?
When I went to summer camp in the summer of '67, I would get *Newsweek* sent to my camp, and the other kids were reading comic books. At home, it would be *Newsweek* every week, *New York Magazine*, *Time* magazine, *The New Yorker*, *The New York Times* every day, and the *New York Post* also. Print was king, and you were very affected by print. When I was 14, I decided for some reason that I would do a cartoon every day. First in pencil, and then I would ink them over, and went to an art supply store and bought a bottle of nibs. I drew on cheap paper, copier paper. By the time I was 16, I went to a local Brooklyn newspaper. And I said, "What do you think?" The guy said, "Would you draw a cartoon every week for us?" So I did that. And he reached in his pocket and gave me a $10 bill. I thought this was the greatest thing that's ever happened. I was a professional.

What influence do you think media outlets have on the content of syndicated political cartoons? What advantages and disadvantages do illustrators have who self-publish?
I don't really self-publish, I have a SubStack, which a lot of writers do. Enough people pay $5 a month for me to augment my income. But everything that I do during the week gets published by *The Nation*. In addition to that, I do what I've always done, which is to contact the *New York Times*, *Washington Post*, *Los Angeles Times*, and I say, "Hey, I've got this idea, what do you think of this?" They'll usually say no, that's normal, but then you take it somewhere else. There's no money, they don't have enough money in the world to pay me for the man hours that I'm going to put into this huge thing that's due in three months. But I'm doing it because it's my art! And how great to have the *Washington Post*, or any of these other places agree that this is worth publishing. I feel I'm doing my thing, but I'm not looking at it to support me anymore, like when print was on fire. And those of us who were successful, we kept getting more and more successful. I am going to be 70 next year, and during that time, I was raising a small child and family and needed to make enough money to live middle class in New York, and I did it.

These days, a lot has been taken away by one hand, but given by the other hand. Maybe five years ago, there were something like 50 or 60 professional political cartoonists working for publications in the United States. Now, I think there's like 20. So what do we do? I was lucky that all these magazines called me at one point or another. I worked for just about every single magazine in the country for 40 years. And little by little, they went away or they shrunk. What's the response to the shrinking of the island? We're like the polar bears. Some people go to gallery work, some people go to academia, which I have done to a certain extent. I love teaching, and I've been teaching for longer than 30 years. Some people retire and stop working altogether. Or they do something else! Trade on the stock market! Because this is something that you only should do if you really want to do this, if you really love it.

As a rule, you're saying what you want to say in conjunction with or sometimes in spite of your employer. There is a chain of command in illustration where you are being commissioned to illustrate a piece of preexisting writing. Your freedom is constrained by what's being written by someone else you generally do not meet. You're then constrained by an art director, but he or she or they are constrained by editors, sometimes two or three editors, who are looking over their shoulder and deciding what can pass, what's fine to go. By the time you've gone through this battalion of fire hoses that are watering everything down, if you can come up with something that's strong, you're pretty good. When you're doing what I do now, I have no constraints. I have no people looking over my shoulder. I just do what I want. When I propose something to the *Washington Post*, or someone else, I'm working with an art director who is going to tell me what he thinks. But it's my writing. It's my project. I've invented it. I wrote it. I pitched it. I sent sketches. How much can they destroy of that? Generally, it's wonderful. Generally, they're on my side. But that's me. I've decided I'm not going to make a great deal of money from this anymore. As I said, because of my stage in life, I just want to have a good time. I want to enjoy everything I do. It depends on what's important to you in the final analysis, when you have an editorial world that is so completely melted away. Your choices are either to do something that you want to do for very little, or do something else. But certainly, I don't feel it's a choice anymore. You can do constipated illustrations for people who are afraid to tell the truth. I will not do that. I did that plenty. I paid in. And I made money. One year, I made a quarter million dollars. Those were the days.

Is there a difference between the style and technique you use to draw a lampoon vs. drawing a portrait meant to honor someone?

If I have compassion for someone and I want to tell that story, I feel like I can tell that story. And if I don't have compassion for a political figure, I render it that way. The pen moves based on what the feeling is. It's an exercise in reflecting how you feel, and how you approach each thing. *Living and Dying in America* started as my blog, which I'm still doing every day, The Greater Quiet. It's mostly people who are victims of the system that is hostile. It started out as COVID victims and then George Floyd to Black Lives Matter people. And yesterday I did someone on Maui who lost everything. And then today I did Trump, and he's continuing his insurrection. You can see in the handling of each face what the intention is. If you can do portraits and caricatures, you should be able to change the temperature.

Do you have thoughts about how Trump and the media had a symbiotic relationship during his campaign and presidency?

What happened here is that it exposed the media for what they really were, and I include myself in this. We all thought that we were a rather circumspect, journalistic entity. What this has revealed is that that can go throw that in the wastepaper basket, if there is enough money on the table. Trump, for conservative and liberal media and other media alike, has been a goldmine. The famous statement by the head of CBS at the time said, "He's the best thing that ever happened to us." CNN, MSNBC, Fox, and the rest of them have a machine. They can see in second-by-second metrics, in real time, how many viewers are coming or going from the show. If there's a guest that's on and is saying things that for some reason is causing the numbers to go down drastically, that guest will never be asked again. And that guest may be offering something very important and very real that your audience just doesn't want to hear. When Trump goes, they'll all be in terrible trouble. They've got nothing else. They've got no other act. It was an overwhelming moment for media, from a showbusiness point of view in selling a product. For Fox, the product is Trump the hero. And on MSNBC, it's how close are we to getting Trump today? I think the whole Trump phenomenon has to do with capitalism, and who's buying on the counter whatever you're selling.

What advice do you have for students who are interested in participating in political illustration?

I think the idea that you're going to have a gorgeous portfolio, and you just send out cards and the world comes round to you, that's over. But it's like the idea that the good Lord closes one door and then opens another. I feel that to be an entrepreneur today, there are opportunities like there never were before. What I do with SubStack is an example, but also what you can do with comics, graphic memoirs, graphic novels, animations, video games. It requires different talents. You're not just a wrist anymore. You are a thinker, an inventor, a writer, a person who has something to say. I think that that is your ticket to having a fascinating, interesting creative life. However, if you are just a renderer, you could have gotten a lot of work back then. They needed renders, they don't anymore. AI is going to take care of all that. You have to love it. You have to not be ashamed to show that you love it. And make sure that you find your cohort of people who agree with you and can share that with you and would be happy to pay X amount of money for what you do. You have to find the thing that is out there that no one's thought of yet. And then sell it.

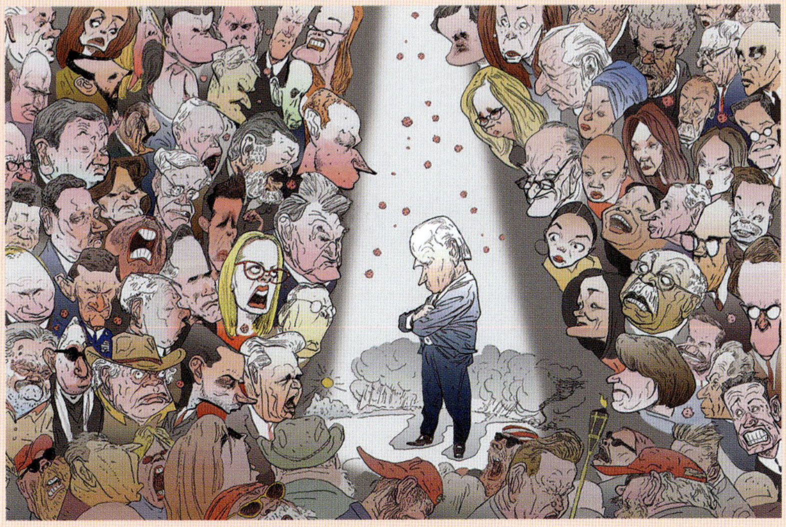

Figure 3.48
Biden's World
© Steve Brodner, 2022

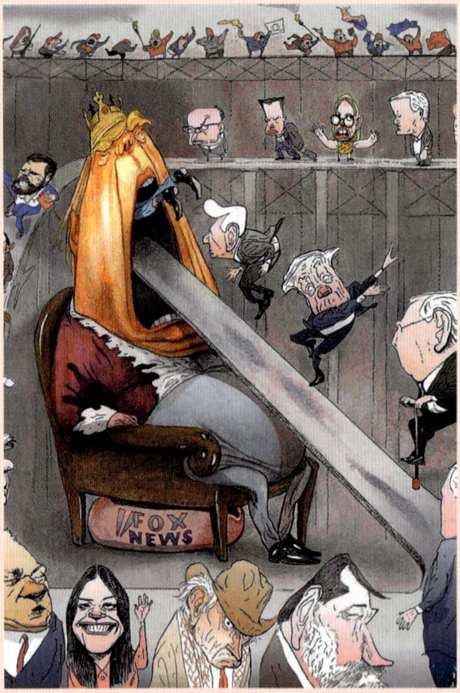

Figure 3.49
Gargantua, *The LA Times*
© Steve Brodner, 2021

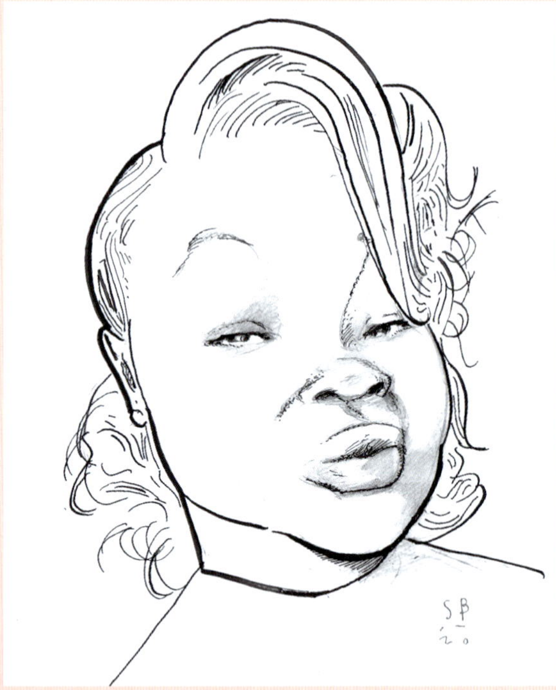

Figure 3.50
Breonna Taylor, *The Greater Quiet*
© Steve Brodner, 2020

Group Activities/Discussion Questions

- Gather examples of contemporary editorial illustrators who work with political themes, and find examples of their work along with any accompanying articles. Then join with a group and share the examples you've found. Choose examples to critique and discuss how these illustrators stand out because of their use of color, shape, composition, and metaphor, and which illustrations succeeded and which did not. If you were art directing this piece, what would you do differently?
- Find a political cartoon created by one of the artists discussed in this chapter. Research what the theme of the cartoon was and the historical context behind it. Present your research to a small group or to the class, and discuss how the artist used visual metaphor to deliver their message.
- Many illustrators draw a different line between what should be drawn and what should remain taboo. Some countries outlaw the display of symbols, such as the Nazi flag in Germany, while others embrace broader free speech. Where do you think the line should be for newspapers, news magazines, satire magazines, or the internet? Is it ever appropriate to curb free speech, for instance, when it puts people in danger?
- Technology has played a large role in the development of political illustration, including photography, different printing technologies such as wood engraving and lithography, and all of the new technologies discussed in the Contemporary Editorial Illustration section. How do you see technology playing a role in the future of distribution of illustration, as well as how that technology may change the style and message of illustration?

Endnotes

1 Andrew Selby, *Editorial Illustration: Context, content, and creation*, (London: Bloomsbury Visual Arts, 2022), 62.
2 Andrew Selby, *Editorial Illustration,* 58.
3 Edmund Lee, "New York Times Hits 7 Million Subscribers as Digital Revenue Rises," *The New York Times*, Last modified November 5, 2020, https://www.nytimes.com/2020/11/05/business/media/new-york-times-q3-2020-earnings-nyt.html.
4 Dan Kennedy, "For Five Years, Trump Outrage Has Fueled Media Profits. So Now What?" *GBH*, Last modified January 27, 2021, https://www.wgbh.org/news/commentary/2021/01/27/for-five-years-trump-outrage-has-fueled-media-profits-so-now-what
5 Kennedy, "For Five Years."
6 Kate Conger, "Twitter's revenue jumps 28 percent in its first post-Trump quarter," *The New York Times*, Last modified April 29, 2021, https://www.nytimes.com/2021/04/29/business/twitter-growth-trump-ban.html.
7 Tali Arbel, "Trump bump? NYT adds subscribers, grows digital revenue," Business, *AP*, Last modified February 6, 2019, https://apnews.com/article/652e36fee140b00ca7074c536e846af9.
8 Megan Brenan, "Americans' Trust In Media Remains Near Record Low," *Gallup*, Last modified October 18, 2022, https://news.gallup.com/poll/403166/americans-trust-media-remains-near-record-low.aspx.
9 Margaret Sullivan, "If Trump Runs Again, Do Not Cover Him the Same Way: A Journalist's Manifesto," *The Washington Post*, Last modified October 12, 2022, https://www.washingtonpost.com/magazine/2022/10/12/margaret-sullivan-how-media-should-cover-trump-next-campaign/.
10 Paul Hogarth, *The Artist as Reporter,* (London: Studio Vista, 1967), 16.
11 Ken Ellingwood, "How US Newspapers Became Utterly Ubiquitous in the 1830s," *Literary Hub*, Last modified May 6, 2021, https://lithub.com/how-us-newspapers-became-utterly-ubiquitous-in-the-1830s/#:~:text=The%20paper%20on%20which%20newspapers,wood%20pulp%20to%20be%20used.
12 "History of Periodical Illustration", *NC State University*, accessed on January 24, 2024, https://ncna.dh.chass.ncsu.edu/imageanalytics/history.php.
13 Joanna Colclough, "Printing Newspapers 1400-1900: A Brief Survey of the Evolution of the Newspaper Printing Press," *Library of Congress Blogs*, Last modified April 21, 2022, https://blogs.loc.gov/headlinesandheroes/2022/04/printing-newspapers-1400-1900/#:~:text=The%20first%20printing%20press%20made,pressed%20side%20of%20a%20paper.
14 Hogarth, *Artist as Reporter,* 23.
15 Hogarth, *Artist as Reporter,* 26–27.
16 "The 'Daily Graphic' of New York Publishes the First Halftone of a News Photograph in a U.S. Newspaper," *Jeremy Norman's HistoryofInformation.com*, accessed January 24, 2024, https://historyofinformation.com/detail.php?entryid=4389.
17 Mia Fineman, "Kodak and the Rise of Amateur Photography," *The Met*, Last modified October, 2004, https://www.metmuseum.org/toah/hd/kodk/hd_kodk.htm#:~:text=By%20far%20the%20most%20significant,100%2Dexposure%20roll%20of%20film.
18 Hogarth, *Artist as Reporter,* 41.
19 Hogarth, *Artist as Reporter,* 52–53.
20 "Ask a Historian: How Many Japanese Americans Were Incarcerated During WWII?" *Densho*, Last modified June 2, 2021, https://densho.org/catalyst/how-many-japanese-americans-were-incarcerated-during-wwii/#:~:text=So%20it%20would%20be%20correct,Authority%20during%20World%20War%20II.%E2%80%9D.
21 Matthew McRae, "Japanese Canadian internment and the struggle for redress," *Canadian Museum for Human Rights*, Last modified on May 19, 2017, https://humanrights.ca/story/japanese-canadian-internment-and-struggle-redress#:~:text=Approximately%2012%2C000%20people%20were%20forced,roadwork%20and%20other%20physical%20labour.
22 "Picturing Japanese American Internment: Dorothea Lange," *PBS Learning Media*, accessed on January 24, 2024, https://gpb.pbslearningmedia.org/resource/lang14.soc.ushist.intern/picturing-japanese-american-internment-dorothea-lange/.
23 "Picturing Japanese American Internment."
24 Tim Chambers, "Dorothea Lange's Censored Photographs of FDR's Japanese Concentration Camps," *Anchor Editions*, Last modified December 7, 2016, https://anchoreditions.com/blog/dorothea-lange-censored-photographs.
25 "Hatsuki Wakasa Shot by M.P.," *National Museum of American History*, accessed January 24, 2024, https://americanhistory.si.edu/collections/search/object/nmah_1812189.

26 Kelly Chicago- Spring, “Miné Okubo,” *National Women's History Museum*, Last modified 2017, www.womenshistory.org/education-resources/biographies/mine-okubo.

27 Scott A. Rosenberg, “Artist Harmony Becker discusses working on ‘They Called Us Enemy’ with George Takei,” Entertainment, *AMNY*, Last modified August 12, 2019, https://www.amny.com/entertainment/george-takei-harmony-becker-they-called-us-enemy-1-34950911/.

28 “Interview: George Takei Talks ‘They Called Us Enemy,’” *Previewsworld*, Last modified on June 8, 2021, https://www.previewsworld.com/Article/231676-Interview-George-Takei-Talks-They-Called-Us-Enemy.

29 Note these numbers are estimates and a topic of debate among scholars.

30 Dan Listwa, “Hiroshima and Nagasaki: The Long Term Health Effects,” *Colombia K=1 Project Center for Nuclear Studies*, Last modified August 9, 2012, https://k1project.columbia.edu/news/hiroshima-and-nagasaki.

31 John W. Dower, “Ground Zero 1945”, *Visualizing Cultures—Image Driven Scholarship*, accessed on January 24, 2024, https://visualizingcultures.mit.edu/groundzero1945/gz_essay.pdf.

32 Janet Farrell Brodie, “Radiation Secrecy and Censorship after Hiroshima and Nagasaki,” *Journal of Social History*, 48, no. 4 (Summer 2015) Pages 842–864.

33 Gabrielle Decamous, “Art, Censorship and Nuclear Warfare,” *Leonardo* 54 no.5 (2021): 537–541.

34 “Caricatures: Sketching out reality,” *Minneapolis Art Institute*, accessed June 4, 2024, https://new.artsmia.org/stories/caricatures-sketching-out-reality.

35 John J. Richetti, *The Cambridge history of English literature, 1660–1780,* (Cambridge: Cambridge University Press, 2005), 85.

36 Frederick Burwick, “Lamb, Hazlitt, and De Quincey on Hogarth,” *The Wordsworth Circle* Vol. 28m No. 1 (WINTER, 1997), p1 https://www.jstor.org/stable/24042524.

37 Richard Godfrey and Mark Hallett, *James Gillray: The Art of Caricature*, (London: Tate, 2001), 30.

38 “Political and Social Satire through Caricature,” *Films On Demand*, 1985, accessed April 26, 2023. https://fod.infobase.com/PortalPlaylists.aspx?wID=96309&xtid=35741.

39 Tim Clayton and Sheila O'Connell, *Bonaparte and the British: Prints and propaganda in the age of Napoleon,* (London: British Museum, 2015), 20.

40 Clayton, *Bonaparte and the British*, 20.

41 W. S. Lewis, *Rescuing Horace Walpole*, (London: Yale University Press, 1978), 220, https://bpb-us-w2.wpmucdn.com/campuspress.yale.edu/dist/3/1856/files/2020/05/Rescuing_HW_Chapter_23-1.pdf

42 Godfrey, *James Gillray*, 176

43 Clayton, *Bonaparte and the British*, 15.

44 Clayton, *Bonaparte and the British*, 24.

45 Timothy Clayton, *James Gillray: A Revolution in Satire*, (London: Paul Mellon Centre, 2022), 331.

46 Clayton, *James Gillray*, 334.

47 Clayton, *James Gillray*, 331.

48 Godfrey, *James Gillray*, 47.

49 Clayton, *Bonaparte and the British*, 26.

50 “Poor John Bull-The free born Englishman-deprived of his seven senses by the six new acts.?,” https://www.britishmuseum.org/collection/object/P_1868-0808-12894

51 Chris Price, “‘Pictorially Speaking, so Ludicrous’: George IV on the Dance Floor,” *Music in Art* 43, no. 1/2 (2018): 49–66: 62.

52 “Political and Social Satire through Caricature,” *Films On Demand.*

53 Donna Lee Owen Petersen, “Napoleonic censorship, 1799–1810,” *Student Work* 402 (1975): 4, https://digitalcommons.unomaha.edu/cgi/viewcontent.cgi?article=1407&context=studentwork.

54 Petersen, “Napoleonic censorship ,” 27

55 “The Pears,” *Art & Popular Culture*, accessed January 24, 2024, http://www.artandpopularculture.com/Les_poires.

56 “Lithography,” Arts & Culture, *Britannica*, Last modified January 9, 2024, https://www.britannica.com/technology/lithography.

57 “Lithography,” History of Science Museum, *University of Oxford*, accessed January 27, 2024, https://www.hsm.ox.ac.uk/lithography#:~:text=Discovered%20in%20Germany%20in%201798,was%20easier%20and%20more%20versatile.

58 “Lithography,” *Britannica.*

59 Colta Ives, “Lithography in the Nineteenth Century,” *The Met*, Last modified October 2004, https://www.metmuseum.org/toah/hd/lith/hd_lith.htm#:~:text=Lithography%20was%20invented%20around%201796,them%20with%20rolled%2Don%20ink.

60 Patricia Mainardi, “Of Pears and Kings,” *The Public Domain Review*, Last modified January 9, 2020, https://publicdomainreview.org/essay/of-pears-and-kings.

61 Mark Summer, "Elephants, Donkeys, and Uncle Sam: The Political Cartoons of Thomas Nast," *Northeast Georgia History Center*, Last modified May 11, 2021, https://www.youtube.com/watch?v=YO473y3zIlE.
62 Colta Ives, "The Print in the Nineteenth Century," *The Met*, Last modified October 2004, https://www.metmuseum.org/toah/hd/prnt2/hd_prnt2.htm.
63 Summer, "Elephants, Donkeys, and Uncle Sam."
64 Clayton, *Bonaparte and the British*, 21
65 Susan Doyle, Jaleen Grove, and Whitney Sherman, *The History of Illustration*, (New York: Fairchild Books, 2018), 174.
66 Clayton, *Bonaparte and the British*, 22
67 Jennifer Davis, "Elbridge Gerry and the Monstrous Gerrymander," *Library of Congress Blogs*, Last modified February 10, 2017, https://blogs.loc.gov/law/2017/02/elbridge-gerry-and-the-monstrous-gerrymander/.
68 Erick Trickey, "Where Did the Term 'Gerrymander' Come From?", *Smithsonian Magazine*, July 20, 2017, https://www.smithsonianmag.com/history/where-did-term-gerrymander-come-180964118/.
69 Fiona Deans Halloran, *Thomas Nast: The Father of Modern Political Cartoons*, (Chapel Hill: University of North Carolina Press, 2013), 101–102.
70 Summer, "Elephants, Donkeys, and Uncle Sam."
71 Steven Brodner, "An introduction to Thomas Nast," *Norman Rockwell Museum*, accessed January 24, 2024, https://www.youtube.com/watch?v=PSJeLRR8seI&t=280s.
72 Diane K. Skvarla and Donald A. Ritchie, *The United States Senate Catalogue of Graphic Art*, (Washington, DC: U.S. Government Printing Office, 2006), 308.
73 Albert Bigelow Paine, *Th. Nast: His Period and His Pictures*, (New York: Macmillan, 1904), 300.
74 "'Compromise with the South' illustration," *Ohio History Connection*, accessed on January 24, 2024, https://ohiomemory.org/digital/collection/p267401coll32/id/16531/.
75 "The Georgetown elections; the Negro at the ballot box," *Library of Congress*, accessed on January 24, 2024, https://www.loc.gov/resource/cph.3c39438/.
76 "'This is a white man's government, 'We regard the Reconstruction Acts [so called] of Congress as usurpation, and unconstitutional, revolutionary, and void'," *Library of Congress*, accessed on January 24, 2024, https://www.loc.gov/resource/cph.3c21735/.
77 "Colored Rule in a Reconstructed [?] State", *Harpers Weekly*, March 14, 1874, https://blackhistory.harpweek.com/7illustrations/reconstruction/coloredrule.htm.
78 Richard Samuel West, "The First 150 Years of the American Political Cartoon," *Politics in Graphic Detail*, accessed on January 24, 2024, http://digitalhistory.hsp.org/hint/politics-graphic-detail/essay/first-150-years-american-political-cartoon.
79 Paul Alkebulan, *The African American Press in World War II: Toward Victory at Home and Abroad* (Lanham, MD: Lexington Books, 2014), 201.
80 Kelly Fazilleau, "The role of the Black Press in America," *Memoire(s), identite(s), marginalite(s) dan le monde occidental contemporain* 7 (2012).
81 "The Double V Victory," *The National WWII Museum*, accessed January 24, 2024, https://www.nationalww2museum.org/war/articles/double-v-victory.
82 Matthew Delmont, "Why African-American Soldiers Saw World War II as a Two-Front Battle," *Smithsonian Magazine*, Last modified August 24, 2017, https://www.smithsonianmag.com/history/why-african-american-soldiers-saw-world-war-ii-two-front-battle-180964616/.
83 "Anne Mergen: First Lady of Editorial Cartoons During World War II," *The National WWII Museum*, Last modified June 25, 2020, https://www.nationalww2museum.org/war/articles/anne-mergen-political-cartoons#:~:text=Anne%20Mergen%20was%20the%20only,the%20WWII%20years%20and%20beyond.
84 Becky Morton, "Tackling the 'boys' club' of political cartoons," *BBC*, Last modified October 30, 2017, https://www.bbc.com/news/uk-politics-41724321.
85 Valeriya Mechkova, Anna Luhrmann, and Staffan I. Lindberg, "How Much Democratic Backsliding?" *The Journal of Democracy* 28, no. 4 (2017): 162–169.
86 Sarah Repucci, "Media Freedom: A Downward Spiral," *Freedom House*, accessed on January 27, 2024, https://freedomhouse.org/report/freedom-and-media/2019/media-freedom-downward-spiral.
87 Marisa Kellam and Elizabeth A. Stein, "Silencing Critics: Why and How Presidents Restrict Media Freedom in Democracies," *Comparative Political Studies* 49, no.1(2016): 36–77.
88 "The Nobel Peace Prize 2021 Press release," *The Nobel Prize*, Last modified October 8, 2021, https://www.nobelprize.org/prizes/peace/2021/summary/.
89 "North Korea," *Freedom House*. Archived from the original on 10 September 2015. Retrieved 27 September 2017, https://freedomhouse.org/country/north-korea/freedom-world/2024.

90 "North Korea," *Freedom House*.
91 Ron Gluckman, "North Korean art captures the world's imagination," *Nikkei Asia*, Last modified June 15, 2020, https://asia.nikkei.com/Life-Arts/Arts/North-Korean-art-captures-the-world-s-imagination.
92 Dagyum Ji, "North Korean art: pure kitsch or misunderstood masterpieces?" *NK News*, Last modified April 19, 2018, https://www.nknews.org/2018/04/north-korean-art-pure-kitsch-or-misunderstood-masterpieces/.
93 Thomas Storey, "Song Byeok, A North Korean Sature," *Culture Trip*, accessed June 4, 2024, https://theculturetrip.com/asia/north-korea/articles/song-byeok-s-satirical-take-on-north-korea#:~:text=Song%20Byeok%20was%20selected%20by,his%20father%20Kim%20Il%2DSung
94 "Song Byeok," *Art in Protest*, accessed June 4, 2024, https://artinprotest.viewingrooms.com/viewing-room/3-song-byeok/
95 Noe Tanigawa, "Byeok Song: N. Korean Propaganda Artist's SOS," *Hawai'i Public Radio*, accessed June 4, 2024, https://www.hawaiipublicradio.org/arts-culture/2019-04-26/byeok-song-n-korean-propaganda-artists-sos
96 Song Byeok, "About," *The Art of Song Byeok*, accessed Jan 29, 2024, https://www.songbyeoktheartist.com/about.
97 "Song Byeok," *Art in Protest*, accessed Jan 29, 2024, https://artinprotest.viewingrooms.com/viewing-room/3-song-byeok/.
98 Anthony Mughan and Richard Gunther, "The Media in Democratic and Nondemocratic Regimes: A Multilevel Perspective," *Democracy and the Media*, ed. Richard Gunther and Anthony Mughan (New York: Cambridge University Press 2000), 1–27.
99 Kellam and Stein, "Silencing Critics."
100 MEE staff, "Naji al-Ali remembered: A Palestinian cartoonist gunned down in London," *Middle East Eye*, Last modified August 30, 2022, https://www.middleeasteye.net/discover/palestine-naji-ali-handala-creator-remembered.
101 Cherian George and Sonny Liew, *Red Lines: Political Cartoons and the Struggle Against Censorship*, (Cambridge: MIT Press, 2021), 12.
102 "Akram Raslan- Syria," *Cartooning for Peace*, accessed January 24, 2024, https://www.cartooningforpeace.org/en/soutiens/akran-raslan/.
103 George, *Red Lines*, 14.
104 "Bangladesh High Court grants bail to imprisoned cartoonist Ahmed Kabir Kishor," *The New Indian Express*, Last modified on March 3, 2021, https://www.newindianexpress.com/world/2021/mar/03/bangladesh-high-court-grants-bail-to-imprisoned-cartoonist-ahmed-kabir-kishore-2271698.html.
105 "The Master Series: An Evening with Steve Brodner," *School of Visual Arts*, Last modified on October 30, 2019, https://www.youtube.com/watch?v=ayckgYmS86k.
106 Tom Kludt, "A newsroom tirade and a controversial hire: tension rises at Pittsburgh newspaper," *CNN Business*, Last modified February 19, 2019, https://www.cnn.com/2019/02/19/media/pittsburgh-post-gazette-john-block/index.html.
107 George, *Red Lines*, 23–25.
108 Jay A. Clarke, "Käthe Kollwitz: An Art of Resistance," *Art Institute Chicago*, Last modified May 4, 2021, https://www.artic.edu/articles/910/kathe-kollwitz-an-art-of-resistance.
109 "Demonstration, final version, 1931," *Käthe Kollwitz Museum Köln*, accessed January 27, 2024, https://www.kollwitz.de/en/demonstration-kn-252.
110 "Henry Luce," Arts & Culture, *Britannica*, accessed January 27, 2024, https://www.britannica.com/biography/Henry-Luce.
111 "Biography," *Bernard Safran: Paintings*, accessed January 31, 2024, http://www.safran-arts.com/bio.html.
112 Elizabeth Malyon, email message to the author, March 2, 2023.
113 Malcolm X, "Malcolm X on Lumumba," *World History Archives*, accessed January 27, 2024, http://www.hartford-hwp.com/archives/45a/459.html.
114 Benjamin P. Russell, "Edel Rodriguez Isn't Afraid to Live With the Consequences," *The New York Times*, Last modified November 9, 2023, https://www.nytimes.com/2023/11/08/books/edel-rodriguez-worm.html.

4

Contentious Politics and the Art of Dissent

Introduction

Throughout our chapter on Media, Censorship, and Taboo, we discussed a number of artists who have experienced censorship and media intervention because of their dissent through **contentious politics**. Contentious politics refers to societal attempts to create governmental change by using disruptive methods and actions outside of formal political institutions. Those engaging in contentious politics can work within the media, including some examples given in the previous chapter, but they often work outside of established organizations so that they can express their opinions more freely. Some of the most impactful and enduring examples of political illustration fall into this category, and will be the primary focus of this chapter. In this chapter, we aim to address the causes and reasons behind this dissent, as well as highlight political activists who use illustration as their medium. We will touch on a few noteworthy examples of dissent art but acknowledge that this is not by any means a comprehensive guide. Some of these examples include interviews with illustrators who embrace the art of dissent and have helped define illustration's role as a primary conduit for expressing contentious politics.

Dissent illustration can take many forms and be created through many types of media. Certainly, the political cartoon, as discussed in the previous chapter, has been used throughout history as a satirical vehicle for dissenting opinions. Another notable medium for political protest art is the poster, which has evolved from simple, printed placards to collected works of art. A poster can be reproduced and distributed but is often limited in size. A work of **street art**, however, while lacking reproducibility, can be produced at a scale which attracts further attention and observers. However, with wheat pasted paper, reproducibility is not impossible, nor is the medium necessarily discernibly different from a poster. We'll harken back to Doyle, Grove, and Sherman's definition of illustration here: that it "intends to communicate specific messages with an intended audience in mind." As many illustrators find street art to be an additional method to distribute intentional messages within a political context, we choose to include that medium within our definition of illustration. We will discuss these mediums as well as others in this chapter.

Latin American Protest Art

Latin American protest illustration emerged in the early 1800s. Miguel Hidalgo y Costilla, considered the "Father of Mexican Independence," used images of the Virgin of Guadalupe during the 1810 uprising against the Spanish.[1] In Argentina, illustrated posters were used to express dissent against the Rosas dictatorship in the 1830s. The **modernismo** movement in Latin American literature, which valued metaphor and symbolism, eventually translated into Latin American art and illustration. One of the form's early influencers was Mexican José Guadalupe Posada, who learned etching and lithography as a teenager and subsequently went on to work for many political newspapers. Posada was estimated to have created over 20,000 images for newspapers, **broadsheets** (newspaper sheet posters), and pamphlets throughout his career.[2] Posada popularized the symbol of the skull, or **calavera**, in Mexican art. One of his most famous creations was *La Calavera Catrina*, which satirized the Mexican upper class. The image of *La Calavera Catrina* was co-opted by other artists, including Diego Rivera, and eventually became a symbol of Mexico itself.[3] This is another good example of how symbols can change over time. Posada would decorate his calaveras with different accessories to poke fun at various archetypes of people in Mexican society, which became a recognizable and popular method of political satire in the country. His 1910 broadsheet *Calavera Maderista* featured a female revolutionary soldier. Posada's broadsheets featuring calavera revolutionaries were some of the few posters created during the Mexican Revolution, and helped to inspire future poster illustrators in Mexico and across the world.[4] (Figure 4.1)

A more popular form of illustration following the Mexican Revolution (which lasted from approximately 1910–1920) was **mural art** (or ***muralismo***). The *Tres Muralistas,* as they were known, Diego Rivera, José Clemente Orozco, and David Alfaro Siqueiros, were formative in creating Mexican visual language and renewing the practice of ancient mural painting. Following the Revolution, the Mexican government commissioned murals to inform illiterate members of the public about its history and their vision for its future. Filled with the idealism of the Revolution, these artists depicted murals that celebrated Mexican farmers, workers, and citizens, often with political connotations. Part of the power of these socialist messages came from the fact that these illustrations were publicly shown, that the art belonged to the people, and everyone had a right to view it. Often the *Muralistas* would insert their own messages into their publicly commissioned murals, and would sometimes experience backlash and censorship over this practice. Orozco openly critiqued the concepts of governmental law and justice in his work.[56] (Figure 4.2) His viewpoint was that the people had been repressed for generations and that the Revolution was the first step towards liberation. Importantly, while the *Muralistas* would also sometimes create placards or postcards, they paved the way for public street art as a means for political illustration and expression for generations to come.

FOCUS ON TECHNOLOGY

Murals

Mural art is one of the earliest forms of human recorded art. The earliest human murals are thought by some anthropologists to not be just purely decorative, but to be communicating messages about hunting, maps, and food sources. These early examples were often created with dirt or natural pigments, and it is thought that saltwater seeping through the limestone helped to preserve them. Mural art continued to evolve through the cultures of ancient Egypt, Mexico, Italy, and others before the 1st century. During the Middle Ages in Europe and in Kerala, India, artists would paint on dry plaster, called **fresco secco**, by mixing paint with a binder and lime. However, these murals were very vulnerable and would often flake and lose their color. By 1300 in Italy, a new technique called **buon fresco** ("buon" meaning "true") was developed, in which the pigments were mixed directly with a thin layer of plaster, making the paint become part of the dried wall, and therefore more durable. Michelangelo's frescoes on the Sistine Chapel and Raphael's *The School of Athens* are both surviving examples of buon fresco. In the early 20th century, the *Tres Muralistas* used a variety of techniques to create their murals, including frescos. Other techniques they used included **mosaics**, in which small bits of ceramic, glass, or stone are placed together to form a larger picture, and **encaustic**, in which colored wax was used to create the image. Today, artists can use durable acrylic paints that stand up well to weather, and can free-hand their murals or transfer their images in a number of ways, either by projecting the images, using a grid, or using the pouncing method described in Chapter 2. Preexisting images can also be printed on paper and **wheat-pasted** to a wall, or digital images can be printed on canvas, textiles, or latex and attached to a wall. Street artists today continue to innovate how new technology and techniques can be used to communicate their messages.

When envisioning Latin American protest illustration, one ubiquitous example likely comes to mind: the 1968 Jim Fitzpatrick screenprint of the controversial Marxist revolutionary Che Guevara. (Figure 4.3) This illustration, based on a photograph by Alberto Korda, has become universally synonymous with countercultural revolutionary movements across the world, and has been displayed (often without copyright attribution) on posters, in street art, in restaurants, and in advertisements. Guevara himself remains controversial. While an advisor to Fidel Castro, Guevara oversaw forced labor camps, mass executions of former government officials, and extreme censorship of the press, and many saw him as an authoritarian, replacing one dictatorship with an even more brutal regime. However, others see him as an anti-imperialist, a figure of liberation, and a socialist martyr. This is especially true in Cuba, where he remains revered and is featured on their currency and in public art. Although dozens of variations have been created by Fitzpatrick and other artists, the most popular version features the bold, flat shapes and colors we associate with Russian Constructivism and Socialist Realism: red, black, and white, with the addition of a yellow star on Guevara's hat. Fitzpatrick made changes to the reference image, including changing the gaze of Guevara's eyes to look up, in a nod to religious figures.[7] The flattening of the shapes, as well as the simplification and abstraction of his visage, are one part of how the portrait has come to symbolize not one person, but an emblem that transcends the man himself. The impact of Fitzpatrick's screenprint goes far beyond its photographic reference, abstracting the figure to not just represent a singular person, but the ideals of socialism. Here we recall Charles Phillipon's argument in the French court that once an illustration is created, a resemblance is simply a resemblance, and instead the image becomes a symbol. Many leftist and socialist idealists who wear and display the image of Guevara have adopted the image to become a symbol of their own ideals, such as the Black Panther Party, discussed later in this chapter.

GLOBAL POLITICS PERSPECTIVE

What Caused the Cuban Revolution?

Between 1953 and 1959, Fidel Castro led Cuba in a revolution against violent dictator Fulgencio Batista, who seized power in Cuba in 1952 in a military coup. During his reign, Batista murdered what is estimated to be up to 20,000 political prisoners, terrorizing the country.[8] During the revolution, Argentine-born Ernesto "Che" Guevara became a prominent military leader, helping to secure Castro's eventual victory in 1959. Prior to the revolution, Che Guevara, while training as a doctor in Argentina, traveled around South and Central America by motorcycle and witnessed extreme poverty across the continent. This experience caused Guevara to recognize that government, as well as medicine, was a factor in saving lives. Under the guise of anti-communism, the United States promoted oligarchies in Latin America that advanced its own economic interests, maintaining power of economic conglomerates, while many people in these countries suffered from poverty and starvation. After observing the United States CIA overthrow of a democratically elected leader in Guatemala, Guevara became convinced the US was an imperialist force. Soon thereafter, in 1955, he was introduced to Fidel Castro and his brother Raúl, and moved to Cuba to assist in their revolution, rising to second in command.[9]

Following the revolution and exile of Batista, Castro implemented a communist government in Cuba, deepening its relationship with the Soviet Union and severing ties to the United States. While Castro's overthrow of the Batista government was welcomed by many, it soon exhibited many of the traits of its predecessor. Guevara was tasked with commandeering the tribunals of the Batista army officers. With the overwhelming support of the public at the time, Guevara led the executions of several hundred people who worked with or fought for Batista, without trial. He also oversaw arbitrary arrests and forced labor camps, while additionally redistributing land, implementing universal education, and making strides towards economic equality.[10,11,12] However, while Guevara believed in Marxism, he grew increasingly disillusioned with the Soviet Union, and in 1965 resigned from his official posts in Cuba to combat imperialism in other parts of the world. In 1967, Guevara was killed by Bolivian soldiers with the assistance of the CIA and Green Berets, becoming a martyr figure throughout the world. From that time until today, Cuba has continued to operate as an authoritarian communist state, and limits freedom of the press, oppositional political parties, labor unions, and human rights organizations.

In 1962, Cesar Chávez and Dolores Huerta founded the National Farm Workers Association (NFWA) in Delano, California. After the NFWA consolidated with the Filipino Agricultural Workers Organizing Committee (AWOC) and the National Farm Workers Association (NFWA), the United Farm Workers Organizing Committee (UFWOC) was born. Chávez urged the Catholic community in the area to move their focus from charity to social justice, using religiously inspired nonviolent tactics to protest the working conditions of low-paid farm workers of Filipino, Mexican, and American Indian descent.[13] Inspired by and working alongside civil rights leaders Dr. Martin Luther King Jr. and Robert Kennedy, the union members fought for better working conditions, better pay, and better treatment.[14] From 1966–1970, the workers mobilized a successful boycott of grapes, marched, and forced corporations to recognize their union, resulting in many corporations signing contracts with the union members. In 1972, the UFWOC became the UFW and continues to work today for the union rights of farmworkers.[15]

Chicano identity was a central visual component of imagery associated with the UFW and its predecessors. Chávez' brother Richard designed the first UFW flag in 1962 with the Aztec eagle, originally on brown wrapping paper. Richard also took reproducibility into consideration when designing the eagle, squaring the edges of the wings so that it could be easily recreated by union members in their own posters. (Figure 4.4) Chávez said of the flag, "A symbol is an important thing and that is why we chose an Aztec eagle. It gives pride...When people see it they know it means dignity."[16] The colors of the flag also held symbolism. The black eagle was supposed to show the dark situation of the farm workers, the white circle was meant to signify aspirations and hope, and the blood red background was meant to symbolize the sacrifices and labor of the union members. Although the Aztec eagle acknowledged the union originated from Mexican farmworkers, the union was far more diverse than just Mexican members.[17] The Aztec symbolism and style was also used in Xavier Viramontes' iconic *Boycott Grapes* poster from 1973. (Figure 4.5) This poster was created in response to the violent and corrupt tactics of the UFW's competing union, the Teamsters. In the poster, a frustrated Aztec figure, haloed by a starburst of geometric shapes, angrily smashes grapes in his fists. The figure stares directly at the viewer, confronting them with blood running from the grapes in between his clenched hands. The blood then drips over the bold yellow words "BOYCOTT GRAPES" at the bottom third of the image, flanked on either side by two copies of Richard Chávez' UFW logo. The muted triadic color scheme of red, blue, and yellow, with hints of bold orange, highlights the face of the farm worker, who is being visually compared to a strong warrior after the efforts they have put in for their rights. The poster, although considered too graphic by the union because of the blood, was a successful mail-order fundraiser.[18] Other posters created by and for the UFW evoked woodblock etching styles that had been popular during the Mexican Revolution. (Figure 4.6)

The traditions of mural art and printmaking that Mexican and Chicano illustrators popularized and developed have been used across Latin America and the world. Latin American posters from the 20th century are notable for their variety of styles and techniques, as demonstrated by the Sam L. Slick Collection of Latin American and Iberian Posters. Jesús Ruiz Durand created a series of posters in Peru in the comic style of Roy Liechtenstein, creating superheroes out of revolutionaries. Some posters borrow the techniques of modern and contemporary artists Seymour Chwast and Pablo Picasso. Others adopted colors and styles from Soviet and Chinese posters.[19] The Aztec eagle and variations of Che Guevara's visage are repeated in posters from Nicaragua to Argentina to Chile. These posters borrowed from a number of different printmaking and poster styles and techniques in order to create something entirely new. Latin American posters and mural art influenced the aesthetics of many countercultural movements of the 20th century.

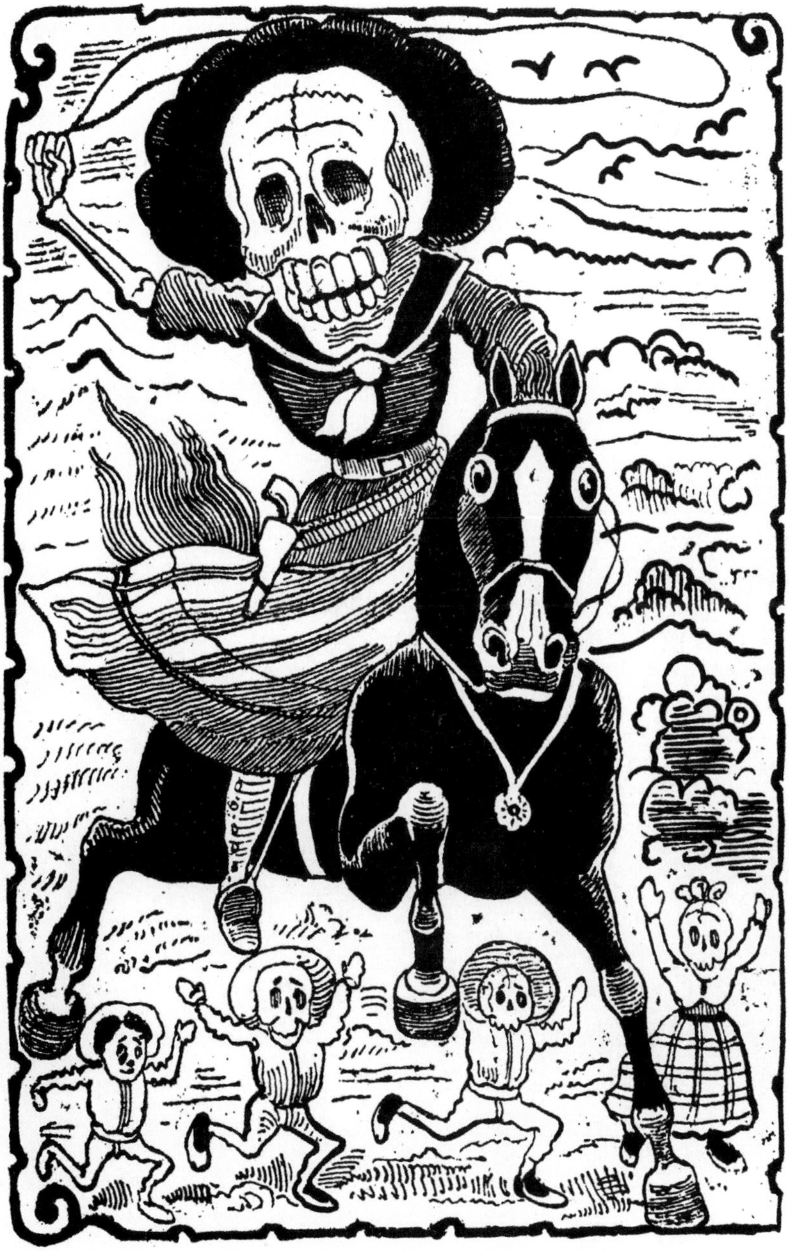

Calavera revolucionaria

Figure 4.1 Guadalupe Posada's 1910 broadsheet *Calavera Maderista* featured a female revolutionary soldier.

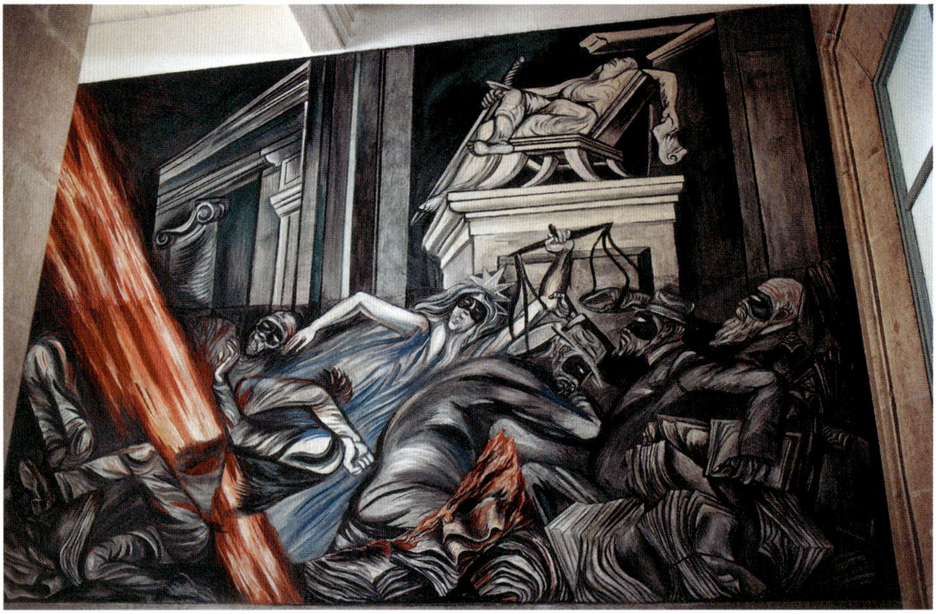

Figure 4.2 José Clemente Orozco openly critiqued the concepts of governmental law and justice in his work, such as in his 1941 mural *Justice*.

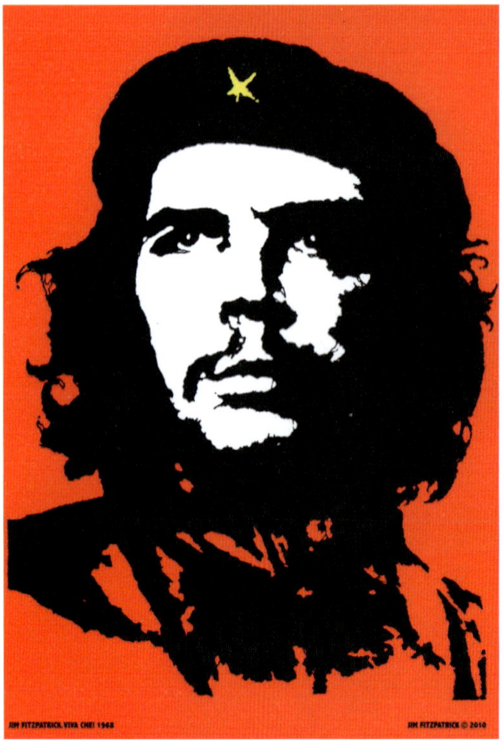

Figure 4.3
Jim Fitzpatrick's 1968 *Viva Che* screenprint became a worldwide recognizable symbol for socialist causes. © Jim Fitzpatrick

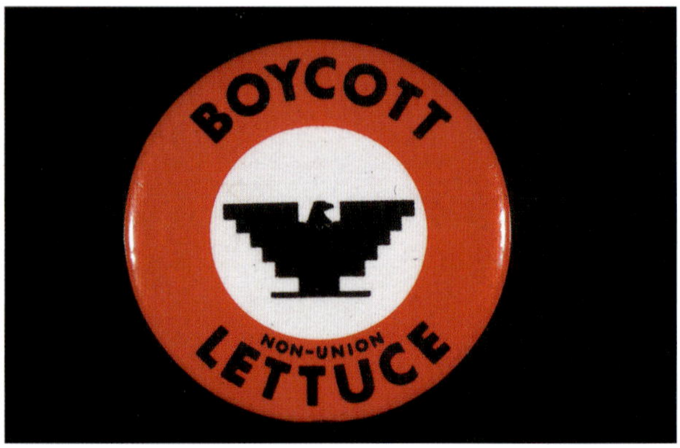

Figure 4.4
Richard Chávez' 1962 logo for the United Farm Workers was simple, easy to reproduce, and endures as the logo for the organization today.

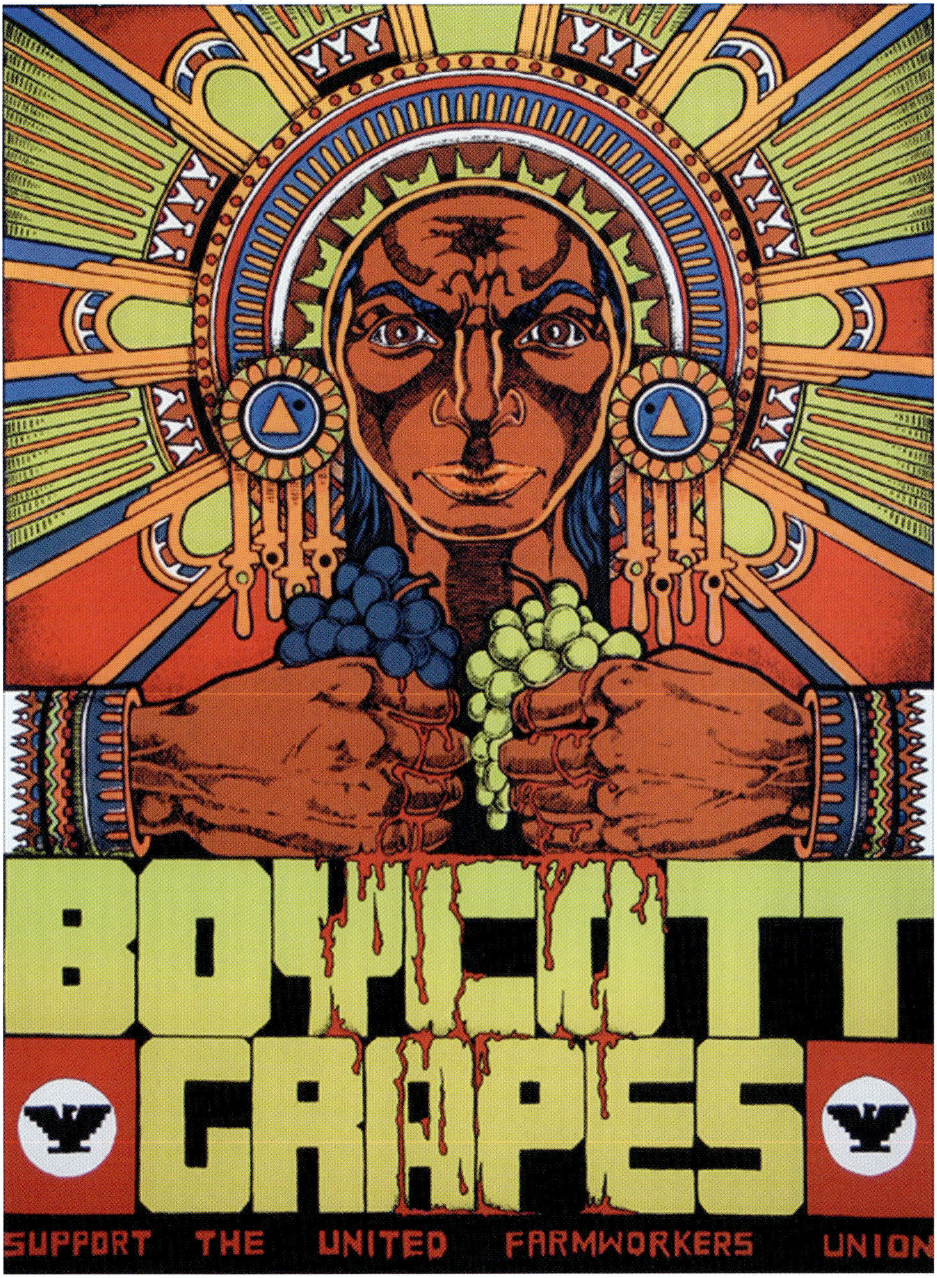

Figure 4.5
Xavier Viramontes' *Boycott Grapes* poster from 1973 became an iconic image of the American union movements and the UFW.

Figure 4.6 This poster for a UFW benefit at the University of Wisconsin – Madison (1977) evoked woodblock etching styles that had been popular during the Mexican Revolution.

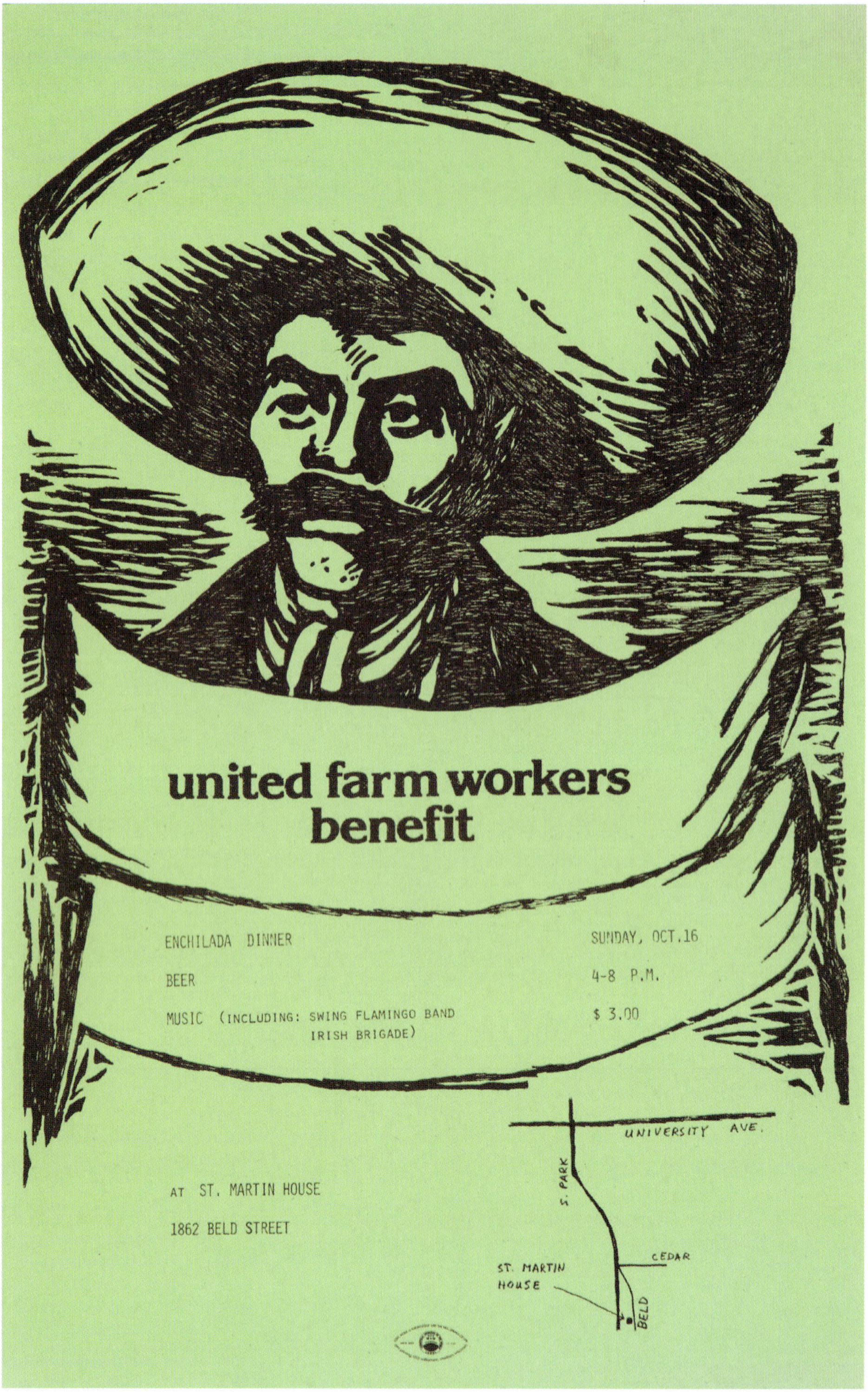

The Vietnam War

Countries across the world participated in grassroots protests of the Vietnam War, but the protests that took place in the US became part of a larger countercultural movement that changed not only the political landscape, but the aesthetic language of the time. The briefly incorporated organization Art Workers' Coalition (AWC) created many works associated with the conflict in Vietnam. The AWC was initially founded to pressure New York City's museums to reform their policies from 1969 to 1971, and successfully lobbied for women and people of color to find more representation at the museums.[20] Because Black and Latino citizens were more likely to be drafted and die in Vietnam, the group's inclusion message was intertwined with an anti-war message.[21] In 1969, the AWC took a disturbing photograph by photographer Ronald L. Haeberle of murdered women and children from the My Lai Massacre and overlaid it with an equally disturbing quote from a CNN interview on the massacre: "Q. And babies? A. And babies." The AWC printed 50,000 copies of this image into a lithography poster to protest the war and pressure art museums to oppose it, and thereby created one of the most enduring illustrations of Vietnam War protest imagery.[22]

GLOBAL POLITICS PERSPECTIVE

What Led to the Vietnam War?

Many Americans are familiar with the 'Vietnam War' through the lens of the 1960s counter-culture movement and the protest movement against the war. What many may not know is that Vietnam had already been the site of violent conflict since it fought for its independence from French colonial rule in the 1940s. After the United States withdrew its forces in 1974, conflict continued throughout the 1980s in different forms. Therefore, Vietnam was the site of war for over forty years, from about 1945 to 1989. In 1945, revolutionary leader Ho Chi Minh and his supporters fought the French colonial rulers, in pursuit of an independent Vietnam with a Communist government. Vietnam was separated in 1954 with French guidance, leaving Minh and the Communists in North Vietnam and an independent Republic of Vietnam in the south. This was a very chaotic event and led to a mass migration of people between the two countries, depending on their political allegiances and economic circumstances.[23] US involvement began gradually as an extension of its new Cold War containment policy; the US wanted to bolster the new Republic of Vietnam, and thus sought to counter the influence of the Soviet Union on the Communist North. American military aid began arriving as early as 1954, but it wasn't until 1961 that American troops were sent to South Vietnam. Revolutionaries from the North had begun making incursions in the South, seeking to reunify the country through insurgent violence and guerilla warfare. In response to the incursions, the United States deployed special forces like the Green Berets in 1961, but within a few years, major American combat and support forces were sent to South Vietnam and the first draft of American civilian men took place in 1964.[24] As American involvement in the conflict increased, so too did public opposition to the war, and to the use of the draft. Students and young people often organized their dissent on college campuses, and became increasingly disillusioned with the political establishment of both major parties due to their commitment to the war.

For both North and South Vietnam, the 1950s and 1960s were politically tumultuous, as hardliners held top government positions in the North, while a series of military coups installed increasingly repressive hardliners in the South. These hardliners were both committed to using violence to defeat their foes. Over the course of the war, civilian casualties were enormous; the Vietnamese government officially stated that as many as 2 million civilians were killed between the years of 1954 and 1975. The US government reports that over 57,000 Americans were killed, and estimates put Vietnamese military deaths, from both the North and the South, at close to 1.3 million. The United States withdrew its forces in 1974, and the South fell to the North within a year, leaving Vietnam as a unified and independent state with a communist regime that remains in place today. Vietnam next fought a war against Cambodia shortly thereafter, invading its neighbor and ultimately toppling the brutal Khmer Rouge regime.[25] It continued to fight both Cambodia and China through the 1980s in limited border skirmishes. The US did not diplomatically recognize this government until 1995, when an American embassy was established in the capital city of Hanoi.

Artist Seymour Chwast has spent decades producing anti-war art, which originated in 1957 with his *Book of Battles* and was popularized with the art he created to protest the Vietnam War. Chwast, along with artists and designers Edward Sorel and Milton Glaser, founded the revolutionary Push Pin Studios in 1954, which purposefully rejected traditional styles, introducing fresh simplicity into the cultural aesthetic. In 2017, Chwast published a compilation of his anti-war work in the book *At War with War.* One of his enduring posters came from a popular anti-war slogan used on buttons during the war: "War is good business, invest your son." (Figure 4.7) In his visually dense poster, Chwast uses lettering reminiscent of Civil War recruitment posters, which tempted viewers with money and values such as honor and commitment. The image also has the bombastic flashiness of circus posters, highlighting the absurdity of the statement. Chwast's work calls out the crooked motivations for war by deep-pocketed politicians and arms salesmen, questioning what commodities we value in society. In his most famous anti-war poster, *End Bad Breath*, Chwast protested the bombing of Vietnam. The poster depicts Uncle Sam, symbolizing Nixon and American politicians, spouting aircrafts and bombs from his mouth. (Figure 4.8) A sunburst brings the viewer's eye to Uncle Sam, who wears a manic expression, highlighting America's power and senselessness. Chwast purports in many interviews that his visual ideas are spontaneous, yet they contain enduring visual truths that have resonated across decades.

INTERVIEW

Seymour Chwast

Steven Heller cites you as helping lead the shift from realism in illustration to "comic expressionism." One focus of the book is how style and technique influence the persuasive messages of political art throughout history. How much does your style and technique influence the messaging in your illustration, and what can looser styles add to the communication of illustrative messages that realism can't?
Yeah, this technique has gotten simpler and more direct, because everybody has less time to concentrate on what is being said and what is being shown. We work with symbols and metaphor, and all those things that get the idea across and in a simple, direct way. Sometimes technique is determined by the media and how the work is being used. But if I do a drawing for *The New York Times* and it's due the next day, I'm going to do a line drawing, and probably keep it simple, but will be concerned about the deadline. And usually there's a sketch that has to be done first, to get approval. So generally, there's a chance to improve on the sketch for the finish. My work is intuitive. And I just do it, because this is what comes out. There are no straightforward rules.

How have you used illustration and text together to communicate a message? Is one more important than the other when creating a composition? What is the relationship between the two?
Sure, they have to work together. Sometimes the type and image are integrated into the work. Sometimes they're completely separate. One is used as a foil for the other. If I do a delicate drawing, I might want the type to be bold. You either balance the type and image or both can be as strong as I want to make it. There are different ways of using it.

How have you used visual concepts and metaphors in your illustrations?
Well, most of the ideas come from the visual language. If I have to represent something, I have to find the best way to do it in a way that people will understand what I'm doing, what I'm talking about. And there are symbols for most things, you know. America is represented by Uncle Sam. It may be a map, there may be a dozen things that could represent the United States that are visual rather than the words. The problem for a designer is finding those things that are not clichés that that can be original, where the context is, is original. So that's what we have to strive for. I used Uncle Sam in a poster that I did, *End Bad Breath*. It was during the Vietnam War, when we were bombing. So that was a way I could easily represent United States in this case in a negative way. It was pure propaganda. I thought for a good cause.

Political themes periodically arise in your work, including many anti-war themes, anti-gun themes, and themes of peace. How has politics played into your career as an illustrator? Were your pieces entirely self-generated, or did you work in partnership with organizations?
I did one poster for a Japanese organization that promotes peace. They come different ways. And *End Bad Breath* was just a

commercial poster done during the period in the 1960s when posters were popular, and people bought them. They were just sold in store, usually rolled up and they were very cheap. The company was called Personality Posters. It was sort of at that time when psychedelic posters were being done promoting music, so that was a market that was big enough to hold political posters as well.

What inspired you to create some of these images? Would you just choose themes that matter to you? Were there any social or market influence that played into creating some of those publications? Did some of your publications such as *At War With War* help you to further explore some of these issues that mattered to you?
Well, since I'm against war, that book allowed me to express that by doing a timeline of every war since 3500 BC, up to the present time, a few years ago, when the book was published. Basically the point was that it never changes. It's all part of a dark side of the human condition.

What advice do you have for students who are interested in pursuing political and editorial illustration?
Well, for students making a living is tough enough. You have to find an outlet where somebody is going to make money off of what you do you know. Magazine publications could be okay. Few posters are being done. There are not many outlets here, so you do as best you can, even if it's for yourself. If you come up with a good book idea that involves text and illustration, fine, then do it. These days, I've been doing a lot of children's books, and other books for grownups. Editorial illustration is difficult. There are a few magazines that do good work, but there are many more illustrators looking for work. It's good time for illustration, but not good for illustrators. In the early 1900s, there were so many magazines using illustration. It's too bad. Photography has just taken over. And now with AI, no illustrator may have a job shortly. It's a problem. I guess I'm concerned about students and people coming up, and if they will be able to satisfy what they are interested in doing. And it is a problem. I guess some of them would go into fine arts and try to sell their work directly. But nothing is easy. Animation may be a good area for some who are inclined, there's a lot of that being done. The students should look around and see where their work is needed and go after it.

Artist and illustrator Martha Rosler utilized collage illustration as a means of distributing her anti-war messages. From 1967 to 1972, Rosler created a series of photomontages entitled *House Beautiful: Bringing the War Home*, playing on the term coined by the U.S. media that the Vietnam War was the "living-room war." Vietnam was the first major American conflict in which Americans could vividly see video coverage of the violence and atrocities of war.[26] Rosler sought to highlight the ironies of affluent Americans passively watching the horrors of war in the comfort of their homes by slicing out images of Vietnamese citizens from *Life* magazine and juxtaposing them with pages of *House Beautiful* magazine. Rosler sought to be more explicit with her work than other artists working at the time, moving away from symbols of America, such as Jasper John's American flags, to force Americans to face the realities of the war.[27] In her work *Tron: Amputee*, a Vietnamese victim of war who has lost her right leg strolls through an elegantly decorated living room with a vaulted ceiling and modernist furniture. (Figure 4.9) A television in the background of the scene is turned off, reminding us of the advantage Americans had (and continue to have) of turning off anything unpleasant and returning to their blissful economic privilege. In another collage, a family of three casually relaxes on a new, king-sized mattress, obliviously reading magazines and playing with toys, while behind them we see a bombed-out, decaying interior of a room. (Figure 4.10) Rosler's work endures into the modern day as the disparities between prosperous Western nations and the rest of the world continue to exist. Rosler distributed these images by Xeroxing copies of the illustrations to hand out at political protests against the war.

Rosler's collage and Xeroxing are an example of how the illustration work of artists during the Vietnam War broke boundaries of what mediums and styles can be used in illustration, contributing to the growth of many countercultural movements at the time. Many student organizations in Europe and the US utilized **screenprinting**, a quick and accessible form of printmaking, as a way of creating protest posters against the war. In Paris, the Atelier Populaire produced silkscreen prints, and in London, the Poster Workshop offered a "pay what you can" model to produce prints for many causes. In America, students at the University of California-Berkeley formed the Free Speech Movement, which protested against the college's free speech restrictions, and utilized posters as a critical communication tool during protests and in the community. At the Rhode Island School of Design (RISD), students also used their silkscreen printmaking skills to produce posters against the war. In 1968–69, RISD students produced a series of eight silkscreened anti-war posters which used simplicity and minimalism to communicate striking messages through visual similarities. In the poster *America?*, the artist uses the visual similarity between the "I" in the word America and the bayonet of a gun, asking the viewer if this violence is how they want America to be represented on the world stage. (Figure 4.11) Even more striking is a poster with simple hand lettering, which parodies an iconic anti-war poster by Lorraine Schneider. (Figure 4.12) In the original poster, Schneider pairs an image of a simple sunflower on a bright, optimistic yellow with the words written in black in the handwriting of a child: "War is not healthy for children and other living things." In the RISD student poster, the cheerful sunflower is removed, and the text, turned to blood red, offers a response: "Peace is not healthy for generals and other killing things." In their illustration, the students placed the onus for peace on what they perceived the real perpetrators of war and violence to be: the politicians and the military-industrial complex.

In 1968, the Black Student Union, Latin American Students Organization, and other student groups at San Francisco State College (now San Francisco State University) joined together to form an organization called the Third World Liberation Front (TWLF). The students who eventually formed the TWLF originally protested the Vietnam War and the draft, including protesting administrators reporting of student academic status to the selective service. The TWLF later protested the lack of diversity on the campus, including the lack of Ethnic Studies and Black Studies departments. The protest actions of the TWLF helped pave the way for the Black Civil Rights Movement and other civil rights movements in history to be placed in college educational curriculum. The TWLF created a larger movement in the Bay Area, and art students Rupert García and Malaquías Montoya led a movement to create posters as fundraisers to bail out strikers who had been jailed. Montoya taught García and other students how to screenprint, which García considered a necessary step to foster political action. García stated that he did not learn to screenprint in school, but learned it as a practical skill from "a need to make multiple images that would support the strike." García was, like Fitzpatrick, inspired by the Korda photo of Che Guevara, beginning his practice of including "individuals who were politically inclined for social change" into his work.[28] The political movements and screenprinting actions of the Bay Area activists helped to raise awareness about international political issues and poster-making techniques, creating an intersectionality of movements brought together through the Civil Rights movement.

FOCUS ON TECHNOLOGY

Silkscreen Printmaking

Silkscreen printmaking, also called serigraphy, has been a longtime favorite medium for printing political posters and flyers. An ancient technique that originated in China during the Song Dynasty, silkscreen printmaking is inexpensive, efficient, and easy to learn. Silkscreen also has an aesthetic that lends itself well to the unflinching messages political posters attempt to convey. Using one color at a time, silkscreen printmaking builds its layers from lightest to darkest, creating bold, flat areas of color that mimic the bold messages that political posters communicate. Silkscreen is so accessible, anyone can set up a silkscreen printmaking workshop in their garage or home. From the late 1970s to early 2000s, the Gocco printmaking machine was estimated to be owned by 1 in 3 Japanese households.[29] Some of the most well-known screenprinting workshops of the 1960s included the Atelier Populaire in Paris, started by students of the École des Beaux-Arts to support striking workers, and the Poster Workshop in Britain, founded by sculptor an expelled Frenchman Jean-Loup Msika. In the US, Pop Artists such as Andy Warhol and Robert Rauschenberg popularized the process among political artists, although it had been previously used by the Works Progress Administration in the mid-1930s.

To create a screenprint, the artist stretches a fine mesh fabric (the "screen") onto a frame, and then applies a stencil using a photographic transfer method. In a darkroom, a fine coat of photosensitive **emulsion** is applied to the screen, and a transparency with a dark image is placed on the screen. The screen is then exposed to light and the uncovered area hardens, while the image area is rinsed away. In the past, instead of using photo emulsion, an artist could simply cut out a stencil and attach it to the screen so ink could only go through the cut area. Once the image is on the screen, the screen is placed on a clamp hinge, and the artist pulls ink across the screen with a squeegee to force it through the screen. When the clamp hinge is lifted, the paper with the printed image is revealed. Prints of multiple colors can be registered (or "lined up") so that darker colors can be printed over lighter colors.

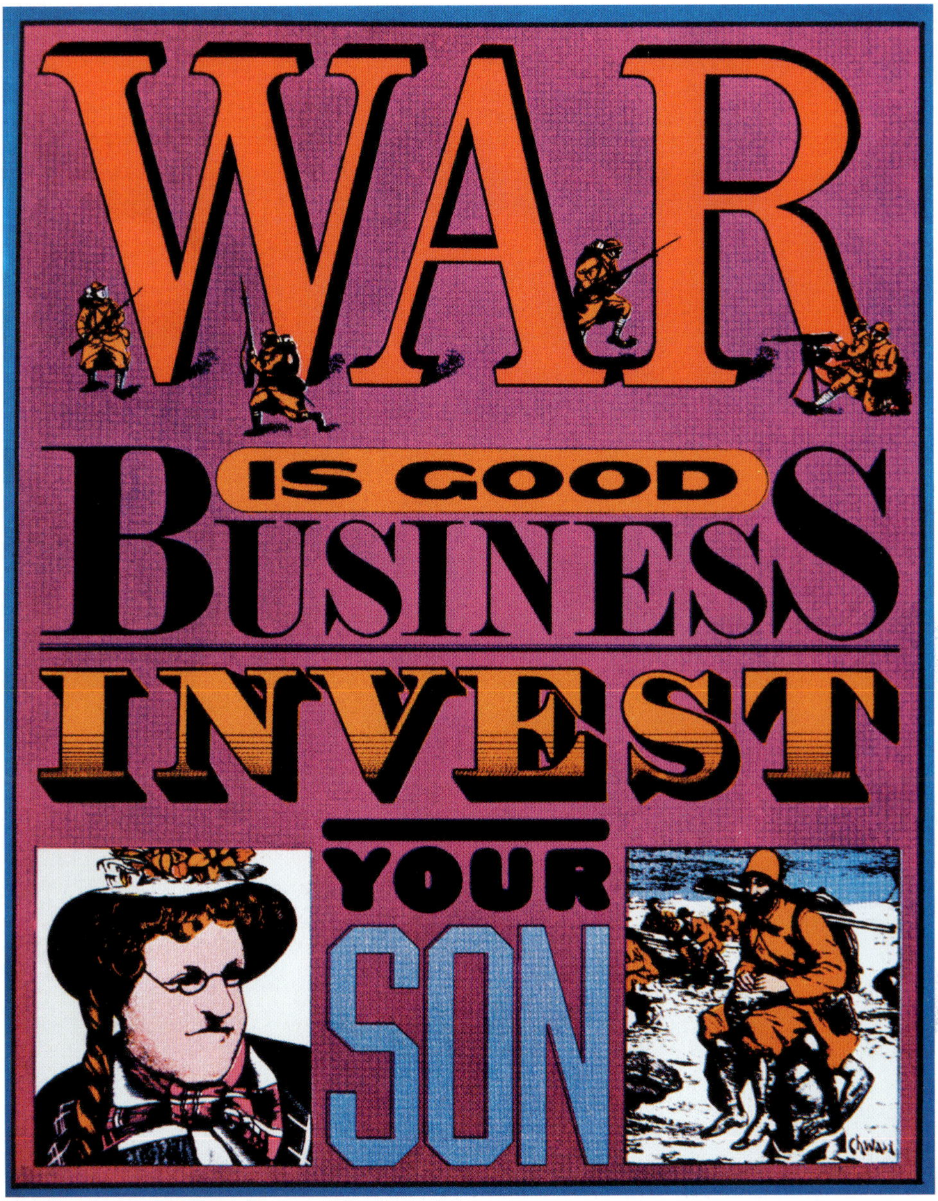

Figure 4.7
Seymour Chwast's 1968 poster *War Is Good Business: Invest Your Son*, like much of the work of PushPin Studios, helped create a change in the American visual aesthetic of the 1960s and 1970s.

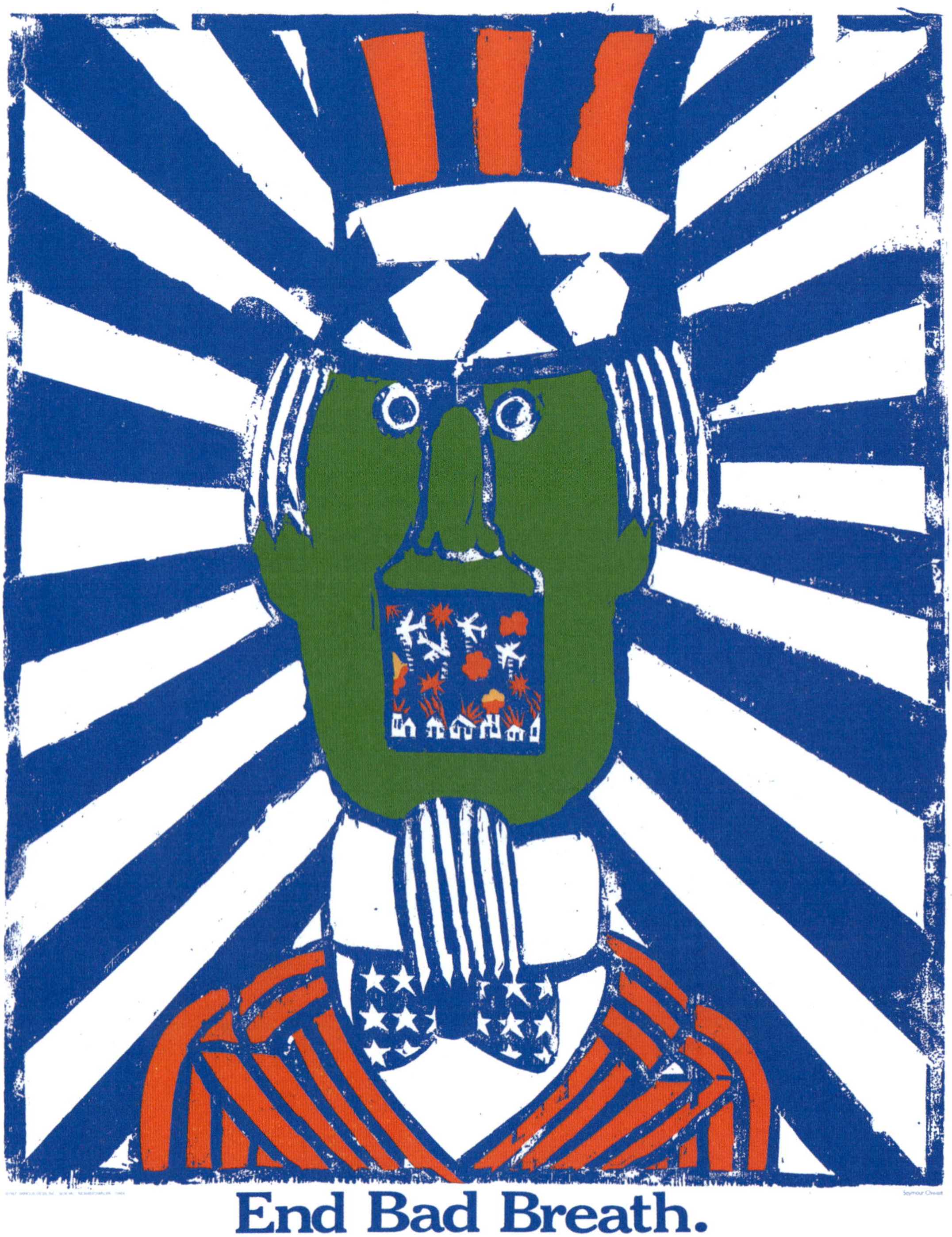

Figure 4.8
In his most famous anti-war poster, *End Bad Breath*, Chwast protested the bombing of Vietnam.

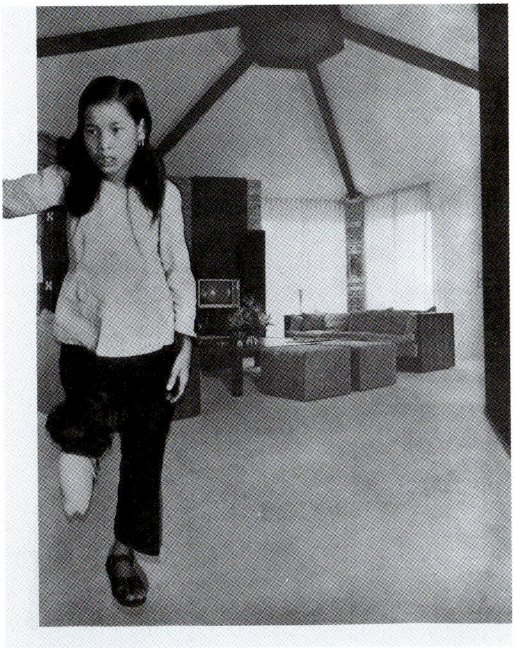

Figure 4.9
Martha Rosler
Tron (*Amputee*), from the series *House Beautiful: Bringing the War Home*. c. 1967-72

Courtesy of the artist and Mitchell-Innes & Nash, New York

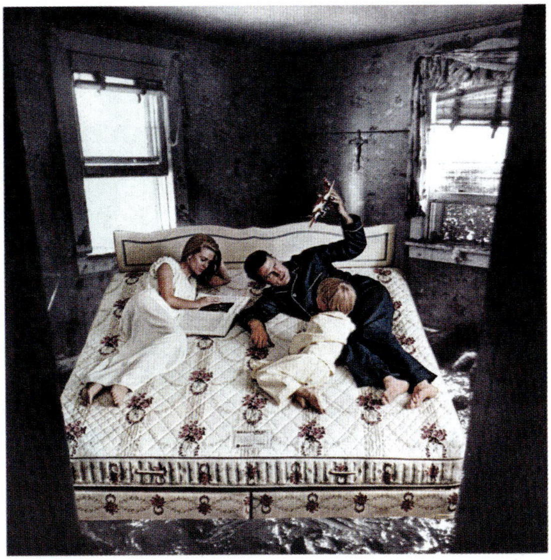

Figure 4.10
Martha Rosler
Beauty Rest, from the series *House Beautiful: Bringing the War Home*. c. 1967-72

Courtesy of the artist and Mitchell-Innes & Nash, New York

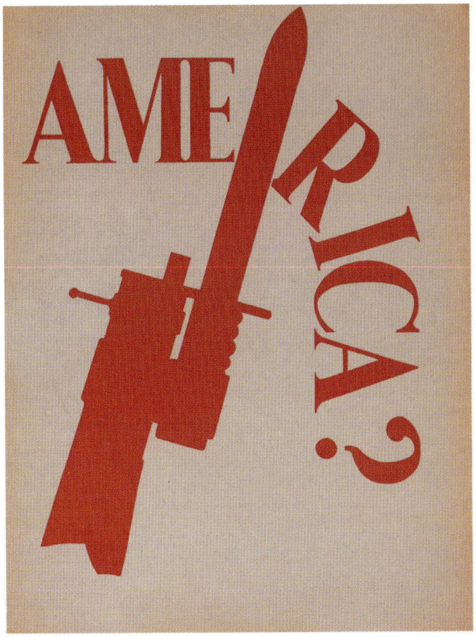

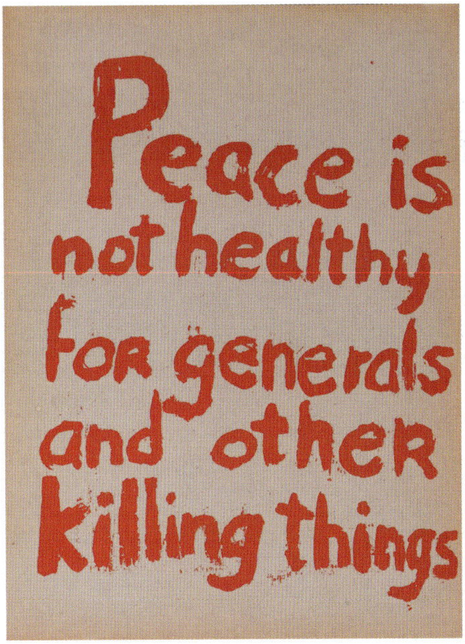

Figure 4.11
(left)
America?
1968–1969, students at RISD

Figure 4.12
(right)
Peace is not healthy for generals and other killing things. 1968-1969, students at RISD

Black Civil Rights

One illustration medium that helped further the Civil Rights Movement may have seemed unconventional for political activism at the time. In 1957, Dr. King and activist Jim Lawson worked together to create a 16-page, 10 cent comic book called *Martin Luther King and The Montgomery Story*. Throughout its pages, it used the popular method of comics as visual storytelling to communicate the story of the Montgomery bus boycott and Walk to Freedom, including depictions of the violence waged on social justice workers. In the book, King describes the story of Gandhi and his tactics of non-violent resistance as an influence. The book concludes with an illustrated "how-to" guide of how to practice non-violent resistance. 250,000 copies of the comic were distributed, and it even inspired non-violent apartheid protests in South Africa, where the government eventually banned the book.[30] Dalia Ziada, an Egyptian activist, had the book translated to Arabic and Farsi and distributed it during the 2011 Arab Spring protests in Egypt. One of the readers of the original book was John Lewis, a founding member of SNCC and its eventual chairman, who represented the organization as a speaker at the 1963 March on Washington. An original Freedom Rider, Lewis led the first March on Selma, known as "Bloody Sunday" for the violent police response. In 2013, when Lewis was a Georgia congressman, he worked with his press secretary Andrew Aydin to create a graphic novel about his experiences in the Civil Rights movement, entitled *March*. (Figures 4.16 and 4.17) Illustrator Nate Powell created over 300 reconstructions of historical figures for the book and vivid scenes from Lewis' descriptions. Lewis said of the book, prior to his death in 2021, "*March* is really so relevant to what is happening right now not only in America, but all over the world. *March* is emerging as the blueprint and as the road map."[31]

Not all civil rights organizations followed the practice of non-violence, and this was reflected in their illustrations as well as their actions. In 1966, in response to police brutality in Oakland, California, Huey P. Newton and Bobby Seale founded a revolutionary political organization named the Black Panther Party. Originally called "The Black Panther Party for Self-Defense," the name originated from the idea that a panther only strikes in self-defense, and not when unprovoked. The logo for the Black Panther Party was borrowed from the Lowndes County Freedom Organization, which was developed by SNCC field secretary Ruth Howard based on the logo of historically Black Clark Atlanta University. (Figure 4.18) The original logo was developed in response to the all-white Southern Democrats' logo, a white rooster, with the metaphor being that the panther would eat the rooster.[32] LCFO co-founder John Hulett said "The black panther is a vicious animal, as you know... He never bothers anything, but when you start pushing him, he moves backward, backward, and backward, and then he comes out and destroys everything that's in front of him."[33] Once the panther logo was adopted by the Black Panther Party, its symbolism, strong value contrast, and foreshortened perspective (indicating a panther leaping out of the page and towards the viewer), made it an enduring symbol of Black protest. It has since appeared on signs, protest posters, and the cover of *The Black Panther* newspaper.

GLOBAL POLITICS PERSPECTIVE

The Black Civil Rights Movement in the United States

The Black American Civil Rights movement gained national and global prominence in the 1950s and 1960s, but its origins began much earlier. One of the oldest organizations committed to racial equality and justice, the National Association for the Advancement of Colored People, or NAACP, was formed at the turn of the 20th century, and many of its initial leaders had ties to the Abolitionist movement against slavery from the pre-Civil War era.[34] It was the end of World War II that helped ignite growing commitment to Black activism in the United States. During the war, some Black service members belonged to integrated units, while others served in segregated units; many were tasked with major roles in Europe and the Pacific. Yet upon returning home to a still-segregated US, their patriotism and pride in their service gave way to frustration and disillusionment. In the southern states, many Black war veterans found that Jim Crow-era laws often prohibited them from voting in elections. This triggered new urgency in the cause for Civil Rights among established groups like the NAACP, and it prompted the creation of new groups, such as the Student Nonviolent Coordinating Committee (SNCC), representing younger activists. (Figure 4.15) In addition, the Southern Christian Leadership Conference (SCLC), with ties to Black Christian leaders like Dr. Martin Luther King Jr., established a connection between faith and activism in advancing the Civil Rights movement.[35]

Globally, social movements may often be united in general causes, but they may differ in their strategies and visions for addressing a cause. Groups like the NAACP, SNCC and SCLC generally focused on nonviolent civil disobedience, using tactics like the Montgomery Bus Boycott and sit-ins at whites-only establishments, to protest segregation and Black disenfranchisement. King himself spoke often of drawing his inspiration from the Indian Independence movement and one of its leaders, Mahatma Gandhi, who had championed peaceful resistance in the push to end British colonialism of India.[36] These groups often sought a fully integrated United States and full equality in opportunities, including voting, access to education, home ownership, and employment opportunities. King and leaders of the NAACP worked within the political establishment to establish allies inside the white political class and inside the presidential administrations of John F. Kennedy and Lyndon B. Johnson. By staying within the confines of the existing political institutions, King and his allies sparked a growing fissure between the different civil rights organizations. A growing group of disillusioned Black civil rights activists, including many young leaders in SNCC like Stokely Carmichael, felt that the goal should not be full equality and integration, but rather Black autonomy and self-reliance. Known as both the Black Power Movement and Black Nationalism, this perspective rested upon a distrust with the existing political institutions and process in the United States, and argued that the only sure way to serve the interests of Black Americans was by creating strong and independent Black communities. Malcolm X emerged as one of the early thought leaders and public figures associated with Black Nationalism in the early 1960s. Malcolm X connected contemporary racial injustice in the US to the marginalization of colonized people in Africa, Asia, and the Middle East and asserted that nonviolence was not the most effective way to achieve Black self-determination. Malcolm X also recognized that a more militant approach to civil rights, might help the cause of the more mainstream groups, stating in 1965, "If white people realize what the alternative is, perhaps they will be more willing to hear Dr. King" (Scott King 1969). Carmichael was the first to use the phrase "Black Power" in 1966. He also admired the work of the NAACP and King, but felt that civil disobedience could only go so far, and was pessimistic that it could cause the moral outrage necessary to compel genuine change.[37]

While the goals and tactics differed, the American Civil Rights Movement is associated with both landmark legislation as well as violence and tragedy. School segregation was overturned in the Brown v. Board of Education ruling in 1954. Poll taxes were outlawed in the ratification of the 24th amendment to the US Constitution in 1964. The Civil Rights Act of 1964 and the Voting Rights Act of 1965 were adopted, establishing legal government protections against discrimination in employment and education, and mandating that southern states guarantee voting rights regardless of race. Yet throughout the movement, peaceful protests were often violently suppressed by law enforcement and white supremacist groups, including at the March on Selma, Alabama in 1964. Innocent children were killed in the bombing of the 16th Street Baptist Church in Birmingham in 1963, and Malcolm X and Dr. Martin Luther King Jr. were both ultimately assassinated, in February 1965 and in April 1968, respectively.

The political illustrations and cartooning traditions started by Black newspapers in the 19th and first half of the 20th century were continued through *The Black Panther* newspaper. The paper was founded in 1967 by Newton and Seale and was a key source of information about the party's activities, beliefs, and history. The newspaper also printed stories about revolutionaries that the party admired, including Patrice Lumumba and Che Guevara. In fact, illustrated posters protesting the jailing of Black Panther Minister of Defense Huey Newton, haloed by a red star, compared him to the Cuban revolutionary. Newton also recreated Guevara's gaze in photographs on the cover of the newspaper, wearing his signature beret. (Recall the upward gaze was Fitzpatrick's edit to the original photograph, a good example of art influencing life.) Sales of the paper were critical to creating funding for the Black Panther's activities, and became a steady source of income for the party. As of 1970, the paper was estimated to have had a circulation of 139,000, with the actual readership being much higher. Originally a four-page 11" × 17" publication, the newsletter eventually grew to a full 32-page newspaper with full-color inserts. Judy Juanita served as the paper's editor-in-chief while a student at San Francisco State. Emory Douglas, the Black Panther Minister of Culture, created the design of the newspaper, which used a variety of typefaces, photographs, cartoons and illustrations to communicate the paper's message.

The pages of the newspaper were filled with an assortment of illustration styles and techniques such as etchings, simple ink cartoons, and two-toned portraits. (Figures 4.19 and 4.20) Many of the illustrations were militant and filled with guns and weapons, including instructions on how to clean and store a gun, and how to make Molotov cocktails and hand grenades. Numerous illustrations of pigs compared them to the police,

President Lyndon B. Johnson, and U.S. imperialism. Solidarity with other oppressed groups was expressed in many illustrations, as were tributes to idealized revolutionary leaders, including, perhaps surprisingly, North Korean dictator Kim Il Sung. Emory Douglas' portraits of leaders and individuals within the party are aesthetically noteworthy, which often graced the back cover of the newspaper. His illustrations earned him the name "the Norman Rockwell of the ghetto."[38] Douglas used bold contour lines, two tone portraits, patterns such as dots, hatches, and checkers, and splashes of color to create visually arresting illustrations.

Another important contributor to the paper was M. Gayle Dickson, also known as Asali. Dickson was the first female illustrator for the paper, creating illustrations between 1972–74 that countered the masculine, violent imagery of Douglas' and other illustrators' previous images. Dickson focused on the subjects of women, children, and the elderly, and her themes revolved around the Black Panthers' community programs like free groceries and promoting voting participation. In one illustration, an elderly woman embraces a bag of groceries, face filled with joy as her hat, jacket, and grocery bag are adorned with political ads.

By 1974, the Black Panther Party had essentially dissolved due to infighting, government interference, and corruption, but the paper continued until 1980. By 1976, the content of the paper had shifted in direction, becoming much more intersectional and pan-national, and the themes of the paper's cartoons lost their previous violence and militarism. Emory Douglas' iconic posters continued to be offered for sale in the back pages of the paper. Following the close of the paper, Douglas worked for the *San Francisco Sun Reporter*, a Black community publication, for 30 years, and continues to create art for activist causes. Douglas' art has become more popular and mainstream, with museums around the world holding exhibitions of his work. Douglas reflected on the value of unvarnished, outsider viewpoints at a talk at the Walker Art Center in Minneapolis in 2015, "When you're an outsider, you can be provocative and do what you do to try to correct injustice. It's no problem to be outside of the context of exploitation, outside of the context of bigotry, outside of a system of institutionalized racism. That's the best place to be."[39] In 2021, a graphic novel history entitled *The Black Panther Party*, was published by author David F. Walker and illustrator Marcus Kwame Anderson.

Today, Black illustrators continue to fight for their civil rights through artistic messaging. The Black Lives Matter movement emerged in 2013, following the acquittal of Trayvon Martin's killer, and the movement grew after the police killings of Michael Brown and Eric Gardner. In Atlanta, the heart of the Civil Rights Movement, many illustrators have used murals and street art to tackle political subjects. In 2020, artist Fabian Williams witnessed the bulldozing of an iconic wall which held a mural of football player Colin Kaepernick. Kaepernick was known for kneeling during the national anthem at a 2016 game as a protest against police mistreatment of Black citizens, which caused widespread controversy. Williams spoke with the owner of the building, who said he had been put under pressure to bulldoze it. Williams believed this was an intentional act of silencing Black dissent because the mural was on the route NFL teams would take to the Atlanta Falcons stadium for the upcoming SuperBowl LI. Williams then led a movement to have seven prominent street artists create Kaepernick murals across the city over the course of three days prior to SuperBowl Sunday, gaining international media attention. Williams said about his response, "This was the first day of Black History Month in America. You mean to tell me you're tearing down the building with Colin Kaepernick, who is protesting against police brutality and systemic racism, on this day? To me, art is communication. So when you destroy a piece of work on a certain day, you are communicating how you feel about that work, about that subject matter, about that person."[40] This story shows the importance of street art as illustration, that it can be, like a political cartoon or quickly illustrated protest poster, made to communicate a direct message to a specific audience.

INTERVIEW

Fabian Williams

Tell me about your work as an illustrator and, previously, as an art director. How has the medium of illustration influenced your mural work today?
I definitely use my education as an illustrator. My degree is in illustration and graphic design from East Carolina University. I started out really trying to do work as an editorial illustrator. I used to look at the illustrator society books and I would picture myself in there as one of those artists. Instead, I ended up doing web design, because those were the jobs that were available. When I was knee deep in doing web design and advertising, I got sick of it. Because I spent so much time online arguing with people about my political views, I quickly discovered that leaving comments and arguing with people on social media doesn't necessarily change the wave or affect culture, so I decided to start doing artwork that addresses those things. To me, the biggest platform for doing something like that without having to go through a middleman is taking it to the street. I started going to buildings in the West End that I felt like were abandoned and started painting. I would just address political topics, or I would paint somebody that I felt needed to be known, like C.T. Vivian, or John Lewis, or Ralph David Abernathy. I was just picking random civil rights leaders who played an important part, but didn't get the media presence that Martin Luther King Jr. got. I wanted to create a campaign of "this is what the city should look like." It's 50% Black. Most of the city's leadership is Black. It should look like that when you ride around town, just like any other city. Then I started getting paid to do murals, but I still keep it geared towards social issues that I'm concerned about.

What was one of your first paid murals?
I want to say, for murals, it was the "Education is not a Crime" or "Paragraphilizer." "Paragraphilizer" is about how African American history has been condensed into a paragraph in US history books. I came up with the concept off the memory of being in the third grade. The teacher was talking about George Washington. And I was like, "Did he own slaves?" The teacher was like, "Yes, but he treated them *well*." You know, as an eight-year-old, it's like, "but how can you treat a slave well, when a slave was a slave? If you're a slave, then in general… things are not good, in the house, in the field." So, you know, later on, you find that George Washington did not, in fact, treat the slaves well. Then you find out that the Nazis got their ideology from Jim Crow. So who's leading who? They don't even count the amount of people that suffered and

died under slavery for hundreds of years in America as some sort of Holocaust equivalent or catastrophe. Imagine if the Holocaust kept on for 400 years. We have truly generational problems. I do things that I don't even understand sometimes, because my family's been through it.

How are you hoping to reach your audience with murals in a way you are unable to reach them with other media?
Street art is ephemeral, it's not there for forever. It comes and goes, like a memory. The landscape is always changing, and your medium is always in transit. The more powerful your message is, the longer it stays. I have a couple of pieces that I painted when I first started, and they're around because people care about them. And they care about them because it connects to something that's deeper than something trivial, like your name or some butterflies. People will fight for something that has historical relevance, or connects a generation to another generation. If someone chooses to remove a piece, sometimes it creates like a reaction. Art is a lot of things, it's a weapon, it's a gift, it's a medium of substance, it's a reflection. If you use it correctly, who knows what could happen?

What's the process of how you select your clients and how they find you?
A lot of times the people that come to me have projects that just align with what I'm doing. But I have had to turn down some projects that just didn't sit right with me. I'm not an ad agency anymore. I don't just take anything just because the money's good. It has to align with my beliefs and goals. Someone wanted me to paint a piece on a newly renovated police station. At first I thought it would be cool, like great to make an image about good Black community policing. But then I was like, "It can be used as propaganda." So I said no.

I have decided recently, in my work, that I'm not going to dwell on the past anymore. I'm gonna focus on the future. Focusing on the future is really hard, because all the data that we're getting right now about the future is super negative, but that is because of who

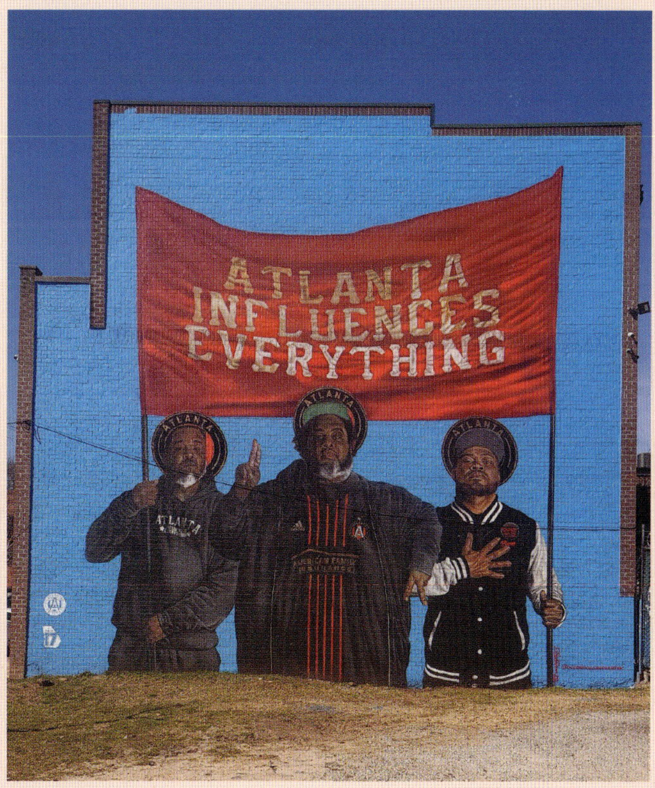

Figure 4.13
Three Wise Men (Atlanta Influences Everything)
© Fabian Williams, Occasional Superstar, 2022

is pushing that narrative. If I understand what I understand about quantum physics, the future is yet to be determined. There are many outcomes for the future. That means the future being broadcast to us not necessarily the future that we have to accept. This is just an option. Or we can create another narrative.

It seems a big part of your work is not just the art itself, but also the process of the creation, curation, and destruction of art, and who has control over this. I think a great example is how you mobilized Black artists in Atlanta after the Colin Kaepernick mural was bulldozed. Could you tell me about that and the powers and symbolism at play?
The day the mural and the building got demolished, I was doing a mural one block down. I just happened to roll up when they were freshly destroying the building. This was the Friday before the Superbowl. It was surreal. I was like, they could just paint it over, but they destroyed the building. It was such an egregious overstep. I knew something was definitely weird because I had met the guy that owned the building. When I talked to him, he said he liked the Colin Kaepernick mural, and that people from the city were trying to get him to paint over it. I told him he didn't have to do any of that, because I was involved in a lawsuit against the city with two other artists, Yoyo Ferro and Peter Ferrari, that said that the city can't tell a private business owner what they can do with their building. The proposed legislation was called the Public Arts Ordinance. So when the piece was getting destroyed, I was like, "Okay, this is weird, and the timing is weird. I don't like it." I decided to make a post, and I took a video while they were demolishing it, and I posted it online. It just caught fire and went viral, and then the news started reporting on it. My homeboy Fahamu [Pecou] called me once he saw the video, "Man, don't let that video be the last thing people see of this mural." I was like, "I'm gonna repaint it, you know, I'm just gonna paint it somewhere else." My manager Ash had a great idea, that we should paint Kaepernick's face all over the city. I thought we needed to get seven businesses to agree to let us paint Kaepernick on them, which ended up being eight, really nine. Sunday morning, I got up at one o'clock in the morning and I painted the first one. He was like Jesus risen on the third day, because it was the third day, which was the Super Bowl. The city really showed up. It was not anything I expected.

Tell me about your process of creating a mural.
I don't necessarily have a dialogue a lot of times, I just have like a dream or a vision. I take a shower, and like something appears to me, and I'll go paint it. That's pretty much what my process was for the first few years. My way of working through a lot of my ideas is my trusty sketchbook. Sometimes I go straight to the wall, depends on how hard ideas are pushing on me. Sometimes, I have a conversation with some of my friends. On the feedback I get, I move forward and work out the details conceptually. Then I go to the wall.

Do you project the images up or do you freehand them?
When I first started I did it, now I use a laser grid. If I should ever teach, I'd have [students] first learn to do it by eye, then learn how to use a projector, then use a laser grid. I'm able to do all three. I can pick any corner and look at it and work it out visually. When you do it by hand, you can get it right, or I mess up and fix it repeatedly. I'm going up and then getting down off the lift or ladder and going back and look across the street and looking at it and say "Is it right?" I did the mural at the King Memorial Marta station by eye in four days. Joe King did the letters, and I did the clouds and the figure. Then Fahamu [Pecou] came over and

did the texture on it. That was the biggest mural I had done up until that date. The biggest one I've done by eye is Hosea Williams on Studioplex.

Do you have any advice for students interested in pursuing political illustration?
Reverse engineer who you are talking to. Put yourself in the shoes of somebody that's going to walk by the mural, and design something that they can understand. Oftentimes in advertising we have a goal. We want this person to buy this thing. We want them to click on this ad. When I was doing banner ads, it was all about getting someone to interact and stall on your ad. It was even better if you get them to interact with it and press the link, which they call it impressions. I treated my murals like banner ads. It's not much different than going to a website. I only have a few seconds. I want you to notice, and then if I can hold your attention, I can get you. I'm going to employ techniques to disrupt your daily routine, like color, metallic paint, or fluorescent paint. Let me turn your eye, and then I got you.

Run it by some people before you throw it up on the wall. Sometimes, creatives fall in love with an idea without fine tuning it. It can be a good idea, but if it's not fine-tuned, you're gonna miss the mark. It's really like engineering. You're playing with the mechanics of the mind. If you can get somebody to buy some shit that they don't need, then you can get them to consider loving their neighbor. And I want you to see visions of people in love, or people connecting in a friendly way. Americans liking Americans. That's my goal, to bring us together.

[Toni] Cade Bambara said, "The artist's job is to make the revolution irresistible." Advertisers know how powerful artists are, the military knows how powerful propaganda is. Government knows how powerful art is. Dictators know how powerful artists are, that's why when they come into power, they get rid of the artists, poets, writers, the painters, the movie makers. They disappear, because that's where the power is. So, what are you using your power for?

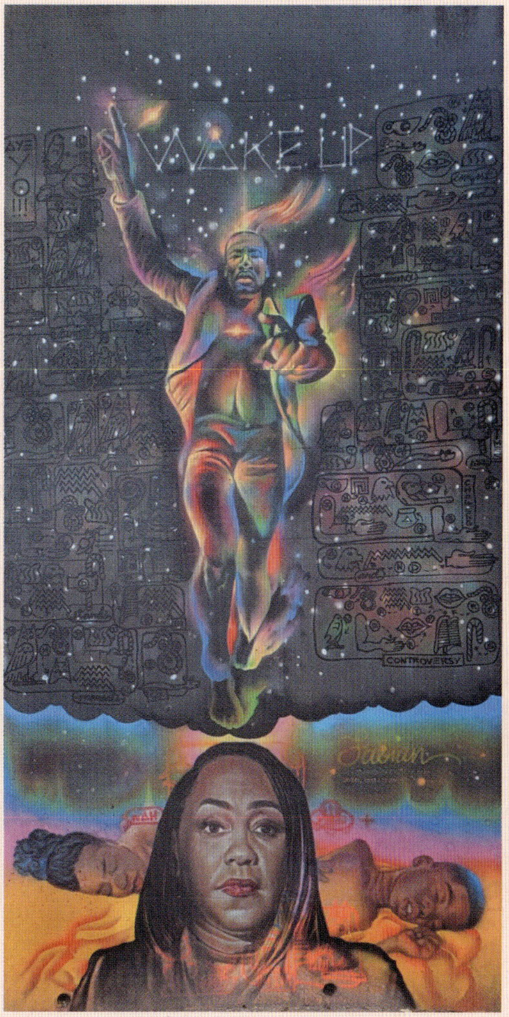

Figure 4.14
Mural of Fani Willis and MLK
© Fabian Williams, Occasional Superstar, 2023

Other forms of illustration have been used to communicate issues of Black Civil Rights, and have also experienced censorship. Illustrator Nikkolas Smith uses the medium of children's books to communicate Black issues, having illustrated books on school desegregation, the history of slavery, the use of the Confederate flag, and other subjects. His book *Born on the Water* by the 1619 Project has been banned in Florida and Texas. Kadir Nelson has illustrated over 30 children's books, as well as multiple covers for *The New Yorker*, and film concept art and posters about Black subjects. In 2019, Liz Montague became the first black female illustrator to draw a cartoon for *The New Yorker*. Many of her cartoons address issues of Blackness in America, including her second cartoon for *The New Yorker* published at the height of the Black Lives Matter movement in 2020. In the cartoon, Montague drew two Black women at a kitchen table, preparing to protest while making signs and buttons, while one of their phones rings. The caption states, "Just ignore it – my white friends keep checking in on me because they think racism is new." Black illustrators from diverse genres and styles were pulled into political messaging because of Black Lives Matter. Fantasy artist and illustrator Lauren Brown had this to say about her piece *We Are Not Prey*, created in 2014: (Figure 4.21)

> "At the start of the BLM movement, I felt a profound sense of powerlessness while I had to witness my Black brothers and sisters getting killed on the streets, broadcasted on national news and watching police officers get away with it. This piece was created to channel that frustration, and speak out that together we could overcome this oppression with fire in our hearts. Even though we were struck down like prey, our fire could strike down the coldness of the apathy against us beyond the shadow of a doubt. We have done and always will fight for better. At the center of it all, a Black woman, as the cornerstone of our fight, of our protection, and of our voices, is the one to project that dream."

In 2020, Brown revived the print as a fundraiser for Black Lives Matter and The Bail Project, which offers free bail assistance in hopes of creating a fairer justice system. Illustration that has documented the Black struggle for justice and civil rights provides us with a historical record that shows these issues are perennial, and contemporary Black illustrators continue to use their craft and voices to share their stories.

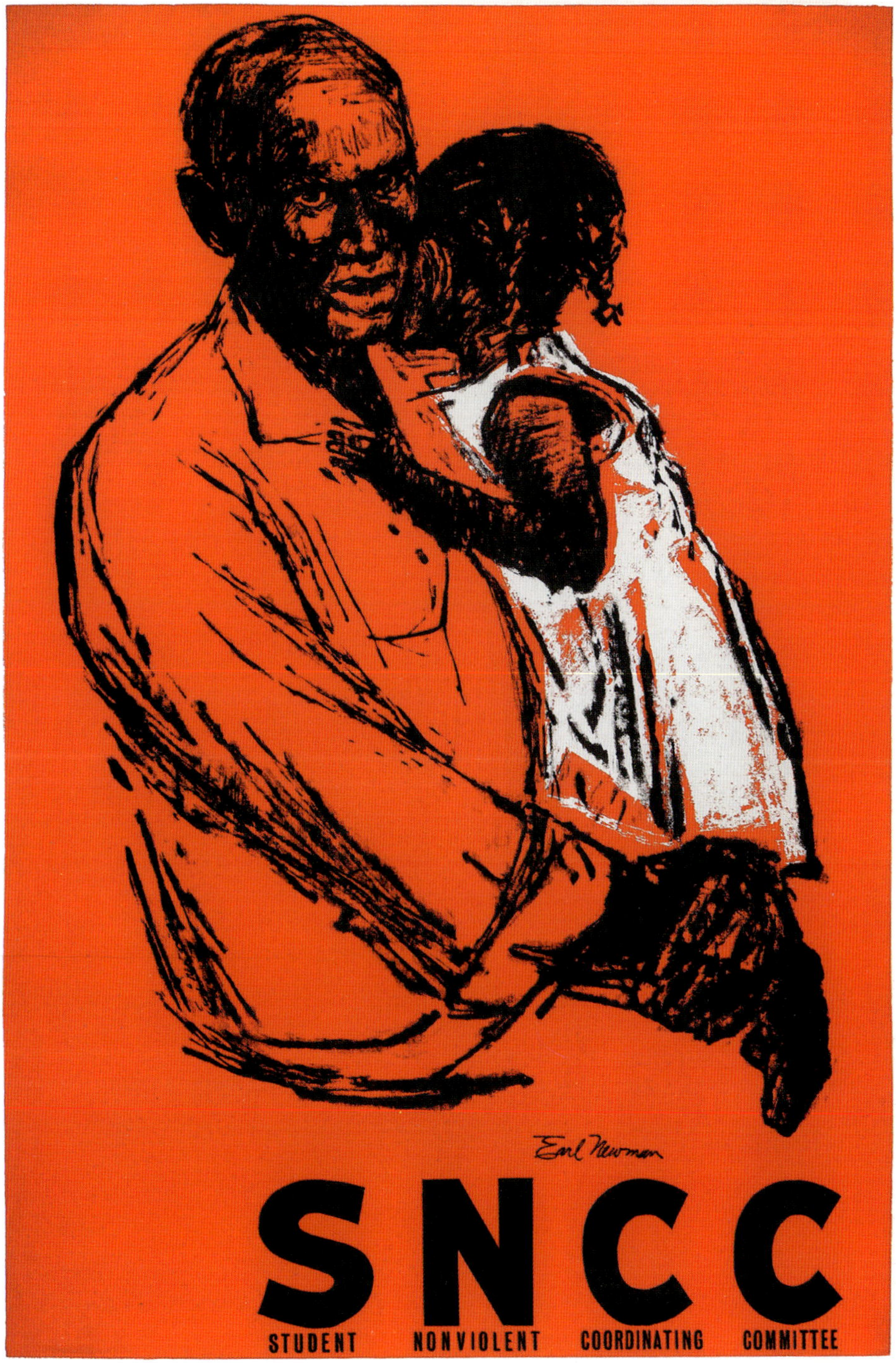

Figure 4.15 A 1964 Student Nonviolent Coordinating Committee (SNCC) poster by Earl Newman.

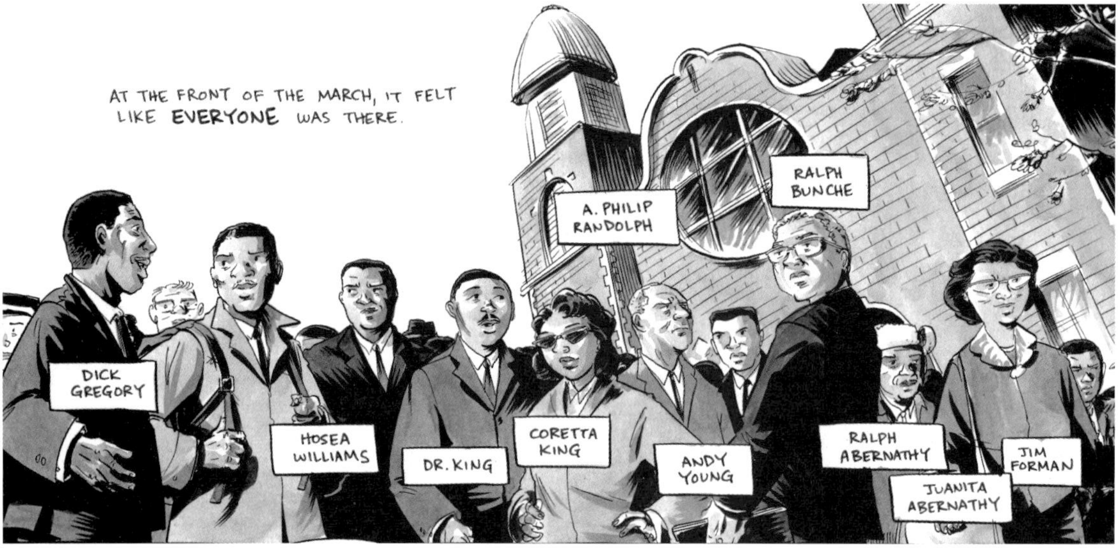

Figure 4.16
Excerpt from the 2013 book *March* by John Lewis and Andrew Aydin, illustrated by Nate Powell

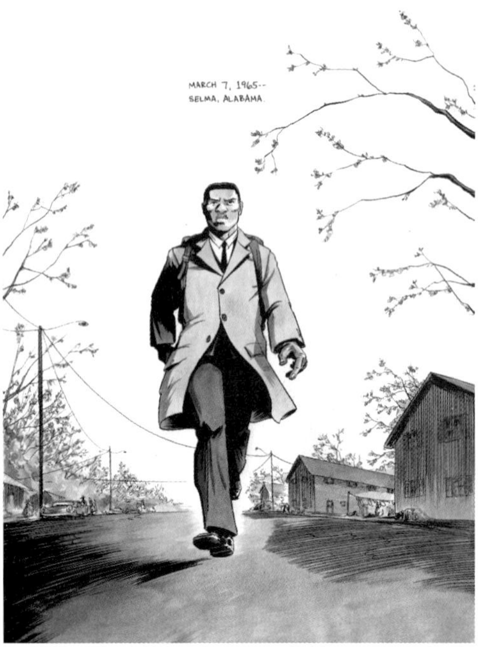

Figure 4.17
Excerpt from the 2013 book *March* by John Lewis and Andrew Aydin, illustrated by Nate Powell

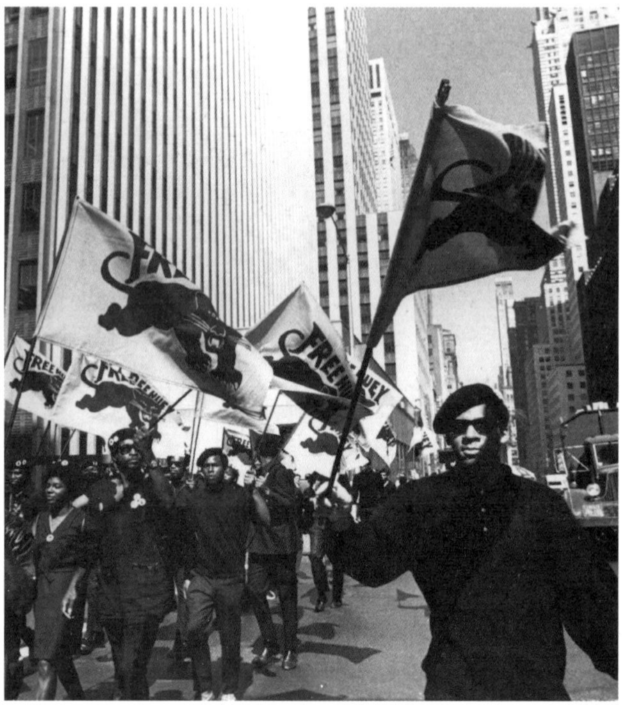

Figure 4.18
The logo for the Black Panther Party was borrowed from the Lowndes County Freedom Organization, which was developed by SNCC field secretary Ruth Howard based on the historically Black Clark Atlanta University logo.

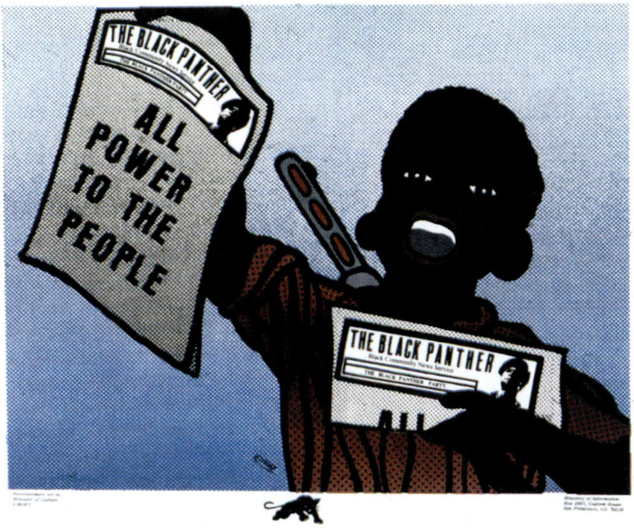

Figure 4.19
An Emory Douglas poster (1968–1969) for the Black Panther Party.

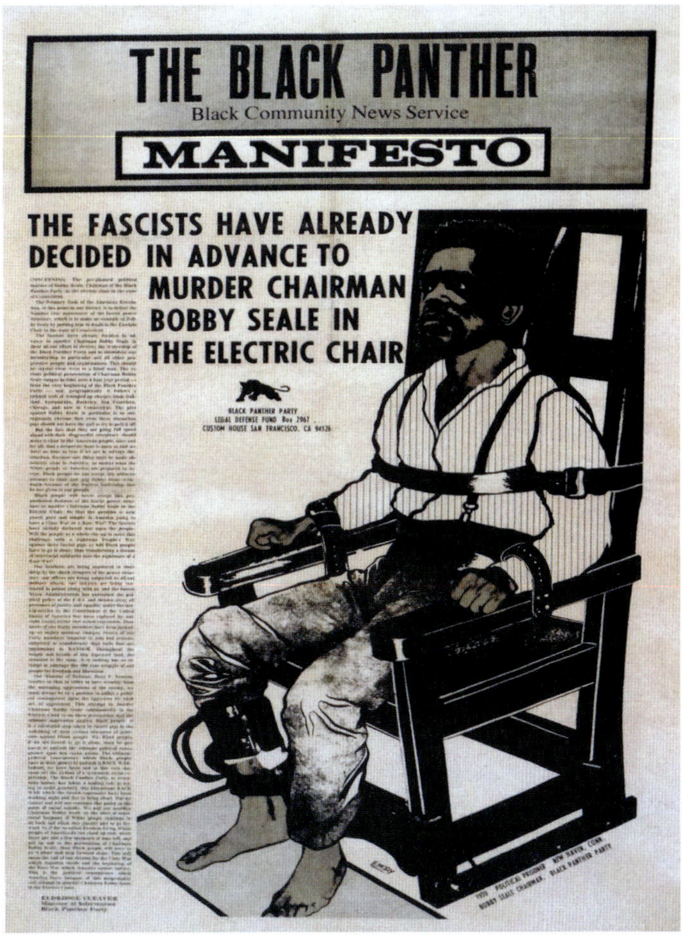

Figure 4.20
A cover of *The Black Panther* newspaper by Emory Douglas (1970). Douglas' prolific illustration and distinctive style defined the aesthetic of the newspaper.

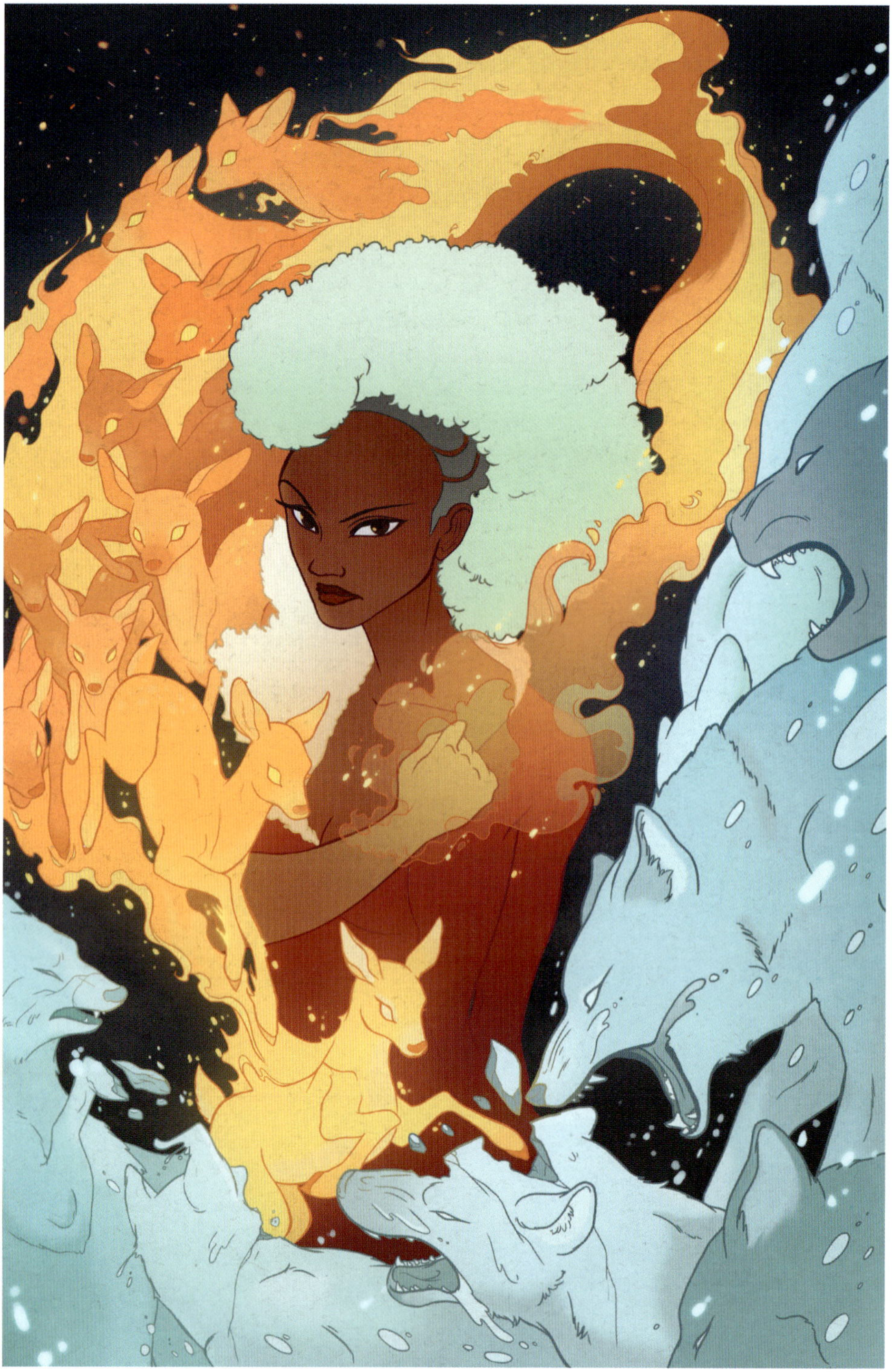

Figure 4.21 We Are Not Prey, 2014 © Lauren Brown, LAB Illustration

LGBTQ+

Religious codes worldwide have admonished same-sex sexual relations throughout history, but it wasn't until the 1530s that discriminatory laws began to be created outside of theocracies. In Great Britain, sodomy remained a crime punishable by death until 1861, and after which, penal codes as punishment for sodomy existed throughout Europe. By the end of the 19th century, gay rights organizations began lobbying for political rights, particularly the Wissenschaftlich-humanitäres Komitee (Scientific-Humanitarian Committee) in Berlin. Although the organization failed to change any laws, it did bring about a degree of tolerance for a gay underground in Germany prior to World War II. As gay organizations began to flourish following World War II, political and police backlash against the organizations rose to meet them.[41]

The late 1950s and 1960s saw violent attacks upon the gay community in the United States, but also saw the rise of publications that advocated for gay rights, including *The Advocate. The Advocate* not only promoted gay rights through articles, but also through the power of political cartoons. John Sam Allen, working under a pseudonym to protect himself from retribution, as many contributors to the paper did, created some of the paper's earliest cartoons, exploring themes of police violence, gay hatred, and personal themes involving the inner struggles of being gay. A powerful 1968 comic entitled *Klan Comic*, shows Klansmen surrounding and burning the Mars symbol, a symbol for man, labeled "hate, ignorance, self doubt, prejudice." The comic becomes even more powerful upon learning Allen committed suicide in 1970.[42] Many cartoonists continued to create cartoons for *The Advocate* and other publications. Illustrator and comic artist Rupert Kinnard, born in 1954, was frustrated with the whiteness of queer events in Portland, Oregon, and took part in creating *Just Out,* the first queer publication in the state. For *Just Out,* Kinnard became known for the first gay and lesbian African American comic strip characters in a strip called "Cathartic Comics." Kinnard also founded the African American Lesbians and Gay United, and went on to work for a number of publications in the San Francisco Bay Area. Kinnard is considered a pioneer of Black gay advocacy and illustration.[43]

Keith Haring began his education as a commercial graphic artist in Pittsburgh, but inspired by the book *The Art Spirit* by Robert Henri, dropped out to pursue art that was created for the masses, instead of hanging it on museum walls. Finding his community in the East Village street art scene in New York City, Haring continued to study on his own and later at the School of Visual Arts, befriending artists Jean-Michael Basquiat and Kenny Scharf. Keith Haring is primarily remembered today for the graphic, bold colors and patterns of his dancing figures, radiating lines, and barking dogs, but also created sexually explicit and erotic art that declared his unashamed identity as a gay man and activist. Committed to sharing art with everyone and providing it at affordable costs, illustration, in its traditional definition, provided Haring with an outlet to practice his beliefs. Haring illustrated posters, toys, clothing, and buttons and sold them at his Pop Shop in Soho, while enduring criticism from the fine art world for "selling out." As Haring's fame grew with many international commissions, he was diagnosed with AIDS in 1988. Despite his diagnosis, Haring committed himself further to AIDS awareness and activism, establishing the Keith Haring Foundation and used his power of popularity, fostered by his illustrated work, to continue to educate through his murals and printed works. One of his most notable prints, created in 1989, a year before his death, *Ignorance = Fear*, features three yellow figures, mimicking the "see no evil, hear no evil, speak no evil" stances, each slashed with a pink X, indicating death by AIDS. (Figure 4.22) The bottom of the poster reads "Silence = Death, Fight AIDS, Act Up," a call to action to bring the verboten conversation of AIDS into the mainstream. Haring passed away from the disease in 1990 at the age of 31. His short life paved the way for gay activists, AIDS research and prevention, social justice causes, and gay visibility. Haring can also be remembered as a champion of illustration, eliminating boundaries between illustrative mediums and genres, and reducing the stigma of illustrative artworks.

Public art as illustration is not limited to paint on walls. In 1985, gay activist Cleve Jones was struck with an idea while planning an annual march to honor gay San Francisco supervisor Harvey Milk and mayor George Moscone, who were assassinated in 1978. When planning the march, Jones learned that 1,000 people had died of AIDS in the past year in San Francisco, and asked marchers to write the names of the people who had died on pieces of paper that were taped to the side of the San Francisco Federal Building. Jones reflected that the names looked like a "patchwork quilt."[44] The first panel for the AIDS Memorial Quilt was created by Jones to honor his friend Marvin Feldman, and he created the panel at 6' × 3', the approximate size of a grave. Jones recalls, "I remember one day exclaiming and raged to my friend, 'You know, if this was a meadow with a thousand corpses rotting in the sun, then people would look at this, they would see it… so each panel is the approximate size of a grave and that was deliberate. I wanted to show how much land would be covered if all of these bodies were lined up head to toe."[45] On October 11th 1987, during the National March on Washington for Lesbian and Gay Rights, the 1,920 panel quilt was displayed for the first time.[46] (Figures 4.23 and 4.24) Sewn into blocks of six panels, the quilt covered a space larger than a football field on the National Mall in Washington DC. Over half a million people visited the quilt during its initial display. Jones hoped that the act of sewing "different colors and different textures" together, a metaphor for the gay community, would be therapeutic and comforting for the participants. The panels show a vast diversity of quilted illustration, typography, design, and style. The illustrations on the quilt include two penguins surrounded by a heart, depictions of music and mountains, an abundance of rainbows, a baby rattle for a child victim, portraits, symbols of many religions and identities, and more. The visual impact of the quilt is two-fold: first, from the sheer size of the quilt, which now includes 50,000 panels representing 110,000 AIDS victims, but also for the visual impact of community and folk art. While the metaphor of each panel was initially meant to represent a grave, each panel represents instead a life, full of color, memories, and stories. In 1988, a panel was received unlike any other previously sent to the project. A stark black panel, inscribed with the words "The Last One," has been saved by the project as a symbol of hope: that one day it will be included as a permanent, final panel in the quilt when the disease is eradicated.

Contemporary LGBTQ+ illustrators have found new freedom and venues for their illustration and political cartoons. Internet outlets, including social media and on-line publications, have become especially valuable in the queer community to help organize events, build community, and share political views through imagery and illustration. The art collective Papi Juice in New York City utilizes illustration on posters and social media to promote political events, causes, and fundraisers, including art by illustrator Mohammed Iman. Illustrator Ryan Hartley Smith uses sketchbook illustration on his website and social media to create what he describes as an "ongoing, informal archive of queer happenings and history." Smith's illustrations include imagery associated with queer protests, demonstrations, public talks, and nightlife in his residence of New York City. (Figure 4.25) Part of Smith's series focuses on creating illustrated portraits of diverse queer activists, politicians, and artists, including Qween Jean, Crystal Hudson, Mike Curato, and others. (Figures 4.26 and 4.27) Quotations accompanying the portraits offer snippets of insight into queer issues in the community. The full collection of illustrations also introduces the viewer to the diversity within the queer community in New York City. Queer and trans owned stationary collective Ash + Chess has successfully created a large business for queer activist art, spanning a variety of mediums such as t-shirts, stickers, posters, and books. Their bright, colorful, and fluorescent aesthetic creates approachable work, while not shying away from serious topics. In 2023, Ash + Chess' collection was pulled from the retail giant Target, after threats were made to the store and its employees. Progressive political cartoon website the Nib also frequently features LGBTQ+ illustrators and topics on its site, including featuring a series of trans illustrators' responses to proposed "bathroom laws," many of which began emerging around 2016. By using the accessible method of storytelling through comics, trans artists were able to express their stories and viewpoints on such laws. Digital activism and the associated visuals have become especially valuable in the queer community, especially because of its reach to parts of the world where queerness is not accepted, and because members of the group are not always physically identifiable. Mishti Ali was quoted in the *Gay Times* as saying, "Without the internet, I don't think people would have as much awareness of non-binary and gender nonconforming identities, which has let people discover who they are – I think that's a huge success."[47]

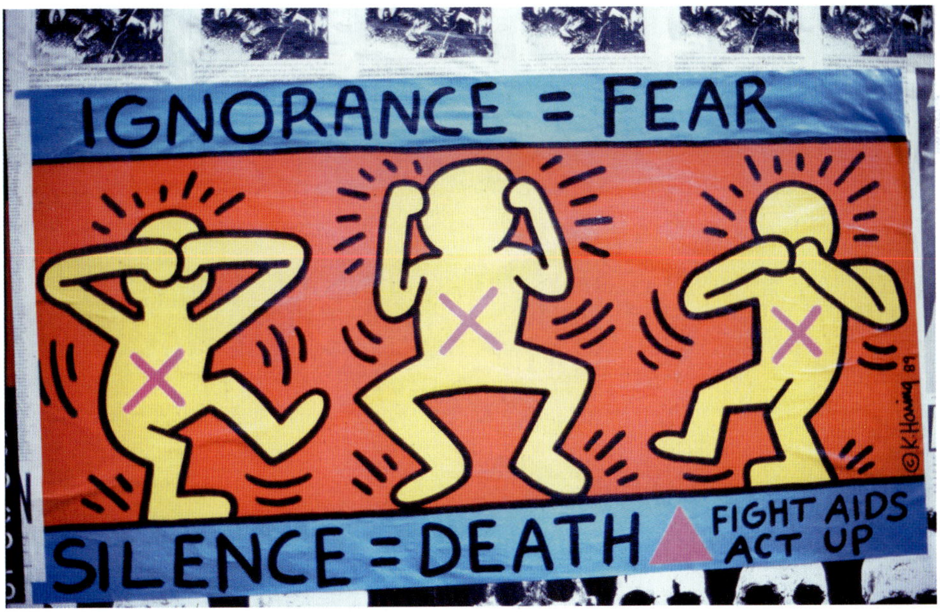

Figure 4.22 Keith Haring's short life paved the way for gay activists, AIDS research and prevention, social justice causes, and gay visibility. Haring can also be remembered as a champion of the medium of illustration, including through his 1989 poster *Act Up*.

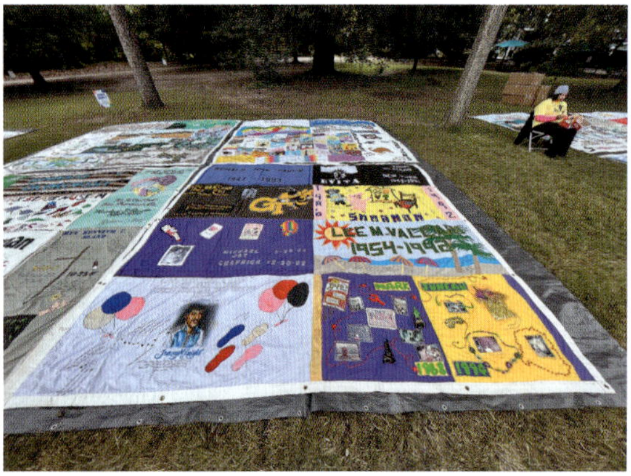

Figure 4.23
Pieces of the AIDS Memorial Quilt are periodically displayed across the country, including these selections at the Atlanta Pride Festival in 2023.
© Jaime Rosegren

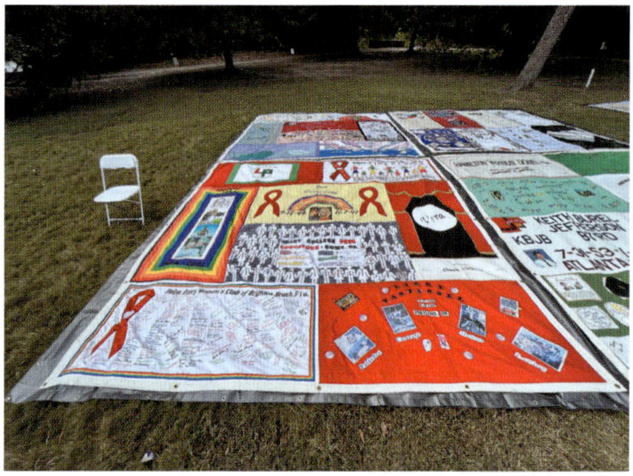

Figure 4.24
Pieces of the AIDS Memorial Quilt are periodically displayed across the country, including these selections at the Atlanta Pride Festival in 2023.
© Jaime Rosegren

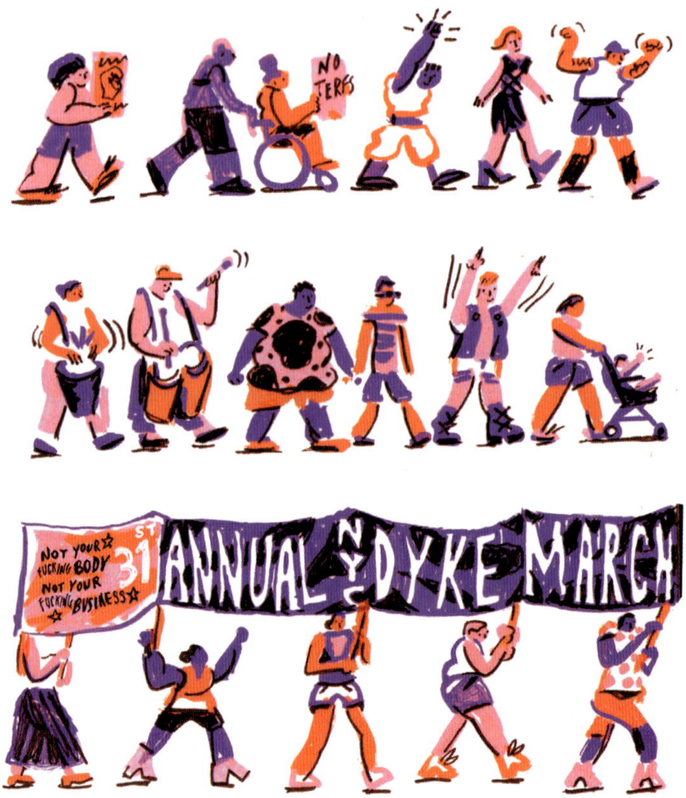

Figure 4.25
2023 Dyke March
© 2023, Ryan Hartley Smith, All Rights Reserved

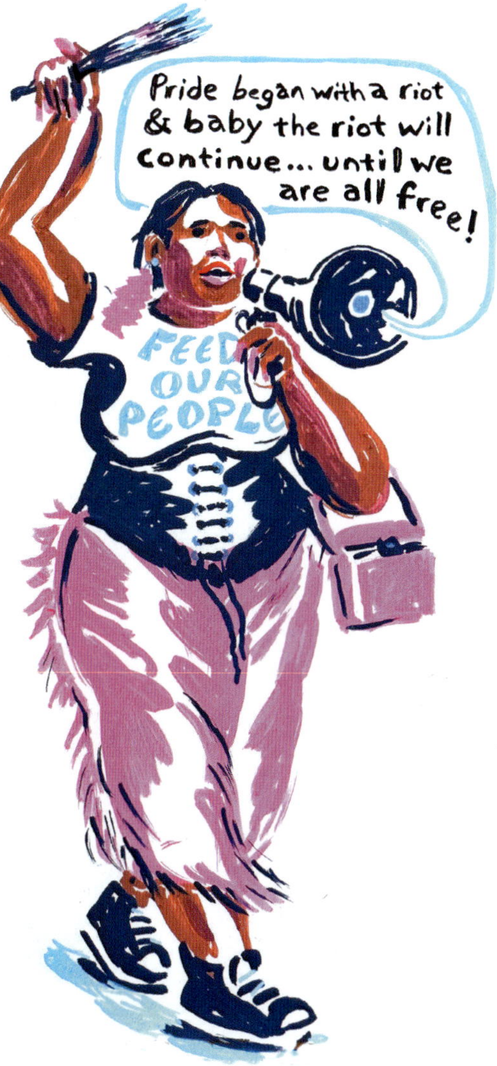

Figure 4.27
Qween Jean Marching in Manhattan

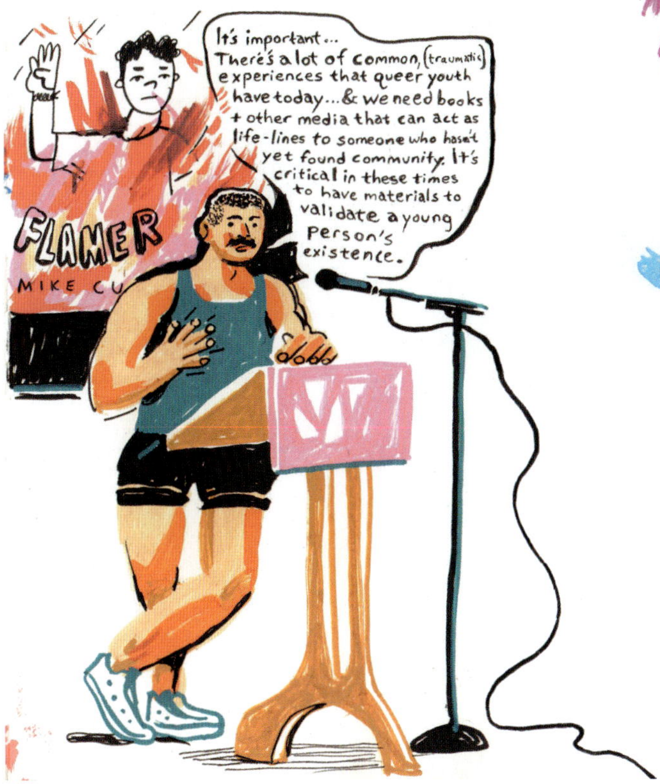

Figure 4.26
Mike Curato Speaking in Provincetown

Indigenous Americans

(Note for this section: We chose to use the term "American Indian" to describe a wide variety of unique and independent tribes and bands of the indigenous people of North America, in accordance with the guidelines from the Smithsonian Museum. We respectfully acknowledge that it is best to use specific names of tribes and bands whenever possible, and that individual tribes and bands may have different preferences for naming this group as a collective.)

GLOBAL POLITICS PERSPECTIVES

The History and Culture of American Indians in the United States

American Indians have fought to preserve their culture, identity, and political standing since European colonists first arrived in North America in the 1500s. When Europeans first made contact, North America was home to hundreds of different nations and languages, each of which had a unique culture, tradition, and background. In the years following first contact, American Indian communities experienced genocide, expulsion, relocation, disease, and, as a result, many lost their identity, history, and languages.[48] Despite this history of hardships, American Indians have survived across the continent and continued to grow and develop their diverse and unique cultures, as well as assert their collective political identity. Upon its creation, the United States of America did not consider American Indians to be part of the country. Its laws and political system explicitly and implicitly excluded American Indians from citizenship and representation. The US Constitution treated the Indigenous tribes and bands as foreign entities, not to be taxed or counted in the population totals that determine representation in the US House of Representatives. The 14th Amendment, ratified in 1868, establishes birthright citizenship and equal treatment under the law for all people in the US, but the legal interpretations at the time determined that it did not apply to American Indians.[49]

Approximately 10,000 American Indians served in the U.S. Army in World War I, but were not given the right to vote until the Citizenship Act of 1919, which gave citizenship to American Indian veterans of World War I.[50] Other American Indians were not given the right to vote until the Indian Citizenship Act of 1924, but this act gave discretionary power to the states, many of which did not allow Indians to vote until the 1950s. The Voting Rights Act of 1965 finally secured the American Indian vote.[51] From the 1940s to 1960s, the American government passed a series of laws attempting to assimilate American Indians, terminate their tribal political rights, and abandon their cultural identity. From 1953 to 1964, the US government ceased to recognize more than 100 tribes. In 1953, the Indian Termination Act (Public Law 280) gave six states the right to criminal jurisdiction over tribal members and reservations. The act violated tribal sovereignty, denied funding for tribal law enforcement, and made minor crimes on reservations punishable by state law.[52] This law was followed in 1956 by the Indian Relocation Act (Public Law 959), which encouraged American Indians to leave reservations to seek vocational training in cities, thereby purposefully weakening tribal and community connections and encouraging assimilation.[53] Around 100,000 American Indians relocated following this event.[54] However, an unintended consequence of this law was the creation of a pan-Indian nationalist movement, due to the relocation of many American Indians from different tribes and bands to urban areas. This helped bring about American Indian activist groups such as the American Indian Movement (AIM) and the National Congress of American Indians (NCAI). These groups made significant progress in asserting treaty rights, social issues such as poverty and education, and preserving American Indian heritage.

The American Indian Movement was established in 1968, inspired by the spirit of many anti-imperialist and civil rights activist movements of the time. In 1972, AIM and other activists demonstrated in Washington, DC in what became known as the Trail of Broken Treaties, occupying the Bureau of Indian Affairs (BIA) and demanding its reform and acknowledgement of harmful federal policies. One result of this demonstration was the 20 Point Proposal, which insisted on treaty making rights, a review of treaty violations, and land reform and restoration, among other points. The activism of AIM, the NCAI, and other groups led Presidents Lyndon B. Johnson and Richard Nixon to enact policies reversing those of termination in the late 1960s and early 1970s. However, the wish for further action led to one of AIM's most remembered actions.

In 1973, members of AIM went to Wounded Knee, South Dakota to protest a controversial Oglala Lakota tribal chairman named Richard Wilson, after a failed impeachment effort. AIM believed that Wilson was putting the interests of the BIA ahead of tribal members, and 200 supporters occupied the town of Wounded Knee because of its historical significance as the site of a massacre of 300 Lakota people by the U.S. Cavalry in 1890. In addition to this symbolism, the Pine Ridge Reservation, on which Wounded Knee is located, had one of the highest poverty rates in the nation. Wilson, however, declared a state of emergency on Pine Ridge and forbade any AIM gatherings, calling in support from U.S. Marshalls. Thus began a 71-day standoff on the reservation and, by the end, two AIM supporters had been killed, and hundreds were arrested. The Department of Justice cut off news media from interacting with AIM, but nevertheless the event attracted international media attention. The following year, actor Marlon Brando, expressing his support for the activists and protesting Hollywood's treatment of American Indians, refused to accept his Oscar for the movie *The Godfather*, and sent Sacheen Littlefeather, an activist for American Indian civil rights, in his place. Vigils and marches across the country in solidarity with the activists took place, and illustrated posters and pins accompanied them. Many of these posters made an effort to show the connection between the government's 1890 massacre and its blockage of American Indian rights in 1973, bringing the events of 83 years earlier back into the American consciousness. Many illustrators created posters, such as Bruce Carter who carved a series of stark, two-tone woodcuts, one showing an American Indian woman and her child looking back at a row of faceless cavalry members. (Figure 4.30) Another poster by an unknown artist uses bold shapes and a red, black, and white color scheme to depict an American Indian man looking warily over his shoulder, surrounded by a red sun halo and Native symbols in the sky. (Figure 4.31) The hand lettering on the poster states "The spirit of the past will rise to claim the future." Commemorative pins and patches of the movement displayed the clever visual metaphor in AIM's unofficial logo. The logo depicts a red hand showing a peace symbol, which also reads as an American Indian face with two feathers coming out of their hair. An illustrated article for the short-lived *Oswatomie* periodical from Marxist militant organization The Weather Underground shows an armed Wounded Knee defender, evoking the collaged style of *The Black Panther* newspaper. (Figure 4.32) The imagery on the associated art helped create empathy for the movement, and connected it to other social justice movements of the era, gaining support from their members, including the Congressional Black Caucus.[55]

In addition to posters, illustrated newspapers became a method of visual communication for American Indian activists. *Akwesasne Notes* was started in 1968 by the Mohawk Nation and became one of the largest Native newspapers, often compiling articles relevant to Native interests from other publications. The newspaper also featured poetry in the tradition of American Indian storytelling traditions.[56] *Akwesasne Notes* abounded with political cartoons calling attention to American Indian causes. The front page of the October 1969 issue featured a cartoon by Ron Cobb of a family praying over Thanksgiving dinner. Ominously, under the floorboards and layers of earth and history, lay the bones of American Indians. Another Thanksgiving themed cartoon from the front page of the September 1970 issue depicts Nixon pouring a cornucopia of "promises" onto Native people, who run away, yelling "spare us!" and "not again!"[57] Other Red Power activist newspapers included *Americans Before Columbus*, the *Indian News*, the *Indian Voice*, and *Warpath*, and American Indian political cartoonists continue to work today.[58] Artist Ricardo Caté is a member of the Santo Domingo Pueblo (or Kewa) tribe of New Mexico, and is the author of the comic *Without Reservations*, the only American Indian cartoon currently featured in a mainstream daily paper, the *Santa Fe New Mexican*.[59] In his comic, Caté explains the indigenous experience through simple, solid colors and biting messages. In one cartoon, a Native man gestures to a wide-open prairie, showing it to his son, and saying, "Someday Son, NONE of this will be yours." Another dark cartoon, with characters drawn similar to the style of the Family Circus, features a blonde boy speaking to a Native boy, saying "My school has a soccer field, a baseball field, and a great big playground!" The Native boy responds darkly, "Mine has a graveyard," alluding to the Indian boarding schools established between 1819 and 1969 meant to assimilate Indian children into white culture. In 2021, one school in Canada found evidence of the remains of a mass grave with 215 children.[60]

The continued attempts by the United States government throughout history to erase Native identity have highlighted the importance of art created by American Indians as a source for establishing and preserving this identity. However, non-Native people have borrowed from varying American Indian aesthetics and art objects for decades to create works for their own profit, finding an appeal by the public for the bold, geometric patterns many Native art traditions use. In 1935, despite previous attempts at eradication of Indian culture, the Indian Arts and Crafts board was established to "promote the economic welfare of Indian tribes and the Indian wards of the Government" and to prevent counterfeit Native artworks. As Native Art continued to be popularized throughout the 20th century by both non-Native artists as well as Native commercial illustrators such as Acee Blue Eagle, the law was updated in 1990 to include more serious fines and punishments for violation. The reestablishment of this law allows greater economic opportunities to American Indian tribes and communities, as well as helps them assert their identity and culture through art.

Art movements from shared causes have also found intersectional relevance in contemporary times. In Eagle Butte, South Dakota, on the Cheyenne River Reservation, the Cheyenne River Youth Center hosts the annual RedCan Graffiti Jam, which draws from graffiti culture and invites both Native and non-Native artists each year for a week of graffiti workshops, traditional drumming and dancing, and painting murals throughout the town of Eagle Butte. Various businesses and tribal buildings donate walls to the event, which brings many outside eyes to the isolated town, located an hour and a half away from South Dakota's capital, Pierre. The event exists to allow youth the opportunity to practice self-expression through art, for mural artists, both non-Native and those from other indigenous tribes, to create messages about Native identity and rights, and allows the community to feel connection with their Lakota heritage and culture. Before creating their works, the artists attend an orientation to learn about Lakota culture and create graffiti that honors Native beliefs. Many murals at RedCan incorporate the illustrated lettering of graffiti with Lakota words that hold significance to their people. In 2023, artists Biafra, Wundr, and Cyfi created a mural spelling out OYATE, which means "our people" in Lakota.[61] The bold letters were filled with illustrated imagery relating to Lakota culture, including animals, drums, and a view of a teepee on the plains. Artists Biafra and Wundr created another mural including the Lakota symbols of an eagle and turtles with the words "ohitika" (courage, freedom, and bravery) and "tiyospaye" (family). Another mural was created by lead artist Desi Mundo, a non-Native participant, assisted by Gilbert Kills Pretty Enemy III and Dakota Stevens. Their mural depicts the word "Wokiksuye" (remembrance) and the Wounded Knee memorial riders, who annually ride in remembrance of the Wounded Knee massacre. (Figure 4.33) Artist and educator Hoka "Infer" Skennandore's work is graffiti inspired. His 2018 RedCan mural spells "Lakota" in sign language, and his 2021 mural says "Takoja," which means grandchild in Lakota. (Figures 4.28 and 4.29) This proud assertion of identity through public murals brings a related political meaning, in bright, vibrant colors, despite centuries of attempts at elimination by the U.S. government, Native people assert that they, and their culture, will not be suppressed.

INTERVIEW

Hoka Skenandore

Tell us about your artwork and background. What role has political messaging played in your previous work?
My first active involvement with art was with Style Writing or Graffiti Art, which began in 1997. I also went to the Institute of American Indian Arts in Santa Fe, New Mexico where I earned a BFA in Studio Arts in 2006 and later attended the University of Oklahoma where I earned my MFA in Painting in 2020. I've worked in both fine art realms as well as in the streets and on public art projects since the late 1990s. I am an enrolled member of the Oneida Nation of Wisconsin and I am also Oglala Lakota, La Jolla Band of Luiseno and Chicano. My heritage is one steeped in politics, as our designation as Indigenous people in the United States is political as much as it is an ethno-religious one, due to our relationship with the government. My work was previously more overt in its messaging and imagery, which has shifted over the decades. The act of creating anything as an Indigenous person is inherently political regardless of the specific imagery or ideas.

How does style play into visual messaging in your work? Does the idea inform the style, or does the style inform the idea?
As the name itself implies, Style Writing requires style, as simple as it sounds. Abstracting lettering requires study of the alphabet and finding the middle ground between pushing the forms to the breaking point, while maintaining the original letters to where they can still be somewhat recognizable. As a muralist one must think of the audience, or how the viewer will perceive the work. I find that each community has different sets of expectations and understandings, and it is best to find a visual language that people can relate to and feel comfortable with. Style Writing is often an art form done for its own purposes and community; however, it is a powerful language that people outside the culture find fascinating. Like all art forms it takes time to understand the motivations, the meanings and eventually to be able to "read" the works themselves. Style Writing has always been in the DNA of my work and has added an element of style to my fine art pieces, murals and especially any extralegal works.

How has your Native identity informed your art, graffiti, and murals? Could you tell us a little about your background and how it inspired you to pursue art as a method of communicating your worldview?
My identity has had a profound impact on my work. There have been stereotypical notions about what Native Art is and what it should look like. I've never been beholden to that way of thinking and have been inspired by individualist artists like TC Cannon, Haley Greenfeather English, Fritz Scholder, America Meredith, Frank Buffalo Hyde, and Daniel McCoy Jr., just to name a few people who inspire a measure of irreverence and an unwillingness to compromise their own specific, acute, and particular Indigeneity. With Style Writing I was introduced to an early and symbolic form of Land Back. For Indigenous and Native Style Writers, our connection to land and place stretches back to time immemorial. Aztec and Mayan Glyphs,

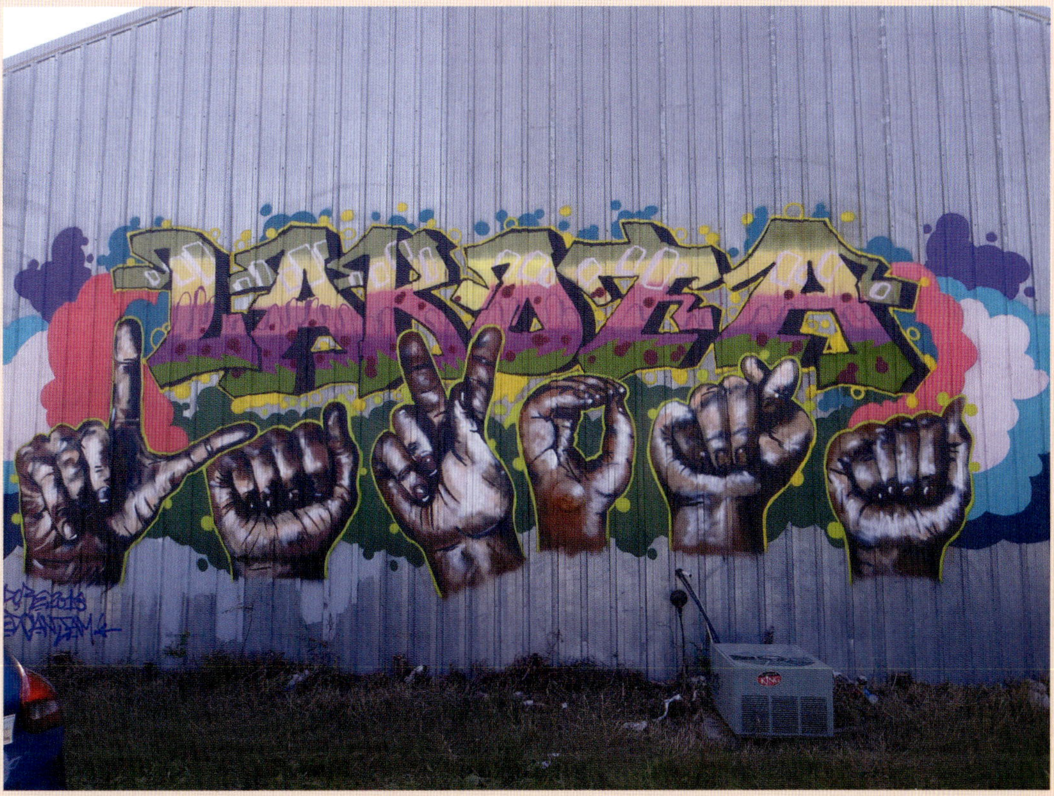

Figure 4.28
Lakota, a 2018 mural for the RedCan Graffiti Jam
© Hoka "Infer" Skenandore

mound building, and the paintings in kivas are all examples of our connection to land, our marking of the land within our relationship to it. Our current mode of creation just happens to involve spray painting surfaces. This is a continuation of a very old connection to land. The act of painting can symbolize a momentary reconnection with and reclaiming of spaces and places, many of which have a complex and troubling history of theft and Indigenous removal.

How has graffiti culture influenced your work? Since Black and Indigenous activist movements have influenced each other throughout the 20th century and beyond, do you think the art styles associated with these movements have also influenced each other?

Style Writing culture is the largest influence on my work and is my personal favorite form of expression. There has been a historical connection of Black and Indigenous communities being involved with one another, the recent documentary *Rumble: The Indians Who Rocked The World* illustrated the connections between Black and Indigenous Music and how both shaped the history of music. There is a deep history of Black and Indigenous and sometimes Afro-Indigenous artists within the history of Style Writing. One of the progenitors of style was Phase 2, who had Indigenous roots. There is a groundswell of Native and Indigenous Style Writers who I feel represent a fascinating part of one of the largest art movements in human history. Few other forms of art can claim to be practiced in most every human community on Mother Earth. All Style Writing originates first from New York and then California, the first generations of kids to create in this style were of varied ethnic backgrounds, but the Black and African American presence is undeniable. In this regard, there absolutely is influence. As time has passed the exchange of ideas and style has been rather fluid.

How has participation in the RedCan Graffiti Jam affected the way you see public art as a means of delivering messages?

It has changed the way I understand art and audience. There is much more connection to be had when the community you work with sees themselves in the work. One of the most profound moments I had was while painting a wall with sign language hands. A small child came over to the wall with his cousins and remarked that the color of the hands was the same as his as he put his hand on the wall. I told him, "Yes, that's you." It is priceless to see yourself in art, especially public art.

Who are your art influences?

I am influenced by a huge number of artists, from mainstream to outsider. Style Writers like Twist and Perish (that list is huge…) Daniel Johnston, R. Crumb, T. C. Cannon, Jean-Michel Basquiat, filmmakers such as Werner Herzog, David Lynch and Terrence Malick, tons of Native and Indigenous Artists including my late Grandmother Rose (Skenandore) Kerstetter and my late mother Olivia Skenandore just to name a small few. The vast histories found in various art forms all have some sort of influence and keep me interested in looking at art.

Do you have any advice for students who are interested in pursuing political illustration?

I don't know if I have any advice specifically for folks interested in political illustration, I will say that one of the most important functions of the artist in society is to speak to your times and lived experience. We should share our perspectives as best we can, as artists we are sensitive to many things, and we perceive the world in unique ways. If we can share that vision and perspective, we might possibly build connections with our fellow travelers in this life.

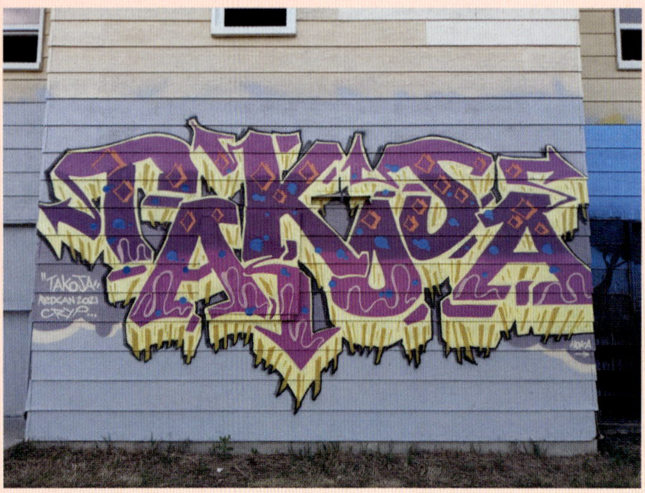

Figure 4.29
Takoja, a mural for the 2021 RedCan Graffiti Jam
© Hoka "Infer" Skenandore

Although American Indians have been able to vote in all states since the Voting Rights Act was passed, they still experience barriers to voting, including isolation from polling places and voter I.D. laws. In 2020, the Amplifier Project, in partnership with the non-profit Illuminative, released four illustrations as 50,000 prints and print-objects, such as stickers and buttons, as well as creating murals in cities across the U.S. to advocate for the Native vote. Three of the illustrations were created by Chichimeca & Apache artist Mer Young and show digital collages of Black and Indigenous activists, and the fourth illustration was created by Shepard Fairey and features hip-hop artist and activist Xiuhtezcatl Martinez. These illustrations use **augmented reality** (AR) to help tell their message. When viewing the image through AR, the portraits become speaking animations, with the recorded voices of the activists they feature. Martinez says in Shepard's animated illustration, "We are flooding the streets, the courthouses and the voting booths by the millions. The power to make a difference doesn't just come from political leaders, it comes from young people like you, your voice and your place in these movements is just as important if not more so than any political leader," and emphasizes the power of young people to use their voice to create political change.[62] Public events, artworks, and illustrations such as these help to cement Native identity, preserve culture, and promote political participation.

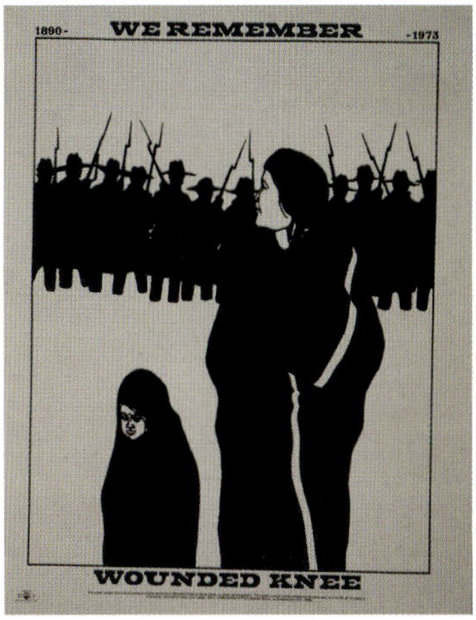

Figure 4.30
We remember Wounded Knee, 1890-1973
Bruce Carter

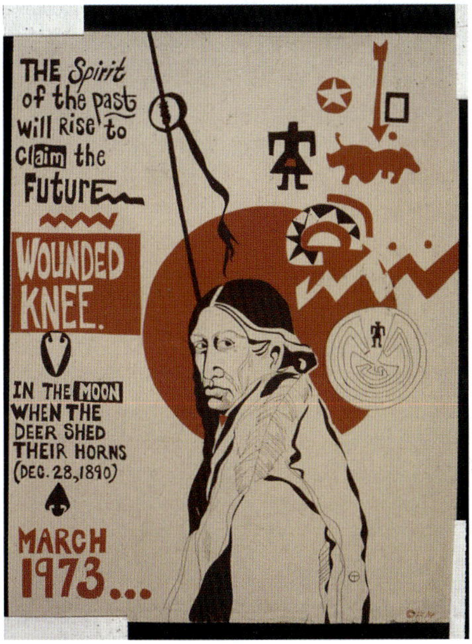

Figure 4.31
March 1973 Wounded Knee Poster

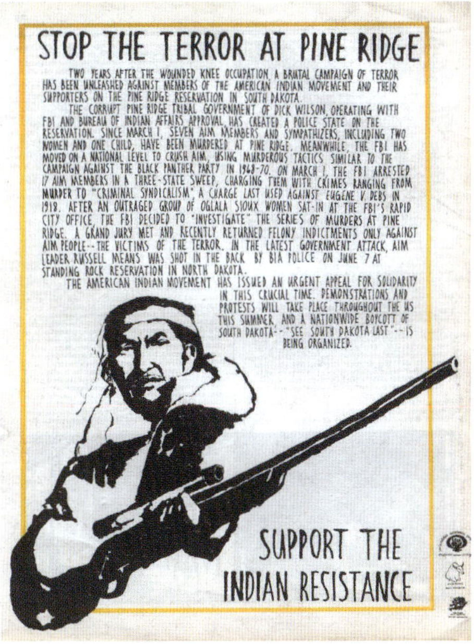

Figure 4.32
An illustrated page from *Osawatomie*, a magazine published by the Weather Underground Organization (WUO).

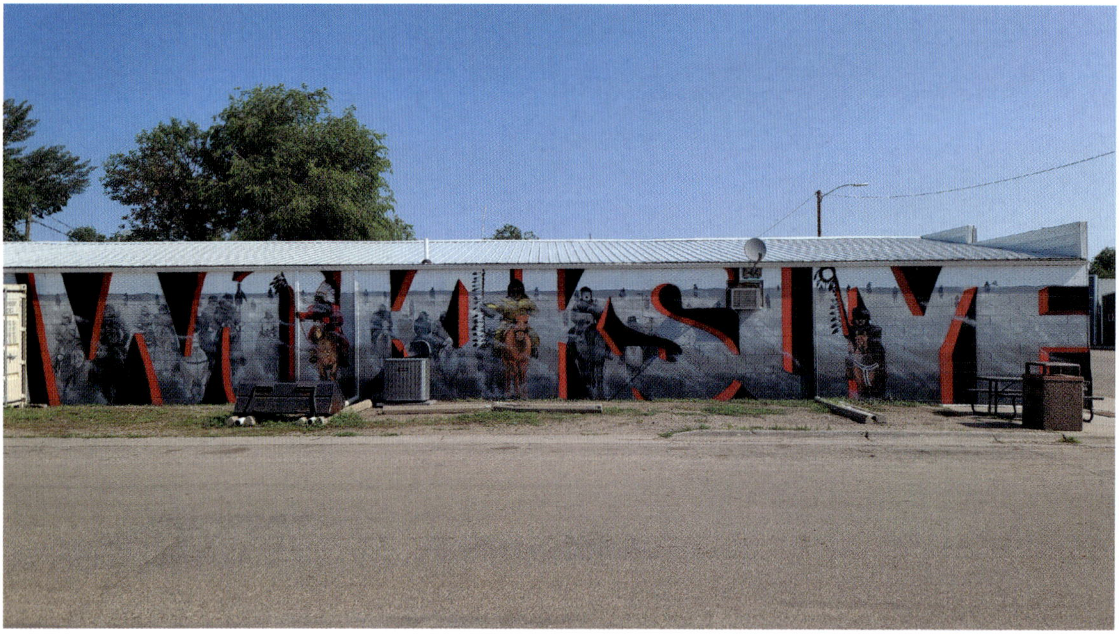

Figure 4.33
Wokiksuye, a 2023 mural for the RedCan Graffiti Jam © Lead Artist Desi Mundo, assisted by Gilbert Kills Pretty Enemy III and Dakota Stevens, supervised by Danny Butcher

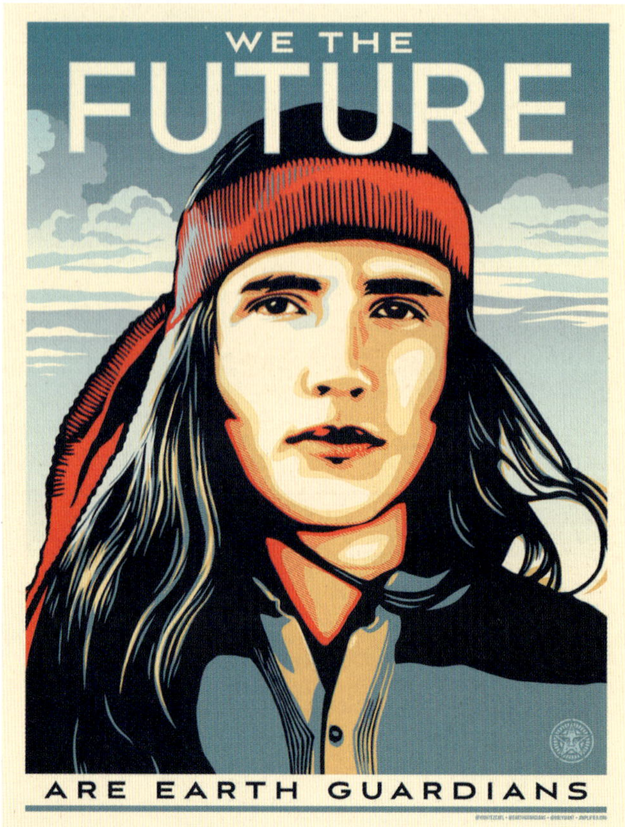

Figure 4.34
We the Future – "Xiuhtezcatl Martinez" 2020 Artwork by Shepard Fairey, courtesy of Amplifier.org

The Arab Spring and the Middle East

GLOBAL POLITICS PERSPECTIVES

The Arab Spring in the Middle East and North Africa

The Arab Spring refers to a series of massive protests that occurred throughout the Middle East and North Africa, primarily in 2011. For decades, this region had been one of predictability, with little societal unrest and virtually no regime changes. The Arab Spring protests turned that reality on its head, in some cases in a matter of weeks. Oftentimes, massive protests are triggered by a particular event that galvanizes the public, and the Arab Spring was no different. This triggering event took place in Tunisia in 2010. A young man, Mohamed Bouazizi, had been making a living as a vegetable vendor on the streets of Ben Arous, just outside Tunis. On the morning of December 17th, police seized his vegetables and cart. Feeling hopeless and without any other options, Bouazizi set himself alight in an act of self-immolation.[63] His struggles and his desperate act resonated with young people in Tunisia, as many were frustrated by high unemployment, limited job opportunities and a corrupt and unresponsive government. The protests swelled in Tunisia and gained massive attention on Twitter and other social media. By January 2011, protests had sprung up throughout the region, including in Egypt, Libya, Bahrain, Yemen, Oman, and Algeria; similar protests took off in Syria in March of 2011.[64] All these countries had a few things in common: they had massive young populations, they experienced high levels of youth unemployment, and they had been ruled by repressive authoritarian rulers.[65] In almost all of these places, the regimes had been seen as invulnerable and public life had been mostly void of any mass demonstrations. The massive protests injected a new volatility into a region that had seemed stable and predictable.

The effects of these protests have been enormous and varied. In some countries, there were significant government changes (Tunisia, Egypt, and Libya) while in other places, nonviolent protests eventually triggered a civil war (Syria, Libya, and Yemen). Both Tunisia and Egypt seemed to be headed towards permanent regime change in 2011, as they worked to establish competitive elections and new constitutions. This was cut short in Egypt in 2013 as the military, led by General Abdel Fattah El-Sisi, retook control of the government in a military coup, and imprisoned leaders of the elected government, including Egyptian President Mohamed Morsi. Tunisia's experiment with democracy lasted much longer. A new constitution was drafted by the Tunisian National Dialogue Quartet, a coalition of civil society groups, lawyers, and religious groups; the Quartet went on to be awarded the Nobel Peace Prize in 2015.[66] Tunisia held multiple successful democratic elections, and by 2020 was the only Arab democracy in the Middle East and North Africa. Yet, by 2021, Tunisian President Kais Saied used the Covid-19 pandemic as a justification to dissolve the parliament, to rule by decree, and to ultimately oversee a constitutional change. As of writing, Tunisia is no longer considered an electoral democracy.[67]

Many artists and illustrators have reacted to the events of the Arab Spring with mediums including street art, political cartooning, and editorial illustration. Street art flourished as a means for illustration communicating public messages during the Arab Spring, including work from artists such as Hossein Amirsadeghi in Tunisia and artists Gazeer and Nadine Abdel Ghaffar in Egypt. Street art especially thrived in Cairo, where some examples played on styles of ancient Egyptian wall art. In 2011, cartoonist Khalid Albaih made a number of cartoons for *Al Jazeera* about the Arab Spring, many of which were repainted as street art across the region. In 2021, ten years after the movement, Albaih revisited some of his cartoons and updated them, reflecting the frustrating lack of progress that the movement made. In one cartoon, the 2011 version shows a person leaning forward pointing, with one large arm pointing to the left, signifying the government, and many smaller arms pointing to the right, symbolizing the public (the directions not to be confused with the symbolism of left/right political leaning). In the 2021 version, the arms pointing to the right were changed to show the fates of the dissenting voices: one arm is cut off, two more are handcuffed together, another has turned the other way, another holds a gun, another holds a phone, symbolizing documentation and on-line activism. A final hand, however, gives a symbol of hope, as it continues to boldly point away from government opinion. Egyptian artist Doaa El-Adl has become a prominent and rare voice for women political cartoonists in Egypt and the Middle East, considered by some to be Egypt's most famous female cartoonist. El-Adl's cartoons have addressed topics ranging from female genital mutilation, criticism of Western media, Brexit, and, most recently, the war in Palestine. (Figure 4.35) Egyptian cartoonist Andeel now lives in France, due to the controversy of his opinions. Andeel has worked in a wide variety of media including film, video, and cartooning to find the best media for the particular message he wishes to communicate. (Figure 4.36)

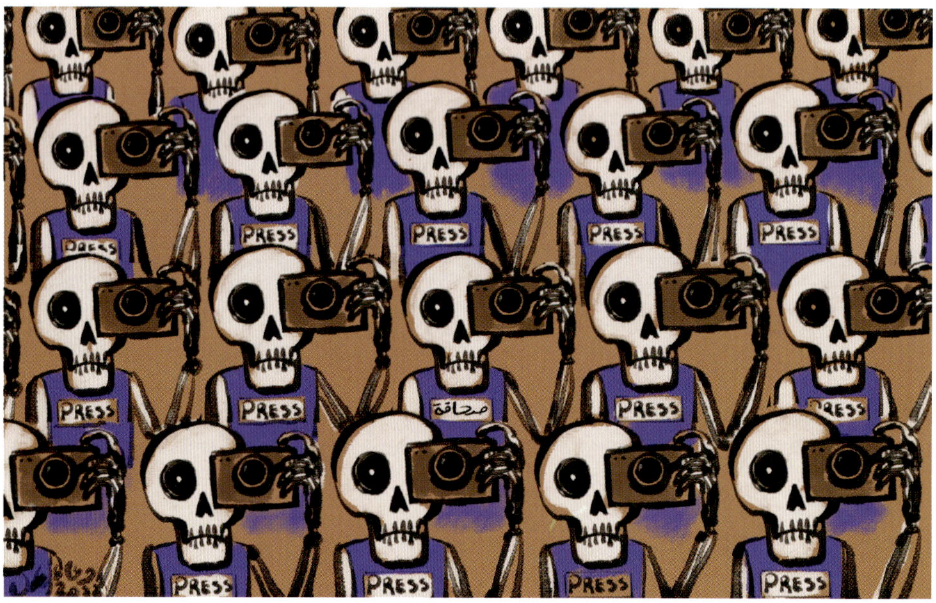

Figure 4.35
Press 2023, Copyright Doaa El-Adl

INTERVIEW

Andeel

Tell me about how you began cartooning. Who are your cartooning influences?
I started in a very early age, and my parents were very helpful. They exposed me to a lot of very useful books and children's magazines. I also was lucky enough to have my first job at 17. I had a lot of opportunity to experiment and make mistakes in very insignificant spaces. I had my first big job in the biggest oppositional newspaper, around 18 or 19 years old, where I worked with some of my childhood stars. I've never imagined that I would see these people in person. That was really helpful and educational. I learned so much just by watching them and the way they work. There was an older veteran cartoonist who I worked with who was really a mentor for me. As I grew older, and he grew older, we had very different opinions and political opinions, but he was responsible for me learning most of the basics of how this artwork works in relation to journalism, the techniques and a lot of the very essential skills needed for it.

Tell me about your experience working with Mada Masr Media as their illustrator and cartoonist, and about founding your comics magazine *Tok Tok*. Since you pursue other media beyond cartooning to deliver your messages, such as script writing and video production, what does the medium of cartooning help communicate that these other mediums do not?
I was part of a team that produced a previous newspaper called *Egypt Independent*, which was the English version of the biggest privately owned newspaper in Cairo. A lot of that team was kicked out, so we sat together and thought about creating a new publication. This is how *Mada* [*Masr*] came about. I was pretty much responsible for a lot of the visual aspects of the new newspaper. I designed the logo and created the visual identity for it, including the first design of the website. While the newspaper was starting, I was also starting to become a lot more involved in writing, so I wrote lots of political articles. I was

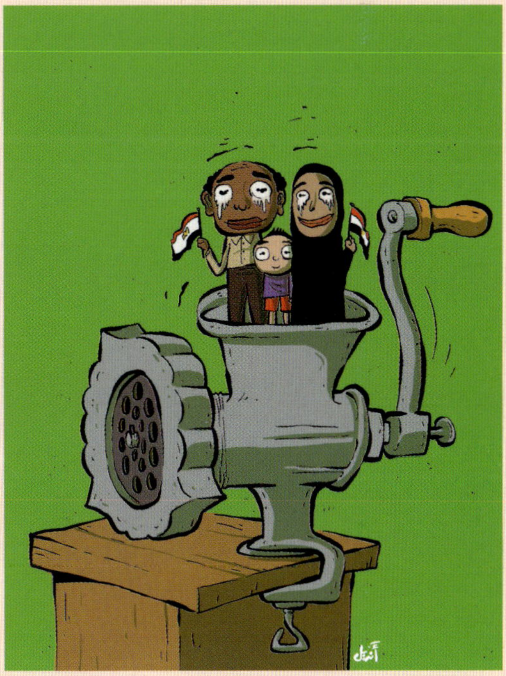

Figure 4.36
Minced Meat
© Artwork by Andeel, published for the first time on *Mada Masr*

writing about cinema a lot, because I was involved in filmmaking in Egypt when I was living there. I also continued making cartoons. Later on, I started to produce a video series where I was playing a fictional character who was a middle aged, Boomer influencer, who is really hates young people and revolution, and has very interesting ideas on how to solve all of Egypt's problems. It was just a continuation of finding other ways to produce satire in journalism, in relation to how the internet was developing. I was originally trained as an as a cartoonist in a very traditional old school journalism style, with mostly hand drawn cartoons and very basic printing techniques. *Tok Tok* was in the bridge between these two worlds because we prepared for its launch in 2011, right before the revolution. It was, for us, an attempt to try and gain more control over editorial work and what we produce. It was quite a challenge because there were lots of difficulties when it comes to production, funding, and printing, as well as distribution and dealing with censorship. Not government censorship, but rather reader censorship. A lot of the styles that you see people using when they're drawing comics are on the innocent and cute kind of side of the visual adaptation. When [that language] is telling stories of something really like dark or unexpected things, it's a very good combination, in my opinion. It's very difficult for an Egyptian audience to process this, because in Egypt comics are usually associated with kids.

What influence do you think media outlets have on the content of political cartoons? How does your style contribute to the message of your cartoons?

[Cartooning] speaks to a certain kind of necessity for art being unintimidating that I find interesting. I'm interested in art in general, and in the way a lot of artworks that seek a very wide reach try to make themselves look very unproblematic. This is something that I find politically interesting: how things get normalized. Things can be marketed or packaged in a certain way where they seem very family friendly or seem very non-controversial or comfortable to look at or to experience.

I don't really think when I'm doing cartoons, because I've been doing them for a really long time. It's a bit like tweeting for me, or like blogging. It's just second nature. I have very easy access to the way I think and the way the pictures formulate themselves. Every now and then I try to stop for a bit and ask, "What am I doing and what is this language and why is it doing what it's doing?" We have been trained to try and make our cartoons comprehensible as quickly as possible. They are being consumed in contexts like newspapers or social media. You must make yourself understood very quickly. There's something that I kind of enjoy in this very deliberate, superficial isolation of politics. I feel like there's something honest about it. I feel very uncomfortable when I'm watching news reports or reading articles that are really good at sounding objective and very factual, but it's obvious that there is an emotional alignment behind them. This is also one of the reasons why I find documentaries very uncomfortable. It suppresses your ability to question, "How was that put together? What was discarded? Why am I watching this and not the other footage? What kind of context is being made out of this?" This is why I feel like there's something kind of cynical in the way cartoons are not pretending to give any information or facts, and are not trying to be objective. They're just a very pure, emotional reaction. They're deliberately reductive.

Has there been a decline of the political cartoon in print publications in Egypt, as there has been in the US?

Journalism is really old, and it's been very

[powerful] for a long time. It was very useful and important, historically and politically, during very important points, like during the British occupation and the liberation movements. All the political struggle during that time was so dependent on strong cartoons. There were lots of strong cartoons, which we call the grandparents of cartooning. Then, after the '52 revolution, there was a new generation of revolution generation cartoons, which were trying to be more progressive and socialist. [However], they were entirely controlled by the state, because they were the voice of the new regime, and Nasir-ism, and pan-Arabism, and all of this. There was a big growth in the volume of the cartoons and the dependency on them in newspapers. After Nasir died, and after the Egyptian political situation changed dramatically, especially towards Israel and America, then it was important for the for the government to suppress this rebellious vibe in Egyptian newspapers, which cartoons were a big part of. Since then, cartoons had a very long winter in Egypt, from the early 70s through the late 90s and early 2000s, where it was very rare to find any good or significant cartoons. They were very boring and very pro-government. It was only in the mid 2000s when newspapers like the one that I worked at came about and cartoons started flourishing again. There was a little bit of a release in terms of freedom of expression that Mubarak's regime needed, which called for more cartoonists and younger people to come and be interested in this job. There has never been money in it, and there will never be, but at least there was an opportunity for people to say something and be noted somehow. Then the revolution happened in 2011 and that encouraged more people to be part of that kind of culture. But then all of this got suppressed again when the coup happened in 2013. 30 years of winter, two years of summer, and then winter again. It's a bit like the weather in Europe. [laughs]

I barely follow what's being published in newspapers, I just follow my cartoonist friends. Certain levels of criticism were accepted when the Brotherhood was in power, for example, which breached certain boundaries or taboos that were impossible to produce in satire in general and in Egypt before that. Now they're just trying to roll things back again. But at the same time, there's so much noise happening on the internet. [The government's] controlling public spheres, but then people are still talking and producing things everywhere.

How has social media affected the distribution of your cartoons?

I definitely owe a lot of my success and the development of my work, as well as the aesthetics of my work, to social media. Since the moment I realized that I can have a direct relationship with the audience and not have to convince an editor that "this cartoon is good because of this and that," my relationship with my work changed completely. However, I am recently starting to revisit that world and try and understand it a little bit more, because I have also been on the receiving end of the madness that exists on the internet. I am now approaching the internet with a lot more caution. I'm trying to experiment a little bit more with how to deal with it, and how to how to deal with the ego and the self-production that it encourages people to do.

Do you have any advice for students who are interested in pursuing political illustration?

Marry rich. [laughs] I don't want to sound cynical... but it's a very tough job. It also depends who I'm talking to and what context they are in. If I'm talking to American students who want to have a role in the politics in

America, I barely know anything about it. Based on a very superficial impression that I get from a lot of political satire that I see in America, either in cartoons or TV shows, there doesn't seem to be any space for anybody who has non-partisan opinions about politics, at least in the mainstream. As soon as you look at the cartoon, it's very easy to know whether the cartoonist is right wing, and most of the times they are left wing, of course. There's this obsession with utilizing cartoons, and making sure that they're useful, or that they are for a cause. It's something that I find very counterproductive and paradoxical, because one of the things that I like about cartoons is that they don't have to conform to journalistic boundaries or journalistic rules. It's an art, and it doesn't have to mean anything, it doesn't have to serve any political agenda or fight for a cause. I think that cartoons have a strong potential for inspiring people to think about these things in different ways by breaking taboos that are really taboo. It's not like the old school, that was like, "Oh my God, you drew Jesus, or you drew Muhammad," but can you really criticize yourself or criticize the way you're consuming politics? Or the way you're talking about politics? Or what is your role as a person in this society? I just think that we have to relearn what a taboo is and be a bit more progressive.

Women's Rights

Women's struggle to gain full political rights began to show progress in the mid-19th century. In 1848 the first women's rights convention in Seneca Falls passed a resolution in support of women's suffrage in the United States. During the following 150 years country by country around the world gradually allowed women to vote in some capacity, with the exception of Vatican City. Despite these colossal gains for women's suffrage, today, millions of women around the world live in societies in which their voting rights are still significantly limited because of their sex or socioeconomic status. Women around the world continue to struggle for voting rights and full legal rights in many societies, including Saudi Arabia, Afghanistan, and Iran. Voting is only the first legal step to women's rights but it does not necessarily fully address the discrimination women face around the world.

Following the Seneca Falls Convention, women's rights advocates in the United States and Britain worked in concert over the following century to gain voting rights in their respective countries. In the UK, the first serious suffrage movement began in the 1860s, when John Stuart Mill presented a women's suffrage petition before Parliament that was handily defeated. Following the enfranchisement of women on the Isle of Man, a British dependency, in 1881, New Zealand in 1893, and South Australia in 1895, Emmeline Pankhurst renewed the British women's suffrage movement by breaking away from the National Union of Women's Suffrage Societies (NUWSS) to form the Women's Social and Political Organization (WSPU) in 1903. The women of the WSPU moved beyond previously practiced tactics and did whatever they could in their power to gain attention for their cause, including practicing direct action and civil disobedience. WSPU members stood on soapboxes to preach their cause, a practice previously only done by men, organized mass demonstrations, and interrupted, and were subsequently ejected, from political meetings.[68] Arrests of the WSPU members were frequent, but the government did not budge on its stance against women's enfranchisement. WSPU members turned to more violent methods to gain attention, including a nationwide bombing and arson campaign. In 1913, Emmeline Pankhurst's daughter Christabel declared, "Why should a woman not make use of the same weapons as men. It is not only war we have declared. We are fighting for a revolution!"[69] WSPU members, once arrested, demanded to be considered political prisoners, which awarded them additional rights. When this was denied, they led a series of hunger strikes, which also gained them plenty of press attention, as well as shaming the government when they were force fed in the jails.[70]

By the end of the 1800s, women had more access to printing presses, and they were able to print and distribute suffragist propaganda. Branding, color, and design were primary concerns of the movement. Co-editor of the WSPU paper *Votes for Women*, Emmeline Pethick-Lawrence, and art editor Ida Proper, designed a color scheme of purple, white, and green, symbolizing dignity and loyalty, purity, and hope, respectively. In response to being portrayed as mannish and boorish in the British press, the British suffragists attempted to hold themselves to strong standards of appearance to fight the stereotypes featured in misogynistic political cartoons and posters. In fact, the term suffragette was originally intended to be a derogatory term by the British press, but was reappropriated by women as a proud moniker. One such derogatory cartoon was published as a postcard in 1909, entitled *Origin and Development of a Suffragette*. (Figure 4.39) Split into four quadrants, the postcard tells the story, "At 15 a little pet. At 20 a little coquette. At 40 not married yet! At 50 A Suffragette." The top two illustrations, depict a 15-year-old girl as the caretaker for a baby doll, replete with full, ribboned hair and daintily crossed ankles, followed by the 20 year old with long lashes, and tiny, delicate features. These illustrations represent the expected roles for women in society at the time, as mother figures and sex objects. The bottom two roles, while displaying ageist caricatures of women, exaggerate lines and wrinkles, giving the women red noses alluding to alcoholism, and sour expressions. By the fourth image, the cartoon is fully caricatured with bug eyes, a claw hand, and an aggressively wielded hatchet.

In contrast, propaganda created by the WSPU strove to represent women as sophisticated, stylish, and noble. Artist Hilda Dallas was a member of the WSPU as well as the Suffrage Atelier, an organization created in 1909 to support artists to "promote the enfranchisement of women, by means of pictorial publication."[71] In 1909, Dallas illustrated the poster *Votes for Women*. (Figure 4.40) Completed in the WSPU green, purple, and white color scheme, the poster depicts a stylishly dressed woman standing in a field, triumphantly holding up the WSPU newspaper. A previous Dallas poster, *Read our Paper*, encouraged sales of the paper among the increasing suffragette population of Britain. Dallas created her posters in woodblock, which was an easy method to learn, and the Suffrage Atelier also put efforts into teaching printmaking to amateur artists. Dallas' distinct **Art Nouveau** style contributed to the perception of the modern suffragette woman of Britain as stylish, elegant, and progressive. In 1912, Emmeline and Frederick Pethick-Lawrence were ousted as the editors of *Votes for Women* because of their opposition to the violent tactics of the WSPU, and Christabel Pankhurst replaced them as editor, renaming the paper *The Suffragette*.[72] When World War I began, the paper went through a final name change as part of an agreement with the British government, calling itself the *Britannia*.[73]

Dora Meeson was another British suffragist who used her artistic talents in service to the cause. Originally born in Australia, Meeson was recruited to the suffragette cause and became a founding member of the Artists' Suffrage League (ASL). Like the Suffrage Atelier, the ASL promoted use of the arts for the cause of women's suffrage, but was founded by the NUWSS, which disagreed with the violent tactics of the WSPU. The ASL strongly believed in the efficacy of propaganda, and created many popular postcards, posters, greeting cards, and illustrated booklets to promote the cause. In 1910, the ASL reported distributing "2,708 posters, 6,488 postcards and 65,000 picture leaflets," along with 70–80 processional banners.[74,75] An early illustration by Meeson depicts *Suffrage Mrs. John Bull*, John Bull being a personification for the United Kingdom. (Figure 4.41) In the illustration, Mrs. John Bull stands proud and upright, firmly denying Britain's parties, unions, and leagues any more political help until she dishes some of her own for the cause of women's suffrage. The poster states, "Now you greedy boys. I shall not give you any more [sic], until I have helped myself." The image of Mrs. John Bull alludes to women's role as homemakers and caretakers, but also to the leadership roles inherent therein. Her depiction of British women shows them neither infantilized, sexualized, nor lampooned, but as a dignified member of society asking for her worth. The children form a triangle, leading to her face, settled on the rule of thirds at the apex of the triangle, with the large red bowl creating a secondary focal point. The gazes of the boys create **psychic lines** leading the viewer's eye further to the subject.

In the United States, a split in the women's suffrage movement occurred when the 15th amendment passed, which gave African American men the right to vote, but did not mention women's suffrage. In protest of the amendment, Susan B. Anthony and Elizabeth Cady Stanton formed the National Woman Suffrage Association (NWSA) in 1869, advocating for women's suffrage. In contrast, the American Woman Suffrage Association (AWSA), founded the same year by Lucy Stone, Julia Ward Howe, Frances Ellen Watkins Harper, and others, supported the 15th amendment and lobbied for universal suffrage. When the groups finally merged in 1890 into the National American Woman Suffrage Association (NAWSA), they concluded to focus primarily on women's suffrage, which many African American women of the movement took offense to, including Harper and Ida B. Wells. In 1896, Harper helped to found the National Association for Colored Women (NACW) to promote both African American women's suffrage and a variety of reforms to improve Black life in America.[76] After founding the nation's first anti-lynching movement, Wells also helped to found Chicago's premiere Black suffrage organization, the Alpha Suffrage Club. In 1913, Wells and the ASC were invited to Washington DC to take part in the Woman Suffrage Procession, organized by white suffragist Alice Paul. Upon arriving in DC, Wells learned that the Black suffrage organizations were to march at the back of the parade and would be left out of the parade program, out of Paul's fear that their participation would anger white Southern suffragettes. Wells refused, and when the Illinois contingent of the parade marched, she boldly joined them part way through the parade.[77] The issues surrounding the intersectionality of suffrage influenced the women's suffrage movement in the years hence, and continue to affect women's rights issues today.

In the United States, artists adopted yellow and gold to represent the suffrage movement, with some adopting the British green, white, and purple, or replacing the green with yellow. This combination was adopted by the National Women's Party for their banner, with the same symbolism as Britain, albeit the yellow replacement representing "the color of light and life."[78] American suffragettes again borrowed from abolitionist causes through the use of Lady Liberty as a symbol of their movement. Liberty was previously used in Thomas Nast's and other illustrators' political cartoons during the Civil War to champion the Black man, such as in his cartoon *Franchise*, where Lady Liberty asks why a Black veteran and amputee should not gain suffrage, because of his sacrifice. In the 1913 Woman Suffrage Procession, suffragettes even dressed as Lady Liberty. The symbol of Columbia was also used in suffragette art as a feminine alternative to Uncle Sam. A key illustrator who helped shape the female symbol of the suffragettes was Nina Allender. As the primary illustrator for Alice Paul's *The Suffragist*, which began publication in 1913, Allender sought to directly counter stereotypes of suffragette women as mannish, ugly, and abandoning their responsibilities of child and home. Allender was a deft cartoonist who created over 200 political cartoons for *The Suffragist* and its successor publication *Equal Rights*.[79] Many of her cartoons featured the American version of what British artists were also attempting to create, a self-confident, proud, stylish, and attractive American suffragette, which became known as the "Allender girl." In a 1915 cartoon *The Spirit of '76.' On to the Senate!*, Allender created a parody of the 1876 painting by Archibald M. Willard, depicting women cheerfully drumming and fifing to petition for a congressional amendment for women's suffrage. (Figure 4.42) In a 1917 cartoon, Allender played on the public's sympathies for imprisoned women, by showing them gripping onto prison bars in her cartoon *President Wilson says 'Godspeed to the Cause'*. (Figure 4.43) Allender answered President Woodrow Wilson's reluctant support of the suffragist's cause, with the Allender girls insisting he take action, "Mr. President, what will you DO for women's suffrage?"

Artist Bertha Margaret Boye began creating art for the movement when she won a contest put on by the College Equal Suffrage League in 1911. Boye won $50 for an iconic design of women's suffrage movement, which framed women's suffrage not as a fight or struggle, as previous art had, but as a noble, inalienable right. Created in the geometric **Art Deco** style, *Votes for Women* uses symmetry to create a regal, meditative, civilized order. (Figure 4.44) The woman pictured does not demand, but simply is, filling the canvas with her size and quiet strength. Her yellow robe alludes to the symbolism American woman placed on the color, projecting light and life. Suffragists called it "the color of success."[80] The red haloed sun behind her head is reminiscent of a Biblical figure or Greek icon.

GLOBAL POLITICS PERSPECTIVES

The Push for Women's Rights in the United States

While pursuing women's suffrage was one of the first major goals of the early Women's Rights movements in the Western world, so-called second wave feminism focused on women's rights in broader society. This included normalizing women's participation in the workforce and in gaining full individual autonomy over financial and legal matters. For example, the creation of no-fault divorce as an option for ending marriages has been seen as a vital legal change that gives women more legal autonomy. In the United States, the Supreme Court ruled in 1973 that abortion was constitutional, and therefore legal, in the case Roe v. Wade, and access to birth control outside of marriage was also legalized. The culmination of this movement was the passage of a new constitutional amendment that would establish women equal to men in the United States. The so-called Equal Rights Amendment (ERA) was brief in its language, stating, "Men and women shall have equal rights throughout the United States and every place subject to its jurisdiction. Congress shall have the power to enforce this article by appropriate legislation". While it was first introduced into Congress in 1972, it was drafted decades earlier in 1923 by women's rights activist Alice Paul.[81] At the time, the amendment was received with bipartisan support and was not considered controversial. To be added to the U.S. Constitution, proposed amendments need to pass both chambers of Congress, the House of Representatives, and the Senate, with a two-thirds majority. Then the amendment needs to be ratified by three-fourths of US states. In 1972, the ERA quickly passed through Congress with the necessary votes, and it was successfully ratified in 25 state legislatures the same year.

While the ERA was introduced with widespread acceptance, a group opposed to its passage emerged and successfully reframed the issue with the public. The conservative-leaning STOP ERA[82] waged a media campaign and propagated misleading information about the implications of the ERA. Led by anti-feminist activist Phyllis Schlafly, the group asserted that the ERA would deny women their right to lead a traditional life of marriage, motherhood, and homemaking. Schlafly's opposition was both moral but also legal. She argued that the ERA would undermine traditional marriage and so-called female privileges, but also that it would create same-sex public restrooms and would require women to register for the draft (in a decade when mandatory military conscription had still been in use). Schlafly's movement generated support with the Republican Party and within many conservative-leaning churches, and it successfully organized greater opposition in southern states that had not yet ratified the amendment[83]. When the ERA was first introduced in 1972, the deadline for ratification was set for 1982. By the end of 1982, only 35 US states had ratified the ERA, just three short of the 38 needed.

Following the U.S. election of Donald Trump in 2016, women began a worldwide protest movement against his misogynistic statements, sexual assault accusations, and the threat of his Republican presidency to abortion rights for women in America. The Women's March on Washington was quickly organized in the short period of three months, and on January 21st, 2017, the day after inauguration day, half a million people gathered in Washington D.C. An additional 3–4 million people participated in local marches across the country, making the march to be the largest demonstration held on one day in U.S. history.[84] Across the world, approximately 200 additional marches took place with over 350,000 attendees.[85] In Unalakleet, Alaska, approximately 39 women marched in −51 Fahrenheit.[86] In Show Low, Arizona, one participant marched.[87] The attendance of the March in D.C. was so far above the expected numbers, that the streets were too full to march and became a standing demonstration. When the event did begin to disperse, many attendees headed to the Capitol and the White House, leaving their protest signs on fences and in piles, creating a new, multicolored and multifaceted artwork containing the same unified message. (Figures 4.45 and 4.46)

As we've seen throughout this chapter, the power and aesthetics of protest sign illustration can flavor the memory and impact of historic events. Much of the visual memory of the Women's March is through the pink "pussy" hats women knitted and crocheted in response to a derogatory comment Trump made about female anatomy. The hats also symbolized a reclaiming of women's crafts, with the hot pink color being a bold identification of femininity. Artist Shepard Fairey created multiple signs in honor of the event, in partnership with the Amplifier Art We the People project and funded by a Kickstarter. (Figure 4.47) March participants were able to download and print the images for free. The series included a set of three posters honoring Muslim, Latina, and Black women in bold, limited colors, and were also available to buy as screen prints and lithographs. Chicano artist Ernesto Yerena created another poster *We the Resilient* in honor of Native American women, and artist Jessica Sabogal created a poster honoring lesbian women *We the Indivisible*, as well as a poster featuring a young Black girl smiling upward, *Women are Perfect*.

Designing a logo and visual brand for the march occurred during a rushed two-week period, with the San Francisco creative agency Big Monocle taking the reins and illustrator Nicole La Rue creating the iconic logo. The muted colors indicated a feminized version of the colors of the American flag, and the three silhouettes looking forward together had subtle differences in facial features and hairstyles that indicated racial diversity. The organization and continuing action of the Women's March crumbled over the following years due to infighting, accusations of exclusivity, and accusations of anti-semitism. In Georgia, discussions about branding for the state march involved the symbolism behind the colors of the suffragettes, eventually adopting gold, purple, and pink as their color scheme, while noting suffragette symbolism historically excluded African American women. The march, however, defied limitations put upon it by national or state branding. Many posters relied on hand-drawn and illustrated type to communicate their urgent messages, while others incorporated drawing, or mashed-up memes from pop culture to fit the context of the march. Some signs recreated imagery from past eras, such as hand-painted versions of the "Keep Abortion Legal" signs issued by the National Organization of Women in the 1970s, the protest "power fist" (popularized in a woodcut version by SNCC Field Secretary Frank Cieciorka in the 1960s), and the iconic J. Howard Miller "We Can Do It!" poster from World War II. Recognizing the visual significance and folk art historical record, museums and collections around the world made a call for posters from the Women's March to include in their collections.

The spirit behind the suffragist movement and Women's March lives on in the continued actions of women around the world and illustration that demand the equal treatment of women and their participation in the political process. In 2020, Meaghan Dee created her poster *To Not Speak is to Speak* as part of a series of posters from the American Institute of Graphic Artists (AIGA) show *Get Out the Vote: Empowering the Women's Vote*, in honor of the centennial anniversary of the ratification of the 19th amendment. (Figure 4.48) Dee's poster illustration was based on Art Nouveau works by Alphonse Mucha and Paul Berthon. Dee visually references Berthon's poster *L'Ermitage*, which symbolizes the ideals of the "happy few" who remained aloof from present turmoil. In Dee's version, she transformed the aloof figure from Berthon's work into the Statue of Liberty, with her eyes closed to injustice. In her hand is a narcissus flower, which represents selfishness. A quote by the German theologian and anti-Nazi activist, Dietrich Bonhoeffer, surrounds the figure. It states: "Not to speak is to speak. Not to act is to act." Dee adds her own commentary on the piece: "Not to vote is to vote."

An issue central to the work of many illustrators who create work about women's rights is that of abortion access. While abortion access has widened across many parts of the world over the past 50 years, in 2022 the U.S. Supreme Court overturned the right to abortion access American women had had since 1973. Illustrator Erin Burns created her image *Reproductive Rights,* using a visual metaphor of the scales of justice to a gynecologist's stirrups. The metaphor conveys the message of a common plea of the pro-abortion movement that the "government does not belong in your doctor's office." (Figure 4.49) In response to the threat to Roe vs. Wade, illustrator Katrina Kopeloff, who works in bright, geometric shapes and lines, created a print called *My Body, My Choice,* which she later turned into stickers to sell and distribute. (Figure 4.50) Cartoonist Robyn Jordan's non-fiction, illustrated essays often address social justice issues through personal narratives and interviews. Jordan used this medium to tell her story of receiving an abortion after an ectopic pregnancy. (Figure 4.51) An ectopic pregnancy occurs when a fertilized egg attaches to the wall of the fallopian tube instead of a uterus. The egg cannot develop normally, and, if not removed, can cause life-threatening bleeding. Jordan's story is an example of how a comic narrative can provide the reader greater understanding and empathy towards larger issues through identification of an individual author.

Canadian Anita Kunz is one of the most prominent women in illustration today, and many of her themes include promoting the interests and politics of women. Kunz' career began in the early 1980s when art director Fred Woodward recognized her work, and she began illustrating covers and interior illustrations for almost every prominent magazine in the US, including *Rolling Stone*, *TIME*, *Vanity Fair*, *The New Yorker*, and others. She has also illustrated book covers and published her own illustrated books, including *Another History of Art* and *Original Sisters: Portraits of Tenacity and Courage.* In 2003, she was the first woman and first Canadian to have a solo show at the Library of Congress in Washington DC.

INTERVIEW

Anita Kunz

Since you've been active in the illustration industry since the late 70s, I think you come from a unique position that you've been able to experience a historical shift in the producers of illustration. How has the experience for women illustrators changed in the industry since you began?
There's a huge difference. I never had a single female teacher in art school. I attended a higher-level illustration workshop after college, but still no women. I suppose I had always assumed equality. My uncle was an illustrator, and I thought that I wanted to do that. Gender was never part of my decision. I just really wanted to be an illustrator. In hindsight, I think I must have been very stubborn. Every indication I had from the industry was that it was advantageous to be a white male. It took me a long time to realize that I was unusual. When I started teaching, I was the only female. I always felt a little out of place. My first book *Another History of Art*, deals with what iconic paintings might look like if they had been painted by a woman, namely me, a modern secular female. Of course, the paintings wouldn't have been made at all: that's the idea behind the book. Now there are a lot of great women illustrators. There has definitely been a shift and things are really starting to improve. And not just for women, for minorities as well. For example, if you look at the Society of Illustrators from way back, they used to have photos on the wall of white men in tuxedos at their "girlie" show. It's come a long way! My second book, *Original Sisters*, is a book of portraits of many incredible women, many of whom are unknown to the general public. There are female illustrators that I'd never heard of, for instance, who worked for the big magazines. And they are every bit as good as the men, and it's shocking that I didn't know that they existed. I think things are changing, thankfully, but it's taking a long time. If it continues on this trajectory, I hope we will see real equality and soon.

I know recently you've put a lot of effort into self-generated work, often with feminist or women-centric themes such as *Another History of Art* and Original Sisters. What motivated these projects and why did you feel that they were important to create?
When I was a student, I was taught a history of art that was presented as THE history of art, and it seemed to me very myopic, very Westernized, Euro-centric, and I remember some lecturers saying "And this is our experience." I remember thinking "That's not MY experience!" Maybe it had to do with the fact that I'm Canadian and I live in a different country, and I always feel like an outsider, but I definitely felt like an outsider in my field. That's what I was thinking about when I was developing the *Another History of Art* project, which later became a book. There was a time around 15 years ago where I thought I would become a fine artist but I failed spectacularly. Nobody in the fine art world wanted an illustrator because, somehow we are disrespected and seen as a lesser form of artist. I thought "this isn't working," but my project might work as a book. I shopped it around and found Fantagraphics. They are

amazing and I owe endless thanks to them for taking a chance on me. The funny thing is, even though I was rejected in the art world, it probably should have always been a book anyway, because it was better as a book. When I produced the second book, *Original Sisters*, I wanted to do something a little more serious, and the long COVID lockdown was looming so I decided to immerse myself in a more comprehensive project. I have painted and written about 400 women now. Interestingly, if I had started out knowing I'd do 400, I would have never have done it. The book and travelling show are a thank you to women on whose shoulders I gratefully stand.

How does that work differ from your illustration work?

I don't come from a lot of money, so I always knew I'd have to earn a living. My illustration work has always been separate from my personal work. In my personal work, I do whatever I want; mainly what I want to visually say about the world. But in the illustration work, I understand that there are limits and there are parameters and I'm really solving someone else's visual problem. I've always done political work, but as an illustrator I've always been reined in regarding how far I could go. When I look at my early work, it seems surprising. We illustrators had autonomy then, we could do whatever we wanted to do. I'm a little shocked

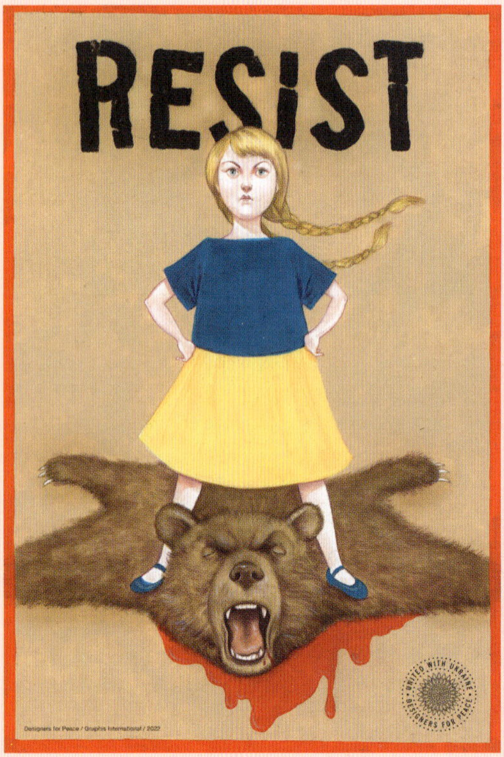

Figure 4.37
Resist
© Anita Kunz

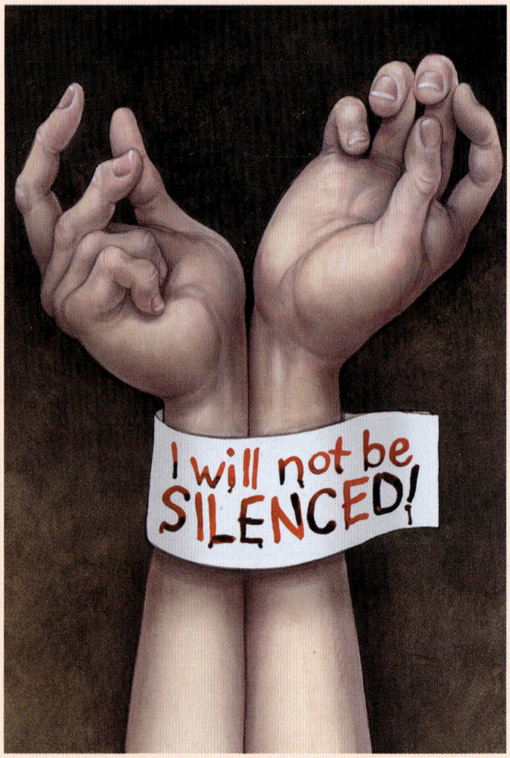

Figure 4.38
I Will Not Be Silenced
© Anita Kunz

when I think of how much freedom we used to have. I used to, for example, paint very dark images with dark subject matter and it was never a problem. I've always worked against whatever boundary was set for me. I stopped doing much illustration work because I don't have as much creative freedom as I used to.

So art directors direct more now, you think?

Absolutely. They micro-manage now. "Can you change this? Can you make it this color?" For decades I could just make any visual statements I wanted to make, so now it's really difficult for me to work under that type of nit picking. That's why I started initiating my own projects. Ultimately, I don't believe my work is any good if I'm always trying to second guess what someone's thinking or what somebody wants; it just dilutes the art. I've had the incredibly good fortune of working with the best art directors; the ones who keep a little bit of distance, so they respect what you do and you respect what they do. That's not to say that it's not a collaboration sometimes, but if somebody is micromanaging, it's just the death of the art!

How do you identify and develop the metaphors and symbols you use in your work?

I've been doing this a very long time, and I approach things differently depending on the audience and what the work is for. I've always identified as a political illustrator, right from the beginning. My heroes were Ralph Steadman and Sue Coe, people who were doing incredible work that had some sort of biting social satire, so those were always the people whose work I admired and wanted to emulate. I think that art can be such a visceral thing, you can get information from illustrations, a feeling, emotions along with intellectual information. I've really used metaphors as a way of making something clearer. I've always tried to do print illustrations in such a way that they were stand-alone and didn't necessarily need to mimic exactly what the text said. I like the use of metaphor; I like trying to figure out different ways to say something. I've thought about this a lot too, I don't know if it's just because I've been working for such a long time, but any time I need to comment on a manuscript, I automatically see pictures in my mind. I think most artists and illustrators do.

How do you make sure that the symbolism is successfully communicated to your audience?

I absolutely think about the audience I'm addressing. I spent a long time working for *Rolling Stone* magazine, and I knew that it was a different audience than *TIME* magazine or the *Atlantic Monthly*. I knew I could get away with more visually and paint something more fun and playful for *Rolling Stone* for example, and I knew it had to be something more serious if it was a strictly a news piece. I've always tried my hardest to make work that is be easily understood. That's the bottom line for me. The work should not be too elitist or strange or something that the audience might not understand. That said, I've run into some problems wherein ideas in different cultures haven't been successfully communicated. When I was working just within Canada and the US, it wasn't so much of a problem. A lot of political cartoonists draw whatever they want. I knew one of the artists murdered in the *Charlie Hebdo* attack in Paris. He was a wonderful man. I just think we have to be mindful that things often can be misinterpreted and I'm of the opinion that I should be very careful. With a wide audience comes a certain responsibility. And I think we should ask ourselves if the work harms or helps. If anyone was ever physically hurt over my work, I couldn't live with myself. *Charlie Hebdo* is the kind of publication that couldn't exist anywhere else except in France. It's such a unique publication, it just has all this harsh satire, but it really is only for the French clientele. George Wolinski, my friend who was murdered, was just a lovely guy, he was a husband and grandfather. His work wasn't even all that scathing. If anything, he did kind of sweet, playboy style cartoons.

Can you describe your own style and technique and how it influences the messaging in your work?
I've been painting pretty much the same way all along. When I started, I was making very tiny paintings because it didn't take as long as larger works and I had deadlines to meet I always worked with watercolors and water-soluble paint. I'm glad I did that because now I have no resulting health issues. When I began working larger, I started experimenting with acrylics and other mediums, but I just needed a way of working so my materials weren't always fighting with me. For my second book, I knew I wanted to many portraits quickly. I aimed to paint one portrait a day, and I discovered a new soft based type of acrylic paint, which is amazing. It's like painting with butter. I started experimenting within what I've always done. I used bright oranges and bright green, which for me is a huge departure from what the somber colors I used in the past. I've always experimented, but it's really about the ends justifying the means. It's always about the idea and intent. I discovered if I do something quickly, I don't agonize over it. If I look at something too much, those little negative thoughts creep in. And I haven't done any typography since college, so I loved hand lettering on the images.

What advice would you give to students interested in pursuing political or editorial illustration?
At this point you can't just be an editorial illustrator. I think you have to do other things. I think that these days you have to construct a career that has a lot of different elements to it. Maybe you're doing editorial illustration but you're also teaching, doing gallery work, selling through an Etsy shop, whatever. When I was young, I just went straight to editorial work, but it was appropriate back then. That's not a strategy I would recommend now. It just doesn't pay enough anymore and there are too many artists and not enough work to specialize that much.

Protests movements, dissent illustration, and contentious politics are practiced worldwide, and we regret that we can only include a small handful of examples in this text. The art movements behind these practices have relied on self-generated imagery, production practices, and means of distribution. Examples in this chapter have explored how internet communication and new technologies have contributed to the efficacy and dissemination of the messages of contentious politics. Our final section will further explore the benefits and dangers of technology on the future of political illustration.

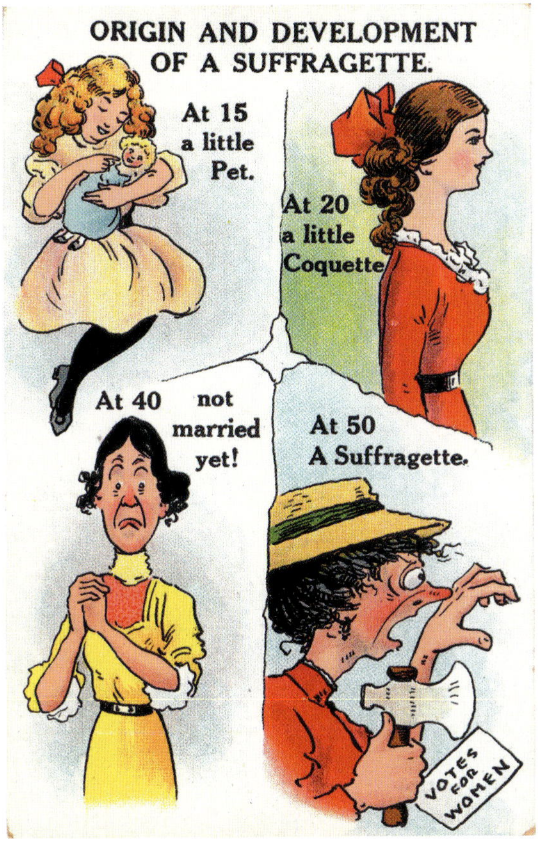

Figure 4.39
A 1909 anti-suffragette postcard, entitled *Origin and Development of a Suffragette*. Split into four quadrants, the postcard reads, "At 15 a little pet. At 20 a little coquette. At 40 not married yet! At 50 A Suffragette."

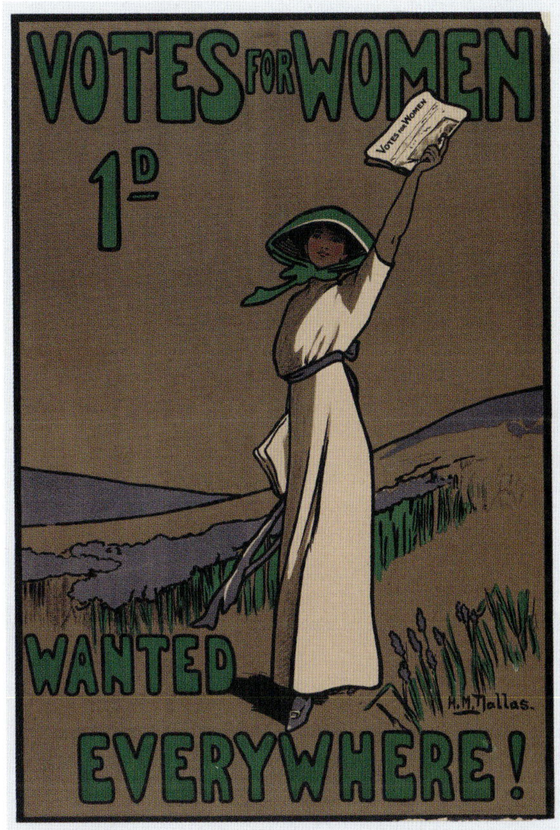

Figure 4.40
Votes for Women! 1909 Hilda Dallas

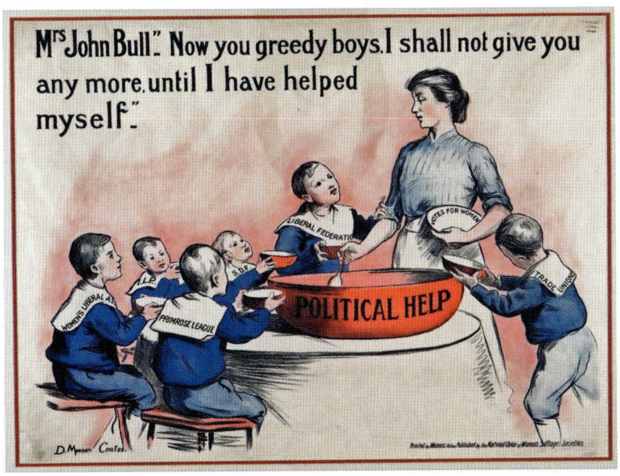

Figure 4.41
A 1900 illustration by Dora Meeson and published by the National Union of Women Suffrage Societies, depicts *Suffrage Mrs. John Bull*, John Bull being a personification for the United Kingdom.

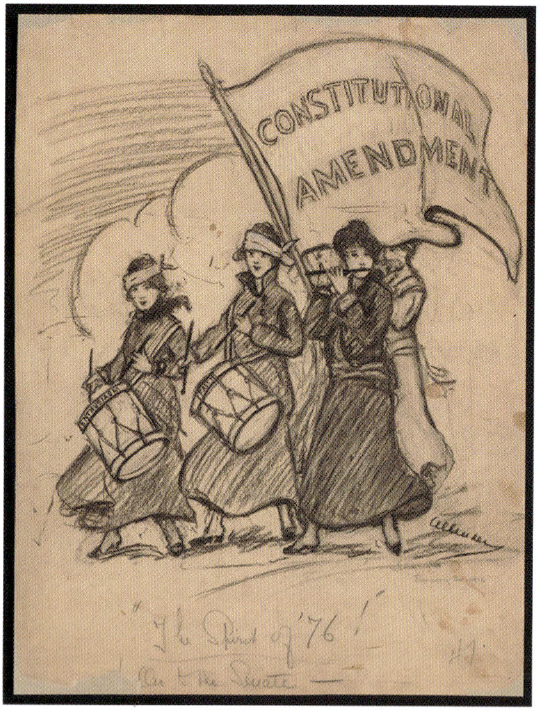

Figure 4.42
Nina Allender's 1915 cartoon *The Spirit of '76.' On to the Senate!*, is a parody of the 1876 painting by Archibald M. Willard, depicting women cheerfully drumming and fifing to petition for a congressional amendment for women's suffrage.

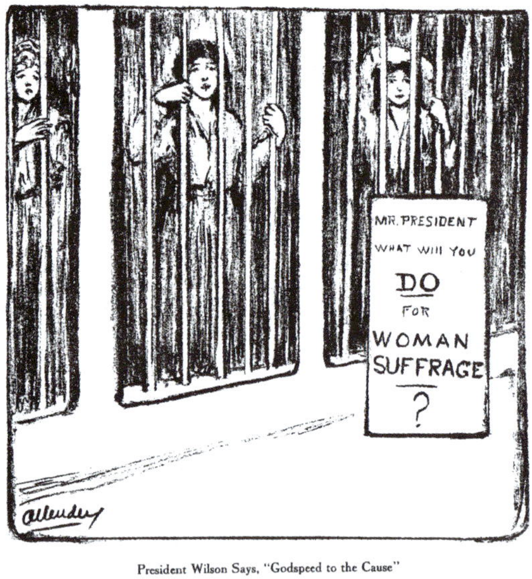

Figure 4.43
In a 1917 cartoon, Allender played on the public's sympathies for imprisoned women, by showing them gripping onto prison bars in her cartoon *President Wilson says 'Godspeed to the Cause'*.

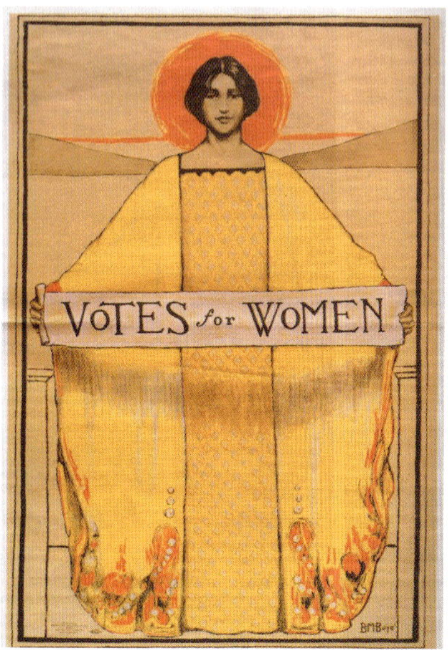

Figure 4.44
Votes for Women 1911
Berthe Boye

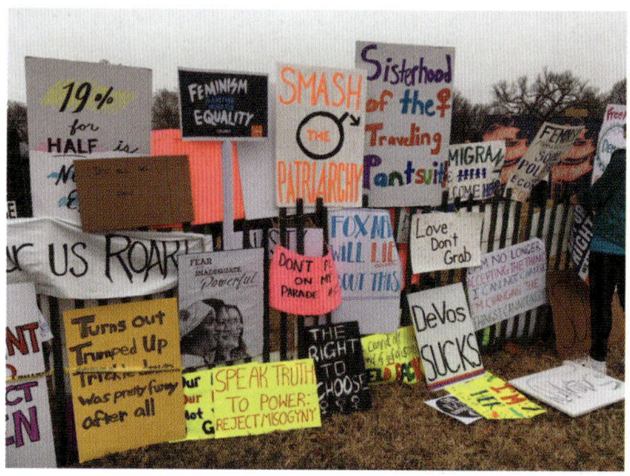

Figure 4.45
Posters from the Women's March at the fence of the US Capitol Building.
Photo © Catherine A. Moore, 2017

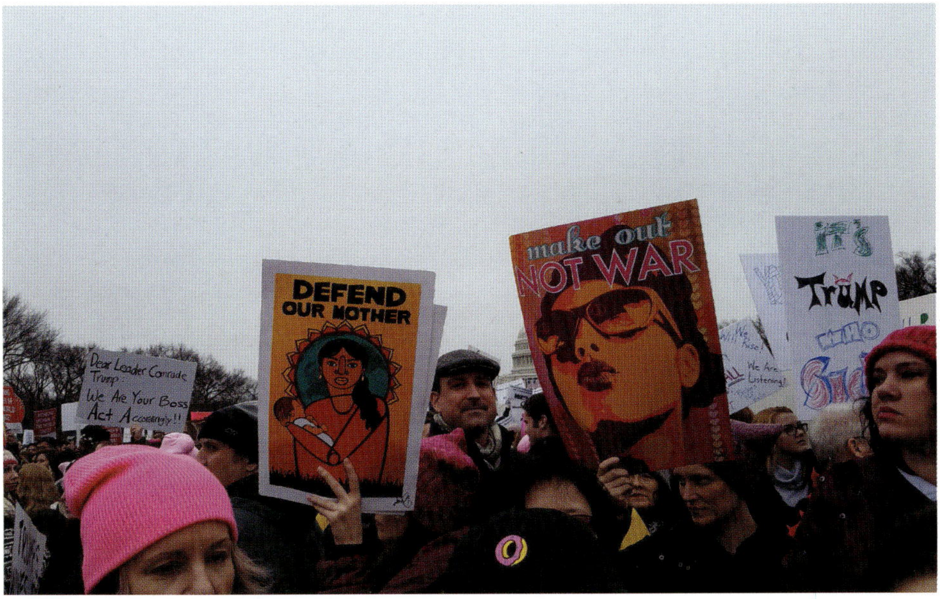

Figure 4.46
Posters from the Women's March
Photo © Maria Geonzcy, 2017

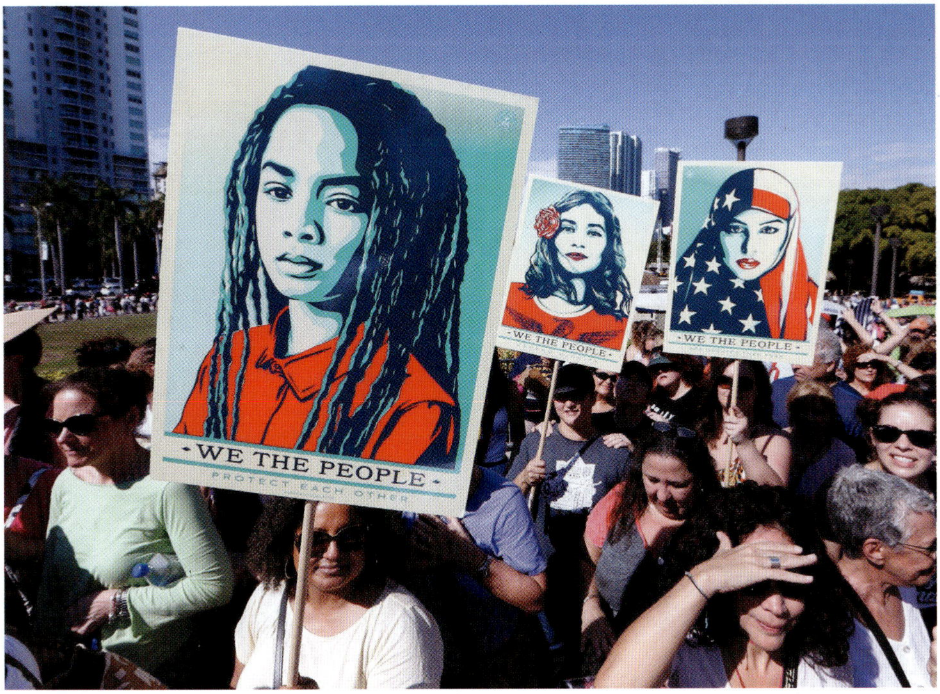

Figure 4.47
Posters by Shepard Fairey from the Women's March in Miami, 2017

Figure 4.48
To Speak is Not to Speak
© Design by Meaghan A. Dee, 2017

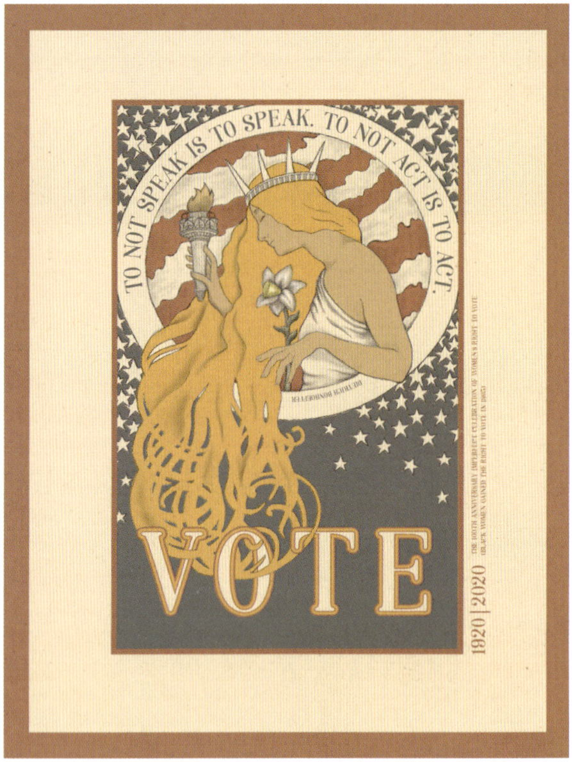

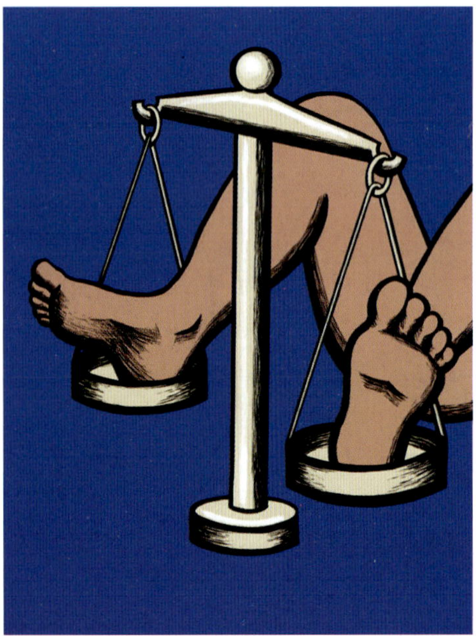

Figure 4.49
Reproductive Rights
© Erin Grace Burns, 2014

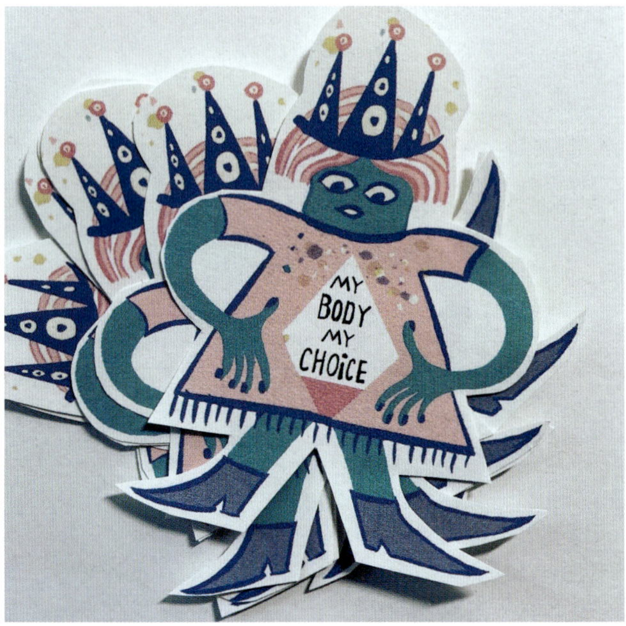

Figure 4.50
My Body, My Choice
© Katrina Kopeloff, 2017

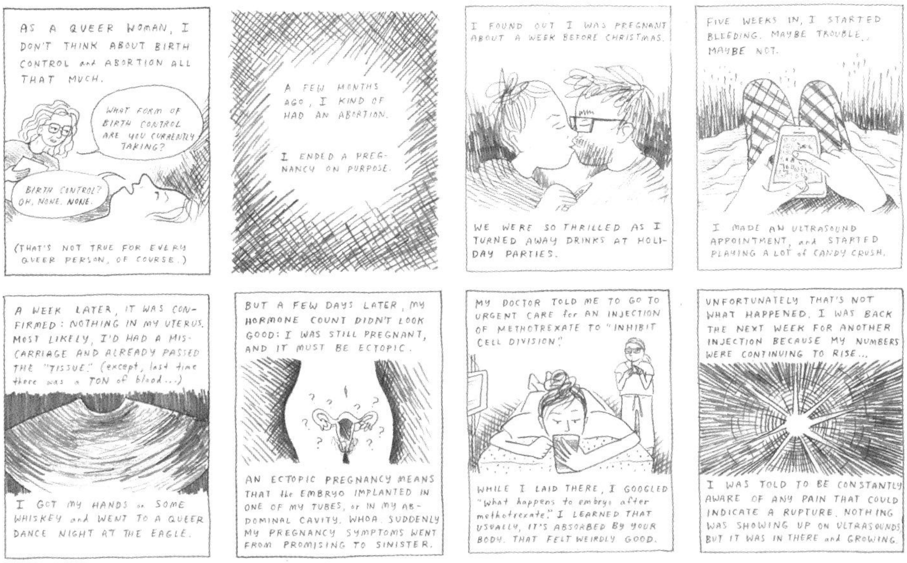

Figure 4.51 *Excerpt from Louder: Shouting my Queer, Sort-of Abortion* © Robyn Jordan, 2016

Group Activities/Discussion Questions

- If you were to make a poster supporting a cause or issue you believe in, how would you create your poster? What visuals or symbolism would you use? What media technique would be the best way of communicating your ideas? How would you copy and distribute your poster so that the most eyes could see it?
- What value does new technology bring to distributing messages of contentious politics? How has the creation and distribution of these messages changed over the past 50 years? The past 100 years?
- Research a dissent artist or movement not mentioned in this chapter. How did this artist or art movement contribute to the canon of dissent art in the world?
- Political illustrators creating dissent art use a variety of distribution techniques to communicate their messages, from Rosler's Xeroxed copies to Fairey's AR poster. What other distribution methods can you think of that one could use to propagate their political messages?

Endnotes

1 Russ Davidson and David Craven, *Latin American Posters: Public Aesthetics and Mass Politics* (Santa Fe: Museum of New Mexico Press, 2006), 27.

2 Carlos Francisco Jackson, *Chicana and Chicano Art: ProtestArte* (Tucson: University of Arizona Press, 2009), 29.

3 Ruben C. Cordova, "José Guadalupe Posada and Diego Rivera Fashion Catrina: From Sellout To National Icon (and Back Again?)," *Glasstire Texas Visual Art*, November 2, 2019, https://glasstire.com/2019/11/02/jose-guadalupe-posada-and-diego-rivera-fashion-catrina-from-sellout-to-national-icon-and-back-again/.

4 Mark McDonald, "Printmaking in Mexico, 1900–1950," *The Met*, September 2016, https://www.metmuseum.org/toah/hd/prmx/hd_prmx.htm.

5 Russ Davidson and David Craven, *Latin American Posters: Public Aesthetics and Mass Politics* (Santa Fe: Museum of New Mexico Press, 2006), 28–29.

6 Dr. Doris Maria-Reina Bravo, "Mexican Muralism: Los Tres Grandes David Alfaro Siqueiros, Diego Rivera, and José Clemente Orozco," *Khan Academy*, accessed January 12, 2024, https://www.khanacademy.org/humanities/ap-art-history/later-europe-and-americas/modernity-ap/a/mexican-muralism-los-tres-grandes-david-alfaro-siqueiros-diego-rivera-and-jos-clemente-orozco.

7 "Che Guevara, Jim Fitzpatrick and the making of an icon," *History of Ireland*, accessed January 12, 2024, https://www.historyireland.com/che-guevara-jim-fitzpatrick-and-the-making-of-an-icon/.

8 "Political Murders in Cuba – Batista Era Compared with Castro Regime," Memorandum, CIA, *CIA Freedom of Information Act Electronic Reading Room*, January 21, 1963, CIA-RDP79T00429A000300030015-8, https://www.cia.gov/readingroom/docs/CIA-RDP79T00429A000300030015-8.pdf.

9 Andrew Annandale Sinclair, "Che Guevara," *Britannica,* December 13, 2023, https://www.britannica.com/biography/Che-Guevara.

10 Alex Gendler, "History vs. Che Guevara," *TedEd,* November 27, 2017, https://ed.ted.com/lessons/history-vs-che-guevara-alex-gendler.

11 "Cuba: Fidel Castro's Record of Repression," *Human Rights Watch,* November 26, 2016, https://www.hrw.org/news/2016/11/26/cuba-fidel-castros-record-repression.

12 "Che Guevara (1928–1967)," *PBS American Experience,* accessed January 12, 2024, https://www.pbs.org/wgbh/americanexperience/features/castro-che-guevara-1928-1967/.

13 "United Farm Workers of America," *National Farm Worker Ministry,* June 2016, https://nfwm.org/farm-workers/farmworker-partners/united-farm-workers-of-america/#:~:text=NFWM%20and%20UFW&text=NFWM%20began%20in%201920%20as,emphasis%20from%20charity%20to%20justice.

14 "1962: United Farm Workers Union," *Library of Congress Research Guides,* accessed January 12, 2024, https://guides.loc.gov/latinx-civil-rights/united-farm-workers-union.

15 "1962: United Farm Workers Union".

16 "Large UFW Flag," *United Farm Workers Store,* accessed January 12, 2024, https://ufwstore.com/x/Large-UFW-Flag.html#:~:text=The%20Aztec%20eagle%20is%20a,circle%20signifies%20hope%20and%20aspirations.

17 "Large UFW Flag."

18 "Boycott Grapes, Support the United Farm Workers Union," *Smithsonian American Art Museum,* accessed January 12, 2024, https://americanart.si.edu/artwork/boycott-grapes-support-united-farm-workers-union-34738.

19 Davidson, *Latin American Posters,* 54.

20 Michelle Elligott, "From the Archives: Faith Ringgold, the Art Workers Coalition, and the Fight for Inclusion at The Museum of Modern Art," *Museum of Modern Art Inside/Out,* July 29, 2016, https://www.moma.org/explore/inside_out/2016/07/29/from-the-archives-faith-ringgold-the-art-workers-coalition-and-the-fight-for-inclusion-at-the-museum-of-modern-art/.

21 Sebastian Smee, "How the Vietnam War Changed Art Forever," *The Washington Post,* March 18, 2019, https://www.washingtonpost.com/entertainment/museums/how-the-vietnam-war-changed-art-forever/2019/03/18/619eff44-4743-11e9-90f0-0ccfeec87a61_story.html.

22 "Q. And babies? A. And babies.", *Smithsonian American Art Museum,* accessed January 12, 2024, https://americanart.si.edu/artwork/q-and-babies-and-babies-111524.

23 Archie Brown, *The Rise and Fall of Communism.*

24 *The Vietnam War,* directed by Ken Burns and Lynn Novick, "Riding the Tiger", Episode 2 (Florentine Films and WETA, 2017), 12:10, https://www.pbs.org/kenburns/the-vietnam-war/.

25 Archie Brown, *The Rise and Fall of Communism.*

26 Jessie Kratz, "Vietnam: The First Television War," *National Archives Pieces of History,* January 25, 2018, https://prologue.blogs.archives.gov/2018/01/25/vietnam-the-first-television-war/#:~:text=Americans%20could%20see%20military%20abuses,U.S%20involvement%20in%20the%20war.
27 Alice Newell-Hanson, "Martha Rosler Wants to Know Why We Still Aren't Outraged," *The New York Times,* August 10, 2023, https://www.nytimes.com/2023/08/10/t-magazine/martha-rosler.html.
28 "Artist Rupert García," *Smithsonian American Art Museum,* accessed January 12, 2024, https://americanart.si.edu/artist/rupert-garcia-1732.
29 *Bliss, Jill (2006). "Long Live Gocco". CRAFT. O'Reilly.* 1 *(1): 50. ISBN 978-0-596-52928-4. Retrieved 2008-05-28.*
30 Christopher Klein, "The MLK Graphic Novel That Inspired Generations of Civil Rights Activists," *History Channel,* December 19, 2023, https://www.history.com/news/civil-rights-graphic-novel-mlk-john-lewis.
31 Lincoln Anthony Blades, "Civil Rights Icon John Lewis Speaks About His 'March' Graphic Novels and Political Activism," *Teen Vogue,* February 9, 2017, https://www.teenvogue.com/story/john-lewis-congressman-civil-rights-icon-march-graphic-novels.
32 John Lewis and Andrew Aydin, *Run,* (New York: Abrams Books, 2021), 47.
33 "Lowndes County Freedom Party," *SNCC Digital Gateway,* accessed on November 16, 2023, https://snccdigital.org/inside-sncc/alliances-relationships/lcfp/.
34 "Our History," *NAACP,* accessed on November 16, 2023, https://naacp.org/about/our-history.
35 Charlie Cobb, "The Story of SNCC," *SNCC Digital Gateway,* accessed on November 16, 2023, https://snccdigital.org/inside-sncc/the-story-of-sncc/.
36 "About Dr. Martin Luther King Jr.", *The King Center,* accessed on November 16, 2023, https://thekingcenter.org/about-tkc/martin-luther-king-jr/.
37 Peniel E. Joseph. *Stokely: A Life.* (London: Civitas Books, 2016).
38 Marianne Combs, "Emory Douglas' art takes him from Black Panthers to the Walker," *Minnesota Public Radio News,* December 18, 2015, https://www.mprnews.org/story/2015/12/18/emory-douglas-walker-art-center.
39 Combs, "Emory Douglas."
40 Jagroop Shinbt, "Colin Kaepernick mural: Fabian Williams on how artists came together in Atlanta," *BBC,* July 24, 2020, https://www.bbc.com/sport/american-football/53415638.
41 Michael Levy, "Gay Rights Movement," *Brittannica,* December 19, 2023, https://www.britannica.com/topic/gay-rights-movement.
42 Michael Macbride, "A History of The Advocate's Earliest Political Cartoons," *The Advocate,* April 26, 2022, https://www.advocate.com/exclusives/2022/4/26/history-advocates-earliest-political-cartoons.
43 Rupert Kinnard." n.d. *The Outwords Archive.* Accessed June 19, 2024. https://theoutwordsarchive.org/interview/rupert-kinnard/.
44 Anne Balsamo and Leticia Ferreira, "Video Essay the AIDS Memorial Quilt: Origins, Legacy, Futures," *ATEC at UT Dallas,* July 5, 2020, https://www.youtube.com/watch?v=7HsDs3YRRZg&t=386s.
45 Rebecca Kesby, producer, "BBC World News Witness History – The AIDS Memorial Quilt," *National AIDS Memorial,* July 4, 2020, https://www.youtube.com/watch?v=hX0Ju8IhoXQ&t=309s, 3:45.
46 "The History of the Quilt," *National AIDS Memorial,* accessed January 15, 2024, https://www.aidsmemorial.org/quilt-history.
47 Zoya Raza-Sheikh, "Digital LGBTQ+ activism: Does it work?", *Gay Times,* February 28, 2022, https://www.gaytimes.co.uk/culture/digital-lgbtq-activism-does-it-work/.
48 "Native American," *Library of Congress,* accessed January 15, 2024, https://www.loc.gov/classroom-materials/immigration/native-american/.
49 NCC Staff, "On this day, all American Indians made United States citizens," *The Constitution Center,* June 2, 2023, https://constitutioncenter.org/blog/on-this-day-in-1924-all-indians-made-united-states-citizens#:~:text=The%2014th%20amendment's%20ratification%20in,most%20of%20them%20from%20citizenship.
50 "H.R. 5007, An Act granting citizenship to certain Indians, September 27, 1919. Serving the Nation: American Indians," *U.S. Capitol Visitor Center Artifact Explorer,* September 27, 1919, https://www.visitthecapitol.gov/artifact/hr-5007-act-granting-citizenship-certain-indians-september-27-1919#:~:text=Though%20they%20were%20not%20granted,Indian%20World%20War%20I%20veterans.
51 "Voting Rights for Native Americans," *Library of Congress,* accessed January 17, 2024, https://www.loc.gov/classroom-materials/elections/right-to-vote/voting-rights-for-native-americans/.
52 "Tribal Crim and Justice: Public Law 280," *National Institute for Justice,* May 19, 2008, https://nij.ojp.gov/topics/articles/tribal-crime-and-justice-public-law-280.

53 Michael C. Walch, "Terminating the Indian Termination Policy," *Stanford Law Review* 35, no. 6 (1983): 1181–1215, accessed January 17, 2024, https://doi.org/10.2307/1228583.

54 Max Nesterak, "Uprooted: The 1950s plan to erase Indian Country," *American Public Media Reports,* November 1, 2019, https://www.apmreports.org/episode/2019/11/01/uprooted-the-1950s-plan-to-erase-indian-country.

55 Dennis Zotigh, "A Return to the Wounded Knee Occupation, 50 Years Later," *Smithsonian Magazine,* February 27, 2023, https://www.smithsonianmag.com/blogs/national-museum-american-indian/2023/02/27/a-return-to-the-knee-occupation-fifty-years-later/.

56 Julia Métraux, "The Importance of Newspapers for the Red Power Movement," *JSTOR Daily,* March 17, 2023, https://daily.jstor.org/the-importance-of-newspapers-for-the-red-power-movement/

57 "Akwesasne Notes vol. 2 no. 5," *American Indian Digital History Project*, September 1970, https://www.aidhp.com/items/show/7.

58 Seonghoon Kim, ""We have Always Had These Many Voices": Red Power Newspapers and a Community of Poetic Resistance," *American Indian Quarterly* 39, no. 3 (2015): 271–301, https://www.jstor.org/stable/10.5250/amerindiquar.39.3.0271?mag=the-importance-of-newspapers-for-the-red-power-movement.

59 Lois Alter Mark, Ricardo Caté Offers Political Cartoons Without Reservations At The Indian Pueblo Cultural Center," *Forbes,* April 18, 2018, https://www.forbes.com/sites/loisaltermark/2018/04/18/ricardo-cate-offers-political-cartoons-without-reservations-at-the-indian-pueblo-cultural-center/?sh=7a5d060e47fa.

60 "Indian/Native American Boarding Schools: Their History, Harm and Impact," *Anti-Defamation League,* August 8, 2022, https://www.adl.org/resources/lesson-plan/indiannative-american-boarding-schools-their-history-harm-and-impact?gad_source=1&gclid=CjwKCAiA9dGqBhAqEiwAmRpTCyE_S49879lkylEhsVFh0c-BD2XWGnrbTQOlCrKQ_cLciTE-8ZRuKxoCMd8QAvD_BwE.

61 Jody Heemstra, "9th annual RedCan brings hundreds to mural sites and Waniyetu Wowapi Art Park," *DRG News,* August 2, 2023, https://drgnews.com/2023/08/02/cheyenne-river-youth-project-releases-short-film-announces-artists-and-guests-for-2023-redcan-invitational-graffiti-jam/.

62 Angie Jaime, "Indigenous Activists Launch Political Art Campaign Ahead of the Election," *Hyperallergic,* November 2, 2020, https://hyperallergic.com/599027/indigenous-activists-launch-political-art-campaign-ahead-of-the-election/.

63 Bouazizi was taken to a hospital on December 17th and died from his injuries on January 4, 2011.

64 Ricardo Rene Laramont, "Revolution, Revolt and Reform in North Africa," in *Revolution, Revolt, and Reform in North Africa: The Arab Spring,* ed. Ricardo Rene Laramont (New York: Routledge 2014), 1–14.

65 Ricardo Rene Laramont, "Demographics, Economics and Technology: Background to the North African revolutions," in *Revolution, Revolt, and Reform in North Africa: The Arab Spring,* ed. Ricardo Rene Laramont (New York: Routledge 2014), 15–29.

66 "The Nobel Peace Prize 2015," *The Nobel Prize,* Last Updated October 10, 2015, https://www.nobelprize.org/prizes/peace/2015/press-release/.

67 Evie Papada, David Altman, Fabio Angiolillo, Lisa Gastaldi, Tamara Kohler, Martin Lundstedt, Natalia Natsika, Marina Nord, Yuko Sato, Felix Wiebrecht, and Staffan I. Lindberg, "Defiance in the Face of Autocratization: Democracy Report 2023," *University of Gothenburg: Varieties of Democracy Institute,* March 2023, https://www.v-dem.net/documents/29/V-dem_democracyreport2023_lowres.pdf.

68 Michelle Ferrari, director, *The Vote*, film, 42nd Parallel Films, American Experience: PBS, 2020, https://www.pbs.org/wgbh/americanexperience/films/vote/.

69 C.J. Bearman, "An Examination of Suffragette Violence," *The English Historical Review* 120, no. 486 (2005): 365–397, accessed January 17, 2024, https://www.jstor.org/stable/3490924.

70 "Winson Green force feeding," *UK Parliament*, accessed January 17, 2024, https://www.parliament.uk/about/living-heritage/transformingsociety/electionsvoting/womenvote/case-study-the-right-to-vote/the-right-to-vote/winson-green-forcefeeding/#:~:text=Hunger%20striking%20was%20an%20important,the%20status%20of%20political%20prisoners.

71 "The Suffragette 1d Weekly (summary)," *Victoria and Albert Museum,* accessed January 17, 2024, https://collections.vam.ac.uk/item/O685356/the-suffragette-1d-weekly-poster-dallas-hilda/#:~:text=Dallas%20was%20a%20member%20of,professional%20artists%20in%20printing%20techniques.

72 "The Suffragette 1d Weekly (summary)"

73 Shana Loudermelk, "Vote for Women / The Suffragette / Britannia (1907–1918)," *Towards Emancipation?,* accessed January 17, 2024, https://hist259.web.unc.edu/vote-for-women-the-suffragette-britannia-1907-1918/.

74 *Woman's Suffrage: The Common Cause of Humanity, Volume 1.* n.d. Accessed June 19, 2024. https://books.google.com/books?id=ISUoAAAAMAAJ&pg=PA599&lpg=PA599&dq=%222,708+posters,+6,488+postcards+and+65,000+picture+leaflets%22&source=bl&ots=gOlPGodXia&sig=ACfU3U3UM5ciDpcfgiI_vicqZC0ll2GdLg&hl=en&sa=X&ved=2ahUKEwiKue-r9OiGAxV1EUQIHQzlD1sQ6AF6BAgMEAM#v=onepage&q=%222%2C708%20posters%2C%206%2C488%20postcards%20and%2065%2C000%20picture%20leaflets%22&f=false.

75 'Artists' Suffrage League.' n.d. Spartacus Educational. https://spartacus-educational.com/Wartists.htm.

76 Allison Lange, "National Association of Colored Women," *National Women's History Museum,* Fall 2015, https://www.crusadeforthevote.org/nacw.

77 Ferrari, *The Vote.*

78 Alden O'Brien, "Part I: Great strides for the "New Woman," suffrage, and fashion," *National Museum of American History,* March 7, 2013, https://americanhistory.si.edu/blog/2013/03/guest-post-great-strides-for-the-new-woman-suffrage-and-fashion.html.

79 "Propagandist Nina Allender (1872–1957)," *Library of Congress,* accessed January 17, 2024, https://www.loc.gov/collections/women-of-protest/articles-and-essays/selected-leaders-of-the-national-womans-party/propagandist/.

80 Jen Johnson, "The Image of Suffrage," *The New Antiquarian,* January 7, 2020, https://www.abaa.org/blog/post/the-image-of-suffrage.

81 Roberta W. Francis, "Equal Rights Amendment Frequently Asked Questions," *Alice Paul Institute,* accessed January 17, 2024, https://www.alicepaul.org/wp-content/uploads/2021/05/FAQ-as-of-2021-05-25.pdf.

82 STOP was an acronym for 'Stop Taking Our Privileges'

83 Donald Crichlow. *Phyllis Schlafly and Grassroots Conservativism: A Woman's Crusade.* (Princeton: Princeton University Press, 2005).

84 John P. Rafferty, "Women's March," *Britannica,* January 14, 2024, https://www.britannica.com/event/Womens-March-2017.

85 Sarah Frostenson, "The Women's Marches may have been the largest demonstration in US History," *Vox,* January 31, 2017, https://www.vox.com/2017/1/22/14350808/womens-marches-largest-demonstration-us-history-map.

86 Laureli Ivanoff, "I'm a strong, beautiful, fierce Inuit woman. Today I march," *Anchorage Daily News,* December 2, 2017, https://www.adn.com/opinions/2017/01/21/im-a-strong-beautiful-fierce-inuit-woman-today-i-march/.

87 Jeremy Pressman and Erica Chenoweth, "Crowd Estimates, 1.21.2017," accessed January 17, 2024, https://docs.google.com/spreadsheets/d/1xa0iLqYKz8x9Yc_rfhtmSOJQ2EGgeUVjvV4A8LsIaxY/edit#gid=0.

Conclusion

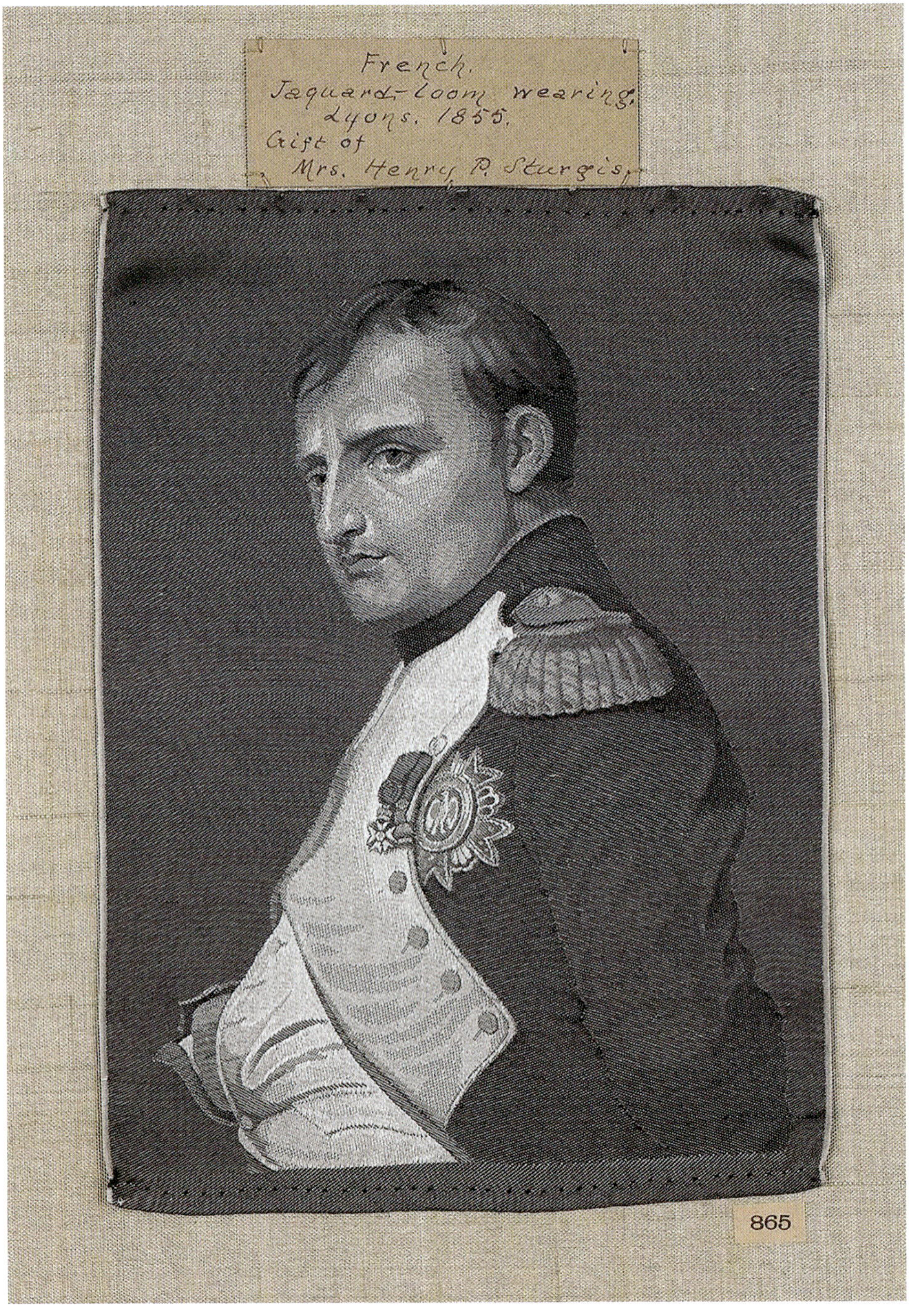

Figure 5.1
A Jacquard loom weaving of Napoleon, 1855

At first glance, you may think that this image is just another etching of Napoleon, but look closer. (Figure 5.1) Upon a more careful inspection, you'll realize the image appears almost pixelated, like a low-quality jpeg viewed on your computer. This is because this image is in fact a highly detailed weaving, created on a Jacquard loom in 1855. Each black dot indicates where a weft thread rises above a warp to create a pixel in the design, continuing line by line as the design emerges, much like a dot matrix printer. The Jacquard loom was a revolution in reproducing works of art and was the first programmable loom capable of weaving any style and structure of cloth without requiring the time-consuming redressing of earlier looms. The loom's designs were created with a chain of punched cards, similar to programming cards used in early computers, which guided the programmable loom, significantly shortening production time.[1] Napoleon himself had an appreciation for science and technology that inspired the period following the Napoleonic Wars, and he also had a fascination with the silk industry. In the early 19th century, Britain and France were in competition for industrial advancement, especially textile manufacturing, with Britain coming out ahead. Napoleon sought to promote technology by instituting exhibitions of French industry, and a weaver by the name of Joseph Marie Jacquard gained success and recognition at these exhibitions.[2] In 1804, the same year Napoleon declared himself to be emperor, Jacquard patented his famous loom, forever changing France's silk industry.[3] The following year, Napoleon and Jacquard met in person for the first time, and Napoleon declared Jacquard's loom public property, awarding Jacquard an annual pension for life of 3000 francs.[4] When Jacquard expressed appreciation for the pension, Napoleon declared to his audience: "Think of all those who incessantly come to me with demands for government grants and other financial favours! And here is a man of vast talent and industry who is happy with so little!"[5]

As discussed in this book, political illustration has advanced and evolved in concert with technology, both in its creation and its distribution. From the printing press advancements discussed in Chapter 2, to photography's impact on reportage illustration discussed in Chapter 3, to screenprinting increasing the accessibility of political posters in Chapter 4, technology has driven illustration forward. Now with the internet, social media, subscriber blogs, and other distribution methods, creating illustration for the masses is easier than ever before. Illustrations can be reproduced and shared around the world within minutes, a significant change from earlier memes, such as the pears scribbled on brick walls in King Louis-Phillipe's France. One example of social media driving illustration was the 2016 election of Donald Trump in the United States, which was, as Doug Chayka put it in an interview with *American Illustration*, "very good for picture making, less good for everything else."[6] Illustrators embraced the opportunity for an easy target by experimenting with a variety of mediums. They had a clear audience for their work, and, most importantly, had an easy and accessible way to communicate their art and their dissent. (Figures 5.2, 5.3, 5.4, 5.5)

Napoleon's comment regarding Jacquard as "a man of vast talent and industry who is happy with so little!" is reflective of the status of editorial political illustration today. Many publications have rejected the idea of inflation, paying the same amount for illustrations that they did in the 1990s. Nevertheless, some illustrators, including Doug Chayka and Miriam Martincic, have found success in a steady flow of editorial illustration jobs. Many of our interviewees for this book balanced cynicism and idealism in their answers about political illustration's financial outlook, agreeing there is not a lot of money in it, yet there can be a lot of honor and satisfaction in the opportunities it provides to speak truth to power. Is there a way to financially succeed in political illustration without compromising your vision or ethics? Many illustrators have found a way. Artists such as Zina Saunders have embraced the internet's opportunities for self-publishing, when she released her book of Sarah Palin illustrations entitled *The Party's Over* in 2008. (Figure 5.6) Steve Brodner utilizes SubStack as a way of collecting income while distributing his message to a fan audience. Anita Kunz, Edel Rodriguez, and Seymour Chwast illustrate and write their own books and participate in gallery shows, and Kunz and Rodriguez continue to work editorially. Fabian Williams found a popular medium in street art where he can make a living distributing messages he believes in, as Andeel has with videos. Many illustrators, including Hoka "Infer" Skenandore, Steve Brodner, Anita Kunz, Miriam Martincic, and Doug Chayka teach alongside illustrating. Some illustrators pursue political illustration for the opportunity to speak their mind, not for the money, such as @9mmBallpoint, who prefers to work anonymously to avoid criticism of his work and opinions. And, of course, there are illustrators who compromise their political and moral ethics to take on paying editorial jobs, whether for the prestige or the money. As we see in this book, this certainly has been done throughout history.

Some of these examples show how technology provides a sense of hope for the future of political illustration, but it can also bring up fears. Internet journalism requires even faster turnovers, but the technology of digital drawing has allowed for this faster turnaround. Meanwhile, those who work in traditional media are forced to speed up their process in any way they can, which can create anxiety as they compete with digital artists for jobs. Internet journalism has, like previous advances in the industry, given opportunities to expand the medium, and created new genres of illustration such as animated illustration. **Animated illustration** differs from traditional animation in that it creates movement while examining time as a cyclical vs. linear element. Animated illustrations tend to loop, capturing a moment and creating a sense of timelessness. Learning this skill can open new avenues for illustrators, and academic analysis of this development in the field has been discussed in the illustration education community. Illustration made through **artificial intelligence**, or AI, has been viewed by many in the illustration community as a threat to their livelihoods and the integrity of illustration. However, it has also renewed illustrators' fervor for creating ethical work and united them in a way that could create further unionization to drive up wages for illustration. AI has also challenged political illustrators to improve their visual communication skills, be clear in their messaging, and determine what is unique about their craft.

Historically, the impact of technology on the field of illustration has required the field to perform a sharp pivot many times before. The advent of photography marked a turning point for illustration, with art directors now having an appealing, more affordable, and quicker alternative for visual content. Even though illustration survived this change, the industry was transformed, and jobs became scarce as this competitor hit the market. Charles Baudelaire, a 19th century art critic, called photography "art's most mortal enemy."[7] The advent of the internet and the fast turnover of internet journalism required the digitization of illustration, and similar critiques were brought about when drawing software including Photoshop, Illustrator, and Procreate hit the market. Around the time Jacquard was working in France, the Luddite movement evolved in Britain. The movement, lasting approximately from 1811 to 1816, consisted of angry workers who would destroy textile machinery to protest the jobs it was replacing. Manufacturers were able to sell the same products for less because they employed fewer skilled workers. Such a protest may have also occurred in Jacquard's workshop as well. A myth from 19th century weaving circles that was often repeated stated that workers assaulted Jacquard and threw him into a river in protest. As author James Essinger states: "the path to acceptance of a new invention in the world at large is rarely a smooth one."[8]

Jacquard was a significant influence on inventor and philosopher Charles Babbage, who invented the idea of the digital programmable computer, and is viewed by many to be the precursor of modern computing technology.[9] The connection between Napoleon's propaganda art and today's AI illustration is shorter than we thought. Technological change has always been a component of illustration, and it is up to the field whether to adapt or become a relic of the past. Politics advances industry, industry advances art, art advances politics… a complicated weaving indeed.

If money is the goal of a particular illustrator, and they have no ethical line, then they can already make a significant profit generating a portfolio of AI generated art. However, most illustrators reading this book likely have different motivations. Students of illustration must be prepared when they enter the field to draw their ethical line and to be aware of their own reasons for creating work. What is your line? AI may come for your job, but it won't come for your purpose. If you know your purpose, as per the examples of illustrators listed above, either you will find the right jobs, or you will make the right job for yourself. Financial success and a principled vision do not always need to be at odds with one another, but financial success without a principled vision may leave an illustrator with an unfulfilling career. We are equipped with the visual literacy skills to create compelling and significant images that, as we have seen throughout this book, sometimes change the course of history. An aspiring political illustrator must ask themselves, as Fabian Williams concluded in his interview, "What are you using your power for?"

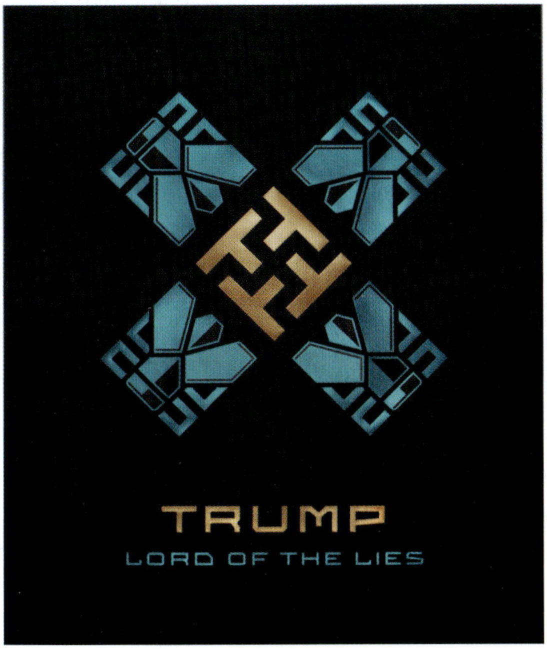

Figure 5.2
Trump: Lord of the Lies
Design © 2020 Mark Fox and Angie Wang, Design is Play (for Lord of the Lies)

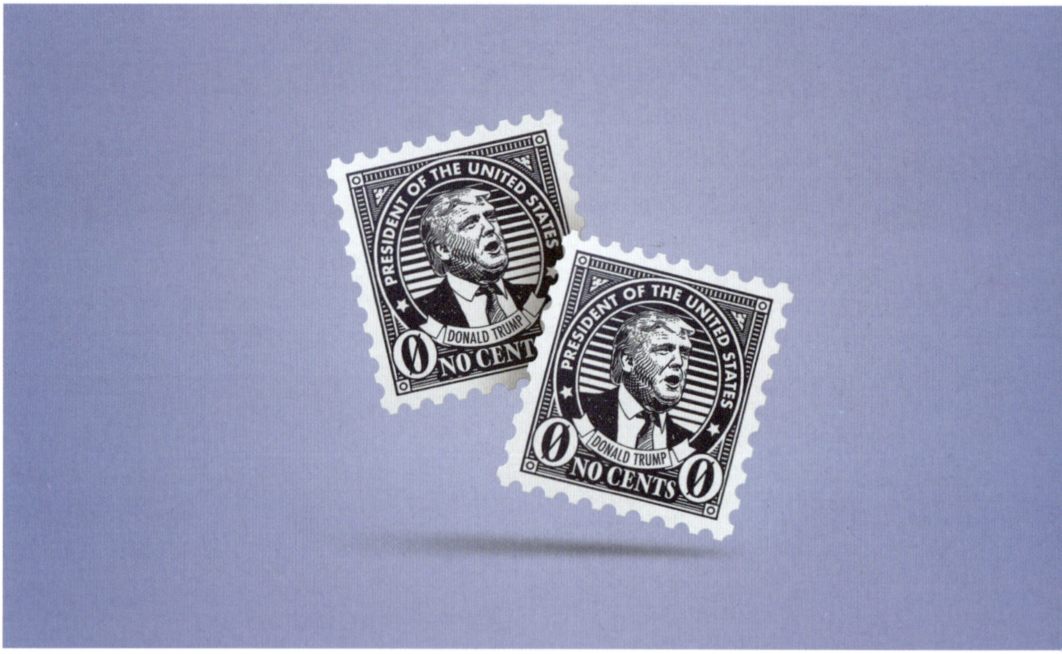

Figure 5.3
Donald Trump "No Cents" Stamp
© Ben Hannam & Bizhan Khodabandeh, 2016

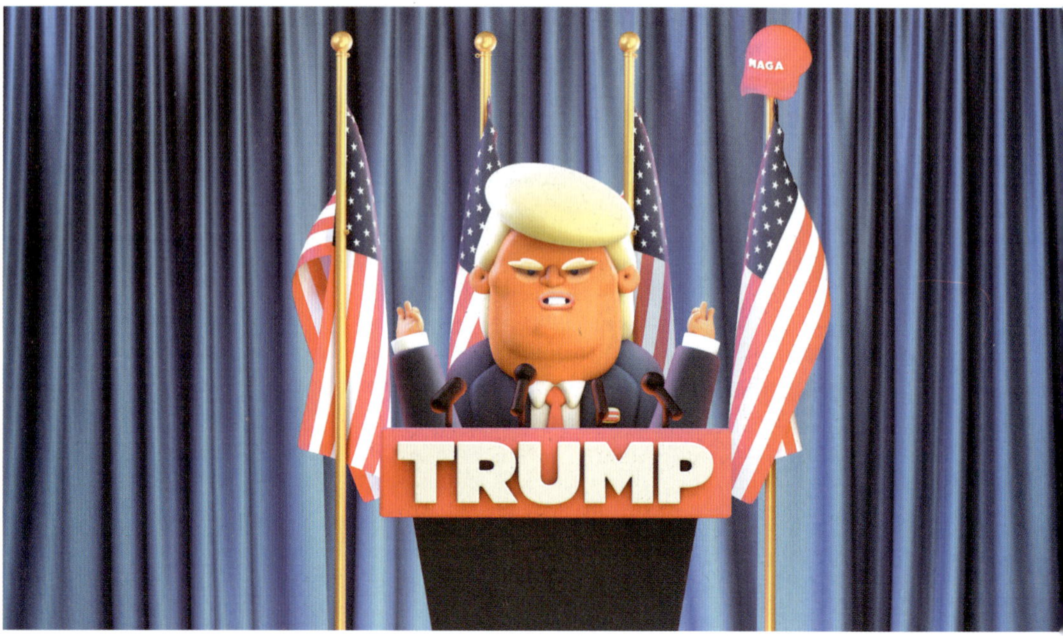

Figure 5.4
Still of "Donald Trump Facts"
© Fraser Davidson, Cub Animation Studio, 2020

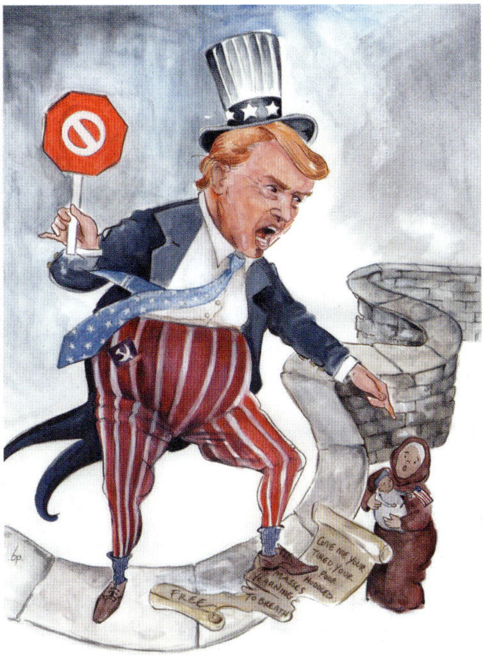

Figure 5.5
TanTrump's Travel Ban
© Printed with the permission of Beth Post, 2017

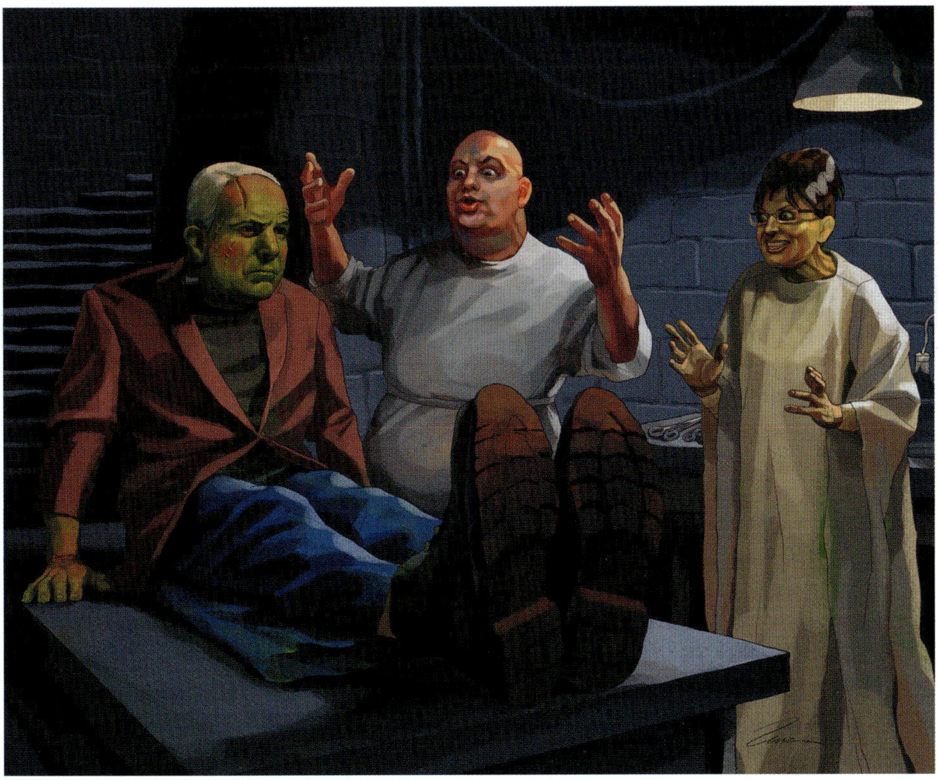

Figure 5.6
McCain Frankenstein
© Zina Saunders, 2008

Endnotes

1 Francesca Elliott, "Weaving Numbers: The Jacquard Loom and Early Computing," *Science and Industry Museum,* October 17, 2017, https://blog.scienceandindustrymuseum.org.uk/weaving-numbers-jacquard-loom-early-computing/.

2 James Essinger, *Jacquard's Web: How a Hand-Loom Led to the Birth of the Information Age* (Oxford: Oxford University Press, 2004), 30.

3 Essinger, 35.

4 Essinger, 39–40.

5 Essinger, 40.

6 B Robert Newman, "Illustrator Profile – Doug Chayka: "I learn with every new assignment," *AI-AP Profiles,* January 18, 2018, Email.

7 Jonathan Mayne, ed, *Charles Baudelaire, The Mirror of Art,* (London: Phaidon Press Limited, 1955).

8 Richard Conniff, "What the Luddites Really Fought Against," *Smithsonian Magazine*, March 2011, https://www.smithsonianmag.com/history/what-the-luddites-really-fought-against-264412/.

9 Elliott, "Weaving Numbers."

Glossary

Agitprop Agitprop is a term that originated in the Soviet Union and refers to media that advances the goals of communism, including flyers, film, and art.

Animated illustration Animated illustration differs from traditional definitions of animation in that it tends to loop, showing a moving moment in time, in comparison to a trajectory through time.

Art Deco Following Art Nouveau, Art Deco was most popular between 1910 and 1930, and used bold, geometric forms as well as symmetry. Art Deco was influenced by Futurism and Cubism and, like Art Nouveau, sought to eliminate barriers between applied arts and fine arts.

Artificial Intelligence (AI) Commercially available AI art and illustration emerged in the 2020s. In AI art, computers gather images from datasets and compile the images via user prompts to create new and unique artworks. AI technology is progressing rapidly and raises many ethical issues about copyright that are still being worked through the courts.

Art Nouveau Art Nouveau was a highly decorative art movement most popular between 1890 and 1910. Art Nouveau sought to eliminate the distinction between applied arts and fine arts, which helped illustration gain popularity in the 20th century. Art Nouveau was often highly detailed and used natural, curving forms.

Augmented reality (AR) Augmented reality (AR) is an interactive method for people to interact with their environment. Using their phones, one can hover over an AR image, which will animate on the phone, sometimes including audio.

Broadsheets Broadsheets are posters made on newspaper, and therefore easy and affordable to print and post.

Buon Fresco Buon fresco is a mural making technique in which paint is mixed with plaster before applying it to a surface. Buon fresco is more durable than fresco secco because the paint becomes part of the surface.

Calavera The Mexican symbol of a calavera, or skull, was popularized by José Guadalupe Posada and has become an enduring symbol in Day of the Dead celebrations in Mexico. Posada's calaveras were meant to mock archetypes of Mexican society, as a message to show we all share death.

Caricature A caricature is a drawing that exaggerates the facial features and other visual characteristics of an individual, often to mock or poke fun at the person, or to lampoon a particular archetype of a person, such as a nobleman or beggar.

Censorship Censorship is the prohibition or suppression of information, which can be enacted by governments, members of the media, or individuals.

Chosonhwa Chosonhwa is a style of North Korean painting that values naturalism and emotional expression. Chosonhwa is similar to Socialist Realism, but incorporates more loose brushwork and impressionistic qualities.

Closure In closure, the brain fills in the visual gaps between disparate pieces of visual information to form a whole. For instance, two dots, a line, and a circle can be perceived as a face.

Color lithography or chromolithography Color lithography (also called chromolithography) is a method of creating prints with multiple colors. Chromolithography is created on flat stones or plates in a chemical process that involves the repulsion of grease and water, and uses multiple plates to print multiple colors. Chromolithographs became very popular in the United States following the Civil War.

Common fate In common fate, the brain perceives objects moving in one direction as a single group. For instance, a flock of birds flying in one direction displays common fate.

Connotation A connotation is the underlying, second meaning of an image.

Constructivism Constructivism is an art movement that developed in Russia during World War I. Constructivism valued abstraction, simplification, and bold geometric shapes, which reflected the aesthetics of the industrial age. Constructivists often created work for a socialist cause.

Contentious politics Contentious politics are when people attempt to create governmental change by using disruptive methods and action. Those engaging in contentious politics can work within the media but often work outside of the media or within organizations that agree with their viewpoints so that they can express their unedited opinions.

Continuation In continuation, the brain fills in the visual gaps in a line or path, and prefers to see lines as smooth and continuous.

Decoder In Stewart Hall's reception theory, a decoder refers to the recipient of a message, who interprets the message.

Democratic backsliding Democratic backsliding refers to an erosion in the quality of democracy in a country. This can occur due to the lessening of the rule of law, the manipulation of elections or the centralization of executive power.

Denotation A denotation is the fixed, literal meaning of the signifier.

Emulsion In screenprinting, an emulsion is a light sensitive substance that creates a barrier between paint and a surface.

Encaustic Encaustic is a three-dimensional illustration technique in which the artist uses wax mixed with color to create an image.

Encoder In Stewart Hall's reception theory, an encoder refers to the sender of a message, who creates coded communications for a particular audience.

Federalism Federalism is a mode of political organization that unites separate states or other polities within an overarching political system in a way that allows each to maintain its own integrity.

Fresco Secco Fresco secco is a mural making technique in which paint is applied to dry plaster. Fresco secco is vulnerable to the elements, and often cracks and chips over time.

Futurism Futurism was an art movement that originated in Italy in the early 1900s on the premise that art should reject all things of the past. Futurism believed art should incorporate industrialism, speed, technology, movement, and science. The movement was later adopted by Russia and spanned a variety of media and styles, but often included indications of repetition indicating movement.

Gestalt theory Developed by Max Wertheimer, Kurt Koffka, and Wolfgang Köhler, Gestalt theory states that the whole is different than the sum of the parts. Gestalt theory states humans perceive information as whole or complete parts versus as individual elements.

Hierarchical scale In hierarchical scale, subjects that are important or powerful are portrayed larger in a composition.

Icon An icon is a semiotic sign in which the signifier directly resembles the signified. For instance, a photograph of a dog is a signifier of a dog (the signified).

Index An index is a semiotic sign in which the signifier indicates or gives evidence of the signified. For instance, a paw print of a dog is a signifier of a dog (the signified).

Invisibility In invisibility, one becomes so immersed in the storytelling experience that the existence of the medium fades.

Market censorship Market censorship is when an individual or publication alters its own speech for financial benefit. Market censorship may lean into social norms to avoid controversy, or, contrarily, embrace shock value content to sell more product.

Media Media refers to the methods or tools used to communicate messages or content. In this book, the term media refers to mass communication methods, while mediums refers to the materials and tools used to create art.

Mediated image A mediated image is an image that has been intervened by the media in which it was presented. Almost all illustrations are mediated images.

Meme A meme is an image, mannerism, or phrase that propagates quickly and widely throughout a society, often carrying symbolic meaning.

Metaphor A metaphor is an image that is meant to stand for another object or concept. Like symbols, metaphors usually require a shared cultural understanding.

Metonym A metonym is an image that is meant to stand for a totality, or a group of things, objects, or ideas.

Modernismo The Modernismo movement originally began as a literary movement in Latin America, and valued metaphor and symbolism. Its ideals were later translated to art and illustration.

Mosaics Mosaics are images created by combining smaller pieces of material to create a larger image. Mosaics are often publicly displayed as flooring or walls, and can be constructed from stone, glass, metal, or other materials.

Mural art (*muralismo*) Mural art, or *muralismo,* in Mexico was the movement led by the Mexican government and the *Tres Muralistas* in the 1920s to create publicly available art through mosaics and paintings. The original goals of *muralismo* were to promote the history and culture of Mexico, as well as the government's vision for the future.

Nationalism Nationalism is loyalty or devotion to a particular nation, sometimes to the detriment of other nations.

Neoclassicism Neoclassicism is a style of art that renewed the artistry and design of Greek and Roman times. It is based on Greco-Roman values of symmetry and simplicity. It lasted from roughly the 1760s through the 1850s.

Offset lithography Offset lithography was an advancement in lithography that used an intermediary plate, so that the original image did not appear reversed on the printed surface.

Photomontage Photomontage is when different photographs are cut up and spliced together. It originated with the Dada art movement and was popularized as an art form during World War I, although other art movements, such as the Surrealists and Constructivists, also practiced photomontage.

Photo references Photo references are tools used by illustrators to help inform their drawing. Illustrators do not copy a single photo, but work from multiple references to design a unique image, making changes in size, emphasis, and lighting to achieve their illustrative goal.

Picture superiority effect The picture superiority effect states that images are remembered and recalled more easily than words, but that the strongest recall and memory effects happen when words and pictures are paired together.

Plakatstil Plakatstil is style of posters originating in Germany in the early 1900s. The style had flat, bold colors, large, distinctive lettering, and often had a large, singular focal point.

Political cartoon Political cartoons are drawings made with the purpose of providing commentary on political events. Political cartoons may be an image alone, but are often paired with words in order to communicate their message. Political cartoons may be made and published by an individual, expressing their own opinion, or mediated by a publication to advance the opinion of a publication.

Pouncing Pouncing is a method of transferring works of art, in which a template is perforated with small holes, through which a fine dust or powder called "pounce" is rubbed. The powder creates a guide on the new drawing surface.

Printing press The printing press was first invented by Johannes Gutenberg circa 1440, which allowed moveable type and the ability to make thousands of copies of a text. The printing press began the era of mass communication and dramatically increased literacy.

Propaganda Images that attempt to persuade, compel, or influence their audience to further an agenda.

Proximity In proximity, the brain perceives items that are close in space as being part of a group. This is a stronger grouping principle than similarity.

Psychic lines A psychic line is a type of implied line that occurs when a subject looks or gestures towards an area or point within a composition, creating a mental connection.

Reportage illustration Reportage illustration is illustration meant to document a particular event or set of events, similar to how photojournalism is used today. Reportage illustration may or may not include the individual opinions of the illustrator on the subject they are documenting.

Reverse censorship Reverse censorship attempts to flood out other opinions by spreading one-sided propaganda, seeking to eliminate dissenting speech.

Screenprinting (also known as *silkscreen printmaking* or *serigraphy*) In screenprinting, a photo emulsion is applied to a screen, and through a photographic process, an image is burned out of the screen. An artist then applies paint to the screen, so the paint only passes through the screen where emulsion is absent, creating an image. Screenprinting is an easy to learn and accessible method of printmaking.

Self-censorship Self-censorship is when an individual or a publication chooses to alter its own speech to adhere to a social or political norm and avoid criticism.

Semiotics Developed by linguists Ferdinand de Saussure and Charles Sanders Peirce, semiotics is the study of signs. In semiotics, there is a signifier, which is the sign, and the signified, which is the thing or concept the sign represents.

Similarity In similarity, the brain perceives similar items as being part of a group. The hierarchy of similarity perception is shape, size, and color.

Socialist Realism Socialist Realism was a style of art that originated in the Soviet Union in the 1930s. Socialist Realism was naturalistic and highly idealistic, creating an optimistic outlook for socialism through portraits, images of workers, and depictions of war and battle. Socialist Realism continued to be practiced in other countries including China and North Korea, and is often associated with communism.

Special Artists Special Artists were reportage illustrators employed by newspapers and publications in the 1800s to go into the field and document the news of the day. Their role is similar to photojournalists today, although Special Artists did not have as much control over how their work would translate into the final publication.

Street art Street art is an art movement that grew out of mural art and graffiti movements and was popularized in in the 1970s and 1980s in New York City. Street art is a blanket term that can encompass a wide variety of styles of art that is publicly displayed and meant for public consumption. Street art may be created by an artist independently, or through a commission from an organization or company.

Suprematism Suprematism was a non-objective, abstract art movement that originated during World War I. Suprematists believed that the experience of art should be based on pure aesthetics, especially geometric shapes and simple colors. The term Suprematism comes from Kazimir Malevich, who believed this type of art was the "supremacy of pure artistic feeling."

Symbol A symbol is a semiotic sign in which the signifier is not directly related to the signified and must be culturally learned. The signified object or concept in the symbol is usually abstract. Words, letters, hand gestures, flags, and culturally learned drawn symbols, such as the peace sign, are all symbols.

Taboo A taboo is a custom that is frowned upon or forbidden by a particular culture or group of cultures. Violating taboos can bring about social exclusion, criticism, or violence.

Texture Texture is a design principle in which a visual effect invokes the sense of touch and brings a sense of three-dimensionality to an illustration. Collage, impasto, and other techniques can be used to create texture in illustrations.

Tusche A tusche is a greasy crayon used as a tool in lithography to draw on a stone or plate. The tusche repels water so that ink can adhere to it.

Verism A style in Roman art in which subjects were portrayed naturalistically. Verism portraits usually include scars, wrinkles, and imperfections.

Visual hierarchy Visual hierarchy refers to the design principle that certain items within an image or design will capture the attention of the viewer more than other parts. Color, size, and contrast can all be elements in creating visual hierarchy.

Visual stereotypes Visual stereotypes are an oversimplified idea or image of a group of people. Visual stereotypes often can have racist or sexist origins. Because of the picture superiority effect, visual stereotypes can be more dangerous than other stereotypes because they can last longer in someone's memory.

Wheatpaste Wheatpaste combines a flour or starch with water to create an adhesive. It is often used to post flyers or posters, and has been used in street art to paste smaller sections of a printed mural on a wall.

Woodblock printing Woodblock printing is one of the oldest types of printmaking. A design is carved out of a wooden block, and ink is applied to the raised areas. Paper or another material are pressed onto the block to transfer the ink to the print.

Xerography A printing process in which paper becomes electrically charged after being exposed to light. A dry toner with an opposite charge to the paper is then exposed to the paper, and sticks to the areas of the paper with an opposite charge. This is commercially known as a Xerox machine.

Selected Bibliography

Alkebulan, Paul. *The African American Press in World War II: Toward Victory at Home and Abroad*. Lanham, MD: Lexington Books, 2016.

Bang, Molly. *Picture This: How Pictures Work*. San Francisco: Chronicle Books, 2016.

Bordes, Phillipe. *Jacques Louis-David: Empire to Exile*. New Haven, Yale University Press, 2005.

Brown, Archie. *The Rise and Fall of Communism*. New York: Harper Collins, 2009.

Burns, Ken and Lynn Novick, dirs. *The Vietnam War*. Walpole, NH: Florentine Films and WETA, 2017. https://www.pbs.org/kenburns/the-vietnam-war/.

Cheles, Luciano and Alessandro Giacone, ed. *The Political Portrait : Leadership, Image and Power*. New York, NY: Routledge, 2020.

Clayton, Timothy. *James Gillray: A Revolution in Satire*. London: Paul Mellon Centre, 2022.

Clayton, Tim and Sheila O'Connell. *Bonaparte and the British: Prints and propaganda in the age of Napoleon*. London: British Museum, 2015.

Dahl, Robert. *Polyarchy: participation and opposition*. New Haven: Yale University Press, 1971.

David: Great Artists (Series 2). Brighton: Seventh Art Productions, 2003. https://fod.infobase.com/PortalPlaylists.aspx?wID=96309&xtid=59675.

Davidson, Russ and David Craven. *Latin American Posters : Public Aesthetics and Mass Politics*. Santa Fe: Museum of New Mexico Press, 2006.

Doyle, Susan, Jaleen Grove, and Whitney Sherman. *The History of Illustration*. New York: Fairchild Books, 2018.

Edwards, Betty. *The New Drawing on the Right Side of the Brain*. Los Angeles: Tarcher, 1999.

Edwards, Marc U. Jr. *Printing, Propaganda, and Martin Luther*. Berkeley: University of California Press, 1994.

Ekman, Paul. *Emotions Revealed*. New York: Owl Books, 2003.

Essinger, James. Jacquard's Web: How a Hand-Loom Led to the Birth of the Information Age. Oxford: Oxford University Press, 2004.

Ferrari, Michelle, dir. *The Vote*. Brooklyn: 42nd Parallel Films and American Experience PBS, 2020. https://www.pbs.org/wgbh/americanexperience/films/vote/.

Fox, Mark and Angie Wang. *Symbols: A Handbook for Seeing*. New York: Monacelli Press, 2016.

Gann, L.H. and Peter Duignan. *Colonialism in Africa 1870-1960: The History and Politics and Colonialism 1870-1914, Volume*. Cambridge: Cambridge University Press, 1969.

Gendler, Alex. "History vs. Che Guevara." *TedEd*. November 27, 2017. https://ed.ted.com/lessons/history-vs-che-guevara-alex-gendler.

George, Cherian and Sonny Liew. *Red Lines: Political Cartoons and the Struggle Against Censorship*. Cambridge: MIT Press, 2021.

Godfrey, Richard and Mark Hallett. *James Gillray: The Art of Caricature*. London: Tate, 2001.

Haidar, Navina Najat and Marika Sardar. *Sultans of Deccan India, 1500-1700: Opulence and Fantasy*. New York: MetPublications, 2015.

Halloran, Fiona Deans. *Thomas Nast: The Father of Modern Political Cartoons*. Chapel Hill: University of North Carolina Press, 2013.

Hassler, Alfred. *Martin Luther King and the Montgomery Story*. Nyack, NY: United States Fellowship for Reconciliation, 1957.

"Helguera, Leon, 1899-1970." *National Archives Catalog*. Accessed January 22, 2024. https://catalog.archives.gov/id/10601387.

Hogarth, Paul. *The Artist as Reporter*. London: Studio Vista, 1967.

Hörmann, André and Anna Samo. *She Was 300 Yards From the Atomic Bomb Center - and Survived*. New York: New York Times Films, 2023. https://www.nytimes.com/video/opinion/100000008818109/obon.html

"How American artists captured the Great War up close." *PBS News Hour*. March 2, 2017. https://www.pbs.org/newshour/show/american-artists-captured-great-war-close#:~:text=KELLI%20MORGAN%3A,in%20particular%20couldn't%20stand.

Lakoff, George and Mark Johnson. *Metaphors We Live By*. Chicago: University Of Chicago Press, 1980.

Leborg, Christian. *Visual Grammar*. New York: Princeton Architectural Press, 2006.

Lewis, John, Andrew Aydin, and Nate Powell. *March Trilogy*. Marietta, GA: Top Shelf Publishing, 2016.

Lewis, John, Andrew Aydin, Nate Powell, and L. Fury. *Run: Book One*. Marietta, GA: Top Shelf Publishing, 2021.

Lidwell, William, Kritina Holden, and Jill Butler. *Universal Principles of Design, Revised and Updated: 125 Ways to Enhance Usability, Influence Perception, Increase Appeal, Make Better Design Decisions, and Teach through Design*. Beverly, MA: Rockport Publishers, 2010.

Likosky, Stephan. *With a Weapon and a Grin: Postcard Images of France's Black African Colonial Troops in WWI*. Atglen, PA: Schiffer Military History, 2017.

Linz, Juan. *Totalitarian and Authoritarian Regimes*. Boulder: Lynne Rienner Publishers, 2000.

Male, Alan. *The Power and Influence of Illustration: Achieving Impact and Lasting Significance Through Visual Communication*. London: Bloomsbury Visual Arts, 2019.

McCloud, Scott. *Understanding Comics: The Invisible Art*. New York City: HarperCollins Publisher, 1993.

Mughan, Anthony and Richard Gunther. 2000. "The Media in Democratic and Nondemocratic Regimes: A Multilevel Perspective". In *Democracy and the Media*, edited by Richard Gunther and Anthony Mughan. New York: Cambridge University Press: (1-27).

Niemann, Christoph. "You Are Fluent In This Language and Don't Even Know It." *Ted*. April 2018. https://www.ted.com/talks/christoph_niemann_you_are_fluent_in_this_language_and_don_t_even_know_it?language=en.

Paine, Albert Bigelow. *Th. Nast: His Period and His Pictures*. New York: Macmillan, 1904.

Pipes, Richard. *Three "Whys" of the Russian Revolution*. Toronto: Vintage Books, 1995.

Political and Social Satire through Caricature. Berlin: Deutsche Grammophon GmbH, 1985. https://fod.infobase.com/PortalPlaylists.aspx?wID=96309&xtid=35741.

Selby, Andrew. *Editorial Illustration: Context, content, and creation*. London: Bloomsbury Visual Arts, 2022.

Sherwood, Marika. "Colonies, Colonials, and World War Two". *BBC*. Accessed on December 29, 2022. https://www.bbc.co.uk/history/worldwars/wwtwo/colonies_colonials_01.shtml#five.

Skocpol, Theda. *States and Social Revolutions*. Cambridge: Cambridge University Press, 1979.

Takei, George, Andrew Eisinger, Steven Scott, and Harmony Becker. *They Called Us Enemy*. Marietta, GA: Top Shelf Publishing, 2019.

Toppins, Aggie. "We Need Graphic Design Histories That Look Beyond the Profession." *AIGA Eye on Design*. June 10, 2021. https://eyeondesign.aiga.org/we-need-graphic-design-histories-that-look-beyond-the-profession/.

Acknowledgments

We are so thankful to everyone who contributed to this book in various ways. Special thanks to the interviewees, Andeel, Anita Kunz, Armando Veve, Doug Chayka, Edel Rodriguez, Fabian Williams, Hoka, Miriam Martincic, Seymour Chwast, Steve Brodner. Special thanks also goes to friends old and new for contributing images: Jaime Anderson, Erin Grace Burns, Jonathan Cumberland, Yamen Elgamal, Lauren Brown, Katrina Kopeloff, Beth Post, Ben Hannam, Fraser Davidson, Robyn Jordan, Meaghan Dee, Ryan Hartley Smith, Mark Fox and Angie Wang, Matt Cook, JP Kelly, Zina Saunders, Jim Fitzpatrick, Desi Mundo, the anonymous @9mmballpoint, and our cover artist, Krishna Chavda. Thank you to Amanda Plumb, Julie Bodam Macartney, Jaime Rosegren, and Maria Geonzcy for providing photographs. Another special thanks goes to the daughters of illustrators Takashi Kono and Bernard Safran, Aoi Huber Kono and Elizabeth Malyon, respectively, for preserving their important work and legacies. Thank you to the Hiroshima Peace Memorial Museum, Freedom House, and Mitchell-Innes & Nash for providing images. Thank you to our editors at Bloomsbury, especially Louise and Leafy, and to our copy editor Sebastian Rydberg. We are also grateful for the helpful feedback from the various anonymous reviewers throughout this process. Thank you to our families for their support over the last three years as we embarked on this journey.

This book grew out of our love for Atlanta, birthplace of the Civil Rights movement, our formative years in Madison, Wisconsin and its history of political activism, and our interest in global politics. Thank you to these communities for our political education.

Additional Acknowledgements, Catherine A. Moore:

Ninety percent of the work on this book was acquiring images, including researching copyright, contacting databases, tracking down the descendants of illustrators who have passed, and writing cold emails. Susan M. Bielstein's book *Permissions: A Survival Guide* was an essential guide during this process, and I recommend this book to anyone gathering images for publication. To the friends, illustration contacts, and total strangers who provided images gratis or at a reduced price due to the book being an educational textbook, we extend our sincere gratitude. For every wall I hit in my research, each of you was an open door, generously sharing your work, inspiration, and insights.

Thank you to Dan Vollaro's students at GGC for proofreading early versions of this book, as well as Kumar Krishnan and Jimmy Lo, and thank you to my mom, Christine Moore, for her very thorough proofread. Thanks also goes to Mandy Horton, Marty Blake, Shreyas Krishnan, and Robyn Phillips-Pendleton for including me in your panels at SECAC and ICON to present portions of the book, and to Laura Franz and Design History Fridays for including me as a presenter. Thank you to Ryan Hartley Smith for inviting me to present about the research process to his class at FIT, Ellen Rafshoon for assisting with interview transcription, and Katie Glusica for teaching me about the Jacquard loom. Thank you to Marika Sardar, Skye Lacerte, Amy Eklund, Kay Chatham, Cynthia Searcy, and Delphine Hirasuna for assistance with research. Thank you to Guin Thompson, Jaime Anderson, Jonathan Cumberland, Meena Khalili, Mandy Horton, and Beth Post for offering to write letters for my sabbatical and/or peer reviewing the original chapter for Bloomsbury, and to Teresa Winterhalter for approving my sabbatical so I could complete the book.

Image Credits

Every effort has been made to trace, clear, and credit the appropriate copyright holders of the images reproduced in this book.

However, if any credits have been inadvertently omitted or in error, the publisher will incorporate amendments in future printings.

Chapter 1. Figure 1.1 © Krishna Chavda, NANU Studio, Figure 1.2 Orson Lowell, Figure 1.3 Christopher Gadsden, Figure 1.4 Design © 2016 Mark Fox and Angie Wang, Design is Play, Figure 1.5 Catherine A. Moore, Figure 1.6 Catherine A. Moore, Figure 1.7 Getty Images, Figure 1.8 © Edel Rodriguez, Figure 1.9 © Doug Chayka, Figure 1.10 Getty Images, Figure 1.11 Thomas Nast, Figure 1.12 Lucas, Figure 1.13 © 2023 Jaime Anderson. All rights reserved., Figure 1.14 20th Century China, Figure 1.15 © Takashi Kono, Figure 1.16 Catherine A. Moore, Figure 1.17 Punch Magazine, Figure 1.18 Scott McCloud, Figure 1.19 Catherine A. Moore, Figure 1.20 © Erin Grace Burns, Figure 1.21 © Erin Grace Burns, Figure 1.22 © Jonathan Cumberland, Figure 1.23 © JP Kelly, Figure 1.24 © Anita Kunz.

Chapter 2. Figure 2.1 © Freedom in the World: Edition 2023 (www.freedomhouse.org), Figure 2.2 Rome, 44BC, Figure 2.3 Getty Images, Figure 2.4 © Julie Bodam Macartney, Figure 2.5 Public Domain, Figure 2.6 Public Domain, Figure 2.7 After a design by William Wyon, Figure 2.8 Byzantine, 500-550 with modern restoration, Figure 2.9 Russian 1797, Figure 2.10 Thomas Fleming, 2.11 Northwestern Litho. Company, Milwaukee, Figure 2.12 Georgii Vladimirovich Kibardin, Figure 2.13 Ruan Zude, 1561 or 1621, Figure 2.14 Hans Holbein the Younger, Figure 2.15 Edo Peoples, 1550-1680, Figure 2.16 Deccan, Bijapur, Figure 2.17 Jacques Louis-David, Figure 2.18 Jacques Louis-David, Figure 2.19 Mitchell Library, State Library of New South Wales, Figure 2.20 Kobayashi Kiyochika, Figure 2.21 Mizuno Toshikata, Figure 2.22 © Megan Hauser, Figure 2.23 © Megan Hauser, Figure 2.24 Prints, Drawings and Watercolors from the Anne S.K. Brown Military Collection. Brown Digital Repository. Brown University Library. 1859, Figure 2.25 Pictures from History / Contributor, 1914, Figure 2.26 Banania Ad, 1915, Figure 2.27 Lucien Jonas, Devambez Imprimerie, Paris (printer), 1917, Figure 2.28 Alfred Leete, Figure 2.29 James Montgomery Flagg, c. 1917, Figure 2.30 Charles Gustrine, Figure 2.31 E.G. Renesch, Figure 2.32 Gustav Klutsis, Figure 2.33 Mayakovsky, Vladimir Vladimirovich, Figure 2.34 Second World War, International War Museum IWM Art.IWM PST 15390, Figure 2.35 William Little, Figure 2.36 J Howard Miller, Figure 2.37 Leon Helguera, Figure 2.38 Leon Helguera, Figure 2.39 Getty Images, Figure 2.40 Tetyana Yablonska, Figure 2.41 Dong Xiwen, Forrest Anderson, Getty Images, Figure 2.42 Photo © Amanda Plumb, Figure 2.43 Jean-Claude Francolon, Figure 2.44 Getty Images, Figure 2.45 Getty Images, Figure 2.46 1840, Public Domain, Figure 2.47 National Museum of American History, Figure 2.48 Getty Images, Figure 2.49 Getty Images, Figure 2.50 Shepard Fairey.

Chapter 3. Figure 3.1 Public Domain, Figure 3.2 Alfred Waud, Figure 3.3 Matt Cook, Figure 3.4 Public Domain, Figure 3.5 Unknown Artist, Photo © Delphine Hirasuna, Figure 3.6 Chiura Obata, Figure 3.7 Harmony Becker, Figure 3.8 YAMADA Sumako, Hiroshima Peace Memorial Museum, Figure 3.9 TAKAKURA Akiko, Hiroshima Peace Memorial Museum, Figure 3.10 Yamen Elgamal, Figure 3.11 Annibale Carracci, Figure 3.12 William Hogarth, Figure 3.13 James Gillray, Figure 3.14 James Gillray, Figure 3.15 James Gillray, Figure 3.16 George Cruikshank, Figure 3.17 Attributed to Auguste Bouquet, Figure 3.18 Honoré Daumier, Figure 3.19 Auguste Bouquet, Figure 3.20 Benjamin Franklin, Figure 3.21 Elkanah Tisdale, Figure 3.22 Thomas Nast, Figure 3.23 Thomas Nast, Figure 3.24 Thomas Nast, Figure 3.25

Thomas Nast, Figure 3.26 Jay Jackson, Figure 3.27 Jay Jackson, Figure 3.28 Freedom in the World: Edition 2019 (www.freedomhouse.org), Figure 3.29 Getty Images, Figure 3.30 @9mmBallpoint, Figure 3.31 Photo © Catherine A. Moore, Figure 3.32 Käthe Kollwitz, Figure 3.33 Käthe Kollwitz, Figure 3.34 BERNARD SAFRAN, Patrice Lumumba (unpublished Time Magazine cover portrait, 1960), oil on illustration board, 43.18cm X 60.96cm, © Estate of Bernard Safran, Figure 3.35 © Catherine A. Moore, Figure 3.36 © Doug Chayka, Figure 3.37 © Doug Chayka, Figure 3.38 © Doug Chayka, Figure 3.39 © Miriam Martincic, Figure 3.40 © Miriam Martincic, Figure 3.41 © Armando Veve, Figure 3.42 © Armando Veve, Figure 3.43 © Armando Veve, Figure 3.44 © Zina Saunders, Figure 3.45 © Zina Saunders, Figure 3.46 © Edel Rodriguez, Figure 3.47 © Edel Rodriguez, Figure 3.48 © Steve Brodner, Figure 3.49 © Steve Brodner, Figure 3.50 © Steve Brodner.

Chapter 4. Figure 4.1 José Guadalupe Posada/Getty Images, Figure 4.2 Jose Clemente Orozco/Getty Images, Figure 4.3 Jim Fitzpatrick, Figure 4.4 Richard Chávez/Getty Images, Figure 4.5 Xavier Viramontes, Figure 4.6 Unknown, Figure 4.7 © Seymour Chwast, Figure 4.8 © Seymour Chwast, Figure 4.9 © Martha Rosler, Courtesy of the artist and Mitchell-Innes & Nash, New York, Figure 4.10 © Martha Rosler, Courtesy of the artist and Mitchell-Innes & Nash, New York, Figure 4.11 Rhode Island School of Design, Figure 4.12 Rhode Island School of Design, Figure 4.13 © Fabian Williams, Figure 4.14 © Fabian Williams, Figure 4.15 Earl Newman, Figure 4.16 © 2013 John Lewis and Andrew Aydin, Figure 4.17 © 2013 John Lewis and Andrew Aydin, Figure 4.18 Getty Images, Figure 4.19 Emory Douglas, Figure 4.20 Emory Douglas, Figure 4.21 © Lauren Brown, LAB Illustration, Figure 4.22 Keith Haring, Figure 4.23 © Jaime Rosegren, Figure 4.24 © Jaime Rosegren, Figure 4.25 © 2023, Ryan Hartley Smith, All Rights Reserved, Figure 4.26 © 2023, Ryan Hartley Smith, All Rights Reserved, Figure 4.27 © 2023, Ryan Hartley Smith, All Rights Reserved, Figure 4.28 © Hoka "Infer" Skenandore, Figure 4.29 © Hoka "Infer" Skenandore, Figure 4.30 Bruce Carter, Figure 4.31 Unknown, Figure 4.32 Weather Underground, Figure 4.33 Lead Artist Desi Mundo, assisted by Gilbert Kills Pretty Enemy III and Dakota Stevens, Figure 4.34 Artwork by Shepard Fairey, courtesy of Amplifier.org, Figure 4.35 © Doaa al Adel, Figure 4.36 © Andeel, Figure 4.37 © Anita Kunz, Figure 4.38 © Anita Kunz, Figure 4.39 Glasgow & London: Millar & Lang, National Series, Figure 4.40 Hilda Dallas, 1909, Figure 4.41 Dora Meeson/Getty Images, Figure 4.42 Nina Allender, Figure 4.43 Nina Allender, Figure 4.44 Bertha Margaret Boye, Figure 4.45 Photo © Catherine A. Moore, 2017, Figure 4.46 Photo © Maria Geonzcy, 2017, Figure 4.47 Getty Images, Figure 4.48 © Meaghan A. Dee, Figure 4.49 © Erin Grace Burns, Figure 4.50 © Katrina Kopeloff, Figure 4.51 © Robyn Jordan.

Conclusion. Figure 5.1 Artist Unknown, © Mark Fox and Angie Wang, Design is Play, Figure 5.3 © Ben Hannam & Bizhan Khodabandeh, Figure 5.4 © Fraser Davidson, Club Animation Studio, Figure 5.5 © Beth Post, Figure 5.6 © Zina Saunders.

Index

Note: Page locators in *italic* refer to figures.